Cognition and
Brain Development

APA HUMAN BRAIN DEVELOPMENT SERIES

Educating the Human Brain
Michael I. Posner and Mary K. Rothbart

Poverty and Brain Development During Childhood: An Approach From Cognitive Psychology and Neuroscience
Sebastián Lipina and Jorge A. Colombo

Child Development at the Intersection of Emotion and Cognition
Edited by Susan D. Calkins and Martha Ann Bell

Self-Regulation: Brain, Cognition, and Development
Andrea Berger

Cognition and Brain Development: Converging Evidence From Various Methodologies
Edited by Bhoomika Rastogi Kar

Cognition and Brain Development

CONVERGING EVIDENCE
FROM VARIOUS METHODOLOGIES

EDITED BY
Bhoomika Rastogi Kar

AMERICAN PSYCHOLOGICAL ASSOCIATION
WASHINGTON, DC

Published by
American Psychological Association
750 First Street, NE
Washington, DC 20002
www.apa.org

To order
APA Order Department
P.O. Box 92984
Washington, DC 20090-2984
Tel: (800) 374-2721; Direct: (202) 336-5510
Fax: (202) 336-5502; TDD/TTY: (202) 336-6123
Online: www.apa.org/pubs/books
E-mail: order@apa.org

In the U.K., Europe, Africa, and the Middle East, copies may be ordered from
American Psychological Association
3 Henrietta Street
Covent Garden, London
WC2E 8LU England

Typeset in Goudy by Circle Graphics, Inc., Columbia, MD

Printer: Edwards Brothers, Inc., Lillington, NC
Cover Designer: Berg Design, Albany, NY

The opinions and statements published are the responsibility of the authors, and such opinions and statements do not necessarily represent the policies of the American Psychological Association.

Library of Congress Cataloging-in-Publication Data

Cognition and brain development : converging evidence from various methodologies / edited by Bhoomika Rastogi Kar.
    p. cm. — (Human brain development series)
  Includes bibliographical references and index.
    ISBN 978-1-4338-1271-2 — ISBN 1-4338-1271-1 1. Cognition. 2. Brain. 3. Cognitive neuroscience. I. Kar, Bhoomika R.

  BF311.C5472 2013
  153—dc23
                              2012029807

British Library Cataloguing-in-Publication Data
A CIP record is available from the British Library.

Printed in the United States of America
First Edition

DOI: 10.1037/14043-000

CONTENTS

Contributors .... *ix*

Foreword .... *xi*
Michael I. Posner

Introduction 3
Bhoomika Rastogi Kar

I. Development of Attention and Control **9**

Chapter 1. Development of Selection and Control 11
            Bhoomika Rastogi Kar and Narayanan Srinivasan

Chapter 2. The Nature and Nurture of Executive
            Attention Development 33
            M. Rosario Rueda and Lina M. Cómbita

Chapter 3. Development of Attention Networks 61
            Michael I. Posner and Mary K. Rothbart

Chapter 4.   Development of Task-Switching Skills 85
              Gijsbert Stoet and Beatriz López

II. Developmental Disorders: ADHD and Autism 103

Chapter 5.   Role of Dopamine in the Pathophysiology
              of Attention-Deficit/Hyperactivity Disorder 105
              Chandan J. Vaidya and Evan M. Gordon

Chapter 6.   The Dopamine Hypothesis of ADHD
              and Brain Response to Stimulant Medication 127
              James M. Swanson, Timothy Wigal, Scott Kollins,
              Jeffrey Newcorn, Gene-Jack Wang, Joanna Fowler,
              and Nora Volkow

Chapter 7.   Exploring Prerequisite Learning Skills
              in Young Children and Their Implications
              for Identification of and Intervention
              for Autistic Behavior 145
              Prathibha Karanth and Archana S

III. Origin of Self, Culture, and Social Cognition 155

Chapter 8.   Self-Consciousness and the Origins
              of an Ethical Stance 157
              Philippe Rochat

Chapter 9.   Learning to Share: The Emergence of Joint
              Attention in Human Infancy 173
              Gedeon O. Deák, Jochen Triesch, Anna Krasno,
              Kaya de Barbaro, and Marybel Robledo

Chapter 10.   Culture and Cognitive Development:
              The Development of Geocentric
              Language and Cognition 211
              Ramesh C. Mishra and Pierre R. Dasen

Chapter 11.   Cultural Differences in Cognitive Styles 231
              Pierre R. Dasen and Ramesh C. Mishra

IV. Language and Reading Development 251

Chapter 12.   Children's Reading Development: Learning About
              Sounds, Symbols, and Cross-Modal Mappings 253
              Sonali Nag and Margaret J. Snowling

Chapter 13.   Young Children's Use of Color Information
                During Language–Vision Mapping 271
                Falk Huettig

Chapter 14.   Functional Magnetic Resonance Imaging
                of Language in Patients With Epilepsy 289
                Jija S. James and Chandrasekharan Kesavadas

Index 311

About the Editor 327

CONTRIBUTORS

Archana S, The Com DEALL Trust, Bangalore, India

Lina M. Cómbita, MA, Departamento de Psicología Experimental, Universidad de Granada, Granada, Spain

Pierre R. Dasen, PhD, Université de Genève, Geneva, Switzerland

Gedeon O. Deák, PhD, Department of Cognitive Science, University of California, San Diego, La Jolla

Kaya de Barbaro, PhD, Department of Cognitive Science, University of California, San Diego, La Jolla

Joanna Fowler, PhD, Department of Chemistry, Brookhaven National Laboratory, Upton, NY

Evan M. Gordon, Georgetown University Medical Center, Washington, DC

Falk Huettig, PhD, Max Planck Institute for Psycholinguistics and Donders Institute for Brain, Cognition, and Behaviour, Nijmegen, the Netherlands

Jija S. James, Sree Chitra Tirunal Institute for Medical Sciences and Technology, Kerala, India

Bhoomika Rastogi Kar, PhD, Centre of Behavioural and Cognitive Sciences, University of Allahabad, Allahabad, India

Prathibha Karanth, PhD, The Com DEALL Trust, Bangalore, India

Chandrasekharan Kesavadas, MD, Sree Chitra Tirunal Institute for Medical Sciences and Technology, Kerala, India

Scott Kollins, PhD, Department of Psychiatry, Duke University Medical Center, Durham, NC

Anna Krasno, Koegel Autism Center, Graduate School of Education, University of California, Santa Barbara

Beatriz López, PhD, Department of Psychology, University of Portsmouth, Portsmouth, England

Ramesh C. Mishra, PhD, Department of Psychology, Banaras Hindu University, Varanasi, India

Sonali Nag, PhD, Centre for Reading and Language, Department of Psychology, University of York, York, England, and The Promise Foundation, Bangalore, India

Jeffrey Newcorn, MD, Department of Psychiatry, Mount Sinai Medical Center, New York, NY

Michael I. Posner, PhD, Institute of Cognitive and Decision Sciences, University of Oregon, Eugene

Marybel Robledo, Department of Cognitive Science, University of California, San Diego, La Jolla

Philippe Rochat, PhD, Department of Psychology, Emory University, Atlanta, GA

Mary K. Rothbart, PhD, Department of Psychology, University of Oregon, Eugene

M. Rosario Rueda, PhD, Departamento de Psicología Experimental, Universidad de Granada, Granada, Spain

Margaret J. Snowling, PhD, Department of Psychology, University of York, York, England

Narayanan Srinivasan, PhD, Centre of Behavioural and Cognitive Sciences, University of Allahabad, Allahabad, India

Gijsbert Stoet, PhD, Institute of Psychological Sciences, University of Leeds, Leeds, England

James M. Swanson, PhD, Child Development Center, Department of Pediatrics, University of California, Irvine

Jochen Triesch, PhD, Frankfurt Institute for Advanced Studies, J. W. Goethe University, Frankfurt, Germany

Chandan J. Vaidya, PhD, Department of Psychology, Georgetown University, Washington, DC

Nora Volkow, MD, National Institute on Drug Abuse and Laboratory of Neuroimaging; National Institute on Alcohol Abuse and Alcoholism, Bethesda, MD

Gene-Jack Wang, MD, Medical Department, Brookhaven National Laboratory, Upton, NY

Timothy Wigal, PhD, Child Development Center, Department of Pediatrics, University of California, Irvine

FOREWORD

Psychology is changing! When I entered the field half a century ago, new ideas in our field came mainly from countries where English was the primary language: the United Kingdom, the United States, and Canada. Although the overwhelming number of new publications are in English, original ideas now come from India, France, Germany, China, Hungary, Russia, and Argentina, among other countries where English is a second or later learned language. Those of us who are native English speakers are fortunate not to have to write in a new language, but we must learn to attend to the new ideas entering the field.

This fifth volume in the American Psychological Association Human Brain Development series points to the international nature of work on brain mechanisms of human development. This volume, edited by Bhoomika Rastogi Kar, includes much more of a South Asian perspective in her chapter with Srinivasan and in other chapters by Indian psychologists. The second volume in the series, on poverty, was written by Sebastián J. Lipina and Jorge A. Colombo from Argentina and included the perspective of developing countries on issues of how poverty shapes development. The fourth volume, on self-regulation, was written by Andrea Berger from Ben Gurion University in Israel.

The topic of this volume is the development of cognition. Part I, which has a heavy emphasis on attention and cognitive control, updates and enlarges some of the discussion found in the first volume of this series, *Educating the Human Brain*, by Michael I. Posner and Mary K. Rothbart. The first three chapters, by Kar and Srinivasan, Rueda and Cómbita, and Posner and Rothbart, feature different aspects of how attention networks develop and influence behavior. Stoet and López deal in Chapter 4 with specific issues related to task switching in late childhood. Task switching is one of the most frequently studied cognitive tasks in adults.

Rueda and Cómbita (Chapter 2) discuss both genetic and training aspects of attentional development. Their work with normal children makes close contact with the studies of attention-deficit/hyperactivity disorder (ADHD) by Vaidya and Gordon (Chapter 5) and Swanson and colleagues (Chapter 6), who connect pathology to neural networks and genetic variation. Swanson is the discoverer of the connection between ADHD and genetic variation in the dopamine 4 receptor gene (*DRD4*), and Chapter 6 provides an accessible summary of this important work. Connecting genetic variation to neural networks as is done in Part II constitutes an important approach to all forms of pathology, including the area of autistic spectrum disorder discussed in Chapter 7 by Karanth and Archana S.

Work on attention also relates to children recognizing their reflection in a mirror, which is traced by Rochat in Chapter 8 dealing with self-consciousness. Rochat also introduces the role of caregivers in joint attention with their children.

A study of joint attention, discussed in Chapter 9 by Deák and associates also provides a clear link between Parts I and II and Berger's volume in the series mentioned earlier. However, none of the previous volumes in this series has emphasized the role of culture as is done in Parts III and IV in this volume, and none provided much material from linguistics and anthropology as is done in Chapters 10 and 11 by Mishra and Dasen.

The presence of such a large number of languages in India and South Asia makes the study of bilingualism and literacy of special relevance in this part of the world. Whereas in the United States bilingual abilities are relatively rare, in India it is often difficult to find people who can serve as monolingual controls. This multilingualism may account for the discussions of language in Parts III and IV in this volume. In Chapter 12, Nag and Snowling deal with reading, a central topic in cognitive studies of language, while Chapter 13, by Huettig, and Chapter 14, by James and Kesavadas, discuss language issues in typically developing children and those with epilepsy, respectively. Studies of culture and of language are intrinsically related, and these two parts emphasize that connection.

Overall this book serves as a useful adjunct to studies of development in its cultural and linguistic context. I was privileged to attend the Allahabad conference and to visit the Centre of Behavioural Sciences located at the University of Allahabad. This volume allows a larger and more diverse audience to benefit from such deliberations. I hope it will serve to increase international collaboration on the important issues of brain and behavioral development.

Michael I. Posner
Series Editor

Cognition and
Brain Development

INTRODUCTION

BHOOMIKA RASTOGI KAR

The essence of development is change. To observe a newborn develop into a toddler, child, and adolescent, and to try to account for the mechanisms of the developing brain and cognition that underlie these changes, are intellectually stimulating as well as emotionally satisfying. The field of cognitive development helps us understand how we learn to think, perceive, reason, talk, learn, and remember. This book conveys the insights gained from recent empirical research in the field of cognitive development and presents a cumulative account of different aspects of the developing brain and cognition. The highlight of the volume is the bringing together of various topics in cognitive development, methodology, developmental stages, and most important, research findings on various populations from both East and West.

The developmental stages of infancy, childhood, and adolescence are characterized by the rapid development of the brain and cognitive processes. Research in the field of cognitive development has been extensive and

DOI: 10.1037/14043-001
Cognition and Brain Development: Converging Evidence From Various Methodologies, B. R. Kar (Editor)

includes studies on infant cognition and the development of specific cognitive processes such as attention, inhibition, executive control, working memory, language, and emotional processing using methodologies such as behavioral experimentation, electrophysiology, and neuroimaging (positron emission tomography, functional magnetic resonance imaging, magnetoencephalography, near-infrared spectroscopy, and diffusion tensor imaging). Studies on cognitive development in normally developing children have informed the profession about the prolonged, progressive nature of developmental patterns and also have helped explain the mechanisms underlying various cognitive processes. Studies on developmental disorders have also provided meaningful insights into the mechanisms of various cognitive processes. Cognitive science offers a wonderful opportunity to investigate cognitive development with diverse approaches and methodologies.

Contributed by a distinguished set of scholars, the chapters in this volume present empirical research in cognitive development and developmental cognitive neuroscience. The book presents recent studies on various cognitive processes, for example, attention, memory, executive control, working memory, joint attention, spatial cognition, the origin of the self and an ethical stance, and lexical access. All of the chapters present empirical research and also relate their findings empirically and theoretically to the understanding of mechanisms underlying these processes. The research presented here also describes the interaction between the development of cognitive processes and variables at the individual and environmental levels, such as temperament, education, parenting style, and so forth.

VOLUME OVERVIEW

The book is organized in four parts. Part I, on the development of attention and control, contains four chapters dealing with the developmental trajectories of the various subprocesses of attention and cognitive control. These chapters serve as a foundation for the subsequent ones.

In Chapter 1, Kar and Srinivasan present an overview of the development of components of selection and control processes, such as selective attention, response inhibition, and task switching. The authors also discuss evidence on the development of affective control, including the contribution of attention.

Chapter 2 focuses on executive attention networks and their role in the development of cognitive and emotional regulation. Rueda and Cómbita provide insight into the implications such an interaction has for training and parenting and address the question of how attention networks are shaped by genes and experience.

The development of attention networks during early childhood is the focus of Chapter 3, with an emphasis on the role of constitutional and environmental factors that affect individual differences in the development of this function. Posner and Rothbart also inform readers about the genetic factors associated with differences in efficiency of attention control, as well as aspects of the environmental and educational contexts that contribute to the development of attention.

In Chapter 4, Stoet and López present results based on studies on the development of task switching in children and adolescents. *Task switching* is a control process that enables flexible switching between task rules and responses. In the task-switching paradigm, people perform two tasks alternately. The time to prepare for the upcoming task is often varied by the experimenter.

Altogether, Part I presents a comprehensive account of the development of attention and control processes covering various components of attention, its developmental trajectories, and the genetic and environmental determinants of such trajectories. It also sets the stage for the sections to follow; for example, in Part II, on developmental disorders, attention-deficit/hyperactivity disorder (ADHD) is described as being a disorder of attention and control, and autism is described as involving difficulties with emotional regulation and control.

Part II begins with Chapter 5, in which Vaidya and Gordon discuss their functional brain imaging studies in children. Their findings have shown that cognitive deficits are associated with reduced involvement of the frontal-striatal regions. To understand the causes of the disorder, they have investigated the extent to which a genetic polymorphism that is associated with ADHD also shows brain and behavioral differences that are observed in ADHD. Their findings suggest a mechanism by which differences in dopamine transporter function may confer some vulnerability to acquiring ADHD.

Chapter 6, by Swanson and colleagues, further discusses studies on the involvement of the dopaminergic systems of the brain in the etiology and treatment of ADHD. These studies are important in part because controlled evaluations of long-term treatment with stimulant medications have been lacking in the literature.

In Chapter 7, Karanth and Archana S use case studies to highlight the need for intervention programs for communication difficulties associated with autism. This chapter highlights the importance of measuring the adequacy of early learning skills in programs for early identification, differential diagnosis, and early intervention to aid in improving long-term outcomes for language and communication as well as for schooling.

Another related aspect of learning is self-exploration. The chapters in Part III, on the origin of self, culture, and social cognition, deal with developmental patterns of the embodied self, the ethical stance, and the effect of culture on cognitive development and social cognitive development in infants and children.

Chapter 8, by Rochat, focuses on the relationship between the emergence of self-consciousness and the emergence of an ethical stance in children. In discussing developmental trajectories of moral identity among infants and children, the author provides a detailed examination of how the emergence of self-consciousness shapes human behavior. Rochat proposes that self-consciousness cannot be separated from one's tendency to take an ethical stance toward others as well as toward the self in terms of one's reputation.

Chapter 9 focuses on infant studies on attention sharing. Deák, Triesch, Krasno, de Barbaro, and Robledo address questions such as the following: How do infants process the complex patterns of their social world? How do they derive new social behavior "policies" for acting effectively with other people? What social experiences facilitate this learning? How does learning relate to individual differences among infants and among their caregivers? The authors propose that an understanding of the development of infant social attention might provide insight into the processes of social development and individual differences. In addition, they propose that a sense of the self as agent in the environment and a sense of mutuality with others are central to the development of the self and an ethical stance.

Chapters 10 and 11 focus on the ecocultural context of cognitive development. In Chapter 10, Mishra and Dasen describe their theoretical framework based on the ecocultural perspective and discuss how culture affects the development of cognitive styles. In Chapter 11, Dasen and Mishra support this framework with evidence from their work on the development of geocentric spatial cognition across different cultural contexts.

Part IV, on language and reading development, comprises three chapters. Chapter 12, by Nag and Snowling, is concerned with the development of reading—particularly the mapping of letters to sound—in studies on Indian languages. The authors discuss how symbols map onto spoken speech in different ways across writing systems. The letters of alphabetical scripts represent sounds at the level of the phoneme, whereas the characters of logographic Chinese represent morphemic information. The authors focus on sound and symbol processing among children learning to read in an alphasyllabic language to clarify the script-specific aspects of learning to read.

Chapter 13 discusses language–vision interaction in infants. Huettig notes that eye movements made by listeners during language-mediated visual searches reveal a strong link between visual processing and conceptual processing.

The final chapter focuses on the use of functional neuroimaging in clinical research and diagnosis in children and adults with neurological/neurosurgical disorders, such as epilepsy, that involve language-related abnormalities. In Chapter 14, James and Kesavadas provide an overview of the use of fMRI as a noninvasive procedure with a focused discussion about presurgical language mapping in epilepsy patients and the concordance between the Wada and fMRI results. The authors provide information about the presurgical evaluation of different aspects of language processing that are affected in patients with epilepsy and how fMRI and diffusion tensor imaging–like techniques can help in understanding the disturbance in language organization among adults and children with epilepsy.

This volume is a collection of chapters based on the proceedings of the International Conference on Cognitive Development held in December 2010 at the Centre of Behavioural and Cognitive Sciences, University of Allahabad, Allahabad, India. Its compilation was an excellent opportunity to put together recent research in developmental cognitive neuroscience with empirical findings based on various methodologies, including behavioral reaction time, imaging, observation, and genetics studies. The findings presented here depict how the interaction between biology and environment produces cognitive development. I sincerely thank all of the authors for contributing their work and all the reviewers for their valuable comments and suggestions. The diverse methodological approaches taken by these experts in their respective areas will benefit researchers and professionals working with children and students of cognitive psychology and cognitive science.

I

DEVELOPMENT OF ATTENTION AND CONTROL

1

DEVELOPMENT OF SELECTION AND CONTROL

BHOOMIKA RASTOGI KAR AND NARAYANAN SRINIVASAN

Mature cognition is characterized by abilities such as being able to select and manipulate appropriate information, to resist inappropriate behaviors, and to quickly and flexibly adapt or modify behavior to changing goals and situations. In other words, we are referring to cognitive processes such as selection, inhibition, and task switching. *Selective attention* enables people to process relevant input and ignore irrelevant or distracting inputs. Selection can be exogenous or automatic—that is, triggered by the presence of salient stimuli in the environment—or it can be endogenous or voluntary—that is, under voluntary or intentional control. Both exogenous selection and endogenous selection are subjected to age-related changes. However, endogenous selection shows greater age-related changes than does exogenous selection because the brain processes mediating controlled processes are the last to mature and the first to deteriorate with age. In addition, it is controlled processing that suffers first in the event of injury or pathology.

DOI: 10.1037/14043-002
Cognition and Brain Development: Converging Evidence From Various Methodologies, B. R. Kar (Editor)

The set of attentional processes also includes processes that are generally referred to as *executive attention* or *cognitive control*. Executive attention refers to processes that control or allow people to inhibit and attend to competing information at the same time. These processes are used to resolve conflicts and produce appropriate actions to achieve the necessary goals of the organism (Hare & Casey, 2005). It is domain general and not task specific. Depending on the type of task and paradigms, many terms are in use that refer to cognitive control, such as *effortful processing, executive control, attention bias,* and *conflict resolution* (Hare & Casey, 2005). Effortful processing is the ability to suppress a dominant response to produce a subdominant response, which demands effort. Similarly, it is sometimes called attention bias in the resolution of conflict between aspects of the stimulus that are attended to and others that are left unattended. Many tasks and paradigms have been used to study different aspects of selection and cognitive control. For example, alertness, selection, and executive attention have been studied with the help of a single task, namely, the attention network task (ANT), based on the combination of flanker and cuing paradigms (Fan, McCandliss, Sommer, Raz, & Posner, 2002). More specifically, selection is studied using paradigms including cuing (both exogenous and endogenous) and visual search tasks (Akhtar & Enns, 1989; Posner, 1980).

Among the many aspects of cognitive control, *task switching* involves the ability to flexibly shift from one mind-set to another, often shifting according to rules incompatible with the previous mind-set. Task switching has been extensively studied in adults, and only a handful of studies have looked at switching abilities in children and adolescents (Cepeda, Kramer, & Gonzalez de Sather, 2001; Crone, Ridderinkhof, Worm, Somsen, & van der Molen, 2004; Gupta, Kar, & Srinivasan, 2009). Switching is fundamentally difficult and requires top-down executive control. Neuroimaging studies confirm that task switching activates the neural system associated with executive function and top-down executive control mediated by the lateral prefrontal cortex and the inferior frontal, premotor, and anterior cingulate cortex (Brass et al., 2003; Dreher & Grafman, 2003).

The interaction between cognitive and emotional processes plays an important role in the development of behavior regulation. Emotions influence many psychological or physiological processes, and these processes in turn influence emotions (Hare & Casey, 2005). *Affective control* refers to the processes involved in regulating emotional processing and responses as well as resolving a conflict in which the emotional valence is present. For example, an emotional conflict task consisted of faces with fearful and happy expressions presented with the words *happy* or *fear* written across them (Etkin, Egner, Peraza, Kandel, & Hirsch, 2006). Subjects were asked to report on the expression of the face while ignoring the words, which were either congruent or incongruent with the facial expression. Incongruent stimuli were thus associated with response conflict that arose from an emotional incompatibility between task-relevant and task-irrelevant dimensions of the stimulus (Etkin et al., 2006).

This chapter discusses salient findings from behavioral, electrophysiological (event-related potential), and neuroimaging studies on the development of selective attention and cognitive control. The ability to select is important for perception, and we provide an overview on the development of processes involved in selection based on findings from different paradigms that involve visual perception. The next section discusses the development of selective attention, followed by discussion on the development of different cognitive control processes. Executive control processes are critical given that they affect other cognitive and affective processes, and the development of those control processes has a significant impact on the development of personality and social skills. We do not focus on all the control processes and paradigms used to study these skills but specifically concentrate on inhibitory processes and situations in which children have to choose and perform one of two possible tasks. This is followed by a discussion of studies looking at the development of affective control. Given that genes and experience affect development, we finally discuss some example studies on the genetics and training of attention. Throughout, the chapter presents developmental data from non-WEIRD (Western, educated, industrialized, rich, and democratic; Henrich, Heine, & Norenzayan, 2010) populations (from India) that would be useful for cross-cultural studies on the development of attention.

DEVELOPMENT OF SELECTIVE ATTENTION

The concept of selection is fundamental to understanding human behavior. And in everyday life, it is clear that there are marked differences in the ability to select across individuals as a function of age. Some differences may reflect a genetically determined plan governing neural growth, maturation, and senescence, whereas others may reflect changes due to training and experience that may interact with genetic capabilities.

Selection can be endogenous or exogenous. There is more age-related change in the two endogenous modes of selection (habit and deliberation) than in the two exogenous modes (reflex and exploration) because the former are driven by specific goals for certain situations (Enns & Trick, 2006). They are also more idiosyncratic because they reflect specific learning histories, which vary as a function of age and experience. In contrast, the two exogenous modes represent innately specified default settings that give certain types of stimuli increased salience in a common way for all humans. Age-related change is also more evident in the two controlled modes of selection (exploration and deliberation) than in the two automatic modes (reflex and habit) because the areas of the brain mediating controlled processes (i.e., prefrontal cortex) are among the last to develop and the first to deteriorate with age. It is controlled processing that suffers first in the event of injury and pathology. By combining the first two principles, we can predict that among the four modes of selection, reflexive selection will show the least change with age, whereas deliberate selection will show the greatest variability and idiosyncrasy.

The measurement of covert orienting is therefore possible only for participants willing and able to perform a target detection or discrimination task. In the study of healthy human children, this usually means that the youngest studied age groups are 3 to 5 years of age (Enns & Brodeur, 1989; Randolph, 2002; Ristic, Friesen, & Kingstone, 2002). Yet, within these constraints, the data have been quite consistent in showing that covert orienting differs little in the course of typical development across the life span and even differs little between the various special populations that have been tested (Burack & Enns, 1997; Plude, Enns, & Brodeur, 1994).

The three major components of attention have been studied using the ANT, which evaluates the alerting, orienting, and executive networks of attention (Fan et al., 2002). The alerting network enables readiness to respond to a target following a warning stimulus; it is associated with the thalamus, frontal, parietal regions and with the distribution of the norepinephrine system in the brain (Marrocco & Davidson, 1998). The orienting network focuses on endogenous orienting, in which a symbolic cue gives information about the location of the stimulus; it is associated with the superior and inferior parietal lobule along with the frontal eye fields and subcortical areas such as the superior colliculus of the midbrain and the pulvinar and reticular nuclei of the thalamus (Corbetta, Kincade, Ollinger, McAvoy, & Shulman, 2000; Corbetta & Shulman, 2002). In terms of development, the alerting network develops later in adulthood without showing any changes from ages 6 to 10 years (Rueda et al., 2004). Although the orienting network did not show any improvement from 6 years of age to adulthood, other developmental studies have indicated a very early development of the orienting network that occurs before 6 years of age (Akhtar & Enns, 1989; Trick & Enns, 1998). Studies on orienting that compared normal children with children with Down syndrome have shown that cuing effects are not different for the two groups, indicating that orienting processes are preserved in children with Down syndrome (Goldman, Flanagan, Shulman, Enns, & Burack, 2005).

One way to study the ability to divide attention and shift attention between locations or objects is using visual search tasks. In *visual search*, observers have to identify a given object among many objects present in the visual display. Typically, the number of objects is manipulated, and identification time as a function of set size is measured. Trick and Enns (1998), in a developmental study, found age-related changes in conjunction search (targets defined by two features), with the children (6, 8, and 10 years) performing less well than the young adults (22 years) and the older adults (72 years). This result indicates that the ability to bind features for identifying an object changes with age. In addition, Trick and Enns found differences in the ability to voluntarily shift attention, with better performance among the young adults as compared with the children and the older adults. The two different developmental trajectories indicate differences in feature integration and endogenous shifts of visual attention.

An important ability in real life is to detect changes that occur in a visual scene. Studies have shown that adults sometimes fail to detect changes (Rensink, 2002). It is important to measure the ability to detect changes under varied conditions. One important factor that determines people's ability to detect changes is attention. Studies have measured the ability to detect changes in children and young adults using a repetition paradigm in which the blank screen duration (50 ms and 250 ms) was manipulated (Shore, Burack, Miller, Joseph, & Enns, 2006). Results showed that children detected changes less easily than adults when the changes involved color change or change in parts (deletion). However, children detected changes in orientation much more easily than adults.

Dye and Bavalier (2010) investigated multiple aspects of visual attention among children and adults. One aspect was the ability to distribute visual attention across the field in searching for a peripheral target among distractors. This aspect was quantified by measuring the useful field of view (UFOV) at the duration in which the participant's performance was at threshold, and there was no significant difference in UFOV across the different age groups. The second aspect investigated was the time required to shift attention to a new target following an already attended target, which was measured using the attentional blink task. Children less than 14 years of age had a much longer recovery time than those more than 14 years of age. The third aspect investigated was the number of objects that could be simultaneously attended to, which was measured by a multiple object visual tracking task. Ability to track multiple objects improved linearly with age. The three different attentional processes showed a different developmental pattern. In addition, those who played action video games (especially the younger children) performed better than those who did not play those games, indicating that experience could also modify these attentional processes.

In a recent study on developmental trajectories, the developmental trajectories of selective and focused attention in children 8 to 15 years of age were examined using the growth curve modeling approach and were found to follow a logistic growth function for selective attention and an exponential growth function for focused attention (Kar, Rao, Chandramouli, & Thennarasu, 2011). The function of selective attention followed the logistic growth model, which signifies a slow initial growth followed by speedy and consistent growth (see Figure 1.1). There were significant differences in performance between 8 and 12 years and at 15 years of age. Focused attention followed the exponential model, depicting a growth pattern that is proportionate to age (see Figure 1.2). There was a significant reduction in response times between 10 and 15 years of age. Some studies have reported that focused attention is mature by 10 years of age (Klenberg, Korkman, & Lahti-Nuuttila, 2001). Age-related differences in performance were present even at 15 years of age. The studies on selection indicate that different aspects of selective attention show different developmental trajectories.

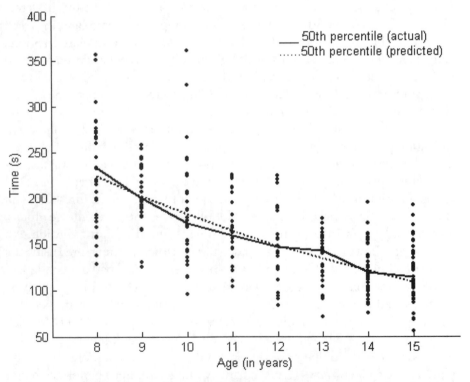

Figure 1.1. Growth patterns of focused attention among children 8 to 15 years of age. From B. R. Kar, S. L. Rao, B. A. Chandramouli, and K. Thennarasu, 2011, "Growth Patterns of Neuropsychological Functions in Indian Children," *Frontiers in Psychology, 2,* p. 240. Copyright 2011 by the authors. Adapted with permission.

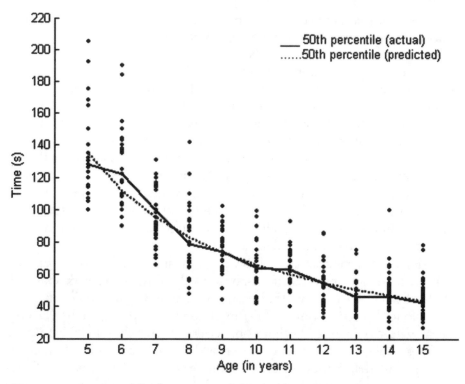

Figure 1.2. Growth patterns of selective attention among children 8 to 15 years of age. From B. R. Kar, S. L. Rao, B. A. Chandramouli, and K. Thennarasu, 2011, "Growth Patterns of Neuropsychological Functions in Indian Children," *Frontiers in Psychology, 2,* p. 240. Copyright 2011 by the authors. Adapted with permission.

DEVELOPMENT OF EXECUTIVE CONTROL

Age-related changes have been identified in executive control processes such as response inhibition, task switching, error monitoring, and working memory, which are critical for all aspects of perception and action. Theories of cognitive development characterize immature cognition as being more susceptible to interference from competing information and actions (Hare & Casey, 2005). Executive attention undergoes changes during the 3rd year of life. By the beginning of the 4th year, children start showing a strikingly different pattern of responses, showing the expected slowing for incompatible relative to compatible trials (Posner & Rothbart, 2000). Thus, younger children have more difficulty in resolving conflicts than older ones, and this ability is further complicated when information has emotional content.

Several studies have used brain imaging methodologies to determine the neural substrates that mediate aspects of cognitive control involved in overriding competing actions in both children and adults. The neural substrates involved in cognitive control include prefrontal-related circuitry, which regulates thoughts and actions and is important for overriding previous information in response to new information. Children recruit the dorsolateral prefrontal cortex more than adults (Hare & Casey, 2005). Initially, the activation in the prefrontal cortex is more diffused, but with age the activation becomes more localized as only relevant connections are strengthened and others are attenuated with maturity. Also in early years of development a higher and more diffused activation is seen in response to a conflict situation, but with age, because irrelevant areas get attenuated, only relevant areas are activated in response to a conflict situation, resulting in a less intense and more focal activation of neural areas.

Following conflicts that typically result in larger numbers of errors, control processes are activated in response to the error (Rieger & Gauggel, 1999). Studies have shown that posterror relative to postcorrect trials led to prolonged reaction times (RTs) in children and young adults (Davies, Segalowitz, & Gavin, 2004; Santesso, Segalowitz, & Schmidt, 2006). These findings imply that an aspect of posterror slowing reflects control processes in children—that is, they can exert cognitive control in this situation. Friedman, Nessler, Cycowicz, and Horton (2009) compared children with young and older adults and reported age-related differences with respect to upregulation of cognitive control in terms of lesser amplitude of medial frontal negativity as an index of response conflict detection. In children and adolescents with attention-deficit/hyperactivity disorder (ADHD), less activation is seen in this region compared with adults (Hare & Casey, 2005).

Executive attention has been studied using the ANT (Fan et al., 2002). The executive network is involved with the complex operations of detecting and resolving conflict required during planning, decision making, and error detection. Executive control can be evaluated with the flanker task (Eriksen, 1995) in which a target is presented with congruent (same as target) or incongruent (different and associated with a different response than the target) distractors. Typically, responses are slower with incongruent compared with congruent distractors because of difficulty in monitoring conflict. The executive network involves the anterior cingulate and lateral prefrontal areas (Matsumoto & Tanaka, 2004) that are linked by the dopamine system. The executive network as tapped by the ANT has been shown to develop up to age 6 or 7 years. From 7 years until adulthood, there is very little difference in performance on executive control (Rueda et al., 2004).

Substantial development of executive control occurs between 3 and 7 years of age. Bunge, Dudukovic, Thomason, Vaidya, and Gabrieli (2002) examined developmental differences in activation during a go/no-go task. They reported greater intensity of activation for children in medial frontal aspects, whereas there was greater intensity of activation for adults in lateral aspects, of the inferior, middle, and superior frontal gyri. Development of executive control continues to occur during adolescence. Adolescence is a period marked by disjunctions among developing brain, cognitive, and behavioral systems that mature along different trajectories and is thus a period of reorganization of regulatory systems (Steinberg, 2005). The developmental patterns of executive control in adolescence are also marked by affective and social context (Crone, 2009). Neuroimaging studies have shown that adolescent development is characterized by immature prefrontal activity and enhanced responses in the subcortical affective system (Hare et al., 2008). Maturation of the frontal cortex facilitates regulatory competence in late adolescence. A study with children and adolescents ages 9 to 17 years reported that performance in a go/no-go task of response inhibition and a digit span task of working memory did not correlate with performance in a gambling task (Hooper, Luciana, Conklin, & Yarger, 2004). However, performance in the response inhibition task improved with age. They concluded that maturation of the ventromedial prefrontal cortex may be developmentally distinct from that of other regions of frontal cortex. These findings have implications for the prolonged development of self-regulation mediated by development of cognitive and affective control.

Development of Response Inhibition

A number of studies have examined the developmental trajectories of attention executive processes in healthy controls (Bunge et al., 2002; Gupta & Kar, 2009). Gupta and Kar (2009) showed the period of 6 through 9 years to be developmentally active with respect to control processes in normal children. Major developments in response inhibition were found to occur between 7 and 8 years of age in normal children. Other studies have also reported that inhibitory control develops over childhood and does not reach full maturity until 12 years of age or later (Bunge et al., 2002). Substantial improvement in inhibitory control occurs during childhood, and it declines during late adulthood (Williams, Ponesse, Schachar, Logan, & Tannock, 1999).

Paradigms such as the go/no-go task, the stop signal task, and the Stroop task have been used to study inhibitory control. Performance on Strooplike tasks improves through 3 to 7 years of age (Gerstadt, Hong, & Diamond, 1994) and declines during late adulthood (Spieler, Balota, & Faust, 1996). Christ, White, Mandernach, and Keys (2001) investigated the ability to inhibit a prepotent response and generate an incompatible response in individuals ranging from 6 to 82 years of age. They found that the inhibitory control effect was larger in children and older adults than for young adults and larger for older adults than children. They further argued that childhood is a critical period in terms of frontal lobe and cognitive development. Thus, changes in inhibitory control could have occurred within the age range of 6 to 15 years. They divided the child group into two age groups: 6 to 9 years and 10 to 15 years. RT data suggested that younger children responded more slowly than older children. To determine if the discrepancy in the magnitude of the effect was attributable to differences in processing speed rather than inhibitory control, the data were reanalyzed following proportional and z-score transformations. Results of the proportional score supported the raw RT data. However, using the more rigorous z-score procedure, group effect and the interaction between group and condition (congruent vs. incongruent) were not found to be significant. These findings indicate that early age-related differences in inhibitory control were due to difference in processing speed rather than true differences in inhibitory control.

In a study on development of response inhibition using the stop signal task, Gupta et al. (2009) observed that major developments in response inhibition occurred between 7 and 8 years of age. Our results indicate that the significant development in error processing, as measured by posterror slowing (PES), takes place between 6 and 10 years of age; an initial increase in PES is followed by a decrease (see Figure 1.3). The decrement was not uniform between 7 and 10 years, with a larger reduction in PES between ages 9 and 10. The study looked at RT distributions for those trials immediately following errors. The distributions revealed that the largest reduction, between 9 and 10 years, was due primarily to a decrease in RTs of the 95th percentile value, indicating a speeding up of the RTs of essentially slow trials. This result indicates that between 9 and 10 years of age, the occasional inability to recover from prior error trials (which result in the larger number of slow trials) gets reduced, with an enhanced ability to respond appropriately in the subsequent trial.

Other developmental studies on inhibitory control have also shown significant development between 7.5 and 9.5 years of age, followed by 9.6 through 11.5 years (Brocki & Bohlin, 2006). Becker, Isaac, and Hynd (1987) reported a developmental transition in inhibitory control between 6 and 8 years of age. Active development of response inhibition between 7 and 8 years of age is consistent with the maturational patterns of the frontal cortex, which mediates inhibitory control (Hudspeth & Pribram, 1992).

Development of Task Switching

The effect of age on task switching has been examined mainly in adults. Only a few studies have examined age-related changes in the switch costs

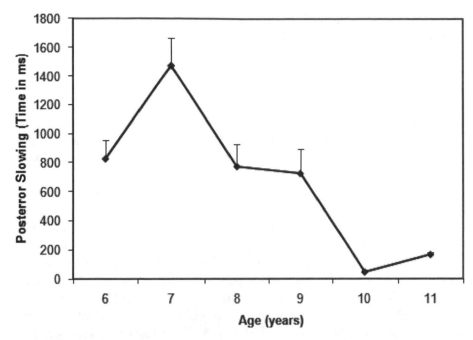

Figure 1.3. Error processing (posterror slowing) among children 6–11 years of age. From R. Gupta, B. R. Kar, and N. Srinivasan, 2009, "Development of Task Switching and Error Monitoring in Children," *Behavioral and Brain Functions, 5,* p. 38. Copyright 2009 by the authors. Adapted with permission.

(i.e., the difference in reaction time when switching between tasks vs. repeating tasks within a mixed task block) in children (Cepeda et al., 2001; Crone, Bunge, van der Molen, & Ridderinkhof, 2006; Dibbets & Jolles, 2006). Different components of task switching have been investigated by manipulating the delay between consecutive trials or between the task cue and the target trials. These manipulations can reveal whether performance deficits are associated with an inability to inhibit the previous task set (i.e., overriding the previously relevant stimulus–response [S-R] rule) or with difficulty in activating the upcoming task set (i.e., rule retrieval). Davidson, Amso, Anderson, and Diamond (2006) examined children 4 through 13 years of age and reported that switching showed a long developmental progression. Even by 13 years, children did not perform at adult levels.

Developmental studies have reported that the switch costs decrease as children grow older (Cepeda et al., 2001), but the underlying processes of this trajectory remain unclear. Cepeda et al. (2001) examined age-related differences in task switching performance in terms of changes in processes responsible for preparation and interference control. They manipulated cue–target interval (CTI) and intertrial interval (ITI) or response–cue interval (RCI) and found that the benefit in increasing the CTI was similar for all the age groups. In contrast, increasing the RCI resulted in a decrease in switch costs for the young adults but not for the children. These results indicated that age did not interact with the preparation time (CTI) and ITI for children, indicating that switching performance was not dependent on CTI or RCI. The effect of both of these variables did not change with age. They observed larger switch costs among young children 7 to 9 years of age, but this effect decreased with age. Performance improved with increased preparation time for the next task. There was a reduction in improvement as the interval between the response to one task and the cue specifying the next task was increased.

It has been suggested that young children probably experience more interference from the previous S-R association, indicating larger carryover effects from the previous trial. Kray, Eber, and Lindenberger (2004) examined the age-related changes in task switching in children (mean age 9.4 years), young adults (mean age 21.5 years), and older adults (mean age 65.3 years) using categorization of pictures by object or by color. The tasks were indicated by semantic instructional cues. Dibbets and Jolles (2006) focused on task switching in children younger than 6 years (58–156 months old) and the development of this ability across childhood. The results indicated that the children younger than 6 years were able to switch between two tasks and that the general performance increased with age. Young children (58–89 months) displayed larger global switch costs than older children (106–156 months)— that is, they made more errors when the tasks were presented randomly compared with the repeated task baseline. These findings suggest that the ability to maintain and manipulate two different tasks in working memory is present, but not fully developed, in young children. These results also indicate that the performance deficits in children are associated with an inability to inhibit the previous task set.

It has been argued that when a task is repeated, individuals benefit from response repetition if the R-S interval is short (called the *automatic facilitation effect*; Soetens, Boer, & Hueting, 1985). However, when a task is not repeated, individuals are hindered by response repetition (called the *reversed repetition effect*), which has been linked to an inhibitory process (Meiran & Gottler, 2001). Both effects are sensitive to developmental changes. For example, Smulders et al. (2005) found that automatic facilitation was larger among younger children (7–9 years of age), indicating larger carryover effects from prior S-R associations. Crone et al. (2006) found greater switch costs with young children (7–8 years of age) compared with adults for task switching with repeating responses. This age difference decreased with the increase in the interval between the previous response and the upcoming stimulus.

It has been argued that inhibition of the task set is one of the contributors to attentional disengagement measured by switch costs (Monsell, 2003).

Cepeda et al. (2001) examined age-related differences in task switching with respect to the processes responsible for preparation and interference control that underlie the ability to flexibly alternate between two different tasks. They observed larger switch costs among young children (7–9 years) that decreased with age. Crone et al. (2006) argued that young children build up stronger transient associations between task sets and response sets that interfere with their ability to switch to currently intended actions. They found greater switch costs and greater carryover effects due to S-R associations for younger children (7–8 years) compared with older children (10–12 years).

The development of task switching and error processing is not gradual (Gupta et al., 2009). We examined whether shared or different mechanisms underlie these processes from a developmental perspective. One hundred eighty children (30 in each of six age groups from 6 to 11 years) participated in the study and performed two tasks: identifying a digit or counting the number of digits. We computed switch costs as a function of response repetition, S-R compatibility, and posterror slowing (Figure 1.4). The results presented in Figure 1.4 demonstrate that reduction in switch costs varied as a function of response repetition or switching. We observed switch costs when the responses were repeated (reversed-repetition effect), and this effect decreased with age. More important, we found that developmental advances in the reversed-repetition effect occurred between 7 to 8 and 9 to 10 years of age. It is possible that children experience greater carryover effects from the S-R association that has been already activated.

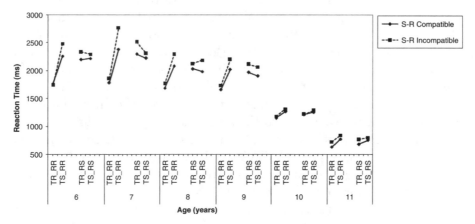

Figure 1.4. Response latencies as a function of task switch/nonswitch, response repetition/response switch, and stimulus–response (S-R) compatibility/incompatibility among children 6–11 years of age. RR = response repetition; RS = response switch; TR = task repetition; TS = task switch. From R. Gupta, B. R. Kar, and N. Srinivasan, 2009, "Development of Task Switching and Error Monitoring in Children," *Behavioral and Brain Functions, 5,* p. 38. Copyright 2009 by the authors. Adapted with permission.

Gupta et al. (2009) also analyzed reaction time distributions. RT distributions showed that the decrement in the switch cost was due to the overall decrease in RTs in fast (5th percentile) trials in 9- to 11-year-olds and slow (95th percentile) trials in children ages 7 to 8 and 9 to 11 years in both the task switch and nonswitch trials. A major reduction in RT was found between 9 and 11 years in both the response type and S-R compatibility conditions. RT distributions for posterror trials revealed that the large decrement seen in children ages 7 to 8 and 9 to 10 years was primarily due to the sudden decrease in RTs in the fast and slow trials, respectively. The developmental pattern of error processing is similar to that of the switch cost of the response repetition condition in task switching, indicating that inhibition could be a common mechanism underlying both processes. The results from the studies discussed so far indicate that the ability to flexibly switch between task rules and responses is sensitive to developmental change and is influenced by working memory and inhibition.

DEVELOPMENT OF AFFECTIVE CONTROL

The interaction between cognitive and emotional processes plays an important role in the development of behavior regulation. Emotions influence many psychological processes, and these processes in turn influence emotions (Hare & Casey, 2005). Younger children have more difficulty in resolving conflicts than older ones (Posner & Rothbart, 2000), and conflict resolution becomes more difficult when emotional content is involved. Developmental studies on affective control have shown distinct patterns of brain activity, with adolescents showing greater activation of the amygdala and adults showing greater activity in the ventral prefrontal cortex (Hare & Casey, 2005). There is a greater susceptibility to attend to irrelevant information and a transition from diffuse to focal patterns of prefrontal activity with development. Another study looking at developmental differences in cognitive control in the context of distracting socioaffective cues compared children (6–13 years) and adults and found that cognitive control of socioaffective processing differs in preadolescent years relative to earlier, in late childhood, and later, in adulthood (Barnes, Kaplan, & Vaidya, 2007).

Mishra and Kar (2010) investigated affective control in children and adults with respect to conflict adaptation using the emotional Stroop paradigm with facial expressions as stimuli comparing positive and negative emotion. They found conflict adaptation effects (trial sequence effects with respect to congruency) in adults as well as children, with more pronounced effects for positive affect (happy) compared with negative affect (sad). Children took more time to resolve a conflict present in the current trial and later to adapt to conflict due to the effect of the previous trial congruence when compared with adults, which shows that the ability to resolve conflicts with respect to affective stimuli develops with age.

One study using the ANT with emotional faces showed that the magnitude of the conflict effect was reduced with age to a greater extent for the happy affect than for the sad affect for children 6 to 8 years and 10 to 13 years of age and for young adults (Kar, Vijay, & Mishra, in press). It was observed that focused attentional strategies were used for the processing of negative affect and distributed attentional strategies for positive affect among both older children and adults. Conflict resolution in a nonemotional ANT also showed significant age effects. Cognitive and affective control in terms of executive attention effects on the ANT was observed to be closer between older children and adults. Temperament was significantly correlated with performance on the ANT with emotional as well as nonemotional stimuli for children in both age groups. Research on the development of cognitive and affective control needs to consider the effect of social and affective context, temperament, and other environmental factors to enhance our understanding of the development of self-regulation of behavior.

GENETIC AND EXPERIENTIAL EFFECTS ON THE DEVELOPMENT OF CONTROL PROCESSES

The development of attention and control processes in childhood and adolescence is shaped by genes and experience. The development of executive attention is mediated by sociodemographic factors such as socioeconomic status and racial differences. Mezzacappa (2004) reported that older children, socially advantaged children, and African American children have better executive control on the ANT, showing better resistance to interference by the competing demands of the flankers. Developmental trajectories interact with environmental factors, such as education and parenting styles, as well as deterministic factors, such as genes and temperament. Individual differences have been found in the efficiency of the executive attention network, which involves the anterior cingulate and prefrontal areas. So far, alleles of four dopamine-related genes have been found to relate to the efficiency of this network (Diamond, Briand, Fossella, & Gehlbach, 2004; Fan, Fossella, Summer, Wu, & Posner, 2003). Substantial development of executive attention required for attentional control has been found to occur during 3 to 7 years of age, and much of this is under genetic control, along with the influence of school and home environment.

In one of their studies, Rueda, Rothbart, McCandliss, Saccomanno, and Posner (2005) explored differences in temperament and genotype as a way of understanding which children might benefit from attention training. They documented the role of temperament and the *DAT1* gene in individual differences in attention and reported that the development of executive attention is under genetic control but is influenced by educational interventions during the course of development in early and middle childhood. In Chapter 2 of this volume, on the nature and nurture of executive attention development, Rueda and Cómbita also report strong effects of education and parenting on the development of the executive attention network. The importance of parenting for behaviors such as activity level and impulsivity shows that the ability of children to handle the school situation may depend on the joint interaction of genes and environment (Posner & Kar, 2010). Rueda et al. (2004) traced the development of executive attention using ANT, finding strong development in the preschool and early school period. Rueda et al. (2005) showed that the brain network underlying executive control and self-regulation can be influenced by training exercises.

There are many forms of attention training, but one form of importance is the practice of meditation. Studies have shown that the practice of meditation affects attentional processes (for a review, see Lutz et al., 2009). Recent studies have looked at the effects of meditation in children, which would affect attentional processes that are already being developed (Baijal, Jha, Kiyonaga, Singh, & Srinivasan, 2011; Flook et al., 2010; Napoli, Krech, & Holley, 2005). A study with adolescents practicing transcendental meditation showed that attentional processes were differentially affected by meditation practice and that these effects are a function of practice and age (Baijal et al., 2011). Different attentional networks were evaluated using the ANT as a function of the practice of transcendental meditation. Results showed that alerting and executive control improved with transcendental meditation practice, but there was no effect on orienting. Studies on meditation training with children indicate that attentional processes that are consistent with the normal developmental pattern can be further strengthened with meditation practice. In addition, meditation practice and other forms of attention training can possibly help with rehabilitation of children with disorders like ADHD.

CONCLUSION

Developmental trajectories of attentional processes including selection, inhibition, and switching reach the most active period at 6 to 9 years and continue to show age-related differences until adolescence. The rapid development of attention and control processes in childhood has implications for understanding the mechanisms underlying developmental cognitive disorders such as ADHD. Understanding and measuring cognitive motivational deficits in ADHD enables researchers to develop a potential diagnostic system for ADHD based on cognitive impairments, particularly control processes such as response inhibition, task switching, and error monitoring (Gupta, Kar, & Srinivasan, 2010). With respect to control mechanisms, development of affective control shows late maturation compared with cognitive control. Future studies need to account for the independent as well as the interactive effects of social and affective context, along with the effects of genes and neural activity, on the development of attention and control. So far, very few studies have been done with such a perspective. Further cross-cultural studies in this field could inform the profession about the differential effects of environment and the interaction between genes and experience on cognitive development across cultures.

REFERENCES

Akhtar, N., & Enns, J. T. (1989). Relations between covert orienting and filtering of visual attention. *Journal of Experimental Child Psychology, 48,* 315–334. doi:10.1016/0022-0965(89)90008-8

Baijal, S., Jha, A., Kiyonaga, A., Singh, R., & Srinivasan, N. (2011). The influence of concentrative meditation training on the development of attention networks in early adolescence. *Frontiers in Psychology, 2,* 153. doi:10.3389/fpsyg.2011.00153

Barnes, K. A., Kaplan, L. A., & Vaidya, C. (2007). Developmental differences in cognitive control of socio-affective processing. *Developmental Neuropsychology, 32,* 787–807. doi:10.1080/87565640701539576

Becker, M. G., Isaac, W., & Hynd, G. W. (1987). Neuropsychological development of nonverbal behaviours attributed to "frontal lobe" functioning. *Developmental Neuropsychology, 3,* 275–298. doi:10.1080/87565648709540381

Brass, M., Ruge, H., Meiran, N., Rubin, O., Koch, I., Zysset, S., . . . von Cramon, D. Y. (2003). When the same response has different meanings: Recoding the response meaning in the lateral prefrontal cortex. *NeuroImage, 20,* 1026–1031. doi:10.1016/S1053-8119(03)00357-4

Brocki, K. C., & Bohlin, G. (2006). Developmental changes in the relation between executive functions and symptoms of ADHD and co-occurring behaviour problems. *Infant and Child Development, 15,* 19–40. doi:10.1002/icd.413

Bunge, S. A., Dudukovic, N. M., Thomason, M. E., Vaidya, C. J., & Gabrieli, J. D. E. (2002). Immature frontal lobe contributions to cognitive control in children: Evidence from fMRI. *Neuron, 33,* 301–311. doi:10.1016/S0896-6273(01)00583-9

Burack, J. A., & Enns, J. T. (Eds.). (1997). *Attention, development, and psychopathology: A merging of disciplines.* New York, NY: Guilford Press.

Cepeda, N. J., Kramer, A. F., & Gonzalez de Sather, J. C. (2001). Changes in executive control across the life span: Examination of task-switching performance. *Developmental Psychology, 37*, 715–730. doi:10.1037/0012-1649.37.5.715

Christ, S. E., White, D. A., Mandernach, T., & Keys, B. A. (2001). Inhibitory control across the life span. *Developmental Neuropsychology, 20*, 653–669.

Corbetta, M., Kincade, J. M., Ollinger, J. M., McAvoy, M. P., & Shulman, G. L. (2000). Voluntary orienting is dissociated from target detection in human posterior parietal cortex. *Nature Neuroscience, 3*, 292–297. doi:10.1038/73009

Corbetta, M., & Shulman, G. L. (2002). Control of goal-directed and stimulus driven attention in the brain. *Nature Reviews Neuroscience, 3*, 201–215. doi:10.1038/nrn755

Crone, E. A. (2009). Executive functions in adolescence: Inferences from brain and behavior. *Developmental Science, 12*, 825–830. doi:10.1111/j.1467-7687.2009.00918.x

Crone, E. A., Bunge, S. A., van der Molen, M. W., & Ridderinkhof, K. R. (2006). Switching between tasks and responses: A developmental study. *Developmental Science, 9*, 278–287. doi:10.1111/j.1467-7687.2006.00490.x

Crone, E. A., Ridderinkhof, R. K., Worm, M., Somsen, R. J. M., & van der Molen, M. W. (2004). Switching between spatial stimulus-response mappings: A developmental study of cognitive flexibility. *Developmental Science, 7*, 443–455. doi:10.1111/j.1467-7687.2004.00365.x

Davidson, M. C., Amso, D., Anderson, L. C., & Diamond, A. (2006). Development of cognitive control and executive functions from 4–13 years: Evidence from manipulations of memory, inhibition and task switching. *Neuropsychologia, 44*, 2037–2078. doi:10.1016/j.neuropsychologia.2006.02.006

Davies, P. L., Segalowitz, S. L., & Gavin, W. J. (2004). Development of response-monitoring ERPs in 7- to 25-year olds. *Developmental Neuropsychology, 25*, 355–376. doi:10.1207/s15326942dn2503_6

Diamond, A., Briand, L., Fossella, J., & Gehlbach, L. (2004). Genetic and neurochemical modulation of prefrontal cognitive functions in children. *American Journal of Psychiatry, 161*, 125–132. doi:10.1176/appi.ajp.161.1.125

Dibbets, P., & Jolles, J. (2006). The switch task for children: Measuring mental flexibility in young children. *Cognitive Development, 21*, 6071.

Dreher, J.-C., & Grafman, J. (2003). Dissociating the roles of the rostral anterior cingulate and the lateral prefrontal cortices in performing two tasks simultaneously or successively. *Cerebral Cortex, 13*, 329–339. doi:10.1093/cercor/13.4.329

Dye, M. W. G., & Bavalier, D. (2010). Differential development of visual attention skills in school-age children. *Vision Research, 50*, 452–459. doi:10.1016/j.visres.2009.10.010

Enns, J. T., & Brodeur, D. (1989). A developmental study of covert orienting to peripheral visual cues. *Journal of Experimental Child Psychology, 48*, 171–189. doi:10.1016/0022-0965(89)90001-5

Enns, J. T., & Trick, L. M. (2006). Four modes of selection. In E. Bialystok & F. I. M. Craik (Eds.), *Lifespan cognition: Mechanisms of change* (pp. 43–56). New York, NY: Oxford University Press. doi:10.1093/acprof:oso/9780195169539.003.0004

Eriksen, C. W. (1995). The Flankers task and response competition: A useful tool for investigating a variety of cognitive problems. *Visual Cognition, 2,* 101–118. doi:10.1080/13506289508401726

Etkin, A., Egner, T., Peraza, D. M., Kandel, E. R., & Hirsch, J. (2006). Resolving emotional conflict: A role for the rostral anterior cingulate cortex in modulating activity in amygdala. *Neuron, 51,* 871–882.

Fan, J., Fossella, J. A., Summer, T., Wu, Y., & Posner, M. I. (2003). Mapping the genetic variation of executive attention onto brain activity. *Proceedings of the National Academy of Sciences of the United States of America, 100,* 7406–7411. doi:10.1073/pnas.0732088100

Fan, J., McCandliss, B. D., Sommer, T., Raz, M., & Posner, M. I. (2002). Testing the efficiency and independence of attentional networks. *Journal of Cognitive Neuroscience, 14,* 340–347. doi:10.1162/089892902317361886

Flook, L., Smalley, S. L., Kitil, J. M., Galla, B. M., Kaiser-Greenland, S., Locke, J., . . . Kasari, C. (2010). Effects of mindful awareness practices on executive functions in elementary school children. *Journal of Applied School Psychology, 26,* 70–95. doi:10.1080/15377900903379125

Friedman, D., Nessler, D., Cycowicz, Y. M., & Horton, C. (2009). Development of and change in cognitive control: A comparison of children, young adults and older adults. *Cognitive, Affective & Behavioral Neuroscience, 9,* 91–102. doi:10.3758/CABN.9.1.91

Gerstadt, C. L., Hong, Y. J., & Diamond, A. (1994). The relationship between cognition and action: Performance of children 31/2–7 years old on a Stroop-like day–night test. *Cognition, 53,* 129–153. doi:10.1016/0010-0277(94)90068-X

Goldman, K. J., Flanagan, T., Shulman, C., Enns, J. T., & Burack, J. A. (2005). Voluntary orienting among children and adolescents with Down syndrome and MA-matched typically developing children. *American Journal on Mental Retardation, 110,* 157–163. doi:10.1352/0895-8017(2005)110<157:VOACAA>2.0.CO;2

Gupta, R., & Kar, B. R. (2009). Development of attentional processes in children with ADHD and normally developing children. In N. Srinivasan (Ed.), *Progress in brain research: Vol. 176. Attention* (pp. 259–276). Amsterdam, the Netherlands: Elsevier.

Gupta, R., Kar, B. R., & Srinivasan, N. (2009). Development of task switching and error monitoring in children. *Behavioral and Brain Functions, 5,* 38. doi:10.1186/1744-9081-5-38

Gupta, R., Kar, B. R., & Srinivasan, N. (2010). Cognitive–motivational deficits in ADHD: Development of a classification system. *Child Neuropsychology, 17,* 67–81. doi:10.1080/09297049.2010.524152

Hare, T. A., & Casey, B. J. (2005). The neurobiology of cognitive and affective control. *Cognition Brain and Behaviour, 9*, 273–286.

Hare, T. A., Tottenham, N., Galvan, A., Voss, H. U., Glover, G. H., & Casey, B. J. (2008). Biological substrates of emotional reactivity and regulation in adolescence during an emotional go-nogo task. *Biological Psychiatry, 63*, 927–934. doi:10.1016/j.biopsych.2008.03.015

Henrich, J., Heine, S. J., & Norenzayan, A. (2010). The weirdest people in the world? *Behavioral and Brain Sciences, 33*, 61–83. doi:10.1017/S0140525X0999152X

Hooper, C. J., Luciana, M., Conklin, H. M., & Yarger, R. (2004). Adolescents' performance on the Iowa Gambling Task: Implications for the development of decision making and ventromedial prefrontal cortex. *Developmental Psychology, 40*, 1148–1158. doi:10.1037/0012-1649.40.6.1148

Hudspeth, W. J., & Pribram, K. H. (1992). Psychophysiological indices of cerebral maturation. *International Journal of Psychophysiology, 12*, 19–29. doi:10.1016/0167-8760(92)90039-E

Kar, B. R., Rao, S. L., Chandramouli, B. A., & Thennarasu, K. (2011). Growth patterns of neuropsychological functions in Indian children. *Frontiers in Psychology, 2*, 240. doi:10.3389/fpsyg.2011.00240

Kar, B. R., Vijay, N., & Mishra, S. (in press). Development of cognitive and affective control brain networks and its influence on decision making. In V. S. Chandrasekhar Pammi & N. Srinivasan (Eds.), *Decision making: Neural and behavioural approaches*. Amsterdam, the Netherlands: Elsevier.

Klenberg, L., Korkman, M., & Lahti-Nuuttila, P. (2001). Differential development of attention and executive functions in 3 to 12 year old Finnish children. *Developmental Neuropsychology, 20*, 407–428. doi:10.1207/S15326942DN2001_6

Kray, J., Eber, J., & Lindenberger, U. (2004). Age differences in executive functioning across the life-span: The role of verbalization in task preparation. *Acta Psychologica, 115*, 143–165. doi:10.1016/j.actpsy.2003.12.001

Lutz, A., Slagter, H. A., Rawling, B. N., Francis, D. A., Greischar, L. L., & Davidson, R. J. (2009). Mental training enhances stability of attention by reducing cortical noise. *Journal of Neuroscience, 29*, 13418–13427. doi:10.1523/JNEUROSCI.1614-09.2009

Marrocco, R. T., & Davidson, M. C. (1998). Neurochemistry of attention. In R. Parasuraman (Ed.), *The attentive brain* (pp. 35–50). Cambridge, England: Cambridge University Press.

Matsumoto, K., & Tanaka, K. (2004, February 13). Conflict and cognitive control. *Science, 303*, 969–970. doi:10.1126/science.1094733

Meiran, N., & Gottler, A. (2001). Modeling cognitive control in task-switching and aging. *Trends in Cognitive Sciences, 13*, 165–186.

Mezzacappa, E. (2004). Alerting, orienting, and executive attention: Developmental properties and sociodemographic correlates in an epidemiological sample of young, urban children. *Child Development, 75*, 1373–1386. doi:10.1111/j.1467-8624.2004.00746.x

Mishra, S., & Kar, B. R. (2010, December). *Conflict adaptation as a measure of affective control*. Poster presented at the International Conference on Cognitive Development, Allahabad, India.

Monsell, S. (2003). Task switching. *Trends in Cognitive Sciences, 7,* 134–140. doi:10.1016/S1364-6613(03)00028-7

Napoli, M., Krech, P., & Holley, L. (2005). Mindfulness training for elementary school students: The attention academy program. *Journal of Applied School Psychology, 21,* 99–125. doi:10.1300/J370v21n01_05

Plude, D. J., Enns, J. T., & Brodeur, D. A. (1994). The development of selective attention: A lifespan overview. *Acta Psychologica, 86,* 227–272. doi:10.1016/0001-6918(94)90004-3

Posner, M. I. (1980). Orienting of attention. *Quarterly Journal of Experimental Psychology, 32,* 3–25. doi:10.1080/00335558008248231

Posner, M. I., & Kar, B. R. (2010). Brain networks of attention and preparing for school subjects. In N. Srinivasan, B. R. Kar, & J. Pandey (Eds.), *Advances in cognitive science* (Vol. 2, pp. 256–269). Delhi, India: Sage.

Posner, M. I., & Rothbart, M. K. (2000). Developing mechanisms of self regulation. *Development and Psychopathology, 12,* 427–441. doi:10.1017/S0954579400003096

Randolph, B. (2002). *Covert orienting across the lifespan.* (Unpublished doctoral dissertation). McGill University, Department of Psychology, Montreal, Quebec, Canada.

Rensink, R. A. (2002). Change detection. *Annual Review of Psychology, 53,* 245–277.

Rieger, M., & Gauggel, S. (1999). Inhibitory after-effects in the stop signal paradigm. *British Journal of Psychology, 90,* 509–518. doi:10.1348/000712699161585

Ristic, J., Friesen, C. K., & Kingstone, A. (2002). Are eyes special? It depends on how you look at it. *Psychonomic Bulletin & Review, 9,* 507–513. doi:10.3758/BF03196306

Rueda, M. R., Fan, J., McCandliss, B., Halparin, J. D., Gruber, D. B., Pappert, L., & Posner, M. I. (2004). Development of attentional networks in childhood. *Neuropsychologia, 42,* 1029–1040. doi:10.1016/j.neuropsychologia.2003.12.012

Rueda, M. R., Rothbart, M. K., McCandliss, B. D., Saccomanno, L., & Posner, M. I. (2005). Training, maturation, and genetic influences on the development of executive attention. *Proceedings of the National Academy of Sciences of the United States of America, 102,* 14931–14936. doi:10.1073/pnas.0506897102

Santesso, D. L., Segalowitz, S. J., & Schmidt, L. A. (2006). Error-related electrocortical responses in 10-year-old children and young adults. *Developmental Science, 9,* 473–481. doi:10.1111/j.1467-7687.2006.00514.x

Shore, D. I., Burack, J. A., Miller, D., Joseph, S., & Enns, J. T. (2006). The development of change detection. *Developmental Science, 9,* 490–497. doi:10.1111/j.1467-7687.2006.00516.x

Smulders, S. F. A., Notebaert, W., Meijer, M., Crone, E. A., van der Molen, M. W., & Soetens, E. (2005). Sequential effects on speeded information processing: A developmental study. *Journal of Experimental Child Psychology, 90*, 208–234. doi:10.1016/j.jecp.2004.10.003

Soetens, E., Boer, L. C., & Hueting, J. E. (1985). Expectancy or automatic facilitation? Separating sequential effects in two-choice reaction time. *Journal of Experimental Psychology: Human Perception and Performance, 11*, 598–616. doi:10.1037/0096-1523.11.5.598

Spieler, D. H., Balota, D. A., & Faust, M. E. (1996). Stroop performance in healthy younger and older adults and in individuals with dementia of the Alzheimer's type. *Journal of Experimental Psychology: Human Perception and Performance, 22*, 461–479. doi:10.1037/0096-1523.22.2.461

Steinberg, L. (2005). Cognitive and affective development in adolescence. *Trends in Cognitive Sciences, 9*, 69–74. doi:10.1016/j.tics.2004.12.005

Trick, L., & Enns, J. T. (1998). Lifespan changes in attention: The visual search task. *Cognitive Development, 13*, 369–386. doi:10.1016/S0885-2014(98)90016-8

Williams, B. R., Ponesse, J. S., Schachar, R. J., Logan, G. D., & Tannock, R. (1999). Development of inhibitory control across the life span. *Developmental Psychology, 35*, 205–213. doi:10.1037/0012-1649.35.1.205

2

THE NATURE AND NURTURE OF EXECUTIVE ATTENTION DEVELOPMENT

M. ROSARIO RUEDA AND LINA M. CÓMBITA

One of the major changes that take place during development over the first years of life has to do with children's ability to regulate behavior in a thoughtful and deliberate manner. During infancy, behavior is regulated, for the most part, by changes in internal or external stimulation and by interactions with caregivers. With age, children become increasingly able to monitor their actions and self-regulate emotions according to their own goals or the requirements of the situation.

Attention is an important mechanism for action monitoring, particularly when responses must be selected in a voluntary and effortful way. When acting in a reflexive or automatic mode, action coordination does not implicate attention control because responses can be automatically triggered by the stimulation. However, attention is needed in a variety of situations in which automatic processing either is not available (e.g., in a novel task) or is

This work was supported by Spanish Ministry of Science and Innovation Grant PSI2011.027746 as well as by funds from the CoEduca Project of the Consolider Ingenio 2010 Program.

DOI: 10.1037/14043-003
Cognition and Brain Development: Converging Evidence From Various Methodologies, B. R. Kar (Editor)

likely to produce inappropriate responses (e.g., difficult tasks, tasks in which there is conflict between possible responses). Posner and Snyder (1975) first argued for the central role of attention for cognitive control. Years later, Norman and Shallice (1986) developed a cognitive model for distinguishing between automatic and controlled processing. According to that model, attention is required when situations call for careful and elaborate responses, such as those involving novelty, error correction, troubleshooting, some degree of danger or difficulty, or the overcoming of strong habitual responses or tendencies.

Attention is also important for the regulation of affect. During infancy, attention orientation often serves as a means for down-regulating babies' distress (Harman, Rothbart, & Posner, 1997). Also, greater flexibility of orienting in infancy is associated with lower parent-reported negative emotionality and better soothing ability (Johnson, Posner, & Rothbart, 1991). Later on, attention and effortful control are involved in the modulation of emotional reactivity (Rothbart & Rueda, 2005). Social contexts (e.g., school) and social interactions impose increasing self-regulation demands, and children must learn to regulate their motivations and emotions in order to accommodate to such demands. Neuroimaging studies in adults have shown that neural structures involved in attention are important for the control of both cognition and emotion (Bush, Luu, & Posner, 2000).

This chapter focuses on the development of attention control during early childhood and the factors, both constitutional and experiential, that affect individual differences in the development of this function. We first introduce the concept of *executive attention* and describe the neural network subserving this function. Next, we discuss the development of executive attention during childhood and describe how individual differences in the efficiency of this system influence a wide range of aspects in children's life, including schooling and socialization. In subsequent sections, we review current evidence on genetic factors associated with differences in efficiency of attention control, as well as aspects of the environmental and educational context of children's development that have been shown to have an impact on the development of attention. Finally, we discuss data provided by recent studies exploring the ways in which genetic variation interacts with experience to determine patterns of behavior and cognitive efficacy related to attention regulation.

EXECUTIVE ATTENTION NETWORK

A variety of cognitive components have been associated with attention from early theoretical accounts, including vigilance, selectivity, and control (James, 1890). According to Posner's neurocognitive model, attention is related to the function of three brain networks (Posner & Petersen, 1990; Posner, Rueda, & Kanske, 2007). The first two of them are involved in reaching and/or maintaining the alerting state (*alerting network*) and orienting toward and/or selecting the source of stimulation (*orienting network*). The third network, the so-called *executive attention network* (EAN), functions to regulate thoughts, emotions, and action. The EAN is not involved in processing information but instead serves the function of monitoring and resolving conflict between processes carried out by other brain networks. Functions associated with the EAN overlap to some extent with the more general domain of executive functions, which encompass a set of interrelated processes involved in planning and carrying out goal-directed actions, including working memory, mental-set switching or attentional flexibility, inhibitory control, and conflict monitoring (Blair & Ursache, 2011; Welch, 2001).

A widely used strategy to study executive attention in cognitive research is to use conflict tasks (Posner & DiGirolamo, 1998). These involve either suppressing processing or responding to information that elicits an incorrect or inappropriate response. One of these is the flanker task (Eriksen & Eriksen, 1974). In this task, a target stimulus is surrounded by stimulation that suggests either the same (congruent) or a different (incongruent) response than the one associated with the target. Suppressing the processing of the distracting information in the incongruent condition requires attentional control and activates the EAN to a greater extent than when there is no conflict between target and flankers (Fan, Flombaum, McCandliss, Thomas, & Posner, 2003). Another widely used conflict task is the Stroop task. Imaging studies have shown that individuals performing the classical color–word Stroop task as well as other variations of the task activate the anterior cingulate cortex (ACC; Bush et al., 2000).

The EAN comprises a circuitry of brain structures involving the ACC and lateral and medial prefrontal regions of the brain (Posner et al., 2007). These structures are target areas of the ventral tegmental dopamine system. Layer 5 of the cingulate contains all of the dopamine receptors, and this node of the EAN is widely connected to many other cortical areas (Goldman-Rakic, 1988). Studies of functional connectivity have shown that lateral and medial frontal areas are strongly connected to parietal structures in neonates. By age 2, the ACC shows stronger connections to lateral parietal and frontal areas (Gao et al., 2009), although connectivity, particularly across more distant areas of the brain, continues to increase during childhood (Fair et al., 2009).

Imaging studies also provide some understanding of the functional role of different areas implicated in the EAN. There is evidence suggesting that the ACC is involved in detecting the occurrence of conflict, which is then conveyed to prefrontal structures in charge of resolving the conflict (Botvinick, Cohen, & Carter, 2004; Fan et al., 2003). Thus, the ACC appears to be the structure involved in monitoring the need for attention control, whereas medial and lateral prefrontal structures may serve the function of holding in mind information relevant to the task and selecting the appropriate action by inhibiting dominant responses in favor of correct ones.

INDIVIDUAL DIFFERENCES IN DEVELOPMENT

Developmental studies have suggested that the three attention networks follow different maturational courses. Whereas the alerting and orienting networks appear to mature to a great extent during infancy and early childhood, the EAN appears to undergo a more progressive maturation, emerging at about the end of the first year of life and continuing during childhood into adolescence (Rueda, Fan, et al., 2004; Rueda & Posner, in press).

However, despite the progressive improvement throughout childhood, executive attention shows a major period of development from about the end of the first year of life up to the end of the preschool years (Rueda, Posner, & Rothbart, 2005). Maturation of this function is related to structural changes in brain areas that are part of the EAN and their connectivity patterns with other brain structures. The developmental course of the EAN and its relation to brain maturation are extensively reviewed in Chapter 3 of this volume.

Aspects of children's temperament have been conceptually and empirically linked to individual differences in executive attention efficiency (Rothbart & Rueda, 2005; Rueda, Posner, & Rothbart, 2011). *Effortful control* (EC) is a dimension of temperament related to the self-regulation of emotional reactivity and behavior (Rothbart, 2007). EC allows increased control over action and adjustment to situational demands in a flexible and willful manner, including both inhibitory control of action (not eating a candy) and activation control (eating a fruit instead). Performance of conflict tasks in the laboratory has been empirically linked to parent- and self-reported EC as assessed with temperament questionnaires. Children who are relatively less affected by conflict receive higher parental ratings of EC and higher scores on laboratory measures of inhibitory control (see Rueda, 2012, for a review). Moreover, variations in the size and structure of the ACC have been related to EC scores obtained in temperament questionnaires, supporting the idea of the EAN as the neural network underlying EC (Posner & Rothbart, 2009; Rothbart & Rueda, 2005).

Given their role in emotion regulation and adjustment, executive attention and EC are considered important contributors to the socioemotional development of the child (Rueda, Checa, & Rothbart, 2010). The ability to regulate behavior in a flexible and controlled mode has proven to be central to many aspects of child development, and in fact, individual differences in efficiency of executive attention appear to play an important role in school competence and socialization (Checa, Rodriguez-Bailon, & Rueda, 2008; Eisenberg, Smith, & Spinrad, 2011; Eisenberg, Valiente, & Eggum, 2010).

In school, control of attention is important to adjust behavior in function of norms and goals, stay focused despite distractions, flexibly allocate attention to information (either internal or external) relevant to current tasks, and persist to complete difficult tasks even when rewards (e.g., learning, good grades) may take time to arrive. Several studies have shown that children with greater executive attention efficiency (i.e., smaller conflict scores) show higher levels of competence at school, with competence being a combination of school achievement and adequate socioemotional adjustment (Blair & Razza, 2007; Bull & Scerif, 2001; Checa et al., 2008). A good example comes from studies examining the role that attention skills play in the achievement of math tasks. Attention has emerged as a potentially robust predictor of arithmetic skills (Fuchs et al., 2005; Russell & Ginsburg, 1984). Pasolunghi, Cornoldi, and De Liberto (1999) showed that children's arithmetic performance is related to the ability to control irrelevant information. In one of their studies, they selected fourth graders according to their ability to solve arithmetic tasks and followed them longitudinally for a 2-year period. Despite the fact that poor problem solvers were able to identify relevant information, they remembered less relevant but more irrelevant information about the arithmetic questions than good problem solvers (Pasolunghi et al., 1999). This finding indicates that children exhibiting poorer arithmetic performance have greater difficulty inhibiting irrelevant information compared with better performers. Other measures tapping the EAN, such as Stroop-like interference and performance on inhibitory control tasks, have shown a consistent relationship with arithmetic competency (Blair & Razza, 2007; Bull & Scerif, 2001; Espy et al., 2004). Recently, Checa and Rueda (2011) showed that the brain reaction to conflict, as measured with event-related potentials (ERPs), also predicts children's grades in math above and beyond general intelligence.

The role of executive attention in school performance and reasoning might also have to do with the anatomical overlap between the EAN and brain areas related to general intelligence and other cognitive demands related to the control of cognition (Duncan & Owen, 2000). Lateral frontal regions of the brain considered to be part of the EAN are activated by marker tasks of general intelligence (Duncan et al., 2000). In our view, efficiency of this brain network results in more successful acquisition and application of knowledge taught in the school, especially in those subjects involving complex reasoning such as mathematics.

On the other hand, individual differences in reactivity and self-regulation, as well as the interactions between them, are involved in the socialization of children and their capacity for socioemotional regulation. When experiencing negative emotions, it is useful to use attention in order to shift thoughts away from the source of distress and to inhibit aggressive impulses and/or mask the expression of negative emotion if needed. In addition, regulation of positive emotions, such as those associated with obtaining desired rewards, often requires reappraising the positive value of immediate or high compensations or rewards taking into consideration that they might lead to more negative consequences in the long term (e.g., eating lots of candy, picking on friends). Flexible allocation of attentional resources facilitates fluent reasoning and helps in connecting current decisions with future consequences. These abilities clearly promote social adjustment, and several studies have supported a key role for executive attention in the use children make of attentional resources. Ellis, Rothbart, and Posner (2004) showed that both mother- and self-reported low EC, together with poor efficiency of executive attention, predicts behavior problems during adolescence. Also, other studies have shown that during childhood, EC is negatively associated with the incidence of externalizing behavioral problems, which are characterized by high levels of aggression and impulsivity, after controlling for other cognitive and social risk factors (Olson, Sameroff, Kerr, Lopez, & Wellman, 2005; Valiente et al., 2003).

Individual differences in executive control are also related to aspects of cognition such as theory of mind (i.e., knowing that people's behavior is guided by their mental state, which includes beliefs, desires, and knowledge; Carlson, Moses, & Claxton, 2004). There is also evidence showing that EC plays an important role in the development of conscience, which involves the interplay between experiencing moral emotions (i.e., guilt/shame or discomfort following transgressions) and behaving morally in a way that is compatible with rules and social norms (Kochanska & Aksan, 2006).

Additional evidence on the role of executive attention in socialization comes from studies looking at brain function directly. An important form of self-regulation is related to the ability to detect and correct self-made errors. Detection and monitoring of errors has been studied using ERPs. A large negative deflection over midline frontal channels is often observed about 100 ms after the commission of an error, called the *error-related negativity* (ERN; Gehring, Gross, Coles, Meyer, & Donchin, 1993). There is evidence that this postresponse signal originates in the ACC (Dehaene, Posner, & Tucker, 1994; Luu, Tucker, Derryberry, Reed, & Poulsen, 2003). The ERN thus provides a means to examine the emergence of this cingulate function during infancy and childhood. In a study conducted with a flanker task and ERPs, it was shown that children who committed more errors on incongruent trials showed smaller amplitudes in the error monitoring wave. This result suggests less sensitivity of the brains of these children to the commission of errors. Also, the amplitude of the ERN was predicted by individual differences in social behavior in that children with poorer social sensitivity, as assessed by a self-report personality questionnaire, were the ones showing ERNs of smaller amplitude (Santesso, Segalowitz, & Schmidt, 2005). Moreover, empathy appears to show a positive relation to amplitude of the ERN (Santesso & Segalowitz, 2009). Children high in EC also appear to be high in empathy and guilt/shame and low in aggressiveness (Rothbart, Ahadi, & Hershey, 1994). Likewise, Eisenberg, Fabes, Nyman, Bernzweig, and Pinuelas (1994) found that 4- to 6-year old boys with good attentional control tended to deal with anger by using nonhostile verbal methods rather than overt aggressive methods. In sum, all this evidence suggests that poor efficiency of the EAN may result in greater difficulty experiencing or appreciating the emotional significance of errors and other unfavorable outcomes leading to higher risk of maladjustment at the school and other social contexts.

NATURE OF EXECUTIVE ATTENTION DEVELOPMENT

In previous sections, we presented evidence establishing a connection between self-regulated behavior and the structural and functional properties of a particular network of brain areas, the EAN. Higher functional efficiency of this network is associated with greater self-regulatory skills. But what makes the brain of an individual more efficient? One possible answer to this question is that neural efficiency is determined by the genetic endowment that is inherited from parents. If this was the case, then the efficiency of the network or the behavior supported by it would have to show some degree of heritability. Heritability of the attention networks was tested in a twin study conducted with the attention network task (ANT). In this study, executive attention scores showed stronger concordance for monozygotic compared with dizygotic twins, indicating a significant level of heritability for this attention function (Fan, Wu, Fossella, & Posner, 2001). Genetic variation may therefore be considered one of the factors accounting for individual differences in the efficiency of the EAN, which in turn determines the ability for attention control that can be directly observed through behavior. Brain function may thus serve as an intermediate link (also called *endophenotype*) between genetic variation and behavioral differences (*phenotype*) in executive attention (Fossella & Casey, 2006). Tracing that link requires a thorough and detailed characterization of the phenotype (through the use of marker tasks and behavioral assessments) as well as the neural mechanisms (circuits and neuromodulators) subserving this function.

Given the role of the neuromodulator dopamine (DA) in the operation of the EAN, various molecular genetic studies have been carried out using behavioral and neurophysiological measures with both adults and children in order to understand the nature of the relationship between DA-related genes and executive control during development. Posner and Rothbart (see Chapter 3, this volume) present an ample review of the relationship between polymorphisms on the dopamine receptor D4 (*DRD4*) gene and the development of the EAN. In this chapter, we focus on two other DA-related genes, catechol-*O*-methyltransferase (*COMT*) and dopamine transporter 1 (*DAT1*), which have been widely studied in past years in relation to cognition.

COMT Gene

Studies of DA diffusion in the brain carried out with animal models have shown that the amount of DA transporter protein expressed along the axons of neurons in the prefrontal cortex (PFC) is significantly low and inconveniently distant from synaptic release sites. As a consequence, extracellular diffusion of DA in the PFC is higher compared with other regions in the brain, and the mechanism to regulate it appears to rely to a greater extent on the action of catabolic enzymes such as COMT (Chen et al., 2004; Sesack, Hawrylak, Matus, Guido, & Levey, 1998).

A common functional polymorphism of the human gene encoding the COMT enzyme protein is related to a methionine (*met*) for valine (*val*) substitution in exon 4 that alters the amino acid codon at position 158 (*val158met*). The more stable *val* allele encodes the enzyme with higher activity, which is associated with less synaptic DA in the PFC (Chen et al., 2004). Given the role of DA-mediated substrates of executive functions in the brain, it was expected that this polymorphism in the COMT gene would be associated with executive attention performance and EAN function. This association has indeed been found in several studies with adults (see Dickinson & Elvevag, 2009, for a review). Individuals homozygous for the *val* allele show increased activity in the ACC associated with poorer performance on an attention control task compared with carriers of the *met* variation (Blasi et al., 2005). Additional research has also shown signs of greater efficiency in the PFC, as well as the ACC, for carriers of the *met* allele when performing attention-related tasks (Heinz & Smolka, 2006).

Studies in typically developing children also provide insights on how genetic polymorphisms that affect the availability of DA in the PFC underlie individual differences in executive attention during development. Diamond, Briand, Fossella, and Gehlbach (2004) found that variations in the COMT enzyme selectively affect performance on a conflict task that indexes executive control but not other tasks targeting memory processes that may also depend on the function of prefrontal structures. In this study, variations in the COMT gene were associated with differences in performance on an inhibition task in a cumulative mode: Children homozygous for the *met* allele performed better than those carrying the *met* variation in just one of the alleles, and the latter in turn performed better than children homozygous for the *val* variation of the gene. Recent advances in pharmacogenetic studies have also determined that the high-activity *val* variation is most frequent among subjects with attention-deficit/hyperactivity disorder (ADHD) compared with healthy subjects. Interestingly, carriers of this variation appear to show better responses to treatment with methylphenidate, with *val/val* homozygous children also displaying less evidence of severe symptoms than those carrying the *met/met* genotype (Kereszturi et al., 2008).

DAT1 Gene

The *DAT1* gene belongs to a family of neurotransmitter transporter genes. The *DAT1* is located on chromosome 5p15.3 and encodes a sodium-dependent dopamine transporter, which terminates the action of DA by reuptaking it into presynaptic terminals. A common polymorphism of the gene consists of a variation in the number of tandem repeats (VNTR) at the 3' untranslated region that varies from three to 11 copies (Vandenbergh et al., 1992), with the 9 and 10 repeats the most frequent variations in humans. Studies of the in vivo availability of striatal DA transporter in humans have found genotype-dependent differences in the density of DA transporter. Individuals carrying the 10-repeat variation show higher DA-transporter availability and thus less synaptic DA than carriers of the 9-repeat version (Heinz et al., 2000). Given the role of DA for modulation of neurotransmission within the EAN, variations in this gene are also expected to affect the efficiency of this network.

Using the ANT, Fossella et al. (2002) found that the presence of the 10-repeat allele in adults is associated with larger flanker interference scores, indicating poorer performance of executive attention. Cómbita, Abundis, Pozuelos, Paz-Alonso, and Rueda (2011) recently replicated this finding with young children. In this study, children performed the child version of the ANT, and higher flanker interference scores were found for carriers of the 10-repeat variation compared with children carrying the 9-repeat variation in at least one of the alleles. Electrophysiological recording was used to examine brain function while children performed the task. Event-related potentials revealed that children homozygous for the 10-repeat variation showed more sustained frontal activation while performing the conflict task, suggesting that they needed to activate the EAN longer in order to achieve the same level of performance as carriers of the 9-repeat variation (Cómbita et al., 2011).

With a large sample ($N = 110$) of children ages 5 to 13 years, Brocki, Clerkin, Guise, Fan, and Fossella (2009) found that children carrying the 10-repeat homozygotes tended to show higher conflict scores (poorer executive attention efficiency) with age than those who carried the 9-repeat homozygotes, despite the fact that they showed smaller conflict scores at younger ages. The changing pattern with age may be related to changes in sensitivity of the organism to DA, in part determined by age-dependent changes in *DAT1* levels (Volkow et al., 2001). Considering the psychopathology of attention, it has been found that the presence of the 10-repeat variation is associated with higher risk of ADHD (Cook et al., 1995). Moreover, ADHD children carrying the 10-repeat variation of the gene also appear to have a smaller volume of the caudate nucleus (Durston et al., 2005).

In summary, genetic variation is shown to influence DA modulation of the EAN and appears to affect its efficiency across development. However, further research is needed in order to fully understand the neurochemical mechanisms underlying such influence.

NURTURE OF EXECUTIVE ATTENTION DEVELOPMENT

The relevance of the biological endowment for executive attention and self-regulation reviewed above could wrongly lead to the impression that attention is not susceptible to experience and cannot be enhanced by intervention. Nevertheless, the extraordinarily plastic capacity of the human nervous system, especially during development (see Posner & Rothbart, 2007), greatly contradicts that idea. Much evidence has been provided in the past years in favor of the susceptibility of systems of self-regulation to the influence of experience. One piece of evidence comes from studies showing the vulnerability of attention to environmental aspects such as parenting and socioeconomic status (SES; Bornstein & Bradley, 2003). Also, in the past years, an increasing number of studies have shown that a broad range of executive functions, including executive attention, working memory, shifting of attention, and reasoning, can be improved during childhood by means of training or interventions at school. In addition, there is some evidence suggesting that susceptibility to the environment might be embedded in genetic endowment because some genetic variations, often under positive selection, appear to make children more susceptible to environmental factors such as parenting (Sheese, Voelker, Rothbart, & Posner, 2007). In this section, we discuss much of the evidence available on how environmental and educational experiences can shape the development of executive attention and EC.

Home Environment

Most parents are concerned with the education of their children and do their best to provide the most favorable opportunities for them to grow into happy and valuable members of society. As was reviewed in previous sections of this chapter, success in the development of attention and EC has many advantages for the child's future. During the first years of life, caregivers regulate most of children's behavior. Parents exert control over most domains of babies' lives, such as their level of arousal, episodes of distress, and sources of sensory input. Progressively, control becomes internalized as toddlers start being able to manage their own emotions and behavior. In this process, caregivers pass on to the child control strategies that are appropriate for a given culture and situation. What aspects of the parent–child interactions are the most successful in this endeavor? Also, is there any information on which aspects of the home environment potentially have beneficial or detrimental effects on the development of self-regulation?

Aspects of parent–child relationships such as attachment security, early positive mutuality, warmth, responsiveness, and discipline have been shown to play a role in the development of regulatory abilities. Recent evidence suggests that autonomy support (i.e., offering children age-appropriate problem-solving strategies and providing opportunities to use them) is the strongest predictor of children's performance on cognitive control tasks (Bernier, Carlson, & Whipple, 2010). In children who are more likely to display externalizing behavior problems, it has been shown that the use of gentle discipline (i.e., giving commands and prohibitive statements in a positive tone) by parents results in the development of greater EC, whereas the use of reasoning explanations and redirections in a neutral tone is associated with poorer EC later on (Cipriano & Stifter, 2010). In line with this, other studies have shown that positive parental control can buffer the risk of developing externalizing behavioral problems in children low in EC (Karreman, van Tuijl, van Aken, & Dekovic, 2009). A similar result is also found for teacher–child relationships. Supportive teaching appears to safeguard the risk of academic failure in children who are low in EC (Liew, Chen, & Hughes, 2010).

However, not only parent–child relationships are important. Home environment is greatly mediated by interparental relationships, and how parents interact also appears to affect their child's development of attention. A recent longitudinal study demonstrated that interparental aggression in infancy predicts reduced attentional skills in toddlerhood. Moreover, two aspects—child's reduced attentional skills and interparental aggression— were associated with increased risk for ADHD symptoms and conduct problems later on (Towe-Goodman, Stifter, Coccia, Cox, & Family Life Project Key Investigators, 2011).

Children's attention is also vulnerable to conditions related to the SES of the family, which typically includes parental education, occupation, and income (McLoyd, 1998). Several studies have reported on the impact of

SES during childhood in a variety of cognitive functions of the individual. The main conclusion is that SES is a significant predictor of neurocognitive function, particularly in language and executive function skills (Hackman & Farah, 2009). Wanless, McClelland, Tominey, and Acock (2011) found that children from low-income families showed poorer behavioral regulation than children from more economically advantaged families. Low income also appears to be associated with children's higher levels of fear and irritability and lower EC, as well as higher levels of rejection by parents and inconsistent discipline (Lengua, 2006). The negative impact of SES on the development of executive functions is observed from early infancy. Infants in the second half of the first year of life coming from low-SES families already show delayed development of cognitive flexibility skills compared with infants from high-SES families (Clearfield & Niman, 2012). Data of this sort suggest that functions of the frontal lobe are the most affected by environmental factors.

The impact of SES on brain function has also been examined. Children whose parents have lower levels of education, for example, have more difficulty selecting out irrelevant information as shown by ERPs than those with highly educated parents (Stevens, Lauinger, & Neville, 2009). Interestingly, in some studies in which brain function was examined, differences in function of SES were found in spite of lack of differences in behavioral performance (Hackman & Farah, 2009). In our lab at the University of Granada, Abundis, Cómbita, Checa, and Rueda (2011) studied differences in patterns of brain activation in preschool children while the children performed a flanker task. The authors examined differences in function of the education level of their parents. Data revealed that children with less-educated parents showed larger and more sustained conflict effects than their peers with more-educated parents, suggesting that their EAN is substantially less efficient when dealing with monitoring and resolving interference from distracting stimulation.

Given the role of attention and EC on socioemotional development, it has been suggested that poor regulatory abilities place the child at risk of developing pathologies such as disruptive behavior problems or ADHD (Nigg, 2006). Aspects of the home environment also appear to be important in the development of behavior problems. In fact, a direct relationship between positive parenting (warmth, positive expressivity) and low levels of externalizing behavior problems has been established. In relation to behavior problems, it is important to distinguish between reactive aggression (emotionally driven conduct problems) and proactive aggression (unprovoked, unemotional aggression that is used for personal gain or to influence and coerce others). EC shows a consistent negative correlation with behavior problems based on reactive aggression but not so much on proactive aggression (Frick & Morris, 2004). Across cultures, it has been found that children who show high levels of emotional reactivity, either in a surge-approaching mode (e.g., impulsivity, sensation, reward seeking) or a negative mode (e.g., anger, frustration), or both, often show externalizing behavior problems when they have poor EC abilities (Eisenberg, Spinrad, & Eggum, 2010). Conversely, children with covert proactive behavior problems, such as stealing, do not always exhibit self-regulation difficulties. Nevertheless, the relationship between parenting style and children's conduct problems appears to be mediated by children's EC (Eisenberg et al., 2005), meaning that positive parenting is facilitated when children show more regulated behavior.

Education

Together with the increased knowledge about the constitutional factors that help in building individual differences in cognitive control, there is growing interest in investigating whether attention skills can be enhanced by educational interventions. First attempts to develop intervention programs to improve attention and test the influence of these programs on cognitive abilities were made in work with patients. For example, Sohlberg, McLaughlin, Pavese, Heidrich, and Posner (2000) used an attention training program (Attention Process Training) in patients with brain injury, who showed specific improvements in executive attention. Kerns, Eso, and Thomson (1999) found improvement in a number of attention measures in children with ADHD after applying an intervention program combining vigilance, selective, and executive attention requirements.

To examine the susceptibility of the EAN to be fostered by experience in normally developing children, we and our colleagues have developed a training program suitable for preschool children. This effort started several years ago in collaboration with Michael Posner, Mary Rothbart, and others (Rueda, Rothbart, McCandliss, Saccomanno, & Posner, 2005; Rueda, Rothbart, Saccomanno, & Posner, 2007). The program comprises exercises of different categories depending on the aspect of attention being trained, and each exercise consists of trials organized in increasing levels of difficulty (see Table 2.1). Most of the exercises have seven levels of difficulty, and in order to go from one level to the next, the child must complete a minimum of correctly responded trials in a row (three, in most exercises).

Using this training program, the efficacy of a very brief 5-day intervention was tested in several experiments with groups of 4- and 6-year-old children. The children were brought to the laboratory for 7 days for sessions each lasting about 45 minutes. Half of the children were trained using the program, and the other half were assigned to a nontrained control group. Children in the control group were watching cartoon videos, which required occasional responses to keep the movie moving forward, for the same number of

TABLE 2.1

Attention Training Exercises Developed by Rueda et al. (2005) for Children Ages 4–7 Years

Category	Exercise name	Exercise requirement
Tracking/ anticipation	Side	The child navigates a cartoon cat to reach areas of grass and avoid muddy areas, which get progressively bigger.
	Maze	The child navigates a cartoon cat through a maze to get food.
	Chase	The child must anticipate the location where a duck that swims across a pond in a straight line will cross in order to chase it.
	Chase Invisible	Same as above, but the duck becomes invisible when entering the pond so that the child cannot see its trajectory.
Focusing/ discrimination	Portraits	This matching-to-sample exercise with cartoon pictures requires the child to click on one of two pictures that look exactly the same as a sample picture.
	Portraits Delay	Same as above, but the sample picture disappears before the two choices appear on the screen, and the child must keep in mind the attributes of the sample picture.
	Shapes[a]	A number of overlapping figures are presented, and the child has to determine which ones are presented by clicking on the appropriate buttons displayed on the sides of the screen.
Conflict resolution	Number of Numbers	Two sets of numbers are presented, and the child has to click in the group containing the larger amount of items. Trials can be congruent (larger group made of numbers of higher value) or incongruent.
	Value Not Size[a]	Various numbers differing in size are presented on the screen. The child is asked to click on the number of higher value, disregarding the size. Size and value can be congruent (higher number is larger in size) or incongruent.
Inhibitory control	Farmer	The child helps a farmer bring sheep inside a fence. Cartoon animals (either sheep or wolves) appear behind a bale of hay. The child is asked to quickly click on the sheep.
Sustained attention	Frog[a]	The child must press a key as fast as possible in order to help a frog catch flies that come out of a bottle. The requirement to sustain attention is increased by enlarging the time interval between targets.

[a]Exercise was added to the original program by Rueda, Posner, and Rothbart (2011).

sessions as the trained group. All sessions were conducted over a 2- to 3-week period. The first and last days were used to assess the effects of the training by means of children's performance on a child-friendly flanker task and a general test of intelligence. Results revealed greater improvement in fluid intelligence in children in the trained groups compared with children in the control groups (Rueda, Rothbart, et al., 2005).

In addition, the effect of training on brain function was characterized with ERPs. Training produced a pattern of brain activation that was more adultlike when compared with the untrained group. Brain activation was registered while children performed a child-friendly flanker task, and changes in brain reaction to conflict were characterized in two dimensions: (a) timing of the conflict effect, which showed a shorter latency after training; and (b) topography of the conflict effect, which moved to posterior leads in the frontal midline with training. In adults, the conflict-related N2 effect has a mid frontoparietal distribution, which has been associated with a source of activation in the ACC (van Veen & Carter, 2002). Reduction of the latency and duration of the conflict effect is a sign of increased efficiency of the underlying brain system, as similar changes happen with maturation (Jonkman, 2006; Ridderinkhof & van der Molen, 1995; Rueda, Posner, Rothbart, & Davis-Stober, 2004).

Recently, in our lab at the University of Granada, we increased the number of exercises included in the original attention training program (new exercises are also presented in Table 2.1). With the extended program, we conducted a new study in which the number of training sessions was increased to 10. In this study, we examined the effect of training in the days that followed completion of the intervention and 2 months later in a follow-up session. Again, we observed that training produced gains on fluid intelligence and, to some extent, on tasks involving regulation of affect (i.e., child gambling and delay of gratification tasks). These tasks require regulating motivational tendencies by inhibiting immediate rewards in the face of obtaining higher rewards in the long term and are thought to rely on attention control skills (Rothbart & Rueda, 2005; Rueda, Posner, & Rothbart, 2011). The effect of training on brain function was also replicated, and more interestingly, clear signs of durability of the effect were observed in the follow-up session (Rueda, Checa, & Cómbita, 2012). We found that the EAN is activated faster and more efficiently after training (see Color Plate 1). Source modeling of the ERP data suggests that training accelerates the involvement of the dorsal portion of the ACC in conflict monitoring. More efficient engagement of the dorsal ACC may also support the transfer of attention training to affect regulation because this structure appears to be involved in reappraising the emotional value of events (Etkin,

Egner, & Kalisch, 2011). Altogether, training studies suggest that the efficiency of the EAN can be enhanced through educational intervention and that other cognitive skills, such as fluid intelligence and regulation of motivation, may also benefit from this type of intervention.

Consistent with our results, other studies have shown beneficial effects of cognitive training on attention and other forms of executive function during development. For instance, auditory selective attention was improved by training with a computerized program designed to promote oral language skills in both language-impaired and typically developing children (Stevens, Fanning, Coch, Sanders, & Neville, 2008). Klingberg and colleagues have shown that training can enhance working memory and that the intervention showed some degree of transfer to aspects of attention (Thorell, Lindqvist, Nutley, Bohlin, & Klingberg, 2009). This group has also shown evidence that training produced changes at various levels of brain function, such as activation (Olesen, Westerberg, & Klingberg, 2004), and in the density of dopamine receptors (McNab et al., 2009) of areas of the cerebral cortex involved in the trained function.

There is also some evidence that curricular interventions carried out in the classroom can lead to improvements in children's cognitive control. Diamond, Barnett, Thomas, and Munro (2007) tested the influence of a specific curriculum on preschoolers' control abilities and found beneficial effects as measured by various conflict tasks. A somewhat indirect but probably not less beneficial form of fostering attention in school could be provided by multilingual education. There is growing evidence that bilingual individuals perform better on executive attention tasks than monolingual individuals (Bialystok, 1999). The idea is that using multiple languages on a regular basis might train executive attention because of the need to suppress one language while using the other. It has been shown that growing up in a bilingual context leads to advantages in executive attention in young children, an effect that appears to transcend that of culture (Yang, Yang, & Lust, 2011).

Although all this evidence shows promising results regarding the effectiveness of interventions and particular educational methods to promote attention control, questions on various aspects of training remain to be answered. Further research is needed to examine whether more extended and systematic interventions would lead to sustained changes in attention skills and other abilities that are thought to rely on attention control and whether benefits would extend to academic competence. Additionally, it will be important to address questions such as whether genetic variation and other constitutionally based variables influence the extent to which the EAN can be modified by experience and whether there are limits to the ages at which training can be effective.

GENE × EXPERIENCE INTERACTIONS

The development of a complex cognitive system such as executive attention cannot be explained by the influence of a single factor such as education, temperament, or genetic variation. Most likely, all these factors interact in many ways to determine the efficiency with which an individual develops his or her cognitive capacities. In consonance with this remark, it has been suggested that children's proficiency in resolving conflict or inhibiting automatic responses is better explained by the interaction between genetic and environmental factors (Belsky, Bakermans-Kranenburg, & van IJzendoorn, 2007).

Kochanska, Philibert, and Barry (2009) recently provided an example of the Gene × Experience interaction on the development of executive attention. In a study with children as young as 25, 38, and 52 months of age, Kochanska et al. found that variation of the serotonin transporter (5HTTPR) gene interacts with early mother–child attachment in predicting later development of regulatory skills. Among children who carried the short variation of the gene, which is associated with risk for poor regulatory control, only those who were insecurely attached developed poor regulatory abilities. The serotonin transporter gene is related to functional and structural differences in brain areas that are part of the EAN (Canli et al., 2005), and the short allele has been linked to diminished dopamine reuptake compared with children homozygous for the long allele.

Among DA-related genes, variations on the DRD4 gene have been shown to moderate the association between environmental factors such as parenting style and behavioral outcomes. For instance, it was reported that carriers of the 7-repeat variation in at least one allele are more susceptible to adverse conditions during early life (Bakermans-Kranenburg & van IJzendoorn, 2006). Also, it was found that the 7-repeat allele of the DRD4 gene interacts with the quality of parenting to influence such temperamental variables in the child as activity level, sensation seeking, and impulsivity (Sheese et al., 2007). More recently, a similar Gene × Parenting interaction has been observed for the COMT gene for 2-year-old children's performance of a visual sequence task thought to involve attention (Voelker, Sheese, Rothbart, & Posner, 2009).

In our lab at the University of Granada, Cómbita et al. (2011) explored interactions between genetic variation and socioeconomic conditions during the development of executive attention. The SES of the family was measured taking into account parental education level, monthly income, and availability of educational resources (e.g. books, computer, Internet connection) at home. Cómbita et al. observed that these aspects of the home environment were associated with children's self-regulatory skills and performance on tests of intelligence. However, genetic variation seemed to modulate the extent to which environmental factors affected the children's skills. The Gene × Experience interaction was observed mostly on the measures of intelligence. Results showed that only carriers of the 7-repeat variation at the *DRD4* gene or the 10-repeat variation of the *DAT1* gene were affected by the home environment, with children being raised in high-SES families showing higher IQ scores than children raised in families with low SES.

CONCLUSION

The process of building neural systems, such as the EAN, throughout development is determined by a multiplicity of factors, including both constitutional dispositions and experience. The function of this network underlies individual differences in the voluntary and effortful regulation of thoughts, emotions, and responses. These capacities are important for a broad range of behaviors that significantly influence children's social adjustment and success in school. The EAN shows a strong maturational progress during early childhood, and it is followed by a more progressive development during late childhood and adolescence as mechanisms related to executive control and connectivity among neural structures become progressively more refined and efficient. Increasing evidence suggests that efficiency of the EAN is partially determined by the genetic endowment of the individual, as variation on DA-related genes is associated with differences in efficiency of this network and risk for developing pathologies that involve this network. However, the relation of genetic factors to attention and self-regulation does not mean that the system cannot be influenced by experience. In this chapter we have reviewed evidence showing that the development of executive attention skills is also affected by environmental factors such as parenting and education.

Susceptibility to experience provides an opportunity to promote attention control and self-regulation by means of appropriate educational interventions. We have been working toward that purpose for several years and have provided evidence on the susceptibility of executive attention to enhancement by training. Nevertheless, we think this is only the starting point. Plasticity of the brain provides an opportunity for curricular improvement, and we hope our work shows a way to begin. Current results point out the potential to produce a greater and more stable impact on children's executive attention and related domains with more extended educational interventions.

REFERENCES

Abundis, A., Cómbita, L. M., Checa, P., & Rueda, M. R. (2011, September). *Neural mechanisms of conflict processing in children from different socio-economic backgrounds*. Paper presented at the 11th International Conference on Cognitive Neuroscience, Palma de Mallorca, Spain.

Bakermans-Kranenburg, M. J., & van IJzendoorn, M. H. (2006). Gene–environment interaction of the dopamine D4 receptor (DRD4) and observed maternal insensitivity predicting externalizing behavior in preschoolers. *Developmental Psychobiology, 48*, 406–409. doi:10.1002/dev.20152

Belsky, J., Bakermans-Kranenburg, M. J., & van IJzendoorn, M. H. (2007). For better and for worse: Differential susceptibility to environmental influences. *Current Directions in Psychological Science, 16*, 300–304. doi:10.1111/j.1467-8721.2007.00525.x

Bernier, A., Carlson, S. M., & Whipple, N. (2010). From external regulation to self-regulation: Early parenting precursors of young children's executive functioning. *Child Development, 81*, 326–339. doi:10.1111/j.1467-8624.2009.01397.x

Bialystok, E. (1999). Cognitive complexity and attentional control in the bilingual mind. *Child Development, 70*, 636–644. doi:10.1111/1467-8624.00046

Blair, C., & Razza, R. P. (2007). Relating effortful control, executive function, and false belief understanding to emerging math and literacy ability in kindergarten. *Child Development, 78*, 647–663. doi:10.1111/j.1467-8624.2007.01019.x

Blair, C., & Ursache, A. (2011). A bidirectional model of executive functions and self-regulation. In K. D. Vohs & R. F. Baumeister (Eds.), *Handbook of self-regulation: Research, theory and applications* (2nd ed., pp. 300–320). New York, NY: Guilford Press.

Blasi, G., Mattay, V. S., Bertolino, A. L., Elvevag, G., Callicot, J. H., Das, S., . . . Weinberger, D. R. (2005). Effect of catechol-O-methyltransferase val158met genotype on attentional control. *Journal of Neuroscience, 25*, 5038–5045. doi:10.1523/JNEUROSCI.0476-05.2005

Bornstein, M. H., & Bradley, R. H. (2003). *Socioeconomic status, parenting, and child development*. Mahwah, NJ: Erlbaum.

Botvinick, M. M., Cohen, J. D., & Carter, C. S. (2004). Conflict monitoring and anterior cingulate cortex: An update. *Trends in Cognitive Sciences, 8*, 539–546. doi:10.1016/j.tics.2004.10.003

Brocki, K., Clerkin, S. M., Guise, K. G., Fan, J., & Fossella, J. A. (2009). Assessing the molecular genetics of the development of executive attention in children: Focus on genetic pathways related to the anterior cingulate cortex and dopamine. *Neuroscience, 164*, 241–246. doi:10.1016/j.neuroscience.2009.01.029

Bull, R., & Scerif, G. (2001). Executive functioning as a predictor of children's mathematics ability: Inhibition, switching, and working memory. *Developmental Neuropsychology, 19*, 273–293. doi:10.1207/S15326942DN1903_3

Bush, G., Luu, P., & Posner, M. I. (2000). Cognitive and emotional influences in anterior cingulate cortex. *Trends in Cognitive Sciences, 4*, 215–222. doi:10.1016/S1364-6613(00)01483-2

Canli, T., Omura, K., Haas, B. S., Fallgatter, A., Constable, R. T., & Lesch, K. P. (2005). Beyond affect: A role for genetic variation of the serotonin transporter in neural activation during a cognitive attention task. *Proceedings of the National Academy of Sciences of the United States of America, 102*, 12224–12229.

Carlson, S. M., Moses, L. J., & Claxton, L. J. (2004). Individual differences in executive functioning and theory of mind: An investigation of inhibitory control and planning ability. *Journal of Experimental Child Psychology, 87*, 299–319. doi:10.1016/j.jecp.2004.01.002

Checa, P., Rodriguez-Bailon, R., & Rueda, M. R. (2008). Neurocognitive and temperamental systems of self-regulation and early adolescents' school competence. *Mind, Brain, and Education, 2*, 177–187. doi:10.1111/j.1751-228X.2008.00052.x

Checa, P., & Rueda, M. R. (2011). Behavioral and brain measures of executive attention and school competence in late childhood. *Developmental Neuropsychology, 36*, 1018–1032. doi:10.1080/87565641.2011.591857

Chen, J., Lipska, B. K., Halim, N., Ma, Q. D., Matsumoto, M., Melhem, S., . . . Weinberger, D. R. (2004). Functional analysis of genetic variation in catechol-O-methyltransferase (COMT): Effects on mRNA, protein, and enzyme activity in post-mortem human brain. *American Journal of Human Genetics, 75*, 807–821. doi:10.1086/425589

Cipriano, E. A., & Stifter, C. A. (2010). Predicting preschool effortful control from toddler temperament and parenting behavior. *Journal of Applied Developmental Psychology, 31*, 221–230. doi:10.1016/j.appdev.2010.02.004

Clearfield, M. W., & Niman, L. C. (2012). SES affects infant cognitive flexibility. *Infant Behavior & Development, 35*, 29–35. doi:10.1016/j.infbeh.2011.09.007

Cómbita, L. M., Abundis, A., Pozuelos, J. P., Paz-Alonso, P. M., & Rueda, M. R. (2011, August). *Interaction of dopamine-related genetic variation and environment on preschoolers' executive function*. Paper presented at the 15th European Conference on Developmental Psychology, Bergen, Norway.

Cook, E. H., Stein, M. A., Krasowski, M. D., Cox, N. J., Olkin, D. M., Kieffer, J. E., & Leventhal, B. L. (1995). Association of attention-deficit disorder and the dopamine transporter gene. *American Journal of Human Genetics, 56*, 993–998.

Dehaene, S., Posner, M. I., & Tucker, D. M. (1994). Localization of a neural system for error detection and compensation. *Psychological Science, 5*, 303–305. doi:10.1111/J.1467-9280.1994.TB00630.X

Diamond, A., Barnett, W. S., Thomas, J., & Munro, S. (2007, November 30). Preschool program improves cognitive control. *Science, 318*, 1387–1388. doi:10.1126/science.1151148

Diamond, A., Briand, L., Fossella, J., & Gehlbach, L. (2004). Genetic and neurochemical modulation of prefrontal cognitive functions in children. *American Journal of Psychiatry, 161*, 125–132. doi:10.1176/appi.ajp.161.1.125

Dickinson, D., & Elvevag, B. (2009). Genes, cognition and brain through a COMT lens. *Neuroscience, 164*, 72–87. doi:10.1016/j.neuroscience.2009.05.014

Duncan, J., & Owen, A. M. (2000). Common regions of the human frontal lobe recruited by diverse cognitive demands. *Trends in Neurosciences, 23*, 475–483. doi:10.1016/S0166-2236(00)01633-7

Duncan, J., Seitz, R. J., Kolodny, J., Bor, D., Herzog, H., Ahmed, A., . . . Emslie, H. (2000, July 21). A neural basis for general intelligence. *Science, 289*, 457–460. doi:10.1126/science.289.5478.457

Durston, S., Fossella, J., Casey, B., Pol, H., Galvan, A., Schnack, H., . . . van Enge-land, H. (2005). Differential effects of DRD4 and DAT1 genotype on fronto-striatal gray matter volumes in a sample of subjects with attention deficit hyperactivity disorder, their unaffected siblings, and controls. *Molecular Psychiatry, 10*, 678–685. doi:10.1038/sj.mp.4001649

Eisenberg, N., Fabes, R. A., Nyman, M., Bernzweig, J., & Pinuelas, A. (1994). The relations of emotionality and regulation to children's anger-related reactions. *Child Development, 65*, 109–128. doi:10.2307/1131369

Eisenberg, N., Smith, C. L., & Spinrad, T. L. (2011). Effortful control: Relations with emotion regulation, adjustment, and socialization in childhood. In K. D. Vohs & R. F. Baumeister (Eds.), *Handbook of self-regulation: Research, theory and applications* (2nd ed., pp. 263–283). New York, NY: Guilford Press.

Eisenberg, N., Spinrad, T. L., & Eggum, N. D. (2010). Emotion-related self-regulation and its relation to children's maladjustment. *Annual Review of Clinical Psychology, 6*, 495–525. doi:10.1146/annurev.clinpsy.121208.131208

Eisenberg, N., Valiente, C., & Eggum, N. D. (2010). Self-regulation and school readiness. *Early Education and Development, 21*, 681–698. doi:10.1080/10409 289.2010.497451

Eisenberg, N., Zhou, Q., Spinrad, T. L., Valiente, C., Fabes, R. A., & Liew, J. (2005). Relations among positive parenting, children's effortful control, and external-izing problems: A three-wave longitudinal study. *Child Development, 76*, 1055–1071. doi:10.1111/j.1467-8624.2005.00897.x

Ellis, L. K., Rothbart, M. K., & Posner, M. I. (2004). Individual differences in execu-tive attention predict self-regulation and adolescent psychosocial behaviors. *Annals of the New York Academy of Sciences, 1021*, 337–340.

Eriksen, B. A., & Eriksen, C. W. (1974). Effects of noise letters upon the identi-fication of a target letter in a nonsearch task. *Perception & Psychophysics, 16*, 143–149. doi:10.3758/BF03203267

Espy, K. A., McDiarmid, M. M., Cwik, M. F., Stalets, M. M., Hamby, A., & Senn, T. E. (2004). The contribution of executive functions to emergent mathematic skills in preschool children. *Developmental Neuropsychology, 26*, 465–486. doi:10.1207/s15326942dn2601_6

Etkin, A., Egner, T., & Kalisch, R. (2011). Emotional processing in anterior cin-gulate and medial prefrontal cortex. *Trends in Cognitive Sciences, 15*, 85–93. doi:10.1016/j.tics.2010.11.004

Fair, D. A., Cohen, A. L., Power, J. D., Dosenbach, N. U. F., Church, J. A., Meizin, F. M., . . . Petersen, S. E. (2009). Functional brain networks develop from a "local to distributed" organization. *PLoS Computational Biology, 5,* e1000381. doi:10.1371/journal.pcbi.1000381

Fan, J., Flombaum, J. I., McCandliss, B. D., Thomas, K. M., & Posner, M. I. (2003). Cognitive and brain consequences of conflict. *NeuroImage, 18,* 42–57. doi:10.1006/nimg.2002.1319

Fan, J., Wu, Y., Fossella, J., & Posner, M. I. (2001). Assessing the heritability of attentional networks. *BMC Neuroscience, 2,* 14. doi:10.1186/1471-2202-2-14

Fossella, J., Sommer, T., Fan, J., Wu, Y., Swanson, J. M., Pfaff, D. W., . . . Posner, M. I. (2002). Assessing the molecular genetics of attention networks. *BMC Neuroscience, 3,* 14. doi:10.1186/1471-2202-3-14

Fossella, J. A., & Casey, B. (2006). Genes, brain, and behavior: Bridging disciplines. *Cognitive, Affective & Behavioral Neuroscience, 6,* 1–8. doi:10.3758/CABN.6.1.1

Frick, P. J., & Morris, A. S. (2004). Temperament and developmental pathways to conduct disorders. *Journal of Clinical Child and Adolescent Psychology, 33,* 54–68. doi:10.1207/S15374424JCCP3301_6

Fuchs, L. S., Compton, D. L., Fuchs, D., Paulsen, K., Bryant, J. D., & Hamlett, C. L. (2005). The prevention, identification, and cognitive determinants of math difficulty. *Journal of Educational Psychology, 97,* 493–513. doi:10.1037/0022-0663.97.3.493

Gao, W., Zhu, H., Giovanello, K. S., Smith, J. K., Shen, D., Gilmore, J. H., & Lin, W. (2009). Evidence on the emergence of the brain's default network from 2-week-old to 2-year-old healthy pediatric subjects. *Proceedings of the National Academy of Sciences of the United States of America, 106,* 6790–6795. doi:10.1073/pnas.0811221106

Gehring, W. J., Gross, B., Coles, M. G. H., Meyer, D. E., & Donchin, E. (1993). A neural system for error detection and compensation. *Psychological Science, 4,* 385–390. doi:10.1111/j.1467-9280.1993.tb00586.x

Goldman-Rakic, P. S. (1988). Topography of cognition: Parallel distributed networks in primate association cortex. *Annual Review of Neuroscience, 11,* 137–156. doi:10.1146/annurev.ne.11.030188.001033

Hackman, D. A., & Farah, M. J. (2009). Socioeconomic status and the developing brain. *Trends in Cognitive Sciences, 13,* 65–73. doi:10.1016/j.tics.2008.11.003

Harman, C., Rothbart, M. K., & Posner, M. I. (1997). Distress and attention interactions in early infancy. *Motivation and Emotion, 21*(1), 27–43.

Heinz, A., Goldman, D., Jones, D. W., Palmour, R. L., Hommer, D., Gorey, J. G., . . . Weinberger, D. R. (2000). Genotype influences in vivo dopamine transporter availability in human striatum. *Neuropsychopharmacology, 22,* 133–139. doi:10.1016/S0893-133X(99)00099-8

Heinz, A., & Smolka, M. N. (2006). The effects of catechol-O-methyltransferase genotype on brain activation elicited by affective stimuli and cognitive tasks. *Reviews in the Neurosciences, 17,* 359–368. doi:10.1515/REVNEURO.2006.17.3.359

James, W. (1890). *The principles of psychology.* New York, NY: Holt. doi:10.1037/11059-000

Johnson, M. H., Posner, M. I., & Rothbart, M. K. (1991). Components of visual orienting in early infancy: Contingency learning, anticipatory looking, and disengaging. *Journal of Cognitive Neuroscience, 3,* 335–344. doi:10.1162/jocn.1991.3.4.335

Jonkman, L. M. (2006). The development of preparation, conflict monitoring and inhibition from early childhood to young adulthood: A go/nogo ERP study. *Brain Research, 1097,* 181–193. doi:10.1016/j.brainres.2006.04.064

Karreman, A., van Tuijl, C., van Aken, M. A., & Dekovic, M. (2009). Predicting young children's externalizing problems: Interactions among effortful control, parenting, and child gender. *Merrill-Palmer Quarterly, 55,* 111–134. doi:10.1353/mpq.0.0020

Kereszturi, E., Tarnok, Z., Bongar, E., Lakatos, K., Farkas, J. G., & Sasvari-Szekely, Z. N. (2008). Catechol-O-methyltransferase val158met polymorphism is associated with methylphenidate response in ADHD children. *American Journal of Medical Genetics, Part B, 147B,* 1431–1435.

Kerns, K. A., Eso, K., & Thomson, J. (1999). Investigation of a direct intervention for improving attention in young children with ADHD. *Developmental Neuropsychology, 16,* 273–295. doi:10.1207/S15326942DN1602_9

Kochanska, G., & Aksan, N. (2006). Children's conscience and self-regulation. *Journal of Personality, 74,* 1587–1618. doi:10.1111/j.1467-6494.2006.00421.x

Kochanska, G., Philibert, R. A., & Barry, R. A. (2009). Interplay of genes and early mother-child relationship in the development of self-regulation from toddler to preschool age. *Journal of Child Psychology and Psychiatry, 50,* 1331–1338. doi:10.1111/j.1469-7610.2008.02050.x

Lengua, L. J. (2006). Growth in temperament and parenting as predictors of adjustment during children's transition to adolescence. *Developmental Psychology, 42,* 819–832. doi:10.1037/0012-1649.42.5.819

Liew, J., Chen, Q., & Hughes, J. N. (2010). Child effortful control, teacher–student relationships, and achievement in academically at-risk children: Additive and interactive effects. *Early Childhood Research Quarterly, 25,* 51–64. doi:10.1016/j.ecresq.2009.07.005

Luu, P., Tucker, D. M., Derryberry, D., Reed, M., & Poulsen, C. (2003). Electrophysiological responses to errors and feedback in the process of action regulation. *Psychological Science, 14,* 47–53. doi:10.1111/1467-9280.01417

McLoyd, V. C. (1998). Socioeconomic disadvantage and child development. *American Psychologist, 53,* 185–204. doi:10.1037/0003-066X.53.2.185

McNab, F., Varrone, A., Farde, L., Jucaite, A., Bystritsky, P., Forssberg, H., & Klingberg, T. (2009). Changes in cortical dopamine D1 receptor binding associated with cognitive training. *Science, 323,* 800–802. doi:10.1126/science.1166102

Nigg, J. T. (2006). Temperament and developmental psychopathology. *Journal of Child Psychology and Psychiatry, 47,* 395–422. doi:10.1111/j.1469-7610.2006.01612.x

Norman, D. A., & Shallice, T. (1986). Attention to action: Willed and automatic control of behavior. In R. J. Davison, G. E. Schwartz, & D. Shapiro (Eds.), *Consciousness and self-regulation* (pp. 1–18). New York, NY: Plenum Press.

Olesen, P. J., Westerberg, H., & Klingberg, T. (2004). Increased prefrontal and parietal activity after training of working memory. *Nature Neuroscience, 7,* 75–79. doi:10.1038/nn1165

Olson, S. L., Sameroff, A. J., Kerr, D. C., Lopez, N. L., & Wellman, H. M. (2005). Developmental foundations of externalizing problems in young children: The role of effortful control. *Development and Psychopathology, 17,* 25–45. doi:10.1017/S0954579405050029

Pasolunghi, M. C., Cornoldi, C., & De Liberto, S. (1999). Working memory and intrusions of irrelevant information in a group of specific poor problem solvers. *Memory & Cognition, 27,* 779–790. doi:10.3758/BF03198531

Posner, M. I., & DiGirolamo, G. J. (1998). Executive attention: Conflict, target detection, and cognitive control. In R. Parasuraman (Ed.), *The attentive brain* (pp. 401–423). Cambridge, MA: MIT Press.

Posner, M. I., & Petersen, S. E. (1990). The attention system of the human brain. *Annual Review of Neuroscience, 13,* 25–42. doi:10.1146/annurev.ne.13.030190.000325

Posner, M. I., & Rothbart, M. K. (2007). *Educating the human brain.* Washington, DC: American Psychological Association. doi:10.1037/11519-000

Posner, M. I., & Rothbart, M. K. (2009). Toward a physical basis of attention and self-regulation. *Physics of Life Reviews, 6,* 103–120. doi:10.1016/j.plrev.2009.02.001

Posner, M. I., Rueda, M. R., & Kanske, P. (2007). Probing the mechanisms of attention. In J. T. Cacioppo, J. G. Tassinary, & G. G. Berntson (Eds.), *Handbook of psychophysiology* (3rd ed., pp. 410–432). Cambridge, England: Cambridge University Press.

Posner, M. I., & Snyder, C. R. R. (1975). Attention and cognitive control. In R. Solso (Ed.), *Information processing and cognition: The Loyola Symposium* (pp. 55–85). Hillsdale, NJ: Erlbaum.

Ridderinkhof, K. R., & van der Molen, M. W. (1995). A psychophysiological analysis of developmental differences in the ability to resist interference. *Child Development, 66,* 1040–1056. doi:10.2307/1131797

Rothbart, M. K. (2007, August). Temperament, development, and personality. *Current Directions in Psychological Science, 16,* 207–212. doi:10.1111/j.1467-8721.2007.00505.x

Rothbart, M. K., Ahadi, S. A., & Hershey, K. L. (1994). Temperament and social behavior in childhood. *Merrill-Palmer Quarterly, 40,* 21–39.

Rothbart, M. K., & Rueda, M. R. (2005). The development of effortful control. In U. Mayr, E. Awh, & S. W. Keele (Eds.), *Developing individuality in the human brain: A tribute to Michael I. Posner* (pp. 167–188). Washington, DC: American Psychological Association. doi:10.1037/11108-009

Rueda, M. R. (2012). Effortful control. In M. Zentner & R. Shiner (Eds.), *Handbook of temperament* (pp. 145–167). New York, NY: Guilford Press.

Rueda, M. R., Checa, P., & Cómbita, L. M. (2012). Enhanced efficiency of the executive attention network after training in preschool children: Immediate changes and effects after two months. *Developmental Cognitive Neuroscience, 2*(Suppl. 1), S192–S204. doi:10.1016/j.dcn.2011.09.004

Rueda, M. R., Checa, P., & Rothbart, M. K. (2010). Contributions of attentional control to social emotional and academic development. *Early Education and Development, 21,* 744–764. doi:10.1080/10409289.2010.510055

Rueda, M. R., Fan, J., McCandliss, B. D., Halparin, J. D., Gruber, D. B., Lercari, L. P., & Posner, M. I. (2004). Development of attentional networks in childhood. *Neuropsychologia, 42,* 1029–1040. doi:10.1016/j.neuropsychologia.2003.12.012

Rueda, M. R., & Posner, M. I., (in press). Development of attention networks. In P. D. Zelazo (Ed.), *The Oxford handbook of developmental psychology*. Oxford, England: Oxford University Press.

Rueda, M. R., Posner, M. I., & Rothbart, M. K. (2005). The development of executive attention: Contributions to the emergence of self-regulation. *Developmental Neuropsychology, 28,* 573–594. doi:10.1207/s15326942dn2802_2

Rueda, M. R., Posner, M. I., & Rothbart, M. K. (2011). Attentional control and self-regulation. In K. D. Vohs & R. F. Baumeister (Eds.), *Handbook of self-regulation: Research, theory, and applications* (2nd ed., pp. 284–299). New York, NY: Guilford Press.

Rueda, M. R., Posner, M. I., Rothbart, M. K., & Davis-Stober, C. P. (2004). Development of the time course for processing conflict: An event-related potentials study with 4 year olds and adults. *BMC Neuroscience, 5,* 39. doi:10.1186/1471-2202-5-39

Rueda, M. R., Rothbart, M. K., McCandliss, B. D., Saccomanno, L., & Posner, M. I. (2005). Training, maturation, and genetic influences on the development of executive attention. *Proceedings of the National Academy of Sciences of the United States of America, 102,* 14931–14936. doi:10.1073/pnas.0506897102

Rueda, M. R., Rothbart, M. K., Saccomanno, L., & Posner, M. I. (2007). Modifying brain networks underlying self-regulation. In D. Romer & E. F. Walker (Eds.), *Adolescent psychopathology and the developing brain: Integrating brain and prevention science* (pp. 401–419). New York, NY: Oxford University Press.

Russell, R. L., & Ginsburg, H. P. (1984). Cognitive analysis of children's mathematical difficulties. *Cognition and Instruction, 1,* 217–244.

Santesso, D. L., & Segalowitz, S. J. (2009). The error-related negativity is related to risk taking and empathy in young men. *Psychophysiology, 46,* 143–152. doi:10.1111/j.1469-8986.2008.00714.x

Santesso, D. L., Segalowitz, S. J., & Schmidt, L. A. (2005). ERP correlates of error monitoring in 10-year olds are related to socialization. *Biological Psychology, 70,* 79–87. doi:10.1016/j.biopsycho.2004.12.004

Sesack, S. R., Hawrylak, V. A., Matus, C., Guido, M. A., & Levey, A. I. (1998). Dopamine axon varicosities in the prelimbic division of the rat prefrontal cortex exhibit sparse immunoreactivity for the dopamine transporter. *Journal of Neuroscience, 18*, 2697–2708.

Sheese, B. E., Voelker, P. M., Rothbart, M. K., & Posner, M. I. (2007). Parenting quality interacts with genetic variation in dopamine receptor D4 to influence temperament in early childhood. *Development and Psychopathology, 19*, 1039–1046. doi:10.1017/S0954579407000521

Sohlberg, M. M., McLaughlin, K. A., Pavese, A., Heidrich, A., & Posner, M. I. (2000). Evaluation of attention process training and brain injury education in persons with acquired brain injury. *Journal of Clinical and Experimental Neuropsychology, 22*, 656–676. doi:10.1076/1380-3395(200010)22:5;1-9;FT656

Stevens, C., Fanning, J., Coch, D., Sanders, L., & Neville, H. (2008). Neural mechanisms of selective auditory attention are enhanced by computerized training: Electrophysiological evidence from language-impaired and typically developing children. *Brain Research, 1205*, 55–69. doi:10.1016/j.brainres.2007.10.108

Stevens, C., Lauinger, B., & Neville, H. (2009). Differences in the neural mechanisms of selective attention in children from different socioeconomic backgrounds: An event-related brain potential study. *Developmental Science, 12*, 634–646. doi:10.1111/j.1467-7687.2009.00807.x

Thorell, L. B., Lindqvist, S., Nutley, S. B., Bohlin, G., & Klingberg, T. (2009). Training and transfer effects of executive functions in preschool children. *Developmental Science, 12*, 106–113. doi:10.1111/j.1467-7687.2008.00745.x

Towe-Goodman, N. R., Stifter, C. A., Coccia, M. A., Cox, M. J., & Family Life Project Key Investigators. (2011). Interparental aggression, attention skills, and early childhood behavior problems. *Development and Psychopathology, 23*, 563–576. doi:10.1017/S0954579411000216

Valiente, C., Eisenberg, N., Smith, C. L., Reiser, M., Fabes, R. A., Losoya, S., . . . Murphy, B. C. (2003). The relations of effortful control and reactive control to children's externalizing problems: A longitudinal assessment. *Journal of Personality, 71*, 1171–1196. doi:10.1111/1467-6494.7106011

Vandenbergh, D. J., Perisco, A. M., Hawkins, A. L., Griffin, C. A., Li, X., Jabs, E. W., & Uhl, G. R. (1992). Human dopamine transporter gene (DAT1) maps to chromosome 5p15.3 and displays a VNTR. *Genomics, 14*, 1104–1106. doi:10.1016/S0888-7543(05)80138-7

van Veen, V., & Carter, C. (2002). The timing of action-monitoring processes in the anterior cingulate cortex. *Journal of Cognitive Neuroscience, 14*, 593–602. doi:10.1162/08989290260045837

Voelker, P., Sheese, B. E., Rothbart, M. K., & Posner, M. I. (2009). Variations in catechol-O-methyltransferase gene interact with parenting to influence attention in early development. *Neuroscience, 164*, 121–130. doi:10.1016/j.neuro-science.2009.05.059

Volkow, N. D., Wang, G., Fowler, J. S., Logan, J., Gerasimov, M., Maynard, L., . . . Franceschi, D. (2001). Therapeutic doses of oral methylphenidate significantly increase extracellular dopamine in the human brain. *Journal of Neuroscience, 21*, RC121.

Wanless, S. B., McClelland, M. M., Tominey, S. L., & Acock, A. C. (2011). The influence of demographic risk factors on children's behavioral regulation in prekindergarten and kindergarten. *Early Education and Development, 22*, 461–488. doi:10.1080/10409289.2011.536132

Welch, M. C. (2001). The prefrontal cortex and the development of executive function in childhood. In A. F. Kalverboer & A. Gramsbergen (Eds.), *Handbook of brain and behavior in human development* (pp. 767–790). Dordrecht, the Netherlands: Kluwer Academic.

Yang, S. J., Yang, H. J., & Lust, B. (2011). Early childhood bilingualism leads to advances in executive attention: Dissociating culture and language. *Bilingualism: Language and Cognition, 14*, 412–422. doi:10.1017/S1366728910000611

3

DEVELOPMENT OF ATTENTION NETWORKS

MICHAEL I. POSNER AND MARY K. ROTHBART

We view attention as an organ system. This idea relates specific brain areas to particular psychological functions (Posner & Fan, 2008). A major advantage of viewing attention as an organ system is being able to trace the ability of children and adults to regulate their thoughts and feelings in relation to the development of brain networks. By *brain networks*, we mean anatomical areas, often remote from each other, that are connected and work together to carry out tasks. This chapter is concerned chiefly with attention networks important for achieving the alert state, orienting to sensory events, and mediating conflict between response tendencies.

This chapter is also concerned with the development of brain mechanisms that allow the children to regulate their behavior. For example, adjacent areas of the anterior cingulate are involved in cognitive and emotional control. Connectivity of these control systems develops over the early life of infants and young children and leads to the ability to regulate other brain networks and thus exercise executive control over emotions, thoughts, and behavior. We

DOI: 10.1037/14043-004
Cognition and Brain Development: Converging Evidence From Various Methodologies, B. R. Kar (Editor)
Copyright © 2013 by the American Psychological Association. All rights reserved.

start in infancy, in which control is largely carried out by the caregiver. The early-developing orienting network serves as the primary control mechanism. Later in childhood, there are significant increases in connectivity of the executive attention network, and this network becomes primary in self-regulation. We introduce a longitudinal study that seeks to determine how experience and genetic variation result in individual differences in the efficiency of self-regulation. We then examine training methods to influence the efficiency of the executive attention network. Finally, we briefly examine the role of self-control in studies of aging.

EMOTIONAL AND COGNITIVE SELF-REGULATION

Even at birth, there are early signs of the ability of infants to orient to environmental events. This early-developing orienting network is used by caregivers in soothing distressed infants. During the first months, the most common method used is holding and rocking, but by 3 months of age and later, parents often also use visual distraction to soothe their infants. Experimentally, the ability of orienting of attention to control distress can be demonstrated in infants as young as 3 months; orienting to a visual stimulus provided by the experimenter produced a powerful, if temporary, soothing of distress (Harman, Rothbart, & Posner, 1997). One of the major accomplishments of the first years of life is for infants to develop the means to achieve this regulation on their own.

There is evidence that one element of the executive attention system, namely, the ability to detect error, is present by at least 7 months and involves the same anterior cingulate brain areas as found in adults (Berger, Tzur, & Posner, 2006). However, the ability of this system to control behavior through remote connections develops slowly over many years.

An early sign of the child's ability to manage cognitive conflict is found in the first year of life (Diamond, 1991; Piaget, 1954). For example, in A-not-B tasks, children are trained to reach for a hidden object at Location A and then tested on their ability to search for the hidden object at a new Location B. Children younger than 12 months tend to look in Location A, even though they have seen the object disappear behind Location B. The previously rewarded location dominates over the response dependent on seeing the object hidden in a new location. After the first year, children develop the ability to inhibit the prepotent response toward the trained Location A and successfully reach for the new Location B (Diamond, 1991).

During this period, infants also develop the ability to resolve conflict between line of sight and line of reach when retrieving an object. At 9 months of age, line of sight dominates completely. If the open side of a box is not in line with the side in view, infants will withdraw their hand from the box and reach directly along the line of sight, striking the closed side (Diamond, 1991). In contrast, 12-month-old infants can simultaneously look at a closed side of the box while reaching through the open end to retrieve a toy.

The attention network test (ANT) has been used to examine the efficiency of three brain networks underlying attention: alerting, orienting, and executive attention (Fan, McCandliss, Sommer, Raz, & Posner, 2002). The task requires the person to press one key if the central arrow points to the left and another key if the arrow points to the right. Conflict is introduced by having flankers surrounding the target point in either direction be in the same (congruent) or opposite (incongruent) direction as the target. Cues presented prior to the target provide information about where or when the target will occur. Reaction times for the separate conditions are subtracted, providing three measures that represent the efficiency of the individual's alerting, orienting, and executive networks.

Rueda et al. (2004) examined the ANT in children from 6 to 10 years of age using a version specifically adapted to them. The results for children of this age are similar to those found for adults using the same children's version of the task. Children's reaction times are much longer, but they show similar independence between the three networks. Children have larger scores than adults for alerting up to age 10 and for conflict up to age 7, suggesting that young children have trouble resolving conflict and that even older children have trouble maintaining the alert state when not warned of the target (Rueda et al., 2004).

Seven-year-old children are amenable to neuroimaging using magnetic resonance imaging (MRI). Children ages 5 to 16 years show a significant correlation between the volume of the area of the right anterior cingulate and the ability to perform tasks requiring focal attention (Casey, Trainor, Giedd, et al., 1997). In a functional MRI study, the performance of children ages 7 to 12 and adults was studied in a go/no-go task. The go/no-go task requires responding to most stimuli but inhibiting responding to certain specified stimuli. In comparison with a control condition in which children responded to all stimuli, the condition requiring inhibitory control activated the prefrontal cortex in both children and adults. The number of false alarms in this condition also correlated significantly with the extent of cingulate activity (Casey, Trainor, Orendi, et al., 1997), consistent with the role of the cingulate in error detection.

EFFORTFUL CONTROL

Effortful control is a higher order factor derived from a number of parent-report, child-report, and adult-report temperament scales that reflect inhibitory, associational, and attentional control. It is related to many important landmarks of development (Rothbart, 2011; Rothbart & Rueda, 2005).

Effortful control is inversely related to negative affect (Rothbart, Ahadi, Hershey, & Fisher, 2001): Children and adults reported to have stronger effortful control showed less negative affect. While in infancy, negative affect is partly controlled by parents' presenting novel objects to their child. Later in life, this regulation seems to be internal, perhaps through the generation of positive thoughts. This relation is in keeping with the notion that attentional skill may help attenuate negative affect while also serving to constrain impulsive approach tendencies.

Empathy is also strongly related to effortful control, with children high in effortful control showing greater empathy. To display empathy toward others requires that one interpret their signals of distress or pleasure. Imaging work with the typically developing brain has shown that sad faces activate the amygdala. As sadness increases, amygdala activation is accompanied by activity in the anterior cingulate as part of the executive attention network (Blair, Morris, Frith, Perrett, & Dolan, 1999). It seems likely that this cingulate activity represents the basis for humans' attention to the distress of others. Cingulate activity is related to regulation of positive as well as negative affect. The effort to control arousal to a sexually stimulating movie, for example, also shows specific activation of this brain network (Beauregard, Levesque, & Bourgouin, 2001).

Developmental studies have found two routes to successful socialization, called *conscience* by Kochanska (1995, 1997). A strongly reactive amygdala indicative of high fear levels would provide the distress signals that would easily allow the child to have empathic feelings toward others. These children would be easy to socialize. For children with low levels of fear, the development of conscience would be more difficult and would rest largely on effortful control. Consistent with the dual-route view of empathy, the internalization of moral principles appears to be facilitated in fearful preschool-age children, especially when their mothers use gentle discipline (Kochanska, 1995). In addition, internalized control is facilitated in children high in effortful control (Kochanska, 1997). Two separable control systems—one reactive (fear) and one self-regulative (effortful control)—appear to regulate the development of conscience.

Individual differences in effortful control are also related to some aspects of metacognitive knowledge, such as theory of mind (i.e., knowing that people's behavior is guided by their beliefs, desires, and other mental states; Carlson & Moses, 2001). Moreover, tasks that require the inhibition of a prepotent response are correlated with performance on theory of mind tasks even when other factors, such as age, intelligence, and working memory, are factored out (Carlson & Moses, 2001). Inhibitory control and theory of mind share a similar developmental time course, with advances in both between the ages of 2 and 5 years.

ERROR CORRECTION

One function that has been traced to the anterior cingulate is the monitoring and correction of errors. Although infants show evidence of detecting and looking longer at error trials (Berger et al., 2006), error correction appears much later. In one study, children played a Simple Simon game in which they were asked to execute a response command given by one puppet while inhibiting commands given by a second puppet (Jones, Rothbart, & Posner, 2003). Children 36 through 38 months of age showed no ability to inhibit their response and no slowing following an error, but at 39 through 41 months, children showed both an ability to inhibit and a slowing of reaction time following an error. These results suggest that early in the fourth year of life, performance changes based on detection of an error response. Because error detection has been studied using scalp electrical recording (Gehring, Gross, Coles, Meyer, & Donchin, 1993; Luu, Collins, & Tucker, 2000) and shown to originate in the anterior cingulate (Bush, Luu, & Posner, 2000), we are able to examine the emergence of this cingulate functioning even during infancy; these findings are discussed below in the report of our longitudinal research.

Studies of error correction provide evidence for early control, particularly of emotion, by the orienting network. Although the executive network is present during infancy at least for the detection of error, it does not seem able to slow behavior based on a previous error. These findings support important development of the executive network during early childhood. Moreover, the development of executive attention contributes to the socialization process by increasing the likelihood of learning important behaviors related to self-regulation and understanding the cognition and emotion of others. It seems likely that understanding the origins of this system in early development could further our understanding of self-regulation.

LONGITUDINAL STUDY OF COGNITIVE AND EMOTIONAL CONTROL

The cross-sectional studies discussed above provide some evidence on the development of attention during later childhood. We began our longitudinal study when the children were about 7 months old and so far have followed the participants until 4 years of age. Several summaries of our findings have become available (Posner, Rothbart, Sheese, & Voelker, 2012; Rothbart, Sheese, Rueda, & Posner, 2011; Sheese, Rothbart, Posner, White, & Fraundorf, 2008; Sheese, Rothbart, Voelker, & Posner, 2012; Sheese, Voelker, Posner, & Rothbart, 2009; Sheese, Voelker, Rothbart, & Posner, 2007; Voelker, Sheese, Rothbart, & Posner, 2009).

The reason we began at 7 months of age was that Berger et al. (2006) had shown the ability of 7-month-old infants to detect errors. It was not until about 3 years of age that children slowed their performance in response to an error (Jones et al., 2003), but even infants seemed to detect error as indicated by increased looking times (Wynn, 1992).

In the Berger et al. (2006) study, infants observed a scenario in which one or two puppets were hidden behind a screen. A hand was seen to reach behind the screen and either add or remove a puppet. When the screen was taken away, either the correct number of puppets or an incorrect number was presented. Wynn (1992) found that 7-month-old infants looked longer when the number was in error than when it was correct. Whether the increased looking time involved the same executive attention circuitry active in adults was unknown.

Berger et al. (2006) replicated the Wynn (1992) study but used 128-channel electroencephalography (EEG) to determine the brain activity that occurred during error trials in comparison with that found when the infant viewed a correct solution. Results indicated that the same EEG component over the same electrode sites differed between conditions for both infants and adults. Because this EEG component had been shown to be related to activity in the anterior cingulate gyrus (Dehaene, Posner, & Tucker, 1994), it appears that the same brain anatomy is involved as in adult studies. Of course, activation of this anatomy has different consequences in adults, who actually slow down after an error and adjust their performance. However, it suggests that even very early in life, at least a part of the executive network is in place.

The development of executive attention can be easily observed using questionnaire and cognitive tasks in preschool and school-age children, when parents can identify the ability of their children to regulate their emotions and control their behavior in accord with social demands. However, in infancy it has been difficult to word questions that refer to effortful control because most regulation seems automatic or involves the caregiver's intervention. Obviously, infants cannot be instructed to press a key in accord with a particular rule. However, the clear evidence on the existence of early error detection makes it seem likely that the executive attention network is partly in place much earlier than we had suspected.

Our longitudinal study involved 70 children observed between 7 months and 4 years of age. We examined various aspects of temperament and behavior and also asked if the genes we had shown to influence attention in adults would have specific roles in the development of self-regulation during infancy and childhood. We retested and genotyped the children at age 2 and tested them a final time at age 4, when they were able perform the children's ANT as a measure of executive attention.

Because infants are not able to carry out voluntary attention tasks, we used a sequence learning visual task. Previous work had shown that the ability to use context to reduce conflict can be traced developmentally using the learning of sequences of locations (Clohessy, Posner & Rothbart, 2001). Infants as young as 4 months anticipate the location of a stimulus, provided the associations in the sequence are unambiguous. In unambiguous sequences, each location is invariably associated with another location (e.g., 1-2-3; Clohessy et al., 2001). Because the location of the current target is fully determined by the preceding location, only one type of information needs to be attended, and therefore there is no conflict (e.g., Location 3 always follows Location 2). Adults can learn unambiguous sequences of spatial locations implicitly even when attention is distracted by a secondary task (Curran & Keele, 1993).

Ambiguous sequences (e.g., 1-2-1-3), however, require attention both to the current association and to the context in which the association occurs (e.g., Location 1 may be followed by Location 2 or by Location 3). Ambiguous sequences pose conflict because for any association, there exist two strong candidates that can be disambiguated only by context. When distracted, adults are unable to learn both ambiguous sequences of length six (e.g., 1-2-3-2-1-3; Curran & Keele, 1993). Because distraction reduces attentional resources, this finding indicates the need for higher level attentional resources to resolve this conflict. Even simple ambiguous associations (e.g., 1-2-1-3) were not learned by infants until about 2 years of age (Clohessy et al., 2001).

At first, we felt that all anticipations could be based on an executive attention system and thus could serve as an early indicant of executive attention. The idea was that the anticipations were voluntary and not forced by the location of the target. The data on 7-month-olds seemed to agree with this idea in that the infants who made the most anticipatory looks also exhibited a pattern of cautious reaching toward novel objects, which predicts effortful control in older children (Rothbart et al., 2001; Rothbart, Ellis, Rueda, & Posner, 2003). In addition, infants with more anticipatory looks showed more spontaneous attempts at self-regulation when presented with somewhat frightening objects.

However, when the infants were 4 years of age and could be tested with the ANT, we found evidence that anticipations at 7 months were related more to orienting network scores on the ANT than to executive attention network scores (Posner et al., 2012; Rothbart et al., 2011). In retrospect, this solution may fit with adult MRI data because adult voluntary shifts of attention based on cues use a portion of the orienting network (Corbetta & Shulman, 2002). Our results may also reflect the closer integration of the two networks during early development that has been noted in functional MRI (fMRI) studies (Dosenbach et al., 2007).

Rothbart and Derryberry (1981) distinguished reactive and self-regulatory aspects of child temperament. They argued that early in life, negative affects—particularly fear—and orienting of attention serve as regulatory mechanisms that are supplemented by parental regulation. Moreover, Rothbart and Bates (2006) argued for developmental change in which effortful control arises only at about 3 to 4 years of age when parents can first report on their children's self-regulatory ability.

Our longitudinal study confirmed but also revised and extended this analysis. We found a negative correlation at 7 months between parent reports of infant orienting of attention and negative affect. Orienting was also correlated positively with reports of positive affect. By age 2, orienting was no longer related to affect, but effortful control began to show modest negative correlations with both positive and negative affect.

Results of our longitudinal study suggest that early in life, the orienting network serves as a regulatory system for both negative and positive affect, with both orienting and executive networks serving parallel regulatory functions during infancy. Later on, executive attention appears to dominate in regulating emotions and thoughts, but orienting still remains as a control system. This conceptualization fits well with a parallel control system view that has been developed in MRI studies (Dosenbach et al., 2007; Fair et al., 2009) and in the parallel control systems discussed in the next section.

PARALLEL CONTROL SYSTEMS

Some studies have examined the brain activity of infants and young children at rest using fMRI (Fair et al., 2009, 2011; Fransson et al., 2007; Gao et al., 2009). These results have shown evidence of sparse connectivity between brain structures during infancy and a strong increase in connectivity at 2 years (Gao et al., 2009) and later (Fair et al., 2007, 2009). In studies of neonates, the parietal areas, prominent in the orienting of attention network, show strong connectivity to lateral and medial frontal areas. By age 2, the anterior cingulate, which has been implicated in self-regulation, shows stronger connections to frontal areas and to lateral parietal areas. In work with older children and adolescents (Fair et al., 2009), these tendencies continue, and the anterior cingulate cortex (ACC) becomes increasingly differentiated from the orienting network as one approaches adulthood. According to Fair et al., (2011),

The data suggested that there might be at least two control networks functioning in parallel. Based on the differences in their functional connectivity and activation profiles we suggested that each network likely exerts distinct types of control on differing temporal scales. The fronto-parietal network was proposed to be important for rapidly adaptive control and to work on a shorter timescale. The cingulo-opercular network was thought to be important for more stable set-maintenance, and to operate on a longer timescale. Since this initial work there have now been several reports supporting this framework. (p. 297)

Note that the frontal parietal network is similar in anatomy to the orienting network, whereas the cingulo-opercular network corresponds to the executive network discussed above.

These findings suggest that control structures related to executive attention and effortful control may be present in infancy but do not exercise their full control over other networks until later in development. The connections indicate that initially the ACC has stronger connections to the orienting network and only later becomes differentiated from it. Error detection activates the midfrontal and/or cingulate areas at 7 months (Berger et al., 2006), although the infant's ability to take action based on errors seems not to be present until 3 to 4 years of age (Jones et al., 2003). These and our other behavioral findings fit with the idea that earlier in life, the orienting network, together with the caregiver, is the basic behavioral control system and plays a role similar to the one later associated with the ACC.

When taken together, the data on resting connectivity and from temperament questionnaires and task performance support the important role of executive attention as a regulatory mechanism by 18 to 20 months and the role of orienting as a control mechanism at 6 to 7 months. It seems likely that the parallel activity of these two networks begins in infancy and continues to adulthood. The strong tendency for adults to look away as a self-regulatory strategy suggests a continued role for orienting even for adults.

Parents appear to have an important role in this change. fMRI studies of adults show that orienting to novel objects tends to recruit the executive system (Shulman et al., 2009). The use of orienting to novelty by adults as a soothing technique for their infants may play a role in training the executive system. Problems in the transition from orienting control to executive control may also contribute to forms of childhood pathologies that involve the executive attention network. Some brain states—for example, hypnotism—may take advantage of these parallel control systems and of the orienting network's close association with sensory input to provide increased control of adult behavior by external events (Posner & Rothbart, 2010). We hope future longitudinal results and additional studies will provide further information on the coordination between these two regulatory networks.

Brain networks of attention are common to all and thus argue strongly for the role of genes in their construction. This probable genetic role has led cognitive neuroscience to incorporate data from the growing field of human genetics. One method for doing this relates individual variations in genes (genetic alleles) to aspects of human behavior. Brain activity can serve as an intermediate level for relating genes to behavior. As one example, the ANT has been used to examine individual differences in the efficiency of executive attention. A number of dopamine and serotonin genes have been associated specifically with the ANT scores on executive attention (Green et al., 2008; Posner, Rothbart, & Sheese, 2007), whereas cholinergic genes have been associated with orienting and noradrenergic genes with alerting (see Green et al., 2008, for a review).

The children from our longitudinal study returned to our laboratory at 18 to 20 months. At this time, the children played with toys in the presence of one of their caregivers. Raters reviewed a videotaped caregiver–child interaction and rated five dimensions of parenting quality: (a) supportive presence (positive regard and emotional support), (b) respect for autonomy (unintrusive in interactions with child), (c) stimulation of cognitive development (directed instruction, teaching), (d) hostility (anger, rejection, negative regard), and (e) confidence (confidence in interactions with child; National Institute of Child Health & Human Development, Early Child Care Research Network, 1993). Although all of the parents were likely concerned and caring, they did differ in their scores, and we divided them at the median of overall parenting quality into two groups reflecting higher and lower quality of parenting.

DRD4

The dopamine 4 receptor gene (DRD4) has long been related both to attention-deficit/hyperactivity disorder (ADHD; Swanson, Flodman, et al., 2000; Swanson, Oosterlaan, et al., 2000; Swanson et al., 1991) and, in conjunction with serotonin genes, to the temperamental dimension of sensation seeking (Auerbach, Benjamin, Faroy, Kahana, & Levine, 2001). DRD4 has several versions that occur with relatively high frequency. These differ in the number of repeats of a 48-base pair part of the gene. Common are 2, 4, and 7 repeats of this portion of the gene. Although the 7-repeat allele of the DRD4 is overrepresented in children with ADHD, it is not related to any deficit in attention as measured by cognitive tasks (Swanson, Oosterlaan, et al., 2000).

In our longitudinal study sample at ages 18 through 20 months, Sheese, Voelker, Rothbart, and Posner (2007) found no evidence of a direct influence of the 7-repeat allele on child temperament but instead found that in the presence of the 7-repeat variant, parenting had a large influence on a set of temperamental dimensions assaying sensation seeking, impulsivity, and related symptoms that are typically found in children with ADHD. In our longitudinal study, however, no children had a diagnosis of ADHD, and they seemed representative of our area of the country. Nonetheless, we found that children with the 7-repeat allele who had somewhat lower quality of parenting in our free play situation had unusually high levels of sensation seeking (including the dimensions of activity level, high-intensity pleasure seeking, and impulsivity). If children did not have a 7-repeat allele, or if they had the allele but also had higher quality parenting, ratings of their behavior on these dimensions were about average.

Because of this finding, we think the paradox of the 7-repeat allele may arise because its presence can produce symptoms of ADHD without attention deficits. However, its presence does not automatically lead to later problems. Whether problems appear or not may depend on features of the child's environment such as parenting. Similar evidence that environment can have a stronger influence in the presence of the 7-repeat allele has been reported by others (Bakermans-Kranenburg & van IJzendoorn, 2006; van IJzendoorn & Bakermans-Kranenburg, 2006), and these findings were reinforced by a study in which children were randomly assigned to parent interventions (Bakermans-Kranenburg, van IJzendoorn, Pijlman, Mesman, & Juffer, 2008). Those with the 7-repeat allele showed significant improvements due to the intervention, whereas those without the 7-repeat allele did not. The use of random assignment of children to groups shows that in this case, those with the 7-repeat variation are more influenced by parent training. The special susceptibility of those with the 7-repeat variation may also extend to adulthood. In one study (Larsen et al., 2010), it was found that young adults carrying the 7-repeat allele were more influenced in their alcohol consumption by the drinking of their peers than those without the 7-repeat allele.

An important feature of the 7-repeat allele is that it appears to have been under positive selection pressure during the past 50,000 years of human evolution (Ding et al., 2002). Theories of positive selection in the *DRD4* gene have stressed the role of sensation seeking in human evolution (B. Wang et al., 2006; E. Wang et al., 2004). For example, people leaving Africa might have been especially strong in this characteristic and were thus successful in coping with aspects of their new environment. Another important idea is that genetic variations such as the 7-repeat allele may produce unusual vulnerability under one environmental circumstance but also produce improvements in others (Belsky & Pluess, 2009). This idea fits well with the finding that positive selection of the 7-repeat allele could arise from sensitivity to environmental influences, especially the influence of parents. Parenting allows the culture to train children in the values that it favors, as found in earlier work in China by Ahadi, Rothbart, and Ye (1993). In recent years, the nature versus nurture interaction has tilted very much to the importance of genes, but if genetic variations are selected according to their sensitivity to cultural influences, this would support a more balanced discussion. Thus, one effect of nature may be to influence the susceptibility of children to their environment. The study on alcohol use cited above suggests that this susceptibility can also influence adult behavior, although in this case the influence is through peers rather than parents. Although this evidence is confined to the *DRD4* gene, Belsky and Pluess (2009) discussed other genes whose effect may be to influence the plasticity of the brain in the face of different environments.

A somewhat surprising aspect of the data on the *DRD4* gene is that its influence on temperament did not appear to be through changes in attention at ages 18 through 20 months. Because our study was longitudinal, it was possible to examine the effects of *DRD4* variation in the same children when they were about 4 years old. Sheese, Rothbart, Voelker, and Posner (2012) related ANT performance at age 4 to parenting quality and genotype. They found that parenting quality at 18 through 20 months influenced effortful control at 4 years. The executive attention network is well set up to mediate environmental influence. The anterior cingulate is known to be an important part of reward and punishment networks. Because the dopamine system modulates the activity of the cingulate, the efficiency of the receptor could modify the effectiveness of rewards and punishments. Thus, a system that modulates the reactivity of the cingulate would be well placed to influence attention and behavior.

COMT

COMT (catechol-O-methyltransferase) plays an important role in dopamine metabolism by modulating extracellular levels of dopamine. The functional *val/met* polymorphism of COMT has a measurable effect on COMT enzyme activity, with the *val* allele degrading extracellular dopamine more quickly than the less enzymatically active *met* allele. A finding from our current longitudinal study is that the COMT gene, which has consistently been shown to be related to executive attention in adults and older children, is also related to aspects of executive attention at 18 through 20 months of age (Voelker et al., 2009). Haplotypes of the COMT gene influenced both anticipatory looking and nesting cup performance (another executive task) at 18 through 20 months.

In children age 7 months, COMT was also related to positive affect as reported by parents. The finding of a relation of COMT to positive affect, together with the influence of this gene on executive attention at 18 through 20 months, could provide a genetic link between reactive emotion and emotional regulation during early development. However, it is also possible that *COMT*'s relation to positive affect in infancy is mediated by regulatory aspects of executive attention. It is likely that an early form of executive attention is regulation of emotion, which may occur in parallel with regulation by orienting. Evidence for this idea is mixed; in our current study, positive affect in infancy was unrelated to later effortful control, but other studies have shown such a connection (Rothbart, 2011).

CHRNA4

The nicotinic cholinergic receptor *CHRNA4* modulates the release of dopamine in the mesolimbic system. As seen in adults, this gene is associated with variation in performance of the orienting network and in brain activity during the performance of visual attention tasks.

Because visuospatial attention requires orienting, we expected the *CHRNA4* polymorphism to influence orienting in our child subjects and thought it might also influence higher order attention via its relation with dopamine. In 7-month-old children, we found that *CHRNA4* is related to more successful anticipatory looking. At 18 through 20 months, the main influence of this gene appeared to be on effortful control linked to executive attention (Sheese et al., 2009).

Although in adults *CHRNA4* seems to be related to tasks that clearly involve the orienting network (see Parasuraman, Greenwood, Kumar, & Fossella, 2005, for a review), these tasks may involve executive attention as well. In their measures of spatial orienting in adults, the C/C allele was related to more benefits from a correct cue and significantly fewer costs from an incorrect one. At 7 months, the T/T allele of *CHRNA4* is related to better performance in anticipatory looking, but at 18 through 20 months, the C/C homozygotes had the highest scores on effortful control (Voelker et al., 2009). At 4 years, the C/C homozygotes showed more correct anticipations on the visual looking task. It appears that there is an important switch between infancy and ages 2 through 4 in the role of *CHRNA4*. In infancy, the T/T homozygotes show evidence of better attention, whereas for older children and adults, the C/C homozygotes do better. Below we explore possible explanations for this switch.

TRAINING ATTENTION AND SELF-REGULATION

Attention and self-regulation develop under the joint influence of genes and environment. The important role of parents in the transition between control systems early in life raises the issue of whether it would be possible to design experiences that would change the executive network. One way of doing this would be to find a way to improve the efficiency of the attention network by strengthening the network through exercising it (Klingberg, Forssberg, & Westerberg, 2002; Rueda, Checa, & Santonja, 2008; Rueda, Rothbart, McCandliss, Saccomanno, & Posner, 2005). The Rueda et al. (2005, 2008) studies indicate an important role for the anterior cingulate in the training effect. There are also important changes with training in frontal and parietal areas (Klingberg et al., 2002). This type of training is called *attention training* and is similar to other forms of practice in that specific networks of attention and memory are improved. Rueda et al. (2005, 2008) argued that these changes in attention and memory also support generalization to other tasks. Attention training is reviewed in Chapter 2 of this volume, by Rueda and Cómbita.

ATTENTION STATE TRAINING

Another approach is to develop a brain state that would be especially conducive to the ability of the executive network to regulate other networks (Tang & Posner, 2009; Tang, Rothbart, & Posner, in press). In the case of changing a brain state, the changes induced would be present even when the person is at rest. We call this approach *attention state training* (Tang & Posner, 2009). In our studies, we train attention state through a form of meditation.

One example of attention state training is a method called *Integrated Body–Mind Training* (IBMT), a form of mindfulness meditation adapted from traditional Chinese medicine (Tang et al., 2007). The IBMT method leads to very rapid change in brain state and performance. Random assignment of persons to experimental and control groups is thus possible. IBMT seeks to develop an optimal state of balance between mind and body. In IBMT, the trainees concentrate on achieving a balanced state of mind while guided by the coach and a CD that teaches them to relax, adjust their breathing, and use mental imagery. Because this approach is suitable for novices, it was hypothesized that a short period of training and practice might influence the efficiency of the executive attention network related to self-regulation (Tang et al., 2007). The control group was given a form of relaxation training that is very popular in the West as a part of cognitive behavior therapy. In relaxation training, people were instructed to relax different muscle groups in turn. They tended to concentrate attention on the instructed muscle group as they relaxed it. In one study, only 5 days of group practice were used, during which a coach answered participants' questions and observed facial and body cues to identify students in need of help with the method.

The two groups were given a battery of tests a week before training and immediately after the final training session. The ANT, Raven's Standard Progressive Matrix (Raven, Raven, & Court, 2004), a standard culture fair intelligence test, an assay of mood state, the Profile of Mood States (Shacham, 1983), and a stress challenge consisting of a mental arithmetic task followed by measures of cortisol and secretory immunoglobulin were given before and after training. All assays were scored objectively by people blind to the experimental condition.

The underlying theory was that IBMT should improve functioning of the executive attention network by changing the brain state. The experimental group showed significantly greater improvement than the control group in the executive attention network, in mood scales related to self-control, and in cortisol and immunoreactivity measures of stress to a mental arithmetic challenge (Tang et al., 2007). These improvements appear to involve a change of state, because there is increased brain activity in areas related to the activation and control of the parasympathetic portion of the autonomic nervous system. Also indicative of a change of brain state is that IBMT alters the resting state (default state) as measured by fMRI.

Further studies have revealed the mechanisms underlying this change of state (Tang et al., 2009, 2010). In one study, 30 days of training was provided, with neuroimaging used to assay brain changes with training. The IBMT group was found to have improved functional connectivity between the ACC and striatum. Moreover, parasympathetic function changed more in the IBMT group than in the controls. Further studies using diffusion tensor imaging revealed that several white matter tracts connecting the ACC to other areas had improved in their efficiency (Tang et al., 2010). These tracts include the anterior corona radiata, which had previously been shown to be specifically related to the executive attention network (Niogi, Mukherjee, Ghajar, & McCandliss, 2010). These findings show that the connectivity related to self-regulation can be altered in adults by training.

Although the bulk of the work has been done with young adults, mindfulness training has recently been applied to young children (Zelazo & Lyons, 2012). This training has potential implications for all aspects of self-regulation, including clinical or educational applications.

AGING

Results achieved with both attention training and attention state training suggest that self-regulation may be modified at any age by the appropriate training method. Important issues nevertheless remain: How long do such improvements last? What are the underlying brain mechanisms changed by these various training methods? Of course, development does not end with young adulthood. There have been many studies documenting an increase in reaction time and a decrease in accuracy and reduction of problem-solving ability and fluid intelligence in older adults when compared with young adults. Because of the time periods involved, these are generally not longitudinal studies, and like all cross-sectional research, they may be subject to bias in the selection of people at various ages. Despite this problem, studies using modern imaging methods with older adults provide insight into changes that occur later in life that are closely related to the brain networks we have been examining.

In one study, Pardo et al. (2007) asked which areas of the brain showed the clearest decline in metabolism with age. They used positron emission tomography to examine metabolism in 46 persons ranging from 18 to 90 years of age. The strongest decline with age was in the anterior cingulate gyrus, suggesting a reason why aging brings difficulty in self-regulation. However, some studies of older adults using the conflict score from the attention network task have found no increase in the time to resolve conflict with age unless the participants had been diagnosed with Alzheimer's disease (Fernandez-Duque & Black, 2006).

Fair et al. (2009) showed that the connectivity between the anterior cingulate and more posterior brain areas when at rest was very poor in early childhood and showed a marked increase for older children and adults. In a study of resting connectivity in aging adults (Andrews-Hanna et al., 2007), it was found that connectivity between the midfrontal and posterior areas showed a marked decline in old age. Although there was some overlap in strength of connectivity between younger and older adults, the older adult showing the strongest connectivity was only at the mean of the younger adults.

Although the genotype stays constant over the life span, the influence of genes may be even greater in old age than for younger persons. Nagel et al. (2008) examined the influence of the COMT gene on executive attention and working memory, finding genetic effects to be even stronger in the older adults than in the younger adults. Frontal white matter connectivity thus shows a long history of development in childhood and adolescence. In addition, the studies of aging tend overall to support the idea that the connections between brain areas that develop slowly may be especially vulnerable to the influence of aging.

CONCLUSION

The use of conflict in neuroimaging studies has made it possible to discover many nodes of the neural network that carry out resolution of conflict, including the important role of anterior cingulate connectivity in influencing brain areas involved in cognition and emotion. This discovery led to a proposed brain circuitry underlying self-regulation. The anterior cingulate has an important evolutionary history, including the presence of special cells unique to areas involved in self-regulation among humans and great apes. Specialization in this area could well be an important part of the unique human ability to delay gratification and to otherwise regulate behavior in the service of long-term goals. This finding provides a renewed opportunity to explore differences between the human and other primate brains.

The association of genetic variations with individual differences in the efficiency of the network provides a further method for discovery of genes that serve to build nodes and connections of executive attention. This link provides a molecular perspective on the physical basis of self-regulation. The ability to find candidate genes related to the attention network rests on pharmacological findings linking different neuromodulators to the functioning of attentional networks. Other methods such as the use of full genome scans, the study of brain pathologies, and comparative studies of animals can also be used to provide appropriate candidate genes.

What illumination will this molecular perspective provide? Evidence for positive selection of alleles of the *DRD4* gene within recent human history has led us to propose the possibility that some alleles increase the influence on the child of cultural factors such as parenting. The ability to have greater cultural influence can provide for improved reproductive success and thus produce positive selection. That the molecule can change cultural influence suggests a strong degree of cooperation between the biological and the social. Although we remain far from having a complete understanding of the physical basis of many psychological concepts, the tools currently available appear adequate to foster this effort.

REFERENCES

Ahadi, S. A., Rothbart, M. K., & Ye, R. (1993). Children's temperament in the U.S. and China: Similarities and differences. *European Journal of Personality, 7*, 359–378. doi:10.1002/per.2410070506

Andrews-Hanna, J. R., Snyder, A. Z., Vincent, J. L., Lustig, C., Head, D., Raichle, M. E., & Buckner, R. L. (2007). Disruption of large-scale brain systems in advanced aging. *Neuron, 56*, 924–935. doi:10.1016/j.neuron.2007.10.038

Auerbach, J. G., Benjamin, J., Faroy, M., Kahana, M., & Levine, J. (2001). The association of the dopamine D4 receptor gene (*DRD4*) and the serotonin transporter promotor gene (*5 HTTL-PR*) with temperament in 12-month-old infants. *Journal of Child Psychology and Psychiatry, and Allied Disciplines, 42*, 777–783.

Bakermans-Kranenburg, M. J., & van IJzendoorn, M. H. (2006). Gene–environment interaction of the dopamine D4 receptor (*DRD4*) and observed maternal insensitivity predicting externalizing behavior in preschoolers. *Developmental Psychobiology, 48*, 406–409. doi:10.1002/dev.20152

Bakermans-Kranenburg, M. J., van IJzendoorn, M. H., Pijlman, F. T. A., Mesman, J., & Juffer, F. (2008). Experimental evidence for differential susceptibility: Dopamine D4 receptor polymorphism (*DRD4 VNTR*) moderates intervention effects on toddlers' externalizing behavior in a randomized controlled trial. *Developmental Psychology, 44*, 293–300.

Beauregard, M., Levesque, J., & Bourgouin, P. (2001). Neural correlates of conscious self-regulation of emotion. *Journal of Neuroscience, 21*, RC165.

Belsky, J., & Pluess, M. (2009). Beyond diathesis stress: Differential susceptibility to environmental stress. *Psychological Bulletin, 135*, 885–908. doi:10.1037/a0017376

Berger, A., Tzur, G., & Posner, M. I. (2006). Infant babies detect arithmetic error. *Proceedings of the National Academy of Sciences of the United States of America, 103*, 12649–12653. doi:10.1073/pnas.0605350103

Blair, R. J. R., Morris, J. S., Frith, C. D., Perrett, D. I., & Dolan, R. J. (1999). Dissociable neural responses to facial expression of sadness and anger. *Brain: A Journal of Neurology, 122*, 883–893. doi:10.1093/brain/122.5.883

Bush, G., Luu, P., & Posner, M. I. (2000). Cognitive and emotional influences in the anterior cingulate cortex. *Trends in Cognitive Sciences, 4*, 215–222. doi:10.1016/S1364-6613(00)01483-2

Carlson, S. M., & Moses, L. J. (2001). Individual differences in inhibitory control in children's theory of mind. *Child Development, 72*, 1032–1053. doi:10.1111/1467-8624.00333

Casey, B. J., Trainor, R., Giedd, J., Vauss, Y., Vaituzis, C. K., Hamburger, S., . . . Rapoport, J. L. (1997). The role of the anterior cingulate in automatic and controlled processes: A developmental neuroanatomical study. *Developmental Psychobiology, 30*, 61–69. doi:10.1002/(SICI)1098-2302(199701)30:1<61::AID-DEV6>3.0.CO;2-T

Casey, B. J., Trainor, R. J., Orendi, J. L., Schubert, A. B., Nystrom, L. E., Giedd, J. N., . . . Rapoport, J. L. (1997). A developmental functional MRI study of prefrontal activation during performance of a go-no-go task. *Journal of Cognitive Neuroscience, 9*, 835–847. doi:10.1162/jocn.1997.9.6.835

Clohessy, A. B., Posner, M. I., & Rothbart, M. K. (2001). Development of the functional visual field. *Acta Psychologica, 106*, 51–68. doi:10.1016/S0001-6918(00)00026-3

Corbetta, M., & Shulman, G. L. (2002). Control of goal-directed and stimulus-driven attention in the brain. *Nature Reviews Neuroscience, 3*, 201–215.

Curran, T., & Keele, S. W. (1993). Attentional and non-attentional forms of sequence learning. *Journal of Experimental Psychology: Learning, Memory, and Cognition, 19*, 189–202. doi:10.1037/0278-7393.19.1.189

Dehaene, S., Posner, M. I., & Tucker, D. M. (1994). Localization of a neural system for error detection and compensation. *Psychological Science, 5,* 303–305. doi:10.1111/j.1467-9280.1994.tb00630.x

Diamond, A. (1991). Neuropsychological insights into the meaning of object concept development. In S. Carey & R. Gelman (Eds.), *The epigenesis of mind: Essays on biology and cognition* (pp. 67–110). Hillsdale, NJ: Erlbaum.

Ding, Y. C., Chi, H. C., Grady, D. L., Morishima, A., Kidd, J. R., Kidd, K. K., . . . Moyzis, R. K. (2002). Evidence of positive selection acting at the human dopamine receptor D4 gene locus. *Proceedings of the National Academy of Sciences of the United States of America, 99,* 309–314.

Dosenbach, N. U. F., Fair, D. A., Miezin, F. M., Cohen, A. L., Wenger, K. K., Dosenbach, R. A. T., . . . Petersen, S. E. (2007). Distinct brain networks for adaptive and stable task control in humans. *Proceedings of the National Academy of Sciences of the United States of America, 104,* 11073–11078. doi:10.1073/pnas.0704320104

Fair, D. A., Cohen, A. L., Power, J. D., Dosenbach, N. U. F., Church, J. A., Miezin, F. M., . . . Petersen, S. E. (2009). Functional brain networks develop from a local to distributed organization. *PLoS Computational Biology, 5*(5), e1000381.

Fair, D. A., Dosenbach, N. U. F., Church, J. A., Cohen, A. L., Brahmbhatt, S., Miezin, F. M., . . . Schlaggar, B. L. (2007). Development of distinct control networks through segregation and integration. *Proceedings of the National Academy of Sciences of the United States of America, 104,* 13507–13512.

Fair, D. A., Dosenbach, N. U. F., Petersen, S. E., & Schlaggar, B. L. (2011). Resting state studies on the development of control systems. In M. I. Posner (Ed.), *Cognitive neuroscience of attention* (2nd ed., pp. 291–311). New York, NY: Guilford Press.

Fan, J., McCandliss, B. D., Sommer, T., Raz, M., & Posner, M. I. (2002). Testing the efficiency and independence of attentional networks. *Journal of Cognitive Neuroscience, 14,* 340–347. doi:10.1162/089892902317361886

Fernandez-Duque, D., & Black, S. E. (2006). Attentional networks in normal aging and Alzheimer's disease. *Neuropsychology, 20,* 133–143. doi:10.1037/0894-4105.20.2.133

Fransson, P., Skiold, B., Horsch, S., Nordell, A., Blennow, M., Lagercrantz, H., & Aden, U. (2007). Resting-state networks in the infant brain. *Proceedings of the National Academy of Sciences of the United States of America, 104,* 15531–15536. doi:10.1073/pnas.0704380104

Gao, W., Zhu, H., Giovanello, K. S., Smith, J. K., Shen, D., Gilmore, J. H., & Lin, W. (2009). Evidence on the emergence of the brain's default network from 2-week-old to 2-year-old healthy pediatric subjects. *Proceedings of the National Academy of Sciences of the United States of America, 106,* 6790–6795. doi:10.1073/pnas.0811221106

Gehring, W. J., Gross, B., Coles, M. G. H., Meyer, D. E., & Donchin, E. (1993). A neural system for error detection and compensation. *Psychological Science, 4,* 385–390. doi:10.1111/j.1467-9280.1993.tb00586.x

Green, A. E., Munafo, M. R., DeYoung, C. G., Fossella, J. A., Fan, J., & Gray, J. A. (2008). Using genetic data in cognitive neuroscience: From growing pains to genuine insights. *Nature Reviews Neuroscience, 9*, 710–720. doi:10.1038/nrn2461

Harman, C., Rothbart, M. K., & Posner, M. I. (1997). Distress and attention interactions in early infancy. *Motivation and Emotion, 21*, 27–43.

Jones, L., Rothbart, M. K., & Posner, M. I. (2003). Development of inhibitory control in preschool children. *Developmental Science, 6*, 498–504. doi:10.1111/1467-7687.00307

Klingberg, T., Forssberg, H., & Westerberg, H. (2002). Training of working memory in children with ADHD. *Journal of Clinical and Experimental Neuropsychology, 24*, 781–791. doi:10.1076/jcen.24.6.781.8395

Kochanska, G. (1995). Children's temperament, mothers' discipline, and security of attachment: Multiple pathways to emerging internalization. *Child Development, 66*, 597–615. doi:10.2307/1131937

Kochanska, G. (1997). Multiple pathways to conscience for children with different temperaments: From toddlerhood to age five. *Developmental Psychology, 33*, 228–240. doi:10.1037/0012-1649.33.2.228

Larsen, H., van der Zwaluw, C. S., Overbeek, G., Granic, I., Franke, B., & Engels, R. C. (2010). A variable-number-of-tandem-repeats polymorphism in the dopamine 4 receptor gene affects social adaptation of alcohol use: Investigation of a gene–environment interaction. *Psychological Science, 21*, 1064–1068.

Luu, P., Collins, P., & Tucker, D. M. (2000). Mood, personality, and self-monitoring: Negative affect and emotionality in relation to frontal lobe mechanisms of error monitoring. *Journal of Experimental Psychology: General, 129*, 43–60. doi:10.1037/0096-3445.129.1.43

Nagel, I. E., Chicherio, C., Li, S. C., von Oertzen, T., Sander, T., Villringer, A., . . . Lindenberger, U. (2008). Human aging magnifies genetic effects on executive functioning and working memory. *Frontiers in Human Neuroscience, 2*, 1–8. doi:10.3389/neuro.09.001.2008

National Institute of Child Health & Human Development (NICHD), Early Child Care Research Network. (1993). *The NICHD study of early child care: A comprehensive longitudinal study of young children's lives*. Washington, DC: Author.

Niogi, S., Mukherjee, P., Ghajar, J., & McCandliss, B. D. (2010). Individual differences in distinct components of attention are linked to anatomical variations in distinct white matter tracts. *Frontiers in Neuroanatomy, 4*, 2. doi:10.3389/neuro.05.021.2009

Parasuraman, R., Greenwood, P. M., Kumar, R., & Fossella, J. (2005). Beyond heritability—Neurotransmitter genes differentially modulate visuospatial attention and working memory. *Psychological Science, 16*, 200–207. doi:10.1111/j.0956-7976.2005.00804.x

Pardo, J. V., Lee, J. T., Sheikh, S. A., Surerus-Johnson, C., Shah, H., Munch, K. R., . . . Dysken, M. W. (2007). Where the brain grows old: Decline in anterior cingulate and medial prefrontal function with normal aging. *NeuroImage, 35,* 1231–1237. doi:10.1016/j.neuroimage.2006.12.044

Piaget, J. (1954). *The construction of reality in the child.* New York, NY: Basic Books. doi:10.1037/11168-000

Posner, M. I., & Fan, J. (2008). Attention as an organ system. In J. R. Pomerantz (Ed.), *Topics in integrative neuroscience* (pp. 31–61). New York, NY: Cambridge University Press. doi:10.1017/CBO9780511541681.005

Posner, M. I., & Rothbart, M. K. (2010). Brain states and hypnosis research. *Consciousness and Cognition, 20,* 325–327.

Posner, M. I., Rothbart, M. K., & Sheese, B. E. (2007). Attention genes. *Developmental Science, 10,* 24–29. doi:10.1111/j.1467-7687.2007.00559.x

Posner, M. I., Rothbart, M. K., Sheese, B. E., & Voelker, P. (2012). Control networks and neuromodulators of early development. *Developmental Psychology, 48,* 827–835. doi:10 1037/a0025530

Raven, J., Raven, J. C., & Court, J. H. (2004). *Manual for Raven's Progressive Matrices and Vocabulary Scales.* San Antonio, TX: Harcourt Assessment.

Rothbart, M. K. (2011). *Becoming who we are.* New York, NY: Guilford Press.

Rothbart, M. K., Ahadi, S. A., Hershey, K. L., & Fisher, P. (2001). Investigations of temperament at three to seven years: The Children's Behavior Questionnaire. *Child Development, 72,* 1394–1408. doi:10.1111/1467-8624.00355

Rothbart, M. K., & Bates, J. E. (2006). Temperament. In W. Damon, R. Lerner, & N. Eisenberg (Eds.), *Handbook of child psychology: Vol. 3. Social, emotional, and personality development* (6th ed., pp. 99–106). New York, NY: Wiley.

Rothbart, M. K., & Derryberry, D. (1981). Development of individual differences in temperament. In M. E. Lamb & A. L. Brown (Eds.), *Advances in developmental psychology* (pp. 37–86). Hillsdale, NJ: Erlbaum.

Rothbart, M. K., Ellis, L. K., Rueda, M. R., & Posner, M. I. (2003). Developing mechanisms of effortful control. *Journal of Personality, 71,* 1113–1144. doi:10.1111/1467-6494.7106009

Rothbart, M. K., & Rueda, M. R. (2005). The development of effortful control. In U. Mayr, E. Awh, & S. W. Keele (Eds.), *Developing individuality in the human brain: A tribute to Michael I. Posner* (pp. 167–188). Washington, DC: American Psychological Association. doi:10.1037/11108-009

Rothbart, M. K., Sheese, B. E., Rueda, M. R., & Posner, M. I. (2011). Developing mechanisms of self-regulation in early life. *Emotion Review, 3,* 207–213. doi:10.1177/1754073910387943

Rueda, M. R., Checa, P., & Santonja, M. (2008, April). *Training executive attention in preschoolers: Lasting effects and transfer to affective self-regulation.* Paper presented at the 2008 Annual Meeting of the Cognitive Neuroscience Society, San Francisco, CA.

Rueda, M. R., Fan, J., Halparin, J., Gruber, D., Lercari, L. P., McCandliss, B. D., & Posner, M. I. (2004). Development of attention during childhood. *Neuropsychologia, 42,* 1029–1040. doi:10.1016/j.neuropsychologia.2003.12.012

Rueda, M. R., Rothbart, M. K., McCandliss, B. D., Saccomanno, L., & Posner, M. I. (2005). Training, maturation and genetic influences on the development of executive attention. *Proceedings of the National Academy of Sciences of the United States of America, 102*, 14931–14936.

Shacham, A. (1983). A shortened version of the Profile of Mood States. *Journal of Personality Assessment, 47*, 305–306.

Sheese, B. E., Rothbart, M. K., Posner, M. I., White, L. K., & Fraundorf, S. H. (2008). Executive attention and self-regulation in infancy. *Infant Behavior and Development, 31*, 501–510.

Sheese, B. E., Rothbart, M. K., Voelker, P., & Posner, M. I. (2012). The dopamine receptor D4 gene 7-repeat allele interacts with parenting quality to predict effortful control in four-year-old children. *Child Development Research, 2012*, 1–6. doi:10.1155/2012/863242

Sheese, B. E., Voelker, P., Posner, M. I., & Rothbart, M. K. (2009). Genetic variation influences on the early development of reactive emotions and their regulation by attention. *Cognitive Neuropsychiatry, 14*, 332–355. doi:10.1080/13546800902844064

Sheese, B. E., Voelker, P. M., Rothbart, M. K., & Posner, M. I. (2007). Parenting quality interacts with genetic variation in dopamine receptor *DRD4* to influence temperament in early childhood. *Development and Psychopathology, 19*, 1039–1046. doi:10.1017/S0954579407000521

Shulman, G. L., Astafiev, S. V., Franke, D., Pope, D. L. W., Snyder, A. Z., McAvoy, M. P., & Corbett, M. (2009). Interaction of stimulus-driven reorienting and expectation in ventral and dorsal frontoparietal and basal ganglia-cortical networks. *Journal of Neuroscience, 29*, 4392–4407. doi:10.1523/JNEUROSCI.5609-08.2009

Swanson, J., Oosterlaan, J., Murias, M., Moyzis, R., Schuck, S., Mann, M., . . . Posner, M. I. (2000). ADHD children with 7-repeat allele of the *DRD4* gene have extreme behavior but normal performance on critical neuropsychological tests of attention. *Proceedings of the National Academy of Sciences of the United States of America, 97*, 4754–4759. doi:10.1073/pnas.080070897

Swanson, J. M., Flodman, P., Kennedy, J., Spence, M. A., Moyzis, R., Schuck, S., . . . Posner, M. (2000). Dopamine genes and ADHD. *Neuroscience and Biobehavioral Reviews, 24*, 21–25. doi:10.1016/S0149-7634(99)00062-7

Swanson, J. M., Posner, M. I., Potkin, S., Bonforte, S., Youpa, D., Fiore, C., . . . Crinella, F. (1991). Activating tasks for the study of visual-spatial attention in ADHD children: A cognitive anatomical approach. *Journal of Child Neurology, 6*, S119–S127.

Tang, Y.-Y., Lu, Q., Geng, X., Stein, E. A., Yang, Y., & Posner, M. I. (2010). Short-term mental training induces white matter changes in the anterior cingulate. *Proceedings of the National Academy of Sciences of the United States of America, 107*, 15649–15652.

Tang, Y.-Y., Ma, Y., Fan, Y., Feng, H., Wang, J., Feng, S., . . . Fan, M. (2009). Central and autonomic nervous system interaction is altered by short-term meditation. *Proceedings of the National Academy of Sciences of the United States of America, 106*, 8865–8870. doi:10.1073/pnas.0904031106

Tang, Y.-Y., Ma, Y., Wang, J., Fan, Y., Feng, S., Lu, Q., . . . Posner, M. I. (2007). Short-term meditation training improves attention and self-regulation. *Proceedings of the National Academy of Sciences of the United States of America, 104*, 17152–17156.

Tang, Y.-Y., & Posner, M. I. (2009). Attention training and attention state training. *Trends in Cognitive Sciences, 13*, 222–227. doi:10.1016/j.tics.2009.01.009

Tang Y.-Y., Rothbart, M. K., & Posner, M. I. (in press). Meditation improves self regulation over the lifespan. *Current Directions in Psychological Science.*

Van IJzendoorn, M. H., & Bakermans-Kranenburg, M. J. (2006). DRD4 7-repeat polymorphism moderates the association between maternal unresolved loss or trauma and infant disorganization. *Attachment & Human Development, 8*, 291–307. doi:10.1080/14616730601048159

Voelker, P., Sheese, B. E., Rothbart, M. K., & Posner, M. I. (2009). Variations in catechol-*O*-methyltransferase gene interact with parenting to influence attention in early development. *Neuroscience, 164*, 121–130. doi:10.1016/j.neuroscience.2009.05.059

Wang, B., Wang, Y. F., Zhou, R. L., Li, J., Qian, Q., Yang, L., . . . Faraone, S. V. (2006). Possible association of the alpha-2 adrenergic receptor gene (ADRA2A) with symptoms of attention-deficit/hyperactivity disorder. *American Journal of Medical Genetics, Part B, Neuropsychiatric Genetics, 141B*, 130–134.

Wang, E., Ding, Y.-C., Flodman, P., Kidd, J. R., Kidd, K. K., Grady, D. L., . . . Moyzis, R. K. (2004). The genetic architecture of selection at the human dopamine receptor D4 (DRD4) gene locus. *American Journal of Human Genetics, 74*, 931–944. doi:10.1086/420854

Wynn, K. (1992, August 27). Addition and subtraction by human infants. *Nature, 358*, 749–750. doi:10.1038/358749a0

Zelazo, P. D., & Lyons, K. E. (2012). The potential benefits of mindfulness training in early childhood: A developmental social cognitive neuroscience perspective. *Child Development Perspectives, 6*, 154–160. doi:10.1111/j.1750-8606.2012.00241.x

4

DEVELOPMENT OF TASK-SWITCHING SKILLS

GIJSBERT STOET AND BEATRIZ LÓPEZ

In this chapter, we address the question of how our capacity to rapidly switch between tasks develops. Unlike some higher cognitive abilities, such as mathematics or reading skills, this capacity is essential for our daily survival. In daily life, we regularly switch between tasks (e.g., we interrupt a task when a child calls our attention for immediate help), and we are capable of scheduling and carrying out multiple tasks. But over the years, task-switching studies have shown that adults show considerable difficulty with switching rapidly between two or more tasks. The aim of this chapter is to review what we know about how this skill develops and to further investigate the topic with a short empirical report. Our data are primarily focused on the question of what improvements occur in task switching between the ages of 9 and 16 years.

Mental flexibility is the capacity to switch attention between different tasks or thoughts. Together with a set of other mental functions, including

We thank Tansy Warrilow, Marcia Pring, and Rachel Lau for helping with data collection. We thank the children, parents, and teachers for their participation and support.

DOI: 10.1037/14043-005
Cognition and Brain Development: Converging Evidence From Various Methodologies, B. R. Kar (Editor)

inhibition, monitoring, short-term storage, and planning, it contributes to executive control (Royall et al., 2002). The study of mental flexibility not only helps the understanding of the basic mental functions that enable us to switch our attention but also contributes to the understanding of mental disorders and conditions that lead to impaired mental flexibility and executive control, including Parkinson's disease (Rogers et al., 1998) and schizophrenia (Meiran, Levine, Meiran, & Henik, 2000; Ravizza, Keur Moua, Long, & Carter, 2010; Stoet & Snyder, 2006). This type of research has also contributed to our understanding of developmental disorders that are associated with impaired mental flexibility, such as autism spectrum disorder (Hill, 2004), attention-deficit/hyperactivity disorder (Cepeda, Cepeda, & Kramer, 2000; Happé, Booth, Charlton, & Hughes, 2006; Hughes, Russell, & Robbins, 1994; Ozonoff, Strayer, McMahon, & Filloux, 1994), general learning disabilities (Snow, 1992), and Down syndrome (Lanfrachi, Jerman, Dal Pont, Alberti, & Vianello, 2010).

Well-known experimental paradigms to study mental flexibility are the task-switching paradigm (Monsell, 2003; Vandierendonck, Liefooghe, & Verbruggen, 2010), the Wisconsin Card Sorting Task (Berg, 1948; Grant & Berg, 1948), and the Trail Making Test (Armitage, 1946; Reitan, 1958). The task-switching paradigm has been around for a long time (Jersild, 1927) but became popular following the seminal publications of Allport, Styles, and Hsieh (1994) and Rogers and Monsell (1995). Subsequently, hundreds of studies have been published on the task-switching paradigm alone, and these studies have all demonstrated that humans have considerable difficulty in switching from one task to another (for reviews, see Monsell, 2003; Vandierendonck et al., 2010). This difficulty, known as the *task-switch cost*, is characterized by a slowing in response speed and an increase in error rate in trials immediately following a task switch. Despite the large number of studies on task switching, there are still a number of open questions, especially in regard to the development of task-switch costs, which is the topic of the current paper.

Only recently have researchers started to investigate the development of task-switching skills. Some of these studies have compared typically and atypically developing children of a similar age (Poljac et al., 2010), and other studies have characterized how the difficulty in rapidly switching between tasks changes with ongoing age. The youngest investigated children capable of task switching were 4 years old (Davidson, Amso, Anderson, & Diamond, 2006; Dibbets & Jolles, 2006). With advancing age, response speed increases and task-switch cost decreases (Cepeda et al., 2000; Cragg & Nation, 2009; Crone, Bunge, van der Molen, & Ridderinkhof, 2006; Davidson et al., 2006; Dibbets & Jolles, 2006; Ellefson, Shapiro & Chater, 2006; Poljac et al., 2010). According to one of the most recent studies in this area, the decrease in task-switch cost is not gradual, but irregular, with a major development between 7 and 10 years of age (Gupta, Kar, & Srinivasan, 2009).

These studies have made a start to increase our understanding of the development of task-switching skills in children, but one of the main limitations in interpreting the findings is that they are difficult to compare with the many studies carried out in adults. The problem is that the paradigms used with children have been far easier than those used with adults. For example, in the study by Dibbets and Jolles (2006), children switched between responding to an orange house when it was displayed in a daylight scene and responding to a blue house when it was displayed in a night scene. In a study by Davidson et al. (2006), children responded by pressing buttons pointed to by arrows (switching between two different ways of how arrows could point to response keys), and stimulus presentation time was more than 3 times longer for the children under 7 years old. The conclusion that the studied children were capable of switching between tasks had certainly to do with the simplicity of these paradigms, and it is not unreasonable to assume that these children would most likely have failed on the more difficult paradigms that are frequently used with adults.

There are two major differences between child and adult task-switching studies. First, typically, in studies with children there are straightforward relationships between task rules and imperative stimuli. For example, in the aforementioned study by Davidson et al. (2006), children pressed a button pointed to by an arrow (Task 1, straight arrows; Task 2, diagonal arrows). In contrast, in paradigms tested on adults, there are no intuitive relationships between task rules and imperative stimuli. For example, in one of the most original and most cited task-switching studies (Rogers & Monsell, 1995), participants responded to odd and even numbers or to consonants and vowels using left- or right-positioned buttons (i.e., these were arbitrarily chosen rules without any intuitive stimulus–response relationships). Second, only in adult studies are the task cue and imperative stimulus presented sequentially without any temporal overlap.

Not so long ago, Welsh and Pennington (1988) noted that research on executive control functions in children often used too-difficult paradigms, so it is important to develop tasks that are appropriate and match children's cognitive development. But it is as important to examine the extent to which the added difficulty in adultlike tasks affects children's ability to switch between tasks as adultlike paradigms resemble more closely the conditions we encounter in everyday life in which the demands on the cognitive system are greater. Until now, there have been no studies addressing this question. Therefore, the current study investigates to what degree the development of task-switching performance in simple and difficult paradigms differs.

The question we address here is how much more difficult the adult version really is for children. We aimed to answer this question using a task-switching paradigm in which the complexity of the cue–stimulus relationship was either transparent (easy) or nontransparent (difficult). In our study, *easy* is implemented in a way similar to the study by Davidson et al. (2006), in which the relationship between task cue and imperative stimulus is embedded in the task cue. *Difficult* is implemented by having arbitrarily chosen relationships between task cues and imperative stimuli.

We assumed that there are two possible ways the difficulty level of task-switching paradigms can relate to the development of task-switching skills (see Figure 4.1). In both scenarios, it is assumed that task-switching skills improve, but in the first scenario the difference between the easy and difficult version remains constant during development, whereas in Scenario 2, the task-switching skills develop at different rates. Only in this latter scenario, the difference between easy and difficult paradigms decreases with age. The reason underlying this prediction is based on the assumption that the youngest children have much more difficulty with task switching than the older ones. Thus, although the prediction according to the scenario is that with ongoing age children improve in both difficult and easy conditions, the improvement in the difficult condition is much more dramatic than in the easy condition, and hence the assumption is that the difference between the two conditions will get smaller over age (although it will not disappear).

In Experiment 1, we demonstrate that the paradigm is capable of registering the effect of difficulty while still being sensitive enough to register task-

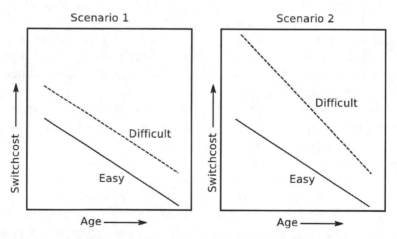

Figure 4.1. Two possible scenarios of results. Scenario 1 (left) depicts the hypothetical situation in which task-switching skills necessary for easy and difficult paradigms develop at a similar rate. Scenario 2 (right) depicts a situation in which the task-switching skills necessary for the difficult task-switching paradigm develop faster.

switch costs in the easy paradigm. In Experiment 2, we used this paradigm with children between 9 and 16 years of age. In statistical terms, we expected that if Scenario 2 were true, we would observe an interaction between task-switching skills, difficulty, and age. Alternatively, for Scenario 1, there would be no interaction between these factors. On the basis of the existing academic literature, no clear predictions for either scenario can be made. Nonetheless, there are good reasons to assume that executive control processes develop throughout adolescence because executive functions depending on prefrontal functions develop well into this period (Luciana, Conklin, Hooper, & Yarger, 2005), and this development is underlined by neurodevelopmental changes in frontal lobe activity (Bunge & Wright, 2007; Olesen, Macoveanu, Tegner, & Klingberg, 2007).

EXPERIMENT 1

The purpose of this experiment is to demonstrate that the task-switching paradigm used in this study is capable of registering task-switch costs in adults in both the easy and the difficult condition.

Method

Participants

Participants were 12 undergraduate students between 18 and 22 years old.

Apparatus and Stimuli

We used a standard personal computer, a standard USB keyboard, and a 17-inch color monitor to run custom software to control the experiment. Response keys were the left- and right-positioned control keys.

Procedure

Participants were seated in a quiet and dimly lit room and received written and verbal instructions from the experimenter. There were 80 training trials, followed by a further 800 trials that were used for the data analyses. The easy and difficult conditions were blocked, and block order was counterbalanced.

In both the easy and the difficult versions of the task-switching paradigm, there was a color task and a shape discrimination task, and these two tasks were randomly interleaved with 650 ms between trials. On each trial, a cue (see Figure 4.2a) informed the participant to carry out the color or shape task, and on each trial, an imperative stimulus followed the cue after 200 ms. The

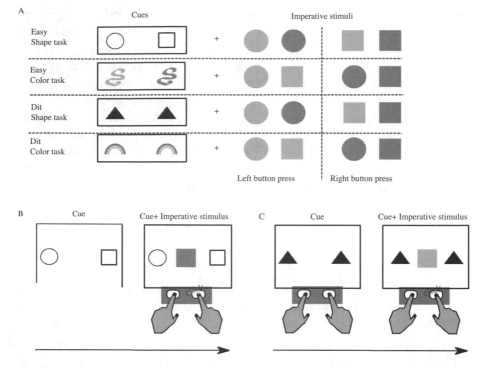

Figure 4.2. Schematic representation of stimuli and trial events. A: In any trial, a left or right button press must be given in response to an imperative stimuli, but because some imperative stimuli have different meanings in the two tasks, it is actually the combination of the cue plus the imperative stimulus that determines the response. On the left (of the plus sign) are the four different cues used in this study (2 tasks × 2 difficulty levels). The cues are used to inform participants about the task to be carried out. On the right are the four different imperative stimuli. At the bottom are the associated responses. In the color task, a red imperative stimulus (here, light gray) required a left button press, and a green one (here, dark gray) required a right button press (irrespective of shape). In the shape task, a round imperative stimulus required a left button press and a rectangular imperative stimulus a right button press (irrespective of color). Congruent stimuli are those that required the same response in both tasks (e.g., red circle and green square). Incongruent stimuli are those that required opposite responses in the two tasks (e.g., red square and green circle). B: Example of an easy shape task trial. The shape task cue helps associate the square with the right button press. C: Example trial of a difficult shape task trial. The look of the cue does not contain any direct information on how to respond to the rectangular stimulus, hence the participant needs to derive this information from memory.

participant then had to press a left- or right-positioned button in response to the imperative stimulus, which was randomly selected from the following four: a red square, a red circle, a green square, or a green circle. The imperative stimulus was presented at the center of the screen. The easy (see Figure 4.2b) and the difficult (see Figure 4.2c) versions differed in the way the cue informed the participant about the task.

In the color task of the easy condition, the task cue was a red scribble on the left side of the screen and a green scribble on the right side of the screen (throughout this study, cues always had a left- and a right-positioned element). The participant had to press the left button if a red imperative stimulus appeared and the right button if a green imperative stimulus appeared (irrespective of its shape). In the shape task, the task cue was a white circle (not filled, on black background) on the left side of the screen and a white square (not filled, on black background) on the right side of the screen. The participant had to press the left button if a circle appeared and the right button if a square appeared (irrespective of color). Hence, for both the easy color task and the easy shape task, the relationships between task cue, imperative stimulus, and responses were transparent.

Likewise, there were a color task and a shape discrimination task in the difficult version, but without transparent relationships between cues, imperative stimuli, and responses. Rather than having a red and green scribble on the left and right of the screen, a rainbow appeared at the left and right of the screen. In a similar fashion, the shape discrimination task was cued by two identical triangles. The relationship between the cues, imperative stimuli, and responses had to be learned during a more elaborate memorization process than that necessary for the easy version of the paradigm.

Easy and difficult trials were performed in separate blocks. Within blocks, trials of the two task types (color task vs. shape task) were randomly interleaved. Each trial had an equal probability of being a color task or a shape task, and the participant could not know what the task type of a trial would be until the task cue appeared. This scheme enabled us to measure task-switch costs, which are defined in terms of both response time (RT) and error rates. Task-switch cost in RT is the difference between the average RT in task-switching trials and in task-repeat trials (error scores were computed similarly).

Apart from task-switch costs, the paradigm was used to measure the difficulty in responding to stimuli that require different responses in the two different task contexts compared with stimuli that always require the same response irrespective of task context (congruent stimuli). *Cost of incongruency* in RT (or error rate) is defined as the difference between the average RT (or error rate) in incongruent trials and the average RT (or error rate) in congruent trials. In a congruent trial, a stimulus should be responded to with exactly the same response irrespective of the task; in an incongruent trial, the response to a stimulus depends on the task condition (see Figure 4.2 for concrete examples). Although this was not the major focus of this study, the difficulty of responding to stimuli with different meanings in different task contexts is an aspect of task-switching paradigms that we analyzed as well, especially because this is an executive function that is playing a role in children's cognitive development (Cepeda et al., 2000).

Results

Analysis of variance (ANOVA) of RT (see Figure 4.3, top) indicated that participants responded 149 ± 32 ms (mean ± 1 standard error of the mean) more slowly in the difficult than in the easy condition, $F(1, 11) = 21.86$, mean squared error (MSE) = 24,367.00, $p < .01$. Participants were 74 ± 12 ms slower in task-switch trials than in task-repeat trials, $F(1, 11) = 37.34$, MSE = 3,481.00, $p < .01$. And they were 36 ± 6 ms slower in incongruent trials than in congruent trials, $F(1, 11) = 32.72$, MSE = 938.40, $p < .01$. Both task-switch costs, $F(1, 11) = 5.00$, MSE = 1,062.40, $p = .05$, and incongruency costs, $F(1, 11) = 13.64$, MSE = 547.30, $p < .01$, were larger in the difficult than in the easy condition (30 ± 13 ms and 35 ± 10 ms larger, respectively).

ANOVAs of error rates showed a similar pattern of significant effects (Figure 4.3, bottom). Participants made 4.5 ± 1.2 percentage points more errors in the difficult block, $F(1, 11) = 14.04$, MSE = 33.94, $p < .01$. Further, we found a main effect of task switching; people made 3.9 ± 1.1 percentage points more errors in the task-switching than in task-repeat condition, $F(1, 11) =$

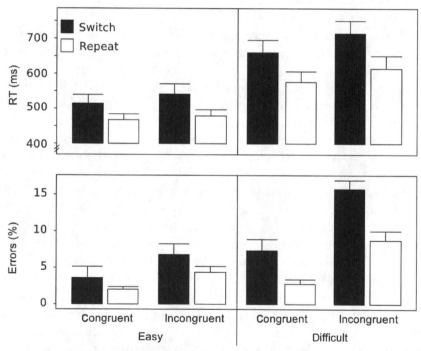

Figure 4.3. Average response times (RT) + 1 standard error of the mean for all conditions. Effects were analyzed as within-subject effects, and because the effect sizes thus cannot be derived from this plot, the magnitude of costs and standard errors are reported in the text.

12.7, MSE = 28.73, $p < .01$, and 5.0 ± 0.7 percentage points more errors in the incongruent than in the congruent condition, $F(1, 11) = 44.8$, MSE = 13.21, $p < .01$. Again, these latter two main effects interacted with difficulty: Task-switch costs increased by 3.8 ± 1.1 percentage points in the difficult block, $F(1, 11) = 11.5$, MSE = 7.57, $p < .01$. Costs of incongruency increased by 4.4 ± 1.2 percentage points, $F(1, 11) = 12.67$, MSE = 9.30, $p < .01$. Further, separate ANOVAs revealed that task-switch costs and incongruency costs could be measured reliably (α criterion of .05) in both the easy and difficult blocks (except for task-switch costs on error rates in the easy block).

In summary, the higher switch and incongruency costs in the difficult version confirm that executive functions are affected by difficulty level. Even though the simple version is easier, it is still sensitive enough to measure the costs of task switching and incongruency. Yet, because error rates were low in both switch and repeat trials of the easy condition, error rates appeared not sensitive enough to express task-switch costs in all conditions.

EXPERIMENT 2

In Experiment 2, we used the same paradigm as in Experiment 1, but with the aim to characterize the relationship between task-switch costs, incongruency costs, difficulty, and age.

Method

Participants

Participants were 65 children (47 boys, 18 girls) between 9 years, 4 months, and 16 years, 6 months, of age. Age was distributed uniformly across participants. Three children (ages 9, 10, 14; two boys, one girl) finished the easy condition without trouble but did not finish the difficult condition. These children with incomplete data sets were excluded from all further analyses.

Procedure

Children were tested in a quiet room of their school. Training was the same as in Experiment 1, but the total number of nontraining trials was 464 instead of 800. Children always started with the easy task to ensure that all had the same level of experience throughout the experiment.

Results

First, we determined whether each child could perform all conditions of the paradigm better than chance level and whether children were more likely to fail in the more difficult paradigm. For each condition of each of the 62 participants who finished all trials, we used a binomial test to determine whether the number of errors was significantly different from the number of errors expected when a participant would guess (a participant could get half the trials correct by just guessing). In the easy condition, two children (3.2% of the sample) performed not significantly different from chance level ($p <$ .05), whereas in the difficult condition, 10 children (16.1% of the sample) performed not significantly different from chance in at least one of the eight conditions. Only one of those children performed not significantly different from chance in both one of the easy conditions and one of the difficult conditions. Altogether, it can be concluded that children were significantly more likely to fail in the difficult than in the easy condition (two vs. 10 out of 62), $\chi^2 (1, N = 62) = 4.5, p = .03$. We excluded the data of the 11 children who failed in the easy condition, the difficult condition, or in both from the subsequent RT analyses.

We combined ANOVA (as in Experiment 1) with general linear regression to determine the effect of the continuous variable age on task performance in the different conditions. An analysis of covariance (ANCOVA; Wildt & Ahtola, 1978) was carried out to determine the effects of the within-subject factors difficulty, task switching, and congruency and the covariate age.

Similar to the findings of Experiment 1, participants responded 311 ± 28 ms (mean ± 1 standard error of the mean) more slowly in the difficult than in the easy condition, $F(1, 49) = 156.17$, MSE = 111820, $p < .01$ (see Figure 4.4). Participants were 179 ± 14 ms slower in task-switching than in task-repeat trials, $F(1, 49) = 174.98$, MSE = 16752, $p < .01$. And they were 83 ± 12 ms slower in incongruent than in congruent trials, $F(1, 49) = 87.60$, MSE = 9559, $p < .01$. Again, there were the interactions between difficulty and these latter two effects; both task-switch costs, $F(1, 49) = 68.3$, MSE = 20653, $p < .01$, and incongruency costs, $F(1, 49) = 19.1$, MSE = 8073, $p < .01$, were larger in the difficult condition (switch cost was 235 ± 28 ms larger; incongruency cost was 78 ± 18 ms larger).

Age affected performance, as revealed by a number of effects. First, response speed decreased with increasing age, $F(1, 49) = 27.36$, MSE = 283317, $p < .01$. Switch cost decreased with increasing age, $F(1, 49) = 5.12$, MSE = 16752, $p = .03$, and so did the cost of incongruency, $F(1, 49) = 3.98$, MSE = 9559, $p = .05$. Neither of the latter two effects interacted with difficulty (see Figure 4.5). The lack of such interactions implies that there is no evidence for the interaction scenario (Figure 4.1, Scenario 2).

A second ANCOVA was applied to the error rates of all participants. It was found that participants made 6.6 ± 0.8 percentage points more errors in the difficult than in the easy condition, $F(1, 60) = 66.74$, MSE = 81.2, $p < .01$. They made 3.4 ± 0.4 percentage points more errors in the task-switching

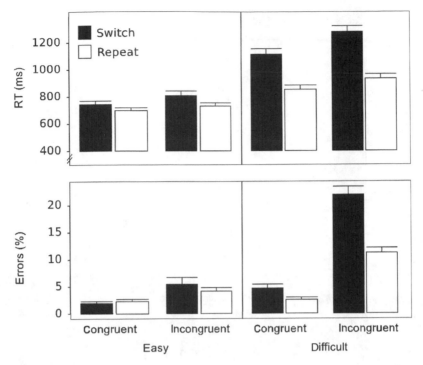

Figure 4.4. Average response times (RT) + 1 standard error of the mean in all conditions. The RT data reflect 51 of the 62 children with complete data sets. The 11 children not included in this figure did not perform significantly different from chance level in at least one of the conditions.

than in the task-repeat trials, $F(1, 60) = 61.19$, MSE = 24.11, $p < .01$, and they made 7.8 ± 0.6 percentage points more errors in the incongruent than in the congruent trials, $F(1, 60) = 165.88$, MSE = 45.5, $p < .01$. Participants made fewer errors with increasing age, $F(1, 60) = 6.63$, MSE = 123, $p = .01$. As for the analysis of RT, no interactions between difficulty, switch costs, and age or between difficulty, costs of incongruency, and age were found.

DISCUSSION

We compared the development of task-switching skills using an easy and a difficult task-switching paradigm. Experiment 1 showed that the easy version is sensitive enough to measure task-switch costs in typically developed adults and that participants showed much larger switch costs in the difficult condition than in the easy condition both in response times and error rates. We also found that the cost of incongruent stimuli was larger in the difficult than in the easy condition. Incongruency costs were just as common

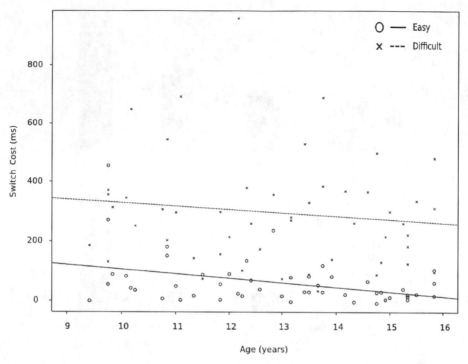

Figure 4.5. Task-switch costs as a function of age. Regression lines for task-switch costs in the easy condition and the difficult condition are shown. The analysis of covariance did not indicate a significant interaction between these two lines.

as task-switching costs (Monsell, 2003; Vandierendonck et al., 2010), and it is no surprise to see that these were also larger in more difficult than in easy trials.

Of special importance to the question of sufficient sensitivity are the error data. Participants made few errors in the easy condition, and the lack of errors made error rates a less sensitive measure of performance than response times. This conclusion is reflected in the lack of task-switch costs in the easy condition in the error rates.

Experiment 2 used the paradigm tested in Experiment 1 to characterize the development of task-switching skills in typically developing children between 9 and 16 years old. Across participants, the pattern of data appeared similar to that of the adults (e.g., larger switch and incongruency costs in the difficult condition).[1] But what was of special interest was that overall, 13 children did not want to or could not perform better than guessing in the

---

[1]From a statistical point of view, one is not allowed to conclude that there really is no difference. Still, it means that if there is a difference, it is incredibly difficult to measure, especially given our relatively large sample.

difficult condition (whereas all the adults in Experiment 1 could). In contrast to the difficult condition, only two children failed in the easy version. The failure of many participants in the difficult condition is an interesting finding in itself, because it begs the question to what degree the easy and difficult versions are comparable.

As argued previously, there are two possible scenarios of how this difference could operate. On the one hand, it would be possible that both easy and difficult task-switching paradigms draw on the same task-switching skills and that the development in both situations is similar (Scenario 1). On the other hand, it would have been possible that task-switching skills required in the difficult task-switching paradigm require special additional switching skills that develop over adolescence (Scenario 2). In this respect, the most important finding of Experiment 2 is that there is a general decrease of task-switch costs with age, and this is in correspondence to the findings of other studies of the development of task-switching costs (Cepeda et al., 2000; Cragg & Nation, 2009; Crone et al., 2006; Davidson et al., 2006; Dibbets & Jolles, 2006; Gupta et al., 2009; Poljac et al., 2010). What is new in our study is that the rate of development of task-switching costs appears similar in both the easy and the difficult condition, which matches Scenario 1. This finding helps us understand the mechanisms underlying the difficulties with task switching, which are particularly obvious in standard (difficult) paradigms carried out with children.

This finding has a number of implications. First, it suggests that developmental studies using simpler paradigms for children can inform us reliably about the development of task-switching skills. If we had found that task-switching skills develop at a different rate for easy and difficult paradigms, it would have been impossible to draw this conclusion.

But despite this advantage, easy task-switching paradigms have their limits. For example, separating task cue and imperative stimulus can sometimes be absolutely necessary to answer how tasks are represented (Stoet & Snyder, 2004). The methodological advantage of the difficult paradigm lies in the certainty with which the researcher can assume which cognitive strategies and processes underlie performance. The difficult condition in the current study is not the most difficult task-switching paradigm available, and yet it already is difficult to perform for many children (16.1%). We expect that the most difficult task-switching paradigm—with a clear temporal separation between task cue and imperative stimulus and multiple cues to cue each task—would be an inappropriate design for participants up to 16 years old. That statement implies that certain developmental questions about task switching cannot be answered (although it is possible that with very long training sessions, even young children can perform well in difficult task-switching paradigms).

There are still a number of outstanding questions. It is unknown what happens at younger ages. Gupta et al. (2009) demonstrated that between

7 and 10 years of age, task-switching skills develop in an irregular way. In other words, the speed of improvement during childhood and adolescence is not constant; therefore, the speed of development before the age of 9 cannot be extrapolated from our data. Further, we wonder at what age children less than 9 years of age will start to be able to carry out difficult (adultlike) task-switching paradigms. And finally, we need to understand the role of training. In the current study and discussion, we assumed that participants were relatively naive in regard to the task requirements. It might be the case that naive 4-year-olds cannot carry out a difficult task-switching paradigm initially, but they might be able to with sufficient training. Given that even rhesus monkeys can be trained to carry out the most difficult task-switching paradigm after sufficient training (Stoet & Snyder, 2003a, 2003b), it is conceivable that 4-year-old children can do this as well. If it is the case that even 4-year-old children can do this (and this is still an open question that we need to address to really understand the development of task-switching skills completely), it would be interesting to differentiate children not just in what they can and cannot do, but in how much time it would cost children of different ages to reach criterion level.

CONCLUSION

We have shown that task-switching skills develop at a similar rate in easy and difficult task-switching paradigms. These findings suggest that task-switching skills develop as an independent function supporting all tasks requiring task-switching skills. This understanding helps us interpret task-switching studies in children and compare them with adult studies. Given that the rate of development in task-switching skills is independent of difficulty level, studies using easier task-switching paradigms can give us reliable insight into the development of task-switching skills. That said, there are questions that cannot be answered with easier task-switching paradigms, and researchers must be careful to assess whether or not to use an easy task-switching paradigm. It might well be possible to use a difficult task-switching paradigm in children, but it is currently entirely unclear how much training would be needed. We hope that future studies will focus especially on how we can study difficult task-switching paradigms in children under the age of 9 with a strong focus on practice and learning.

REFERENCES

Allport, A., Styles, E. A., & Hsieh, S. (1994). Shifting intentional set: Exploring the dynamic control of tasks. In C. Umilta & M. Moscovitch (Eds.), *Attention and performance* (Vol. 15, pp. 421–452). Cambridge: MIT Press.

Armitage, S. G. (1946). An analysis of certain psychological tests used for the evaluation of brain injury. *Psychological Monographs, 60,* 1–48. doi:10.1037/h0093567

Berg, E. A. (1948). A simple objective technique for measuring flexibility in thinking. *Journal of General Psychology, 39,* 15–22. doi:10.1080/00221309.1948.9918159

Bunge, S. A., & Wright, S. B. (2007). Neurodevelopmental changes in working memory and cognitive control. *Current Opinion in Neurobiology, 17,* 243–250. doi:10.1016/j.conb.2007.02.005

Cepeda, N. J., Cepeda, M. L., & Kramer, A. F. (2000). Task switching and attention deficit hyperactivity disorder. *Journal of Abnormal Child Psychology, 28,* 213–226. doi:10.1023/A:1005143419092

Cragg, L., & Nation, K. (2009). Shifting development in mid-childhood: The influence of between-task interference. *Developmental Psychology, 45,* 1465–1479. doi:10.1037/a0015360

Crone, E. A., Bunge, S. A., van der Molen, M. W., & Ridderinkhof, K. R. (2006). Switching between tasks and responses: A developmental study. *Developmental Science, 9,* 278–287. doi:10.1111/j.1467-7687.2006.00490.x

Davidson, M. C., Amso, D., Anderson, L. C., & Diamond, A. (2006). Development of cognitive control and executive functions from 4 to 13 years: Evidence from manipulations of memory, inhibition, and task switching. *Neuropsychologia, 44,* 2037–2078. doi:10.1016/j.neuropsychologia.2006.02.006

Dibbets, P., & Jolles, J. (2006). The switch task for children: Measuring mental flexibility in young children. *Cognitive Development, 21,* 60–71. doi:10.1016/j.cogdev.2005.09.004

Ellefson, M. R., Shapiro, L. R., & Chater, N. (2006). Asymmetrical switch costs in children. *Cognitive Development, 21,* 108–130. doi:10.1016/j.cogdev.2006.01.002

Grant, D. A., & Berg, E. A. (1948). A behavioral analysis of the degree of reinforcement and ease of shifting to new responses in a Weigl-type card-sorting problem. *Journal of Experimental Psychology, 38,* 404–411. doi:10.1037/h0059831

Gupta, R., Kar, B. R., & Srinivasan, N. (2009). Development of task switching and post-error-slowing in children. *Behavioral and Brain Functions, 5,* 38. doi:10.1186/1744-9081-5-38

Happé, F., Booth, R., Charlton, R., & Hughes, C. (2006). Executive function deficits in autism spectrum disorders and attention-deficit/hyperactivity disorder: Examining profiles across domains and ages. *Brain and Cognition, 61,* 25–39. doi:10.1016/j.bandc.2006.03.004

Hill, E. L. (2004). Executive dysfunction in autism. *Trends in Cognitive Sciences, 8,* 26–32. doi:10.1016/j.tics.2003.11.003

Hughes, C., Russell, J., & Robbins, T. W. (1994). Evidence for executive dysfunction in autism. *Neuropsychologia, 32,* 477–492. doi:10.1016/0028-3932(94)90092-2

Jersild, A. T. (1927). Mental set and shift. *Archives of Psychology, 89,* 1–81.

Lanfrachi, S., Jerman, O., Dal Pont, E., Alberti, A., &Vianello, R. (2010). Executive functions in adolescents with Down syndrome. *Journal of Intellectual Disabilities*, *54*, 308–319.

Luciana, M., Conklin, H., Hooper, C., & Yarger, R. (2005). The development of nonverbal working memory and executive control processes in adolescents. *Child Development*, *76*, 697–712. doi:10.1111/j.1467-8624.2005.00872.x

Meiran, N., Levine, J., Meiran, N., & Henik, A. (2000). Task set switching in schizophrenia. *Neuropsychology*, *14*, 471–482. doi:10.1037/0894-4105.14.3.471

Monsell, S. (2003). Task switching. *Trends in Cognitive Sciences*, *7*, 134–140.

Olesen, P. J., Macoveanu, J., Tegner, J., & Klingberg, T. (2007). Brain activity related to working memory and distraction in children and adults. *Cerebral Cortex*, *17*, 1047–1054.

Ozonoff, S., Strayer, D., McMahon, W., & Filloux, F. (1994). Executive function abilities in autism and Tourette syndrome: An information processing approach. *Journal of Child Psychology and Psychiatry*, *35*, 1015–1032. doi:10.1111/j.1469-7610.1994.tb01807.x

Poljac, E., Simon, S., Ringlever, L., Kalcik, D., Groen, W. B., & Buitelaar, J. K. (2010). Impaired task switching performance in children with dyslexia but not in children with autism. *Quarterly Journal of Experimental Psychology*, *63*, 401–416. doi:10.1080/17470210902990803

Ravizza, S. M., Keur Moua, K. C., Long, D., & Carter, C. S. (2010). The impact of context processing deficits on task-switching performance in schizophrenia. *Schizophrenia Research*, *116*, 274–279. doi:10.1016/j.schres.2009.08.010

Reitan, R. M. (1958). Validity of the trail making test as an indicator of organic brain damage. *Perceptual and Motor Skills*, *8*, 271–276.

Rogers, R. D., & Monsell, S. (1995). Costs of a predictable switch between simple cognitive tasks. *Journal of Experimental Psychology: General*, *124*, 207–231. doi:10.1037/0096-3445.124.2.207

Rogers, R. D., Sahakian, B. J., Hodges, J. R., Polkey, C. E., Kennard, C., & Robbins, T. W. (1998). Dissociating executive mechanisms of task control following frontal lobe damage. *Brain: A Journal of Neurology*, *121*, 815–842. doi:10.1093/brain/121.5.815

Royall, D. R., Lauterbach, E. C., Cummings, J. L., Reeve, A., Rummans, T. A., Kaufer, D. I., . . . Coffey, C. E. (2002). Executive control function: A review of its promise and challenges for clinical research. a report from the Committee on Research of the American Neuropsychiatric Association. *Journal of Neuropsychiatry and Clinical Neurosciences*, *14*, 377–405. doi:10.1176/appi.neuropsych.14.4.377

Snow, J. H. (1992). Mental flexibility and planning skills in children and adolescents with learning disabilities. *Journal of Learning Disabilities*, *25*, 265–270. doi:10.1177/002221949202500408

Stoet, G., & Snyder, L. H. (2003a). Executive control and task-switching in monkeys. *Neuropsychologia*, *41*, 1357–1364. doi:10.1016/S0028-3932(03)00048-4

Stoet, G., & Snyder, L. H. (2003b). Task preparation in macaque monkeys (*Macaca mulatta*). *Animal Cognition, 6,* 121–130.

Stoet, G., & Snyder, L. H. (2004). Single neurons in posterior parietal cortex (PPC) of monkeys encode cognitive set. *Neuron, 42,* 1003–1012. doi:10.1016/j.neuron.2004.06.003

Stoet, G., & Snyder, L. H. (2006). Effects of the NMDA antagonist ketamine on task-switching performance: Evidence for specific impairments of executive control. *Neuropsychopharmacology, 31,* 1675–1681. doi:10.1038/sj.npp.1300930

Vandierendonck, A., Liefooghe, B., & Verbruggen, F. (2010). Task switching: Interplay of reconfiguration and interference control. *Psychological Bulletin, 136,* 601–626. doi:10.1037/a0019791

Welsh, M. C., & Pennington, B. F. (1988). Assessing frontal lobe functioning in children: Views from developmental psychology. *Developmental Neuropsychology, 4,* 199–230. doi:10.1080/87565648809540405

Wildt, A. R., & Ahtola, O. T. (1978). *Analysis of covariance.* London, England: Sage.

II

DEVELOPMENTAL DISORDERS: ADHD AND AUTISM

5

ROLE OF DOPAMINE IN THE PATHOPHYSIOLOGY OF ATTENTION-DEFICIT/HYPERACTIVITY DISORDER

CHANDAN J. VAIDYA AND EVAN M. GORDON

The genesis of the association between catecholamines (norepinephrine and dopamine) and attention-deficit/hyperactivity disorder (ADHD) can be traced to an early report by Bradley (1937). Bradley examined the effect of Benzedrine, a racemic mixture of amphetamine, on the cognitive and emotional functioning of 30 children of normal intelligence ages 5 to 14 years who exhibited externalizing behavior problems, including motor hyperactivity, impulsivity, and distractibility—symptoms we now associate with ADHD. The majority of these children improved in school performance and socioemotional functioning after Benzedrine administration, with 14 to 15 improving markedly, seven to eight less so, two to three showing no effect, and one showing a worsening of symptoms; different children showed these responses to different degrees. Bradley noted that the changes in behavior appeared 30 to 45 minutes following administration, peaked in 2 to 3 hours,

Preparation of this manuscript was supported by National Institute of Mental Health Grants MH086709 and MH084961 to Chandan J. Vaidya and National Research Service Award Grant MH088066 to Evan M. Gordon.

DOI: 10.1037/14043-006
Cognition and Brain Development: Converging Evidence From Various Methodologies, B. R. Kar (Editor)

and dissipated in 6 to 12 hours. He also noted loss of appetite and sleep disturbances in some children.

Since then, Bradley's (1937) observations regarding efficacy, individual variation, pharmacodynamics, and side effects have been confirmed by decades of randomized controlled trials of stimulants (Spencer et al., 1996). Further work has revealed that such stimulants enhance dopamine and norepinephrine neuronal signaling in the brain, leading Wender (1971) to propose that alterations in catecholamine neurotransmission mediate the therapeutic effect of stimulants on ADHD symptoms. Bradley, commenting on his seemingly paradoxical observation that a stimulant "subdued" externalizing behavior, surmised that stimulation of inhibitory functions of the central nervous system reduced overactive behavior by increasing voluntary control. His speculation proved to be farsighted, as the application of modern functional brain imaging tools revealed that stimulants enhance the involvement of circuitry mediating voluntary control.

This chapter reviews evidence supporting the role of the dopaminergic system in the pathophysiology of ADHD. First, we briefly describe the clinical and cognitive profile of ADHD. Second, we review the anatomy and physiology of the dopamine neurotransmitter system as it relates to ADHD. Third, we review empirical evidence directly assessing the role of dopamine in ADHD.

ADHD: CLINICAL AND COGNITIVE CHARACTERISTICS

ADHD is one of the most common disorders of childhood, occurring in 8.6% of 8- to 15-year-old children in the United States (Merikangas et al., 2010) and in 4% of adults worldwide (Faraone, Sergeant, Gillberg, & Biederman, 2003). Its core symptoms include inattention (e.g., careless mistakes, difficulty concentrating), hyperactivity (e.g., fidgeting, excessive running or climbing), and impulsivity (e.g., difficulty waiting one's turn, talking excessively). These symptoms, first described by Still (1902), were formally recognized as the core features of the condition now referred to as ADHD in the second edition of the *Diagnostic and Statistical Manual of Mental Disorders* (*DSM*) under the label "Hyperkinetic Disorder of Childhood" (American Psychiatric Association, 1968). Guided by research showing that attention deficits feature prominently in the symptoms, the third edition relabeled the condition "Attention Deficit Disorder" with two subtypes, with and without hyperactivity, and including impulsivity as common to both subtypes (American Psychiatric Association, 1980). In the next revision, the *DSM–III–R*, motor hyperactivity was again recognized as the primary feature, and "Attention Deficit Hyperactivity Disorder" was adopted as the label (American Psychiatric Association, 1987). That label was retained in the fourth and most current edition (*DSM–IV*; American Psychiatric Association, 1994), with the inclusion of three subtypes based on factor analyses showing loadings on two distinct dimensions: (a) inattention and (b) a dimension reflecting both hyperactivity and impulsivity (Lahey et al., 1994). The three subtypes include (a) combined type (meeting the criterion of six out of nine symptoms for both inattention and hyperactive–impulsive), (b) predominantly inattentive, and (c) predominantly hyperactive–impulsive (meeting criteria for either one dimension only). Other criteria include the expression of symptoms for at least 6 months in two settings (home and school) and onset prior to age 7 years. This nomenclature resembles that followed in Europe under "Hyperkinetic Disorder" in the *International Classification of Diseases* (*ICD–10*; World Health Organization, 1990), with some important exceptions: The *ICD–10* requires clinician observation rather than parent or teacher report of symptoms with onset before 6 years and recognizes the combined type only.

Some variables can complicate the diagnosis of ADHD. First, where a child is assessed influences how stringently the diagnostic criteria are applied. Primary care physicians, psychiatrists, and neurologists rely primarily on parent and teacher reports, whereas specialty care settings such as neuropsychology services supplement those reports with performance-based measures of cognitive functioning, academic achievement, and symptoms (e.g., Test of Variables of Attention; Chan, Hopkins, Perrin, Herrerias, & Homer, 2005; Rushton, Fant, & Clark, 2004). Second, symptom expression may differ by gender (e.g., greater motor restlessness in boys but excessive talking in girls), age (e.g., reduced motor restlessness in adolescence relative to childhood), and context (e.g., reduced symptoms in structured environments). Third, symptoms of ADHD are also observed in a number of psychiatric conditions, namely mood disorders (e.g., depression, anxiety), conduct disorder, oppositional defiant disorder, obsessive–compulsive disorder, Tourette's disorder, developmental dyslexia, and autism spectrum disorders, as well as nonpsychiatric conditions such as sleep disorders. This comorbidity makes it difficult to resolve whether ADHD is primary or secondary to other conditions.

Researchers and clinicians agree that a primary area of dysfunction in ADHD is executive function. *Executive function* refers to processes that guide goal-directed behavior such as inhibitory control (e.g., suppressing prepotent or irrelevant responses), working memory (e.g., temporary maintenance and/ or manipulation of information), sustained attention or vigilance, and switching of task set (e.g., adapting to changing task demands). A meta-analysis of 83 studies involving 6,700 subjects reported reductions in all executive operations sampled, with effect sizes ranging from 0.4 to 0.7 (Willcutt, Doyle, Nigg, Faraone, & Pennington, 2005). ADHD and control groups differed most reliably in spatial working memory ($d = 0.85–1.14$; Martinussen, Hayden,

Hogg-Johnson, & Tannock, 2005) and response inhibition ($d = 0.58$; Lijffijt, Kenemans, Verbaten, & van Engeland, 2005). However, there is considerable heterogeneity among children, as distributions of performance on executive tasks overlap between children with ADHD and controls, and not all executive operations are impaired in all children with ADHD. For example, of five executive processes examined, only 10% of children with ADHD were impaired on all five, and 21% of children with ADHD and 53% of control children were unimpaired on all five processes (Nigg, Willcutt, Doyle, & Sonuga-Barke, 2005). Thus, executive function impairment is neither necessary nor sufficient for an ADHD diagnosis.

There is growing evidence suggesting that cognitive deficits in ADHD extend beyond executive function. First, several properties of reaction time performance are atypical in ADHD. Specifically, go trials on go/no-go tasks were slower in children with ADHD than in the control group ($d = 0.58$; Lijffijt et al., 2005). Reaction time performance of children with ADHD deteriorated over the course of the task (Sergeant, van der Meere, & Oosterlaan, 1999), was slow on initial trials (suggesting underarousal; Oosterlaan & Sergeant, 1998), and was more variable from trial to trial compared with control children (Castellanos et al., 2005). Second, children with ADHD perform poorly on tasks of time estimation, time duration, and motor timing (reviewed in Toplak, Dockstader, & Tannock, 2006). Third, children with ADHD exhibit deficits on reward-related decision-making tasks, including delay aversion (the preference for immediate small rewards over delayed larger rewards) and increased risky decision making on gambling tasks (reviewed in Luman, Oosterlaan, & Sergeant, 2005). Fourth, spatial selective attention shows some differences between children with ADHD and control children. Children with ADHD had a rightward attentional bias (i.e., left-sided inattention) relative to controls (Bellgrove et al., 2008; Chan et al., 2009). Fifth, studies of skill learning showed that automatic acquisition of cognitive skills, both with higher and lower working memory demands, was slower in children with ADHD (Huang-Pollock & Karalunas, 2010). Further, implicit learning was selectively impaired for perceptual–motor sequences but not for visual context (Barnes, Howard, Howard, Kenealy, & Vaidya, 2010). Overall, this research demonstrates that cognitive impairment in ADHD is not limited to executive and motivational function but extends to perceptual–motor, temporal, and selective attention processes.

Diagnostic criteria for ADHD have been refined over the past decades, with the current taxonomy in the United States (*DSM–IV*) recognizing three subtypes whereas others (*ICD–10*) recognize only the most common one, the combined type. However, decisions about affected versus unaffected status are confounded by phenotypic variability and comorbidity with other psychiatric and nonpsychiatric conditions. Cognitive sequelae of ADHD include executive function as well as nonexecutive functions and motivational behavior.

DOPAMINE: ALTERED ANATOMY AND FUNCTION IN ADHD

Dopaminergic projections are organized into pathways, each anatomically distinct (having different cell body locations and target projection sites) and functionally specific. The three pathways, nigrostriatal, mesolimbic, and mesocortical, function in an integrated manner to control action, attention, and decision making, and each is implicated in ADHD. Evidence for dysfunction in ADHD comes from structural and functional brain imaging studies showing atypicalities in children with ADHD relative to controls. This work is reviewed briefly here (for in-depth recent reviews, see Vaidya, 2011; for developmental studies, see Makris, Biederman, Monuteaux, & Seidman, 2009; for others, see Vaidya & Stollstorff, 2008).

Nigrostriatal Pathways

The nigrostriatal dopamine system projects from the substantia nigra pars compacta in the midbrain into the striatum (the caudate and putamen), which is part of the basal ganglia. This system regulates voluntary motor movement, as well as the learning of motor programs and habits. Such learning, measured on a modified serial reaction time task, was reduced in children with ADHD relative to controls (Barnes et al., 2010).

There are numerous studies reporting volume reductions of basal ganglia structures, including the caudate and putamen, in subjects with ADHD (reviewed in Seidman, Valera, & Makris, 2005; Shaw & Rabin, 2009). Meta-analyses showed reduced volumes of the putamen/globus pallidus (Ellison-Wright, Ellison-Wright, & Bullmore, 2008) and the caudate (Valera, Faraone, Murray, & Seidman, 2007) in the right hemisphere of subjects with ADHD. Developmentally, caudate volume differences were pronounced in childhood but overlapped with controls in adolescence, suggesting differences in the maturational time course of this region (Castellanos et al., 2002). Functionally, numerous studies have reported reduced engagement of the caudate in children and adults with ADHD relative to controls during response inhibition tasks (Dickstein, Bannon, Castellanos, & Milham, 2006).

Mesolimbic Pathway

The mesolimbic dopamine system projects from the ventral tegmental area situated near the midbrain into the nucleus accumbens/ventral striatum, amygdala, hippocampus, and medial prefrontal cortex, including the anterior cingulate cortex. Dopamine projections into the ventral striatum and nucleus accumbens are believed to signal the presence or possibility of reward. Activity in this target region has been associated with both rewards and the motivation to work toward a future reward (Knutson, Adams, Fong, & Hommer, 2001), whereas a reduction of activity occurs when an expected reward is not delivered (Breiter, Aharon, Kahneman, Dale, & Shizgal, 2001). Such activity is accompanied by increased dopamine release in the same region, suggesting that the reward response is strongly dopamine driven (Pappata et al., 2002). Reward processing is atypical in ADHD, such that subjects demonstrate aversion to delayed rewards and hypersensitivity to gains but hyposensitivity to losses, resulting in risky decision making (reviewed in Luman et al., 2005).

Structural imaging studies indicate differences between children with ADHD and controls in the volumes of regions that make up the mesolimbic pathway. Children with ADHD had smaller bilateral ventral striatal regions, and the size of this region in the right hemisphere correlated negatively with ratings of hyperactivity and impulsivity (Carmona et al., 2009). Children with ADHD had larger bilateral hippocampi, and this enlargement in the right hemisphere correlated negatively with ADHD symptoms on the Conners Parent Rating Scale (Conners, Sitarenios, Parker, & Epstein, 1998), suggesting that enlargement may be compensatory in the disorder; further, analysis of surface morphology indicated reduced basolateral amygdala size in ADHD, although overall amygdala volume was similar in ADHD and control groups (Plessen et al., 2006). This study also reported volumetric reduction of the orbitofrontal cortex in children with ADHD. In contrast to controls, children with ADHD did not show positive correlation between orbitofrontal cortex volume and amygdala volume, suggesting disrupted connectivity of this circuit.

Functional imaging studies of reward processing show a mixed pattern revealing both reduced and increased involvement of mesolimbic pathway regions in ADHD relative to control adults. Ventral striatal activation was reduced during anticipation of reward (Scheres, Milham, Knutson, & Castellanos, 2006; Ströhle et al., 2008) for both immediate and delayed rewards (Plichta et al., 2009). However, other regions of this pathway showed greater activation, including the orbitofrontal cortex in response to reward delivery (Ströhle et al., 2008) and the amygdala for delayed rewards (Plichta et al., 2009). During decision making based on the evaluation of rewards, activation was reduced in the medial temporal lobe regions but increased in the anterior cingulate in subjects with ADHD relative to controls (Ernst et al., 2003). Greater reliance on one region of the circuit in the face of reduced reliance on another region within the circuit suggests alterations in functional connectivity within this pathway.

Mesocortical Pathway

The mesocortical dopamine system projects from the ventral tegmental area in the midbrain to the lateral prefrontal cortex. This pathway contributes to cognitive functions such as working memory and executive control, and it functions in close association with the nigrostriatal pathway during response control and with the mesolimbic pathway during decision making. Increased dopamine release within the dorsal striatum and frontal cortex has been observed during working memory (Aalto, Bruck, Laine, Nagren, & Rinne, 2005), directed attention (Reeves et al., 2005), and set shifting (Monchi, Hyun Ko, & Strafella, 2006). Additionally, greater frontal and dorsal striatal dopamine release has been associated with superior performance on executive control tasks such as working memory (Landau, Lal, O'Neil, Baker, & Jagust, 2009) and set shifting (Lumme, Aalto, Ilonen, Nogren, & Hietala, 2007). Indeed, dopamine-driven responses in prefrontal and dorsal striatal regions are believed to interact with each other during cognition (Hazy, Frank, & O'Reilly, 2007). In ADHD, as reviewed above, there is a large body of work indicating impairment in executive function and decision making.

Anatomically, both longitudinal and cross-sectional structural imaging studies show reduced volumes (Castellanos et al., 2002) and a thinner cortical mantle (Shaw, Eckstrand, et al., 2007) of the frontal lobes, as well as the other lobes, in ADHD. Specifically, the precentral gyrus and superior and medial prefrontal cortex showed more pronounced cortical thinning in children with ADHD relative to controls (Shaw et al., 2006). In typical development, a slower rate of frontal lobe cortical mantle thinning was associated with higher hyperactivity/impulsivity, a behavior defining ADHD (Shaw et al., 2010). Further, hemispheric asymmetries in the thickness of the frontal cortex varied between ADHD and control groups, such that as children entered adolescence, cortical thickness increased in the right orbital and inferior frontal cortex in controls but not in children with ADHD (Shaw et al., 2009). In addition to these differences in gray matter, several studies have observed thinner corpus collosum in children with ADHD, particularly in posterior aspects (for a review, see Konrad & Eickhoff, 2010). Further, the integrity of frontal white matter (Ashtari et al., 2005) and that of tracts connecting the frontal lobes to posterior lobes (Makris et al., 2008) was reduced in adults and children with ADHD relative to controls.

Functional imaging of executive function shows reduced engagement of various components of the mesocortical pathway in ADHD. Specifically, reduced engagement in striatal, thalamic, and cerebellar regions that are important for output of responses has been observed in subjects with ADHD during tasks of response inhibition (e.g., stop signal, go/no-go, and Stroop tasks), working memory (e.g., n-back task, paced auditory serial addition test, mental rotation), interference control (e.g., flanker task, multisource interference task), and response switching (e.g., Meiran switch task; for a meta-analysis, see Dickstein et al., 2006). Other component processes engaged by such tasks are associated with specific frontal regions, such as the dorsal anterior cingulate for monitoring response conflict, the ventrolateral prefrontal cortex for inhibition and selection of responses, and the dorsolateral prefrontal cortex for maintaining information in working memory. However, the activation patterns in these frontal regions appear to be moderated by the individual level of performance, such that lower performing adolescents with ADHD (and those with persisting symptoms) activated inferior ventrolateral and frontopolar cortices to a greater extent than controls in some studies (Schulz et al., 2004; Schulz, Newcorn, Fan, Tang, & Halperin, 2005).

In evaluating the structural and functional evidence, it is important to note that findings of alterations in ADHD are not limited to these dopaminergic pathways but extend beyond to include parietal, temporal, and occipital cortices and thalamic and cerebellar regions. Relative to controls, children with ADHD had approximately 4% smaller volumes of the total cerebrum, cerebellum, and the four lobes, as well as total and lobular gray and white matter, despite adjusting for differences in vocabulary scores, medication status, and height (Castellanos et al., 2002). As dopamine is not the primary neurotransmitter outside the frontal cortex, altered extrafrontal function weakens support for the dopamine system as a primary site of dysfunction in ADHD. However, there are pervasive and complex interactions between the dopamine system and other neurotransmitters such as norepinephrine and glutamate, and therefore it is possible that dopamine dysfunction plays a part in that broader picture of altered brain anatomy and function in ADHD.

Summary

A large body of structural and functional imaging studies point to alterations of structures comprising the three pathways of dopaminergic projections from the midbrain to striatal, limbic, and frontal structures. However, alterations in ADHD are not limited to these pathways but extend beyond to include other lobes and the cerebellum.

DOPAMINE: ALTERED PHYSIOLOGY IN ADHD

Like most neurotransmitters, dopamine is released into the synaptic cleft on stimulation of the presynaptic neuron, and it acts on the postsynaptic neuron by coupling with dopamine-specific receptors on that neuron. Dopamine continues to act on those postsynaptic receptors as long as it is present within the synaptic cleft—a state that is terminated either by breaking dopamine down or by transporting it away from the cleft. Within this sequence of events, a number of key molecular actors can substantially affect the strength of the dopamine signal on the postsynaptic neuron and, consequently, the function of the various dopamine-dependent neurocognitive systems.

Physiologically, synaptic levels of dopamine and effects on dopamine signaling are regulated via multiple agents. Dopamine synthesis consists of a multistage process in which the key actor is tyrosine, an amino acid that is the basis for the synthesis of new dopamine. Dopamine receptors are the mechanism through which released dopamine acts on the postsynaptic neuron. There are two main classes of dopamine receptors—D1 and D2.

The D1 family includes D_1 and D_5 subtypes, whereas the D2 family includes D_2, D_3, and D_4 subtypes. Interestingly, D2 receptors are also often present as autoreceptors on the presynaptic nerve terminal and are known to modulate dopamine synthesis and release rates. The density of dopamine receptors varies regionally in the brain (e.g., D_3 expression is higher in the striatum, whereas D_4 expression is higher in prefrontal cortex). While dopamine receptors are stable, prolonged or acute increases or decreases in dopamine levels (e.g., due to pharmacological manipulation) can result in increases (up-regulation) or decreases (down-regulation) in numbers of receptors. Dopamine reuptake or degradation removes dopamine from the synaptic cleft and ends its action on the postsynaptic neuron. Several different mechanisms bring about this removal. Monoamine oxidase, an enzyme found throughout the brain, breaks down dopamine in the synapse into a nonneuroactive substance that is recycled to later form more dopamine. The enzyme catechol-O-methyltransferase (COMT) performs a similar action, but its distribution is primarily restricted to the prefrontal cortex. By contrast, the dopamine transporter (DAT) is a protein found primarily within the striatum (Hall et al., 1999) that removes dopamine from the synapse by transporting it back into the presynaptic neuron rather than by breaking it down. A reduction in the activity of any of these mechanisms has the net effect of increasing the dopamine signal to the postsynaptic neuron (as the dopamine can stay in the synaptic cleft longer). Indeed, the function of many stimulants (e.g., cocaine, methylphenidate, amphetamine) is to increase dopamine signaling in the striatum by blocking the action of DAT.

Ligand-Based Functional Imaging in ADHD

The most direct examination of alterations of dopamine physiology in ADHD comes from imaging of dopamine synthesis or transport using radiolabeled ligands with positron emission tomography or single-photon emission tomography. These findings can be grouped in two, those showing reductions and those showing increased levels of dopamine in subjects with ADHD relative to controls.

Evidence for ADHD as a hypodopaminergic condition comes from the following studies. First, higher expression of DAT in the striatum in subjects with ADHD has been reported in many studies (for a review, see Krause,

Dresel, Krause, la Fougere, & Ackenheil, 2003). Higher transporter activity is thought to result in higher reuptake and thus reduced synaptic dopamine. Second, D_2/D_3 activity and DAT were reduced in midbrain and striatal regions and correlated with inattention symptoms (Volkow et al., 2009). Further, reduced receptor activity in those regions also correlated positively with trait motivation (Volkow et al., 2010). Third, reduced dopamine synthesis was observed in prefrontal cortex in subjects with ADHD (Ernst, Zametkin, Matochik, Jons, & Cohen, 1998). Together, these findings suggest that a deficit in midbrain-striatal-prefrontal dopamine function is associated with ADHD.

In contrast, ADHD as a hyperdopaminergic condition is suggested by the following studies. First, DAT expression was reduced in the striatum (Volkow et al., 2007) and midbrain (Jucaite, Fernell, Halldin, Forssberg, & Farde, 2005) or was no different (van Dyck et al., 2002) in subjects with ADHD relative to controls. Second, midbrain dopamine synthesis was higher in adolescents with ADHD (Ernst et al., 1999). Third, measurements of homovanillic acid, a metabolite of dopamine in cerebrospinal fluid, were higher in children with ADHD than in controls (Castellanos et al., 1996); these levels correlated with symptoms and were reduced following stimulant treatment.

Although this evidence contradicts a dopamine deficit, it is important to note that synthesis and receptor/transporter activity may reflect compensatory or adaptive changes in response to deficits or increases in other aspects of dopamine functions. For example, higher dopamine synthesis may result from reduced extracellular dopamine or increased transporter activity. Further, ligand-based imaging is invasive, and therefore studies have been limited to children of higher ages, adolescents, or adults. The extent to which these findings extend to young children is not known.

Dopaminergic Candidate Genes in ADHD

Molecular genetic studies show an association of ADHD with polymorphisms of genes coding for molecules important in dopamine signaling for a review, see Faraone et al., 2005). Genes coding for receptors D_4 (*DRD4*) and D_5 (*DRD5*), dopamine transporter (*DAT1*), and dopamine-beta-hydroxylase (*DBH*) have alleles that are overtransmitted in ADHD. However, genetic association for ADHD is not limited to dopaminergic genes but also includes other polymorphisms (serotonin transporter *5-HTT*, serotonin-1B-receptor *HTR1B*, and *SNAP-25*) and rare chromosomal deletions and duplications known as copy number variations (Williams et al., 2010).

Examining structural and functional brain characteristics associated with risk alleles of dopaminergic candidate genes has provided clues about the neuropathophysiological pathway mediating risk for ADHD. Two structural imaging studies showed that children with ADHD, as well as control children who had two copies of the 10-repeat allele (10/10) of the *DAT1* gene, had smaller volumes of the head of caudate relative to carriers of one copy of the 10-repeat allele (9/10; Durston et al., 2005; Shook et al., 2011). Further, the volume of prefrontal cortex and the thickness of the cortical mantle—specifically in the right orbitofrontal and inferior frontal cortex, as well as in the posterior parietal cortex—were reduced in carriers of the 7-repeat *DRD4* allele; caudate volumes did not differ by *DRD4* alleles (Durston et al., 2005; Shaw, Gornick, et al., 2007). Functional imaging studies showed that the caudate involvement was reduced during inhibitory control not only in 10/10 carriers diagnosed with ADHD (Durston et al., 2008) but also in control children (Stollstorff et al., 2010) relative to 9/10 carriers. Therefore, prefrontal-striatal dopaminergic function mediated by dopamine transporter and the D_4 receptors is one neuropathological pathway for developing ADHD.

Pharmacological Manipulation of Dopamine in ADHD

The primary evidence for dopamine dysfunction in ADHD comes from the observation that symptoms of ADHD are temporarily alleviated by the administration of methylphenidate hydrochloride (MPH), which increases striatal synaptic dopamine by blocking DAT, or by administration of amphetamines, which increase synaptic dopamine by both blocking DAT and stimulating release. In adolescents with ADHD, increased extracellular dopamine in the striatum following administration of MPH correlated with severity of impulsivity and inattention (Rosa-Neto et al., 2005). More indirectly, dopamine levels have been associated with executive and motivational functions, known to be affected in ADHD. Reducing dopamine production in the brain in healthy adults, accomplished by ingesting an amino acid–laden cocktail without dopamine precursors (tyrosine and its precursor, phenylalanine), decreased spatial working memory performance (Harmer et al., 2001) and reduced prefrontal and striatal activation during reward processing (da Silva Alves et al., 2011). These findings parallel those observed in subjects with ADHD, suggesting a strong association between these executive and motivational functions and levels of dopamine in the brain.

Several functional imaging studies have found that administration of MPH normalized activation of regions that were either under- or over-activated in subjects with ADHD relative to controls. MPH increased activation in striatal and frontal regions during response inhibition (Vaidya et al., 1998), divided attention (Shafritz, Marchione, Gore, Shaywitz, & Shaywitz, 2004), and interference control (Bush et al., 2008). Further, MPH also increased suppression of medial prefrontal regions during response inhibition (Peterson et al., 2009). During sustained attention, MPH increased involvement of multiple cortical regions but reduced involvement of orbitofrontal and superior temporal regions (Rubia et al., 2009). Similar to these studies examining effects of acute administration, prolonged MPH treatment also showed that regions that were overactivated relative to controls during spatial attention, including the insula and putamen, showed reduced activity after 1 year of MPH treatment (Konrad, Neufang, Fink, & Herpertz-Dahlmann, 2007). Together, these results have been interpreted as suggesting that MPH brings about its therapeutic effects by enhancing dopamine signaling in circuitry important for executive control.

Summary

Direct imaging of transporter/receptor activity provides evidence for altered dopamine function in ADHD. Further, studies of candidate genes suggest that vulnerability to ADHD is mediated by dopamine transporter and D_4 receptor function. Modulation of dopamine signaling by MPH enables typical functional engagement of cortical-striatal circuits underlying executive control. Although it is difficult to reconcile whether ADHD represents a hypo- or hyperdopaminergic state, one model posits an imbalance between tonic and phasic dopamine activity that is corrected by MPH (Seeman & Madras, 2002). This view posits that ADHD reflects reduced tonic but enhanced phasic dopamine release, and MPH serves to enhance tonic dopamine activity, which stimulates autoreceptors that serve to reduce phasic release.

CONCLUSION

Although evidence supporting dopamine dysfunction in ADHD is strong, a complete model of ADHD pathophysiology ought to consider the following factors. First, the dopaminergic system is sensitive to context and varies across individuals. Behaviorally, symptom improvement after MPH administration was greater in a classroom than a playground setting (Swanson et al., 2002). In the brain, dopamine release following MPH administration varied with subjects' reports of interest during a mathematical task (Volkow et al., 2004). Thus, the efficacy of MPH for modulating dopamine levels is not dependent solely on intrinsic factors but also on the activities the child is engaged in. Intrinsic factors also differ across individuals, as the magnitude of extracellular dopamine increase induced by MPH varied across subjects due to differences in rates of DA cell firing, though those subjects were at similar levels of DAT blockade (Volkow et al., 2002). Thus, sources of individual differences ought to be considered in accounts of the nature of dopamine dysfunction in ADHD.

Second, ADHD symptoms do not respond to pure dopamine agonists such as levodopa (Overtoom et al., 2003), suggesting that other catecholamines play a role in the neuropathology of ADHD. Indeed, MPH enhances norepinephrine in the prefrontal cortex (Berridge et al., 2006), and norepinephrine agonists (e.g., atomoxetine, which inhibits the norepinephrine transporter, and guanfacine, which stimulates a-2 adrenoreceptors) are effective for some individuals with ADHD (Spencer & Biederman, 2002). Further, serotonin dysfunction has been implicated in motivational deficits seen in ADHD, as individual differences in delay aversion of reward were associated with a polymorphism of the serotonin transporter genotype but not *DAT1* (Sonuga-Barke et al., 2011). Thus, future research efforts ought to consider the role of other neurotransmitters in the pathophysiology of ADHD.

REFERENCES

Aalto, S., Bruck, A., Laine, M., Nagren, K., & Rinne, J. O. (2005). Frontal and temporal dopamine release during working memory and attention tasks in healthy humans: A positron emission tomography study using the high-affinity dopamine D2 receptor ligand [11C]FLB 457. *Journal of Neuroscience, 25,* 2471–2477. doi:10.1523/JNEUROSCI.2097-04.2005

American Psychiatric Association. (1968). *Diagnostic and statistical manual of mental disorders* (2nd ed.). Washington, DC: Author.

American Psychiatric Association. (1980). *Diagnostic and statistical manual of mental disorders* (3rd ed.). Washington, DC: Author.

American Psychiatric Association. (1987). *Diagnostic and statistical manual of mental disorders* (3rd ed., rev.). Washington, DC: Author.

American Psychiatric Association. (1994). *Diagnostic and statistical manual of mental disorders* (4th ed.). Washington, DC: Author.

Ashtari, M., Kumra, S., Bhaskar, S. L., Clarke, T., Thaden, E., Cervellione, K. L., . . . Ardekani, B. A. (2005). Attention-deficit/hyperactivity disorder: A preliminary diffusion tensor imaging study. *Biological Psychiatry, 57,* 448–455. doi:10.1016/j.biopsych.2004.11.047

Barnes, K. A., Howard, J. H., Jr., Howard, D. V., Kenealy, L., & Vaidya, C. J. (2010). Two forms of implicit learning in childhood ADHD. *Developmental Neuropsychology, 35,* 494–505. doi:10.1080/87565641.2010.494750

Bellgrove, M. A., Barry, E., Johnson, K. A., Cox, M., Daibhis, A., Daly, M., . . . Kirley, A. (2008). Spatial attentional bias as a marker of genetic risk, symptom severity, and stimulant response in ADHD. *Neuropsychopharmacology, 33,* 2536–2545. doi:10.1038/sj.npp.1301637

Berridge, C. W., Devilbiss, D. M., Andrzejewski, M. E., Arnsten, A. F., Kelley, A. E., Schmeichel, B., . . . Spencer, R. C. (2006). Methylphenidate preferentially increases catecholamine neurotransmission within the prefrontal cortex at low doses that enhance cognitive function. *Biological Psychiatry, 60,* 1111–1120. doi:10.1016/j.biopsych.2006.04.022

Bradley, C. (1937). The behavior of children receiving Benzedrine. *American Journal of Psychiatry, 94,* 577–585.

Breiter, H. C., Aharon, I., Kahneman, D., Dale, A., & Shizgal, P. (2001). Functional imaging of neural responses to expectancy and experience of monetary gains and losses. *Neuron, 30,* 619–639. doi:10.1016/S0896-6273(01)00303-8

Bush, G., Spencer, T. J., Holmes, J., Shin, L. M., Valera, E. M., Seidman, L. J., . . . Biederman, J. (2008). Functional magnetic resonance imaging of methylphenidate and placebo in attention-deficit/hyperactivity disorder during the multi-source interference task. *Archives of General Psychiatry, 65,* 102–114. doi:10.1001/archgenpsychiatry.2007.16

Carmona, S., Proal, E., Hoekzema, E. A., Gispert, J. D., Picado, M., Moreno, I., . . . Vilarroya, O. (2009). Ventro-striatal reductions underpin symptoms of hyperactivity and impulsivity in attention-deficit/hyperactivity disorder. *Biological Psychiatry, 66,* 972–977. doi:10.1016/j.biopsych.2009.05.013

Castellanos, F. X., Elia, J., Kruesi, M. J., Marsh, W. L., Gulotta, C. S., Potter, W. Z., . . . Rapoport, J. L. (1996). Cerebrospinal fluid homovanillic acid predicts behavioral response to stimulants in 45 boys with attention deficit/hyperactivity disorder. *Neuropsychopharmacology, 14,* 125–137. doi:10.1016/0893-133X(95)00077-Q

Castellanos, F. X., Lee, P. P., Sharp, W., Jeffries, N. O., Greenstein, D. K., Clasen, L. S., . . . Rapoport, J. L. (2002). Developmental trajectories of brain volume abnormalities in children and adolescents with attention-deficit/hyperactivity disorder. *JAMA, 288,* 1740–1748. doi:10.1001/jama.288.14.1740

Castellanos, F. X., Sonuga-Barke, E. J., Scheres, A., Di Martino, A., Hyde, C., & Walters, J. R. (2005). Varieties of attention-deficit/hyperactivity disorder-related intra-individual variability. *Biological Psychiatry, 57,* 1416–1423. doi:10.1016/j.biopsych.2004.12.005

Chan, E., Hopkins, M. R., Perrin, J. M., Herrerias, C., & Homer, C. J. (2005). Diagnostic practices for attention deficit hyperactivity disorder: A national survey of primary care physicians. *Ambulatory Pediatrics, 5,* 201–208. doi:10.1367/A04-054R1.1

Chan, E., Mattingley, J. B., Huang-Pollock, C., English, T., Hester, R., Vance, A., & Bellgrove, M. A. (2009). Abnormal spatial asymmetry of selective attention in ADHD. *Journal of Child Psychology and Psychiatry, 50,* 1064–1072. doi:10.1111/j.1469-7610.2009.02096.x

Conners, C. K., Sitarenios, G., Parker, J. D., & Epstein, J. N. (1998). The revised Conners' Parent Rating Scale (CPRS-R): Factor structure, reliability, and criterion validity. *Journal of Abnormal Child Psychology, 4,* 257–268. doi:10.1023/A:1022602400621

da Silva Alves, F., Schimitz, N., Figee, M., Abelling, N., Hasler, G., van der Meer, J., . . . van Amelsvoort, T. (2011). Dopaminergic modulation of the human reward system: A placebo-controlled dopamine depletion fMRI study. *Journal of Psychopharmacology, 25*, 538–549.

Dickstein, S. G., Bannon, K., Castellanos, F. X., & Milham, M. P. (2006). The neural correlates of attention deficit hyperactivity disorder: An ALE meta-analysis. *Journal of Child Psychology and Psychiatry, 47*, 1051–1062. doi:10.1111/j.1469-7610.2006.01671.x

Durston, S., Fossella, J. A., Casey, B. J., Hulshoff Pol, H. E., Galvan, A., Schnack, H. G., . . . van Engeland, H. (2005). Differential effects of *DRD4* and *DAT1* genotype on fronto-striatal gray matter volumes in a sample of subjects with attention deficit hyperactivity disorder, their unaffected siblings, and controls. *Molecular Psychiatry, 10*, 678–685. doi:10.1038/sj.mp.4001649

Durston, S., Fossella, J. A., Mulder, M. J., Casey, B. J., Ziermans, T. B., Vessaz, M. N., & Van Engeland, H. (2008). Dopamine transporter genotype conveys familial risk of attention-deficit/hyperactivity disorder through striatal activation. *Journal of the American Academy of Child & Adolescent Psychiatry, 47*, 61–67. doi:10.1097/chi.0b013e31815a5f17

Ellison-Wright, I., Ellison-Wright, Z., & Bullmore, E. (2008). Structural brain change in attention deficit hyperactivity disorder identified by meta-analysis. *BMC Psychiatry, 8*, 51. doi:10.1186/1471-244X-8-51

Ernst, M., Kimes, A. S., London, E. D., Matochik, J. A., Eldreth, D., Tata, S., & van Engeland, H. (2003). Neural substrates of decision making in adults with attention deficit hyperactivity disorder. *The American Journal of Psychiatry, 160*, 1061–1070. doi:10.1176/appi.ajp.160.6.1061

Ernst, M., Zametkin, A. J., Matochik, J. A., Jons, P. H., & Cohen, R. M. (1998). DOPA decarboxylase activity in attention deficit hyperactivity disorder adults. A [fluorine-18]fluorodopa positron emission tomographic study. *Journal of Neuroscience, 18*, 5901–5907.

Ernst, M., Zametkin, A. J., Matochik, J. A., Pascualvaca, D., Jons, P. H., & Cohen, R. M. (1999). High midbrain [18F]DOPA accumulation in children with attention deficit hyperactivity disorder. *The American Journal of Psychiatry, 156*, 1209–1215.

Faraone, S. V., Perlis, R. H., Doyle, A. E., Smoller, J. W., Goralnick, J. J., Holmgren, M. A., & Sklar, P. (2005). Molecular genetics of attention-deficit/hyperactivity disorder. *Biological Psychiatry, 57*, 1313–1323. doi:10.1016/j.biopsych.2004.11.024

Faraone, S. V., Sergeant, J., Gillberg, C., & Biederman, J. (2003). The worldwide prevalence of ADHD: Is it an American condition? *World Psychiatry, 2*, 104–113.

Hall, H., Halldin, C., Guilloteau, D., Chalon, S., Emond, P., Besnard, J. C., . . . Sedvall, G. (1999). Visualization of the dopamine transporter in the human brain postmortem with the new selective ligand [125I]PE2I. *NeuroImage, 9*, 108–116. doi:10.1006/nimg.1998.0366

Harmer, C. J., McTavish, S. F., Clark, L., Goodwin, G. M., & Cowen, P. J. (2001). Tyrosine depletion attenuates dopamine function in healthy volunteers. *Psychopharmacology, 154*, 105–111.

Hazy, T. E., Frank, M. J., & O'Reilly, R. C. (2007). Towards an executive without a homunculus: Computational models of the prefrontal cortex/basal ganglia system. *Philosophical Transactions of the Royal Society: B. Biological Sciences, 362*, 1601–1613. doi:10.1098/rstb.2007.2055

Huang-Pollock, C. L., & Karalunas, S. L. (2010). Working memory demands impair skill acquisition in children with ADHD. *Journal of Abnormal Psychology, 119*, 174–185. doi:10.1037/a0017862

Jucaite, A., Fernell, E., Halldin, C., Forssberg, H., & Farde, L. (2005). Reduced midbrain dopamine transporter binding in male adolescents with attention-deficit/hyperactivity disorder: Association between striatal dopamine markers and motor hyperactivity. *Biological Psychiatry, 57*, 229–238. doi:10.1016/j.biopsych.2004.11.009

Knutson, B., Adams, C. M., Fong, G. W., & Hommer, D. (2001). Anticipation of increasing monetary reward selectively recruits nucleus accumbens. *Journal of Neuroscience, 21*, RC159.

Konrad, K., & Eickhoff, S. B. (2010). Is the ADHD brain wired differently? A review on structural and functional connectivity in attention deficit hyperactivity disorder. *Human Brain Mapping, 31*, 904–916. doi:10.1002/hbm.21058

Konrad, K., Neufang, S., Fink, G. R., & Herpertz-Dahlmann, B. (2007). Long-term effects of methylphenidate on neural networks associated with executive attention in children with ADHD: Results from a longitudinal functional MRI study. *Journal of the American Academy of Child & Adolescent Psychiatry, 46*, 1633–1641. doi:10.1097/chi.0b013e318157cb3b

Krause, K. H., Dresel, S. H., Krause, J., la Fougere, C., & Ackenheil, M. (2003). The dopamine transporter and neuroimaging in attention deficit hyperactivity disorder. *Neuroscience and Biobehavioral Reviews, 27*, 605–613. doi:10.1016/j.neubiorev.2003.08.012

Lahey, B. B., Applegate, B., McBurnett, K., Biederman, J., Greenhill, L., Hynd, G. W., . . . Shaffer, D. (1994). *DSM–IV* field trials for attention deficit hyperactivity disorder in children and adolescents. *The American Journal of Psychiatry, 151*, 1673–1685.

Landau, S. M., Lal, R., O'Neil, J. P., Baker, S., & Jagust, W. J. (2009). Striatal dopamine and working memory. *Cerebral Cortex, 19*, 445–454. doi:10.1093/cercor/bhn095

Lijffijt, M., Kenemans, J. L., Verbaten, M. N., & van Engeland, H. (2005). A meta-analytic review of stopping performance in attention-deficit/hyperactivity disorder: Deficient inhibitory motor control? *Journal of Abnormal Psychology, 114*, 216–222. doi:10.1037/0021-843X.114.2.216

Luman, M., Oosterlaan, J., & Sergeant, J. A. (2005). The impact of reinforcement contingencies on AD/HD: A review and theoretical appraisal. *Clinical Psychology Review, 25*, 183–213. doi:10.1016/j.cpr.2004.11.001

Lumme, V., Aalto, S., Ilonen, T., Nogren, K., & Hietala, J. (2007). Dopamine D2/D3 receptor binding in the anterior cingulate cortex and executive functioning. *Psychiatry Research, 156*, 69–74. doi:10.1016/j.pscychresns.2006.12.012

Makris, N., Biederman, J., Monuteaux, M. C., & Seidman, L. J. (2009). Towards conceptualizing a neural-systems based anatomy of attention deficit/hyperactivity disorder. *Developmental Neuroscience, 31*, 36–49. doi:10.1159/000207492

Makris, N., Buka, S. L., Biederman, J., Papadimitriou, G. M., Hodge, S. M., Valera, E. M., . . . Seidman, L. J. (2008). Attention and executive systems abnormalities in adults with childhood ADHD: A DT-MRI study of connections. *Cerebral Cortex, 18*, 1210–1220. doi:10.1093/cercor/bhm156

Martinussen, R., Hayden, J., Hogg-Johnson, S., & Tannock, R. (2005). A meta-analysis of working memory impairments in children with attention-deficit/hyperactivity disorder. *Journal of the American Academy of Child & Adolescent Psychiatry, 44*, 377–384. doi:10.1097/01.chi.0000153228.72591.73

Merikangas, K. R., He, J. P., Brody, D., Fisher, P. W., Bourdon, K., & Koretz, D. S. (2010). Prevalence and treatment of mental disorders among US children in the 2001–2004 NHANES. *Pediatrics, 125*, 75–81. doi:10.1542/peds.2008-2598

Monchi, O., Hyun Ko, J., & Strafella, A. P. (2006). Striatal dopamine release during performance of executive functions: A [11C] raclopride PET study. *NeuroImage, 33*, 907–912. doi:10.1016/j.neuroimage.2006.06.058

Nigg, J. T., Willcutt, E. G., Doyle, A. E., & Sonuga-Barke, E. J. (2005). Causal heterogeneity in attention-deficit/hyperactivity disorder: Do we need neuropsychologically impaired subtypes? *Biological Psychiatry, 57*, 1224–1230. doi:10.1016/j.biopsych.2004.08.025

Oosterlaan, J., & Sergeant, J. A. (1998). Effects of reward and response cost on response inhibition in AD/HD, disruptive, anxious, and normal children. *Journal of Abnormal Child Psychology, 26*, 161–174. doi:10.1023/A:1022650216978

Overtoom, C. C., Verbaten, M. N., Kemner, C., Kenemans, J. L., van Engeland, H., Buitelaar, J. K., . . . Koelega, H. S. (2003). Effects of methylphenidate, desipramine, and L-dopa on attention and inhibition in children with attention deficit hyperactivity disorder. *Behavioural Brain Research, 145*, 7–15. doi:10.1016/S0166-4328(03)00097-4

Pappata, S., Dehaene, S., Poline, J. B., Gregoire, M. C., Jobert, A., Delforge, J., . . . Syrota, A. (2002). In vivo detection of striatal dopamine release during reward: A PET study with [11C]raclopride and a single dynamic scan approach. *NeuroImage, 16*, 1015–1027. doi:10.1006/nimg.2002.1121

Peterson, B. S., Potenza, M. N., Wang, Z., Zhu, H., Martin, A., Marsh, R., . . . Yu, S. (2009). An fMRI study of the effects of psychostimulants on default-mode processing during Stroop task performance in youths with ADHD. *The American Journal of Psychiatry, 166*, 1286–1294. doi:10.1176/appi.ajp.2009.08050724

Plessen, K. J., Bansal, R., Zhu, H., Whiteman, R., Amat, J., Quackenbush, G. A., . . . Peterson, B. S. (2006). Hippocampus and amygdala morphology in attention-deficit/hyperactivity disorder. *Archives of General Psychiatry, 63*, 795–807. doi:10.1001/archpsyc.63.7.795

Plichta, M. M., Vasic, N., Wolf, R. C., Lesch, K. P., Brummer, D., Jacob, C., & Grön, G. (2009). Neural hyporesponsiveness and hyperresponsiveness during immediate and delayed reward processing in adult attention-deficit/hyperactivity disorder. *Biological Psychiatry, 65,* 7–14. doi:10.1016/j.biopsych.2008.07.008

Reeves, S. J., Grasby, P. M., Howard, R. J., Bantick, R. A., Asselin, M.-C., & Mehta, M. A. (2005). A positron emission tomography (PET) investigation of the role of striatal dopamine (D2) receptor availability in spatial cognition. *NeuroImage, 28,* 216–226. doi:10.1016/j.neuroimage.2005.05.034

Rosa-Neto, P., Lou, H. C., Cumming, P., Pryds, O., Karrebaek, H., Lunding, J., . . . Gjedde, A. (2005). Methylphenidate-evoked changes in striatal dopamine correlate with inattention and impulsivity in adolescents with attention deficit hyperactivity disorder. *NeuroImage, 25,* 868–876. doi:10.1016/j.neuroimage.2004.11.031

Rubia, K., Halari, R., Cubillo, A., Mohammad, A. M., Brammer, M., & Taylor, E. (2009). Methylphenidate normalises activation and functional connectivity deficits in attention and motivation networks in medication-naive children with ADHD during a rewarded continuous performance task. *Neuropharmacology, 57,* 640–652. doi:10.1016/j.neuropharm.2009.08.013

Rushton, J. L., Fant, K. E., & Clark, S. J. (2004). Use of practice guidelines in the primary care of children with attention-deficit/hyperactivity disorder. *Pediatrics, 114,* e23–e28. doi:10.1542/peds.114.1.e23

Scheres, A., Milham, M. P., Knutson, B., & Castellanos, F. X. (2006). Ventral striatal hyporesponsiveness during reward anticipation in attention-deficit/hyperactivity disorder. *Biological Psychiatry, 61,* 720–724.

Schulz, K. P., Fan, J., Tang, C. Y., Newcorn, J. H., Buchsbaum, M. S., Cheung, A. M., Halperin, J. M. (2004). Response inhibition in adolescents diagnosed with attention deficit hyperactivity disorder during childhood: An event-related fMRI study. *American Journal of Psychiatry, 161,* 1650–1657. doi:10.1176/appi.ajp.161.9.1650

Schulz, K. P., Newcorn, J. H., Fan, J., Tang, C. Y., & Halperin, J. M. (2005). Brain activation gradients in ventrolateral prefrontal cortex related to persistence of ADHD in adolescent boys. *Journal of the American Academy of Child & Adolescent Psychiatry, 44,* 47–54. doi:10.1097/01.chi.0000145551.26813.f9

Seeman, P., & Madras, B. (2002). Methylphenidate elevates resting dopamine which lowers the impulse-triggered release of dopamine: A hypothesis. *Behavioural Brain Research, 130,* 79–83. doi:10.1016/S0166-4328(01)00435-1

Seidman, L. J., Valera, E. M., & Makris, N. (2005). Structural brain imaging of attention-deficit/hyperactivity disorder. *Biological Psychiatry, 57,* 1263–1272. doi:10.1016/j.biopsych.2004.11.019

Sergeant, J. A., van der Meere, J., & Oosterlaan, J. (1999). Information processing and energetic factors in attention-deficit/hyperactivity disorder. In H. C. Quay & A. E. Hogan (Eds.), *Handbook of disruptive behavior disorders* (pp. 75–104). New York, NY: Kluwer/Plenum. doi:10.1007/978-1-4615-4881-2_4

Shafritz, K. M., Marchione, K. E., Gore, J. C., Shaywitz, S. E., & Shaywitz, B. A. (2004). The effects of methylphenidate on neural systems of attention in attention deficit hyperactivity disorder. *The American Journal of Psychiatry, 161,* 1990–1997. doi:10.1176/appi.ajp.161.11.1990

Shaw, P., Eckstrand, K., Sharp, W., Blumenthal, J., Lerch, J. P., Greenstein, D., . . . Rapoport, J. L. (2007). Attention-deficit/hyperactivity disorder is characterized by a delay in cortical maturation. *Proceedings of the National Academy of Sciences of the United States of America, 104,* 19649–19654. doi:10.1073/pnas.0707741104

Shaw, P., Gilliam, M., Liverpool, M., Weddle, C., Malek, M., Sharp, W., . . . Giedd, J. (2010). Cortical development in typically developing children with symptoms of hyperactivity and impulsivity: Support for a dimensional view of attention deficit hyperactivity disorder. *The American Journal of Psychiatry, 168,* 143–151.

Shaw, P., Gornick, M., Lerch, J., Addington, A., Seal, J., Greenstein, D., . . . Rapoport, J. L. (2007). Polymorphisms of the dopamine D4 receptor, clinical outcome, and cortical structure in attention-deficit/hyperactivity disorder. *Archives of General Psychiatry, 64,* 921–931. doi:10.1001/archpsyc.64.8.921

Shaw, P., Lalonde, F., Lepage, C., Rabin, C., Eckstrand, K., Sharp, W., . . . Rapoport, J. (2009). Development of cortical asymmetry in typically developing children and its disruption in attention-deficit/hyperactivity disorder. *Archives of General Psychiatry, 66,* 888–896. doi:10.1001/archgenpsychiatry.2009.103

Shaw, P., Lerch, J., Greenstein, D., Sharp, W., Clasen, L., Evans, A., . . . Rapoport, J. (2006). Longitudinal mapping of cortical thickness and clinical outcome in children and adolescents with attention-deficit/hyperactivity disorder. *Archives of General Psychiatry, 63,* 540–549. doi:10.1001/archpsyc.63.5.540

Shaw, P., & Rabin, C. (2009). New insights into attention-deficit/hyperactivity disorder using structural neuroimaging. *Current Psychiatry Reports, 11,* 393–398. doi:10.1007/s11920-009-0059-0

Shook, D., Brady, C., Lee, P. S., Kenealy, L., Murphy, E. R., Gaillard, W. D., . . . Vaidya, C. J. (2011). Effect of dopamine transporter genotype on caudate volume in childhood ADHD and controls. *American Journal of Medical Genetics. Part B, Neuropsychiatric Genetics, 156B,* 28–35.

Sonuga-Barke, E. J., Kumsta, R., Schlotz, W., Lasky-Su, J., Marco, R., Miranda, A., . . . Faraone, S. V. (2011). A functional variant of the serotonin transporter gene (SLC6A4) moderates impulsive choice in attention-deficit/hyperactivity disorder boys and siblings. *Biological Psychiatry, 70,* 230–236. doi:10.1016/j.biopsych.2011.01.040

Spencer, T., & Biederman, J. (2002). Non-stimulant treatment for attention-deficit/hyperactivity disorder. *Journal of Attention Disorders, 6,* S109–S119.

Spencer, T., Biederman, J., Wilens, T., Harding, M., O'Donnell, D., & Griffin, S. (1996). Pharmacotherapy of attention-deficit hyperactivity disorder across the life cycle. *Journal of the American Academy of Child and Adolescent Psychiatry, 35,* 409–432. doi:10.1097/00004583-199604000-00008

Still, G. (1902). The Goulstonian lectures: On some abnormal psychical conditions in children. *The Lancet, 159,* 1008–1013. doi:10.1016/S0140-6736(01)74984-7

Stollstorff, M., Foss-Feig, J., Cook, E. H., Jr., Stein, M. A., Gaillard, W. D., & Vaidya, C. J. (2010). Neural response to working memory load varies by dopamine transporter genotype in children. *NeuroImage, 53*, 970–977.

Ströhle, A., Stoy, M., Wrase, J., Schwarzer, S., Schlagenhauf, F., Huss, M., . . . Heinz, A. (2008). Reward anticipation and outcomes in adult males with attention-deficit/hyperactivity disorder. *NeuroImage, 39*, 966–972. doi:10.1016/j.neuroimage.2007.09.044

Swanson, J. M., Gupta, S., Williams, L., Agler, D., Lerner, M., & Wigal, S. (2002). Efficacy of a new pattern of delivery of methylphenidate for the treatment of ADHD: Effects on activity level in the classroom and on the playground. *Journal of the American Academy of Child and Adolescent Psychiatry, 41*, 1306–1314. doi:10.1097/00004583-200211000-00011

Toplak, M. E., Dockstader, C., & Tannock, R. (2006). Temporal information processing in ADHD: Findings to date and new methods. *Journal of Neuroscience Methods, 151*, 15–29. doi:10.1016/j.jneumeth.2005.09.018

Vaidya, C. J. (2011). Neurodevelopmental abnormalities in ADHD. *Current Topics in Behavioral Neuroscience, 9*, 49–66.

Vaidya, C. J., Austin, G., Kirkorian, G., Ridlehuber, H. W., Desmond, J. E., Glover, G. H., & Gabrieli, J. D. E. (1998). Selective effects of methylphenidate in attention deficit hyperactivity disorder: A functional magnetic resonance study. *Proceedings of the National Academy of Sciences of the United States of America, 95*, 14494–14499. doi:10.1073/pnas.95.24.14494

Vaidya, C. J., & Stollstorff, M. (2008). Cognitive neuroscience of attention deficit hyperactivity disorder: Current status and working hypotheses. *Developmental Disabilities Research Reviews, 14*, 261–267. doi:10.1002/ddrr.40

Valera, E. M., Faraone, S. V., Murray, K. E., & Seidman, L. J. (2007). Meta-analysis of structural imaging findings in attention-deficit/hyperactivity disorder. *Biological Psychiatry, 61*, 1361–1369. doi:10.1016/j.biopsych.2006.06.011

van Dyck, C. H., Quinlan, D. M., Cretella, L. M., Staley, J. K., Malison, R. T., Baldwin, R. M., . . . Innis, R. B. (2002). Unaltered dopamine transporter availability in adult attention deficit hyperactivity disorder. *The American Journal of Psychiatry, 159*, 309–312. doi:10.1176/appi.ajp.159.2.309

Volkow, N. D., Wang, G. J., Fowler, J. S., Logan, J., Franceschi, D., Maynard, L., . . . Swanson, J. M. (2002). Relationship between blockade of dopamine transporters by oral methylphenidate and the increases in extracellular dopamine: Therapeutic implications. *Synapse, 43*, 181–187. doi:10.1002/syn.10038

Volkow, N. D., Wang, G. J., Fowler, J. S., Telang, F., Maynard, L., Logan, J., . . . Swanson, J. M. (2004). Evidence that methylphenidate enhances the saliency of a mathematical task by increasing dopamine in the human brain. *American Journal of Psychiatry, 161*, 1173–1180. doi:10.1176/appi.ajp.161.7.1173

Volkow, N. D., Wang, G. J., Kollins, S. H., Wigal, T. L., Newcorn, J. H., Telang, F., . . . Swanson, J. M. (2009). Evaluating dopamine reward pathway in ADHD: Clinical implications. *JAMA, 302*, 1084–1091. doi:10.1001/jama.2009.1308

Volkow, N. D., Wang, G. J., Newcorn, J., Fowler, J. S., Telang, F., Solanto, M. V., . . . Pradhan, K. (2007). Brain dopamine transporter levels in treatment and drug naive adults with ADHD. *NeuroImage, 34*, 1182–1190. doi:10.1016/j.neuroimage.2006.10.014

Volkow, N. D., Wang, G. J., Newcorn, J. H., Kollins, S. H., Wigal, T. L., Telang, F., . . . Swanson, J. M. (2010). Motivation deficit in ADHD is associated with dysfunction of the dopamine reward pathway. *Molecular Psychiatry, 16*, 1147–1154.

Wender, P. (1971). *Minimal brain dysfunction*. New York, NY: Wiley.

Willcutt, E. G., Doyle, A. E., Nigg, J. T., Faraone, S. V., & Pennington, B. F. (2005). Validity of the executive function theory of attention-deficit/hyperactivity disorder: A meta-analytic review. *Biological Psychiatry, 57*, 1336–1346. doi:10.1016/j.biopsych.2005.02.006

Williams, N. M., Zaharieva, I., Martin, A., Langley, K., Mantripragada, K., Fossdal, R., . . . Thapar, A. (2010). Rare chromosomal deletions and duplications in attention-deficit hyperactivity disorder: A genome-wide analysis. *Lancet, 376*, 1401–1408. doi:10.1016/S0140-6736(10)61109-9

World Health Organization. (1990). *International classification of diseases*. Geneva, Switzerland: Author.

6

THE DOPAMINE HYPOTHESIS OF ADHD AND BRAIN RESPONSE TO STIMULANT MEDICATION

JAMES M. SWANSON, TIMOTHY WIGAL, SCOTT KOLLINS, JEFFREY NEWCORN, GENE-JACK WANG, JOANNA FOWLER, AND NORA VOLKOW

This chapter describes a program of research conducted by the collaborative multidisciplinary ADHD Network that was formed in 2001 with support from the National Institute of Mental Health. The ADHD Network consisted of groups of investigators from clinical programs who evaluated adults with attention-deficit/hyperactivity disorder (ADHD), led by Jeffrey Newcorn at Mount Sinai School of Medicine; Timothy Wigal at the University of California, Irvine; Scott Kollins at Duke University; and a group of investigators located at Brookhaven National Laboratory (BNL) that specialized in brain imaging with positron emission tomography (PET), led by Nora Volkow, Joanna Fowler, and Gene-Jack Wang. The collaboration allowed us to evaluate adults diagnosed with ADHD at the three clinical sites who traveled to BNL for the PET imaging and participated in our research. This research focused on the dopamine (DA) hypothesis of ADHD and brain response to stimulant medications. In this

This chapter was written by the authors for the ADHD network.

DOI: 10.1037/14043-007
Cognition and Brain Development: Converging Evidence From Various Methodologies, B. R. Kar (Editor)

chapter, the background for these two topics is presented, followed by the results from studies the ADHD Network conducted and published over the decade from 2001 to 2010.

DOPAMINE HYPOTHESIS OF ADHD

Our ADHD Network focused on two important pathways of the brain that involve the neurotransmitter DA and define multiple cortical-striatal circuits that connect the frontal cortex to the striatum (see Figure 6.1). These cortical-striatal loops have been associated with the neurophysiological basis of attention and motivation. The striatum is the location of two brain structures that are critical for understanding ADHD: the caudate nucleus and the nucleus accumbens. The circuit that contains the caudate nucleus is often called the *attention circuit*, and the circuit that contains the nucleus accumbens is often called the *reward/motivation circuit*. The DA hypothesis proposes that certain components of these brain circuits are abnormal in individuals with ADHD and that this represents the neurobiological basis for the symp-

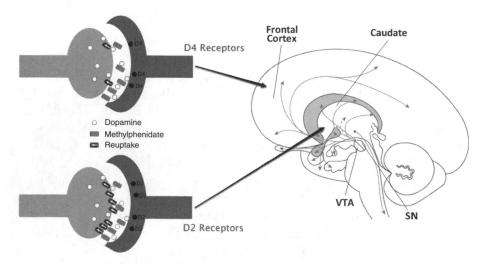

Figure 6.1. Some good hypotheses exist about the biological basis of attention deficit/hyperactivity disorder (ADHD) due to the site of action of medications used to treat this disorder (dopamine agonist drugs) and the magnetic resonance imaging (MRI) studies that have documented anatomical abnormalities in brain regions where dopamine receptors and transporters are dense. The dopamine (DA) hypothesis of ADHD suggests that abnormalities in the synaptic mechanisms of DA transmission may be disrupted. A DA deficit has been proposed (Levy, 1991), and hypotheses about abnormalities in DA receptors and DA transporters have been proposed (Swanson et al., 1998). SN = substantia nigra; VTA = ventral tegmental area.

toms of this disorder (i.e., in the domains of inattention, impulsivity, and hyperactivity).

Which components of these neural circuits might be abnormal in individuals with ADHD? Consider the pathways shown at the right of Figure 6.1. DA neurons with cell bodies in the ventral tegmental area and substantia nigra project up into the striatum and then to the frontal cortex, where DA is released when the neuron is activated. Synapses in these brain regions are shown on the left side of Figure 6.1, with both presynaptic and postsynaptic membranes depicted. The neuronal targets of the released neurotransmitter are DA receptors that are shown on the postsynaptic membrane. There are multiple types of DA receptors (D1, D2, D3, D4, and D5) on the postsynaptic side, and the density of the various DA receptors varies by brain region. Two types of receptors are shown in Figure 6.1 (D2 and D4). DA transporters (DAT) located on the presynaptic side are also shown. In the caudate nucleus, D2 receptors are colocalized with DAT, and the densities of both are very high. Not all released DA molecules reach their targets (e.g., the DA receptors). Some are recycled by the action of the DAT, which attaches to the DA molecule and escorts it back into the presynaptic terminal by a process called *reuptake*. Reuptake limits the spatial and temporal presence of DA in the synapse after it is released. This process is essential for the proper operation of DA in its role of signaling salience at a particular time for a particular duration and for sustaining attention to tasks deemed salient.

Our ADHD Network used PET imaging to investigate these synaptic components of the DA neuron. Since the early 1990s, the BNL group has been developing and using PET ligands (drugs with radioactive labels) to study the neurophysiology and function of DA in the human brain. Three ligands labeled with carbon 11 (^{11}C) have been used: ^{11}C-methylphenidate, ^{11}C-cocaine, and ^{11}C-raclopride. The PET scanning process starts with an intravenous injection of one of the PET ligands, which is taken to the brain by blood flow. The different ligands are designed to bind to specific synaptic components of the DA synapse: ^{11}C-methylphenidate and ^{11}C-cocaine bind to DAT, and ^{11}C-raclopride binds to D2 and D3 (identified in the text as *D2/D3*) receptors. The PET scanner measures the concentration of the emitted photons that result when the positron, which is released from the radioligand, collides with an electron. This information is color coded to form brain images. The PET images shown on the right side of Color Plate 2 are for the ^{11}C-methylphenidate ligand and DAT (top) and the ^{11}C-raclopride ligand and the D2/D3 receptor (bottom).

An early and innovative study by Dougherty et al. (1999) led to our initial hypothesis. This study used a similar method for brain imaging (but less sensitive than PET), single photon emission tomography (SPECT), and another ligand that binds selectively to the DA transporters in the brain (^{123}I-altropane). They conducted a study of six adults with ADHD and reported that DAT density in the striatum was extraordinarily high in the group of subjects with ADHD—70% higher compared with existing norms for historical controls without ADHD that were acquired at a different point in time. This was a plausible finding because (theoretically) a high density of DAT would recycle DA too quickly, which could create a functional deficit in DA and attention. This was potentially a major finding in the ADHD area because it offered evidence of a biological basis of the disorder, so it demanded special scrutiny (see Swanson et al., 1999). In addition to concern about a small sample ($N = 6$), we were concerned that most of the participants (four of six) had histories of treatment with stimulants and that participants were being compared with historic rather than contemporary controls. To address these concerns, in 2001 our ADHD Network initiated a study using PET and the ligand ^{11}C-cocaine (to improve the resolution for estimating DAT density) and stimulant-naive adults with ADHD (to avoid possible confounding with prior treatment) and using parallel recruitment and imaging of matched controls (to balance for drift in equipment or methods). After accumulating a sample of 20 stimulant-naive and 25 control participants, in 2007, Volkow, Wang, Newcorn, Fowler, et al. reported that DAT density was lower in the stimulant-naive subjects with ADHD in striatal brain regions. The direction of this finding was opposite to that of Dougherty et al. (1999), which had been readily accepted by most in the field of ADHD. Based on the logic and hypothesis proposed by Dougherty et al., our finding could be interpreted as evidence that ADHD was characterized by a DA excess (related to decreased reuptake) rather than a DA deficit (related to increased reuptake). Alternatively, we speculated that DAT density might reflect the density of DA terminals reaching the stratum, suggesting that our finding could also be interpreted as the result of decreased striatal innervation by DA neurons.

Our ADHD Network continued this study, and in the next publication, Volkow et al., (2009) we reported findings based on 53 adults with ADHD and 44 controls without ADHD. We also obtained PET scans before and after a year of treatment with clinically titrated regimens of methylphenidate. We obtained two PET images from each participant—one with ^{11}C-cocaine to estimate DAT density and another with ^{11}C-raclopride to estimate D2/D3 receptor availability. In addition, we targeted not only the caudate nucleus but also the nucleus accumbens, defining circumscribed regions of interest that are shown in the middle of Color Plate 3, with the color blue designating the caudate nucleus and the color pink designating the nucleus accumbens. We targeted these two components of the striatum on the basis of the emerging concept that ADHD symptoms may be the result of a motivation deficit involving an abnormality in the nucleus accumbens as well as an attention deficit involving an abnormality of the caudate nucleus.

In Color Plate 3, a PET image for the DAT is shown on the left and one for the D2/D3 receptor is shown on the right. In the middle, the overlay for regions of interest is shown that was used to estimate the values for density in the caudate nucleus and nucleus accumbens. Our findings from the larger sample confirmed our interim findings: There were statistically significant differences in DAT densities due to lower values—not higher values, as predicted by Dougherty et al. (1999)—for the ADHD group compared with the non-ADHD group. Another important finding emerged from this study: The effect size was as large for the nucleus accumbens as for the caudate nucleus (both were about 0.6). The findings were similar for D2/D3 receptor availability: There was also a statistically significant difference due to lower values for the ADHD group, and the effect size was about the same (~0.6) for the nucleus accumbens and for the caudate nucleus.

These findings were somewhat controversial and generated commentaries in Letters to the Editor of the journal where it was published. The following are some of the main points of our article and our responses to these commentaries:

- Our sample size was large enough for a rigorous evaluation of differences between groups and provided evidence of lower, not higher, DAT density in the ADHD group.
- The effects noted (e.g., lower DAT density, lower D2/D3 receptor availability) were equal in size for regions of interest assumed to be important for reward/motivation (nucleus accumbens) and for attention (caudate nucleus).
- Our revised DA-deficit hypothesis suggested that ADHD could be a motivation-deficit disorder as well as an attention-deficit disorder.
- The concept of motivation-deficit disorder suggests that stimulant medication may not only increase attentional abilities of an individual with ADHD but also enhance motivation of the individual to apply existing abilities for longer periods of time. Consistent with this, we had previously shown that in healthy controls, methylphenidate-induced DA increases were associated with an enhanced interest and motivation for the task (Volkow et al., 2004).

On the basis of these and other PET studies conducted by the BNL research program, our ADHD Network developed a new version of the DA-deficit hypothesis of ADHD. We proposed that the DA system might be controlled by a homeostatic tendency that can produce either lower- or higher-than-normal densities of DAT and D2/D3 receptors. We proposed the following:

- An abnormality in release of DA may create an underlying deficit in synaptic DA in the striatal regions of the brain (Volkow, Wang, Newcorn, Telang, et al., 2007).
- Low synaptic DA levels may result in a decrease in DAT density to reduce reuptake in a homeostatic reaction to increase the low synaptic DA level (Volkow, Wang, Newcorn, Fowler, et al., 2007; Volkow et al., 2009).
- Treatment with clinical doses of stimulant medication produces a massive increase in synaptic DA levels (Volkow et al., 2002).
- Treatment-related high DA levels may result in an increase in DAT density to increase reuptake (Wang et al., 2009) in a homeostatic reaction to decrease the synaptic DA level associated with chronic treatment with stimulant medications, just as has been shown in preclinical studies that treated rodents chronically with stimulant drugs.

On the basis of this revised DA hypothesis, we propose that low DAT density characterizes stimulant-naive adults with ADHD, and high DAT density characterizes long-term stimulant-treated adults with ADHD.

RESPONSE TO STIMULANT MEDICATION

Since the 1970s, it has been assumed that stimulant drugs (methylphenidate and amphetamine) are particularly effective in the treatment of ADHD because they are DA agonists. These drugs act by increasing synaptic DA (by blocking the DAT or increasing release of DA from presynaptic terminals), which is assumed to correct an underlying neural deficit in individuals with ADHD. Also, the general consensus has been that in clinical use for the treatment of ADHD, tolerance to these medications did not occur. However, this consensus was challenged by Swanson, Lerner, and Cantwell (1986), who noticed and described some characteristics of clinical use of methylphenidate (and another stimulant, pemoline) that suggested the presence of tolerance in the context of clinical use. First, starting treatment with standard optimal clinical doses often elicited transient side effects (e.g., motor tics, appetite suppression) that dissipated with extended exposure, suggesting tolerance to side effects of these drugs. Second, initial clinical response often waned over time. Third, aggressive increases in dose in some clinical practices (see Davy and Roger, 1989) resulted in extremely high doses (50–100 mg of methylphenidate per administration, three to five times per day) in some children with ADHD (Swanson et al., 1986).

To study these special cases, pharmacokinetic (PK) and pharmacodynamic (PD) methods were developed and used to describe properties of methylphenidate. In PK/PD studies, blood samples are obtained at various times after administration and are assayed to determine how much drug is in the blood (*PK effects;* see Chan et al., 1983), and the time course of behavioral effects is measured in a laboratory setting to relate blood levels to observable responses (*PD effects;* see Swanson et al., 1983). In a study of children aggressively treated with extremely high doses by a community clinician (see Swanson, 1988), PK analyses showed that the serum concentrations of methylphenidate were also very high, so the need for high clinical doses was not explained by altered metabolism of the drug. PD analyses revealed a similar time course for clinical response as for standard doses (onset in 1 to 2 hours and a half-life of 2 to 3 hours) and confirmed that efficacy was reduced when the very high dose was lowered under double-blind conditions. These findings led to the suggestion that long-term tolerance may occur to certain regimens of stimulant medications that are used in the treatment of ADHD (Swanson, 1988; Swanson et al., 1986).

At the time, it was a mystery why some stimulants (i.e., cocaine) had high abuse potential whereas others (i.e., methylphenidate) did not. In the 1990s, the BNL group initiated a research program to address this mystery by investigating the primary site of action of methylphenidate and comparing it with the primary site of action of cocaine (see Volkow et al., 1995b). The methods for this important study are summarized in Color Plate 4. Presented in the middle are serial PET images that are color coded to show binding of ^{11}C-cocaine (at the top) and ^{11}C-methylphenidate (at the bottom) to DA transporters in the striatum (caudate nucleus). On the right side, a graph shows the quantitative estimate of binding to DAT (the ordinate of the graph) that is plotted versus time (the abscissa of the graph). Volkow et al. (1995b) used these serial PET images to calculate how long it takes for these drugs to get to their sites of action in the brain and how long these drugs stay there before the brain level drops by 50% (the brain half-life). Instead of relying on regular PK measures to document the peripheral effects of methylphenidate in the blood along with mathematical modeling to estimate the central effects in the brain, Volkow et al. (1995a) showed how serial PET images with ^{11}C-methylphenidate could be used to obtain brain PK/PD properties of methylphenidate directly in the brain rather than indirectly through plasma and peripheral measurements.

The findings were surprising: Methylphenidate had the same site of action as cocaine (both blocked the DAT) and was about equal in potency. The quantification of the time course of DAT binding (the dark blue lines) established brain PK functions: Intravenous (iv) methylphenidate entered the brain very fast (about as fast as iv cocaine) but remained in the brain for a relatively long time (the brain half-life was much longer than for cocaine). The quantification of the subjective experience (light blue line) established PD functions: The initial effect of iv methylphenidate (euphoria) dissipated even while the brain levels of methylphenidate remained high. This suggested that acute tolerance developed over a short period of time (minutes) and muted the initial PD effect.

In a crucial follow-up study, Volkow et al. (1998) evaluated the brain PK/PD properties of an oral dose of methylphenidate. The methods for this study were innovative. Pretreatment (before the administration of the PET ligand, iv ^{11}C-cocaine) with oral methylphenidate creates competitive inhibition at the common site of action of these drugs. By varying the pretreatment dose, the degree of blockade of DAT by oral methylphenidate was estimated. A standard clinical oral dose (0.6 mg/kg) was sufficient to produce the maximum or asymptotic brain response (80% blockade of DAT).

PK/PD modeling could be used to study, indirectly, some intervening processes in the brain. Swanson et al. (1999) showed how this could be accomplished in a study of acute tolerance in children with ADHD in a laboratory school setting. This method allowed measurement of PD responses with control over timing and context to evaluate several different and innovative ways to administer methylphenidate. Using the procedure developed by Porchet, Benowitz, and Sheiner (1988) to study acute tolerance to another drug (nicotine), time between multiple doses administered across the day was varied in a systematic way. As shown in Table 6.1, methylphenidate was administered in the standard three-times-a-day (TID) regimen with equal doses at 7:30 a.m., 11:30 a.m., and 3:30 p.m., separated by a constant time (4 hours). To establish conditions to evaluate acute tolerance, another regimen was used to administer a middle dose earlier or later than the standard time (e.g., at 1:30 p.m. instead of 11:30 a.m.), which was intended to create the same peak concentrations shifted in time. As shown on the left side of Figure 6.2, after the initial dose at 7:30 a.m., the initial peak blood concentration (about 4.5 ng/ml at 9 a.m.) elicited a large PD response (a drug–placebo difference of about 1.5 units on the SKAMP rating scale), but after the third dose, when the peak blood concentration was almost twice as high (about 8 ng/ml at 4 p.m.), the PD response was about the same as for the lower concentration, suggesting acute tolerance. The right side of Figure 6.2 presents the same data expressed in a hysteresis curve (a plot of PK concentration vs. PD effect, with time coded by arrows and its progression by the serial position of the points). After an initial counterclockwise hysteresis loop (attributed to the absorption and distribution properties of oral methylphenidate), the concentration–effect relationship suggested the presence of acute toler-

TABLE 6.1
Experimental Doses to Evaluate Acute Tolerance to Methylphenidate

Time	Three-times-a-day dose	Morning variation	Afternoon variation
0700			
0730	10 mg	10 mg	10 mg
0800	0	0	0
0830	0	0	0
0900	0	0	0
0930	0	6.4 mg	0
1000	0	0	0
1030	0	0	0
1100	0	0	0
1130	10 mg	0	0
1200	0	0	0
1230	0	0	0
1300	0	0	0
1330	0	0	11.8 mg
1400	0	0	0
1430	0	0	.0
1500	0	0	0
1530	10 mg	13.6 mg	8.2 mg
1600			
1630			
1700			

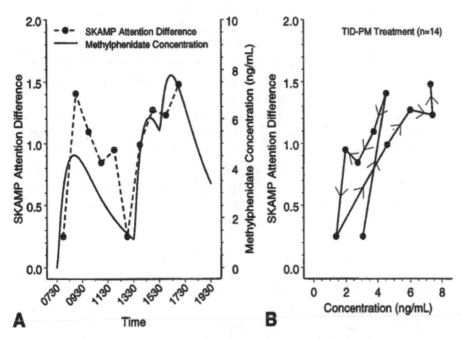

Figure 6.2. Study 2: Time–response (A) and concentration–effect plots (B) for the three-times-a-day afternoon treatment (*n* = 16).

ance. Aoyama, Yamamoto, Kotaki, Sawada, and Iga (1997) also investigated the PK/PD properties of methylphenidate using an animal (rat) model that allowed for direct measurement of brain levels of DA. In an elegant analysis of blood levels of methylphenidate and brain levels of DA, a clockwise hysteresis loop was observed, suggesting acute tolerance to high doses of iv methylphenidate.

If acute tolerance occurs to clinical doses of methylphenidate and undermines efficacy, then an obvious strategy—an increase in dose—is indicated to overcome it and maintain efficacy. This suggested an ascending drug delivery profile, with higher doses in the afternoon than in the morning, which was opposite of the conventional wisdom at the time, which was to reduce the afternoon dose in the TID regimen of immediate-release methylphenidate (see Greenhill et al., 2001).

The discovery of acute tolerance to clinical doses of methylphenidate (Swanson et al., 1999) led to the development of second-generation, long-acting formulations for methylphenidate (Concerta) and amphetamine (Adderall XR) with ascending PK profiles. The first-generation formulations intended for once-a-day administration (Ritalin SR and Dexedrine Spansules) were not effective and never were widely adopted in clinical practice (see Greenhill & Osman, 2000). Concerta (Pelham et al., 2001; Swanson et al., 2000, 2003) and Adderall XR (Greenhill et al., 2003; McCracken et al., 2003; McGough et al., 2003; Swanson et al., 1998) both used an ascending drug concentration profile to overcome tolerance. These second-generation long-acting formulations of stimulant medications revolutionized the use of stimulant medications in the treatment of ADHD. Within a year after they gained approval by the U.S. Food and Drug Administration in 2000 and 2001 and became available for clinical use, there was a rapid shift in clinical practices in the United States from immediate-release formulations to sustained (controlled) release formulations, and this practice has been maintained for more than a decade (see Swanson & Volkow, 2009).

The method for achieving an ascending PK profile of Concerta was developed by Alza Corporation using a controlled-release formulation of methylphenidate with several modifications of the original Osmotic Release Oral System (OROS). These modifications included an elongated rather than the original round shape (to increase pressure during expansion) and a two-layer reservoir of methylphenidate (with a higher concentration in the second layer), in combination with the standard OROS components (an overcoat of immediate-release methylphenidate, a semipermeable membrane, and a water-sensitive expandable polymer). This formulation (see the left side of Figure 6.3) produced the optimal PK profile (see the right side of Figure 6.3), proposed by the proof-of-principle study by Swanson et al. (1999), which cuts across the peaks and troughs but maintains the overall ascending trajectory of

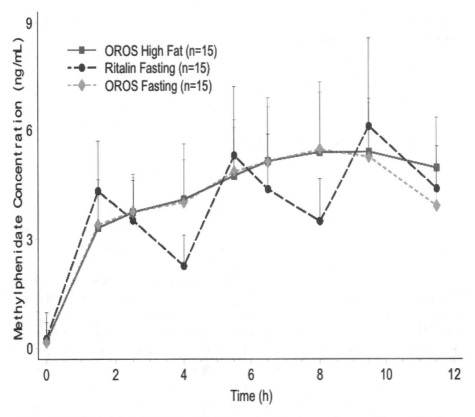

Figure 6.3. Methylphenidate blood levels across the day under conditions of fasting (Ritalin immediate release vs. OROS extended release) or a high-fat meal (OROS only). OROS = Osmotic Release Oral System.

the TID administration of three equal doses of immediate release (IR) methylphenidate. The PD profile from the laboratory school setting revealed rapid onset of full efficacy within 1.5 to 2.0 hours (attributed to the IR overcoat) and a long duration of action that equaled the planned 10-hour duration (attributed to the ascending drug concentrations produced by the modified OROS formulation).

The predicted neural basis of acute tolerance (blockade of DAT) was confirmed by Spencer et al. (2006) in a PET PK/PD study in adults with ADHD. This study documented that the PK profile of Concerta was ascending over the 8 hours after a morning administration but that the brain PK effect (blockade of DAT) measured by PET revealed a constant level over the same period. Also, evidence of acute tolerance was provided by analysis of the PD effect measured in this study (likeability of the drug): The high concentration at the end of the day (produced by the ascending drug delivery profile of Concerta) elicited a very different PD response (low likeability) than the same concentration rapidly achieved in the morning by the high IR dose of methylphenidate (high likeability).

Our ADHD Network is conducting another study of tolerance to methylphenidate in the context of long-term treatment. The participants in the PET study of stimulant-naive adults with ADHD (Volkow, Wang, Kollins, et al., 2009; Volkow, Wang, Newcorn, Telang, et al., 2007) were offered a year of long-term clinical treatment, and we are evaluating the data from this follow-up phase of the project. Wang et al. (2009) reported the preliminary results of the initial 12 participants who were treated for a year with methylphenidate and then reassessed by PET. ^{11}C-methylphenidate PET images for stimulant-naive individuals with ADHD evaluated at baseline and again after a year of treatment and for untreated healthy controls evaluated at the same time points revealed an increase in striatal DAT density in the treated individuals with ADHD but not in the untreated control participants.

We have speculated that this neural adaptation may have an impact on long-term efficacy, but we have not yet documented this key association. However, other findings suggest similar speculations. The Multimodal Treatment Study of ADHD (MTA) evaluated the long-term effects of stimulant medication (Jensen et al., 2007; Molina et al., 2007, 2009; Swanson, Hinshaw, et al., 2007). The MTA was initiated in 1994 as a randomized controlled trial of 579 children 7 to 10 years of age to evaluate long-term effects of established treatments for ADHD: stimulant medication (Med), behavior modification (Beh), the combination (Comb), and treatment as usual for a community comparison (CC). At the end of a 14-month treatment-by-protocol phase of the trial, the two groups treated with medication (Med and Comb) showed greater improvement than the other two (Beh and CC). This provided support for the long-term efficacy of stimulant medication and bolstered its status the first-line treatment for ADHD. However, in monthly medication visits to monitor status, regular clinical adjustments were made with the intent to maintain full efficacy in the Med condition, which resulted in an increase in dose by about 20% over a year. This finding is consistent with the emergence of long-term tolerance.

In the observational follow-up phase that was initiated to extend the study from childhood through adolescence and into adulthood, medication monitoring was not provided by MTA personnel, and regular increases in dose did not occur. By the longer term 36-month follow-up, the relative superiority that manifested initially (at the 14-month assessment) had dissipated (Jensen et al., 2007; Molina et al., 2007; Swanson, Hinshaw, et al., 2007), which also is consistent with the emergence of long-term tolerance. This pattern continued and was still manifested in the very-long-term 8-year follow-up when the participants were 15 to 18 years of age (Molina et al., 2009). Neither initial assigned treatment nor current observed treatment with stimulant medication provided better outcomes than other modalities of treatment on the basis either of ratings of ADHD symptoms as anticipated or of the emergence of serious conditions (e.g., substance use, delinquency) as expected from the literature.

CONCLUSION

Volkow et al. (1995a) identified an important neural site of action of methylphenidate in the human brain (blockade of DAT), which was the same for both iv and oral doses. The brain effect (blockade of DAT) was rapid, but the clearance from the brain was relatively slow. Although the high brain level of DAT blockade was maintained, acute tolerance developed.

The brain PK/PD approach using the PET ligand ^{11}C-methylphenidate identified a possible neural basis for tolerance to methylphenidate, a topic that has now been under investigation for almost a decade (see Swanson et al., 1986) with traditional PK/PD methods (Chan et al., 1983; Swanson et al., 1983). On the basis of a common interest in tolerance to methylphenidate, collaborative studies were conducted to investigate this topic in more detail, which opened up a new way to conduct PK/PD studies that has been described in several journal articles (e.g., Swanson & Volkow, 2002, 2003; Volkow & Swanson, 2003) and chapters in textbooks (e.g., Volkow & Swanson, 2008).

PK/PD studies of methylphenidate and amphetamine led to new formulations of stimulant medications (Concerta, Adderall XR, and Metadate CD) with ascending PK profiles intended to overcome the emergence of acute tolerance across the day. This development revolutionized the treatment of children with ADHD in clinical practice by providing effective once-a-day administration that replaced the usual regimens of twice or three times daily administration of IR formulations.

In the 1990s, evaluation of long-term treatment with stimulant medications was lacking in the literature. The historic MTA provided some needed information. It indicated clear initial relative superiority of pharmacological (stimulant medication) over nonpharmacological (behavior modification) intervention, but over a period of 2 to 3 years, the relative superiority dissipated. We speculate that one possible contributing factor may have been the emergence of long-term tolerance. Of course, other explanations are also viable, and our group has entertained several hypotheses that are still under investigation.

Our PET studies have documented long-term effects of clinical treatment with methylphenidate on DAT density (Wang et al., 2009). We have speculated that this plasticity of the DA system may account for tolerance in the long term and contribute to the absence of long-term benefits, despite the clear short-term benefits of clinical use of this drug. However, we have not yet performed the studies to confirm or refute our hypothesis. This research addressed several questions and generated many more about the involvement of the DA systems of the brain in the etiology and treatment of ADHD. This chapter described how some of these current questions emerged from a decade of collaborative work by our ADHD Network using PET imaging and PK/PD studies of behavioral and brain responses to stimulant medication.

REFERENCES

Aoyama, T., Yamamoto, K., Kotaki, H., Sawada, Y., & Iga, T. (1997). Pharmacological modeling of change of locomotor activity by methylphenidate in rats. *Pharmaceutical Research*, *14*, 1601–1606. doi:10.1023/A:1012186519946

Chan, Y. P., Swanson, J. M., Soldin, S. S., Thiessen, J. J., MacLeod, S. M., & Logan, W. (1983). Methylphenidate hydrochloride given with or before breakfast: Part II. Effects on plasma concentration of methylphenidate and ritalinic acid. *Pediatrics*, *72*, 56–59.

Davy, T., & Rodgers, C. L. (1989). Stimulant medication and short attention span: A clinical approach. *Journal of Developmental and Behavioral Pediatrics*, *10*, 313–318.

Dougherty, D. D., Bonab, A. A., Spencer, T. J., Rauch, S. L., Madras, B. K., & Fischman, A. J. (1999). Dopamine transporter density in patients with attention deficit hyperactivity disorder. *The Lancet*, *354*, 2132–2133. doi:10.1016/S0140-6736(99)04030-1

Greenhill, L., & Osman, B. (2000). *Ritalin: Theory and practice* (2nd ed.). Larchmont, NY: Mary Ann Liebert.

Greenhill, L. L., Swanson, J. M., Steinhoff, K., Fried, J., Posner, K., Lerner, M., . . . Tulloch, S. (2003). A pharmacokinetic/pharmacodynamic study comparing a single morning dose of Adderall to twice-daily dosing in children with ADHD. *Journal of the American Academy of Child & Adolescent Psychiatry*, *42*, 1234–1241. doi:10.1097/00004583-200310000-00015

Greenhill, L. L., Swanson, J., Vitiello, B., Davies, M., Clevenger, W., Wu, M., . . . Wigal, T. (2001). Impairment and deportment responses to different methylphenidate doses in children with ADHD: The MTA titration trial. *Journal of the American Academy of Child & Adolescent Psychiatry*, *40*, 180–187. doi:10.1097/00004583-200102000-00012

Jensen, P. S., Arnold, L. E., Swanson, J. M., Vitiello, B., Abikoff, H. B., Greenhill, L. L., . . . Hur, K. (2007). 3-yr follow-up of the NIMH MTA study. *Journal of American Academy of Child & Adolescent Psychiatry*, *46*, 989–1002.

Levy, F. (1991). The dopamine theory of attention deficit hyperactivity disorder (ADHD). *Australian and New Zealand Journal of Psychiatry*, *25*, 277–283.

McCracken, J. T., Biederman, J., Greenhill, L. L., Swanson, J. M., McGough, J. J., Spencer, T. J., . . . Tulloch, S. (2003). Analog classroom assessment of a once-daily mixed amphetamine formulation, SLI381 (Adderall XR), in children with ADHD. *Journal of the American Academy of Child & Adolescent Psychiatry, 42*, 673–683. doi:10.1097/01.CHI.0000046863.56865.FE

McGough, J. J., Biederman, J., Greenhill, L. L., McCracken, J. T., Spencer, T. J., Posner, K., . . . Swanson, J. M. (2003). Pharmacokinetics of SLI381 (Adderall XR), an extended-release formulation of Adderall. *Journal of the American Academy of Child & Adolescent Psychiatry, 42*, 684–691. doi:10.1097/01.CHI.0000046850.56865.CB

Molina, B. S., Flory, K., Hinshaw, S., Greiner, A., Arnold, L., Swanson, J., . . . Wigal, T. (2007). Delinquent behavior and emerging substance use in the MTA at 36 months: Prevalence, course, and treatment effects. *Journal of the American Academy of Child & Adolescent Psychiatry, 46*, 1028–1040. doi:10.1097/chi.0b013e3180686d96

Molina, B. S., Hinshaw, S. P., Swanson, J. M., Arnold, L. E., Vitiello, B., Jensen, P. S., . . . Houck, P. R. (2009). The MTA at 8 years: Prospective follow-up of children treated for combined type ADHD in a multisite study. *Journal of the American Academy of Child & Adolescent Psychiatry, 48*, 484–500. doi:10.1097/CHI.0b013e31819c23d0

Pelham, W. E., Gnagy, E. M., Burrows-Maclean, L., Williams, A., Coles, E. K., Panahon, C. J., . . . Morse, G. D. (2001). Once-a-day Concerta methylphenidate versus three-times-daily methylphenidate in laboratory and natural settings. *Pediatrics, 107*, e105. doi:10.1542/peds.107.6.e105

Porchet, H. C., Benowitz, N. L., & Sheiner, L. B. (1988). Pharmacodynamic model of tolerance: Application to nicotine. *Journal of Pharmacology and Experimental Therapeutics, 244*, 231–244.

Spencer, T. J., Biederman, J., Ciccone, P. E., Madras, B. K., Dougherty, D. D., Bonah, A. A., . . . Fischman, A. J. (2006). PET study examining pharmacokinetics, detection, and likeability and dopamine transporter receptor occupancy of short- and long-acting oral methylphenidate. *American Journal of Psychiatry, 163*, 387–395.

Swanson, J. M. (1988). Measurement of serum concentrations and behavioral response in children to acute doses of methylphenidate. In L. Bloomingdale (Ed.), *Attention deficit disorder, Volume III: New research in attention, treatment, and psychopharmacology* (pp. 107–126).

Swanson, J. M., Greenhill, L., Pelham, W., Wilens, T., Wolraich, M., Abikoff, H., . . . Winans, E. (2000). Initiating Concerta (OROS methylphenidate HC1) qd in children with attention-deficit hyperactivity disorder. *Journal of Clinical Research, 3*, 9–76.

Swanson, J. M., Gupta, S., Guinta, D., Flynn, D., Agler, D., Lerner, M., . . . Wigal, S. (1999). Acute tolerance to methylphenidate in the treatment of attention deficit hyperactivity disorder in children. *Clinical Pharmacology and Therapeutics, 66*, 295–305. doi:10.1016/S0009-9236(99)70038-X

Swanson, J. M., Gupta, S., Lam, A., Shoulson, I., Lerner, M., Modi, N., . . . Wigal, S. (2003). Development of a new once-a-day formulation of methylphenidate for the treatment of ADHD: Proof-of-concept and proof-of-product studies. *Archives of General Psychology, 60*, 204–211. doi:10.1001/archpsyc.60.2.204

Swanson, J. M., Hinshaw, S. P., Arnold, L. E., Gibbons, R. D., Marcus, S., Hur, K., . . . Wigal, T. (2007). Secondary evaluations of MTA 36-month outcomes: Propensity score and growth mixture model analyses. *Journal of the American Academy of Child & Adolescent Psychiatry, 46*, 1003–1014. doi:10.1097/CHI.0b013e3180686d63

Swanson, J. M., Lerner, M., & Cantwell, D. (1986). Blood levels and tolerance to stimulants in ADDH children. *Clinical Neuropharmacology, 9*(Suppl. 4), 523–525.

Swanson, J. M., Sandman, C. A., Deutsch, C., & Baren, M. (1983). Methylphenidate hydrochloride given with or before breakfast: Behavioral, cognitive, and electrophysiologic effects. *Pediatrics, 72*, 49–55.

Swanson, J. M., & Volkow, N. D. (2002). Pharmacokinetic and pharmacodynamic properties of stimulants: Implications for the design of new treatments for ADHD. *Behavioural Brain Research, 130*, 73–78. doi:10.1016/S0166-4328(01)00433-8

Swanson, J. M., & Volkow, N. D. (2003). Serum and brain concentrations of methylphenidate: Implications for use and abuse. *Neuroscience and Biobehavioral Reviews, 27*, 615–621. doi:10.1016/j.neubiorev.2003.08.013

Swanson, J. M., & Volkow, N. D. (2009). Psychopharmacology: Concepts and opinions about the use of stimulant medications. *Journal of Child Psychology and Psychiatry, 50*, 180—193.

Swanson, J. M., Wigal, S., Greenhill, L., Browne, R., Waslik, B., Lerner, M., . . . Cantwell, D. (1998). Analog classroom assessment of Adderall in children with ADHD. *Journal of the American Academy of Child & Adolescent Psychiatry, 37*, 519–526. doi:10.1097/00004583-199805000-00014

Volkow, N. D., Ding, Y.-S., Fowler, J. S., Gatley, J. S., Logan, J., Ding, Y.-S., . . . Pappas, N. (1998). Dopamine transporter occupancies in the human brain induced by therapeutic doses of oral methylphenidate. *The American Journal of Psychiatry, 155*, 1325–1331.

Volkow, N. D., Ding, Y.-S., Fowler, J. S., Wang, G.-J., Logan, J., Gatley, S. J., . . . Pappas, N. (1995a). A new PET ligand for the dopamine transporter: Studies in the human brain. *Journal of Nuclear Medicine, 36*, 2162–2168.

Volkow, N. D., Ding, Y.-S., Fowler, J. S., Wang, G.-J., Logan, J., Gatley, J. S., . . . Wolf, A. P. (1995b). Is methylphenidate like cocaine? Studies on their pharmacokinetics and distribution in the human brain. *Archives of General Psychiatry, 52*, 456–463. doi:10.1001/archpsyc.1995.03950180042006

Volkow, N. D., & Swanson, J. M. (2003). Variables that affect the clinical use and abuse of methylphenidate in the treatment of ADHD. *The American Journal of Psychiatry, 160*, 1909–1918. doi:10.1176/appi.ajp.160.11.1909

Volkow, N., & Swanson, J. (2008). Basic neuropsychopharmacology. In M. Rutter, D. Bishop, D. S. Pine, S. Scott, J. Stevenson, E. Taylor, & A. Thapar (Eds.),

Rutter's child and adolescent psychiatry (5th ed., pp. 212–233). Malden, MA: Blackwell. doi:10.1002/9781444300895.ch16

Volkow, N. D., Wang, G.-J., Fowler, J. S., Logan, J., Franceschi, D., Maynard, L., . . . Swanson, J. M. (2002). Relationship between blockade of dopamine transporters by oral methylphenidate and the increases in extracellular dopamine: Therapeutic implications. *Synapse, 43,* 181–187. doi:10.1002/syn.10038

Volkow, N. D., Wang, G.-J., Fowler, J. S., Telang, F., Maynard, L., Logan, J., . . . Swanson, J. M. (2004). Evidence that methylphenidate enhances the saliency of a mathematical task by increasing dopamine in the human brain. *The American Journal of Psychiatry, 161,* 1173–1180. doi:10.1176/appi.ajp.161.7.1173

Volkow, N. D., Wang, G.-J., Kollins, S. H., Wigal, T. L., Newcorn, J. H., Telang, F., . . . Swanson, J. M. (2009). Evaluating dopamine reward pathway in ADHD: Clinical implications. *JAMA, 302,* 1084–1091. doi:10.1001/jama.2009.1308

Volkow, N. D., Wang, G.-J., Newcorn, J., Fowler, J. S., Telang, F., Solanto, M. V., . . . Pradhan, K. (2007). Brain dopamine transporter levels in treatment and drug naïve adults with ADHD. *NeuroImage, 34,* 1182–1190. doi:10.1016/j.neuroimage.2006.10.014

Volkow, N. D., Wang, G. J., Newcorn, J., Telang, F., Solanto, M. V., Fowler, J. S., . . . Swanson, J. S. (2007). Depressed dopamine activity in caudate and preliminary evidence of limbic involvement in adults with attention-deficit/hyperactivity disorder. *Archives of General Psychiatry, 64,* 932–940. doi:10.1001/archpsyc.64.8.932

Wang, G.-J., Volkow, N., Wigal, T., Kollins, S., Newcorn, J., Telang, F., . . . Swanson, J. M. (2009, December). *Chronic methylphenidate treatment increases striatal dopamine transporter availability in patients with attention deficit hyperactive disorder.* Poster session presented at the meeting of the American College of Neuropsychopharmacology, Hollywood, FL.

7

EXPLORING PREREQUISITE LEARNING SKILLS IN YOUNG CHILDREN AND THEIR IMPLICATIONS FOR IDENTIFICATION OF AND INTERVENTION FOR AUTISTIC BEHAVIOR

PRATHIBHA KARANTH AND ARCHANA S

Communication skills lie at the core of human development and contribute to all aspects of a child's development. Communication development, in turn, is dependent on other skills, like increasing attention to specific tasks (attention span), the ability to make and sustain eye contact, gaze patterns such as following the gaze of the speaker, and the ability to sit at a place or task (sitting behavior) and follow instructions (compliance). These abilities are seen in children prior to language acquisition and are considered precursors of language learning and communication skills. Because these skills are required to be in place before linguistic skills can develop and form the basis for language and communication development, they are often referred to as *prerequisite learning skills*. These prerequisite skills facilitate learning in general and the development of language and communication skills in particular. Failure in the development of these skills can and does affect acquisition of speech, language, communication, and related skills, leading to delay in language development and impaired communication

DOI: 10.1037/14043-008
Cognition and Brain Development: Converging Evidence From Various Methodologies, B. R. Kar (Editor)

skills, social learning, and literacy development, as seen in many children with developmental disorders. These skills are also known to be affected in children with autism.

RESEARCH ON PREREQUISITE LEARNING SKILLS AND DEFICITS

In the recent past, researchers in the area of speech–language pathology have recognized the importance of infant and caregiver interactions, which play a significant role in language and communication outcomes in young children. This recognition led researchers to attempt to describe prerequisite learning behaviors such as early nonverbal gestures and vocalizations and their role in later language development. Research has shown that infant gaze following and pointing predict subsequent language development. Brooks and Meltzoff (2008) studied eye gaze following and pointing and reported that infants who engaged in longer visual inspection of the target of the adult's gaze and used pointing at the target object had significantly faster vocabulary growth than infants with shorter looks and less pointing. Impairment in these skills and their developmental manifestations in children with developmental disorders are also being looked into.

The last couple of decades have also witnessed a substantial increase in the number of children being identified with difficulties in language and communication skills without any clear identifiable biological cause that accounts for it. These children are referred to as having developmental language disorders. Among the several developmental disorders of childhood, one category that has gained the maximum attention of late is the group of childhood disorders known as autism spectrum disorders (ASDs) or pervasive developmental disorders (PDDs). These disorders have become the focus of much debate and research.

A number of recent studies have shown that young children with autism display deficits in both initiating and responding to joint attention. Adamson, Bakeman, Deckner, and Romski (2009) documented deficits in coordinating attention to a shared object and the partner in children with autism when compared with typically developing (TD) children. Using home videotapes, parental questionnaires, and laboratory-based studies, several researchers have noted that children with ASDs do not look to others very often, point to objects, show toys to the caregiver, or initiate or respond to joint attention and do not attempt to direct another's attention. These early learning differences in gaze, joint attention, and social communication are seen specifically in children with autism and are now being seen as early indicators of autism (Bacon, Fein, Morris, Waterhouse, & Allen, 1998; Charman, 1997, 1998; Dawson, Meltzoff, Osterling, & Rinaldi, 1998; Dawson et al., 2002, 2004).

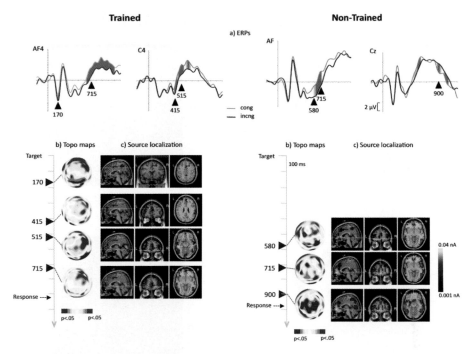

Color Plate 1. Effect of training on the activation of the executive attention network during performance of the child attention network task by 5-year-old children. (a) Event-related potentials (ERPs) showing significant amplitude differences between congruent (cong) and incongruent (incong) trials; (b) Topographic (Topo) maps of voltage differences between conditions; and (c) source models of times in which significant differences between conditions were observed. Trained children showed faster engagement of the executive attention network than untrained children. From M. R. Rueda, P. Checa, & L. M. Cómbita, 2012, "Enhanced Efficiency of the Executive Attention Network After Training in Preschool Children: Immediate Changes and Effects After Two Months," *Developmental Cognitive Neuroscience, 2*(Suppl. 1), pp. 198–199. Copyright 2012 by Elsevier. Adapted with permission.

Imaging Studies of the DA System in ADHD

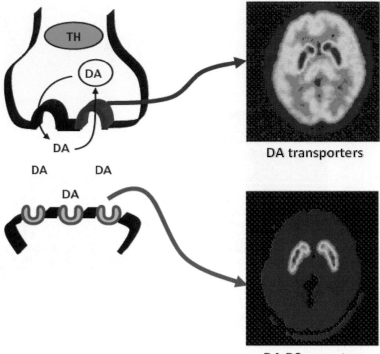

DA transporters

DA D2 receptors

Color Plate 2. Dopamine (DA) D2/D3 receptor and dopamine transporter availability in adults with attention deficit/hyperactivity disorder (ADHD) and controls. TH = tyrosine hydroxylase.

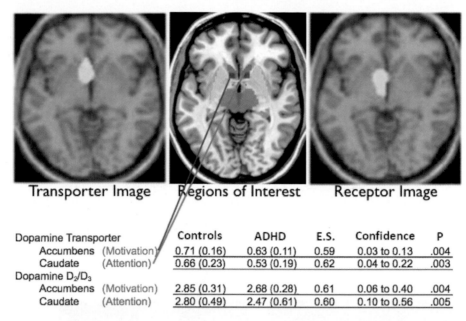

| Transporter Image | Regions of Interest | Receptor Image |

Dopamine Transporter		Controls	ADHD	E.S.	Confidence	P
Accumbens	(Motivation)	0.71 (0.16)	0.63 (0.11)	0.59	0.03 to 0.13	.004
Caudate	(Attention)	0.66 (0.23)	0.53 (0.19)	0.62	0.04 to 0.22	.003
Dopamine D_2/D_3						
Accumbens	(Motivation)	2.85 (0.31)	2.68 (0.28)	0.61	0.06 to 0.40	.004
Caudate	(Attention)	2.80 (0.49)	2.47 (0.61)	0.60	0.10 to 0.56	.005

Color Plate 3. Regions of interest were specified, including the nucleus accumbens, which is an important component of the dopamine reward or motivation pathway of the brain. With relatively large samples (for a positron emission tomography study) of medication-naive subjects, we showed dopamine deficits in both the nucleus accumbens (the "hub" of a motivation network) as well as the caudate nucleus (the "hub" of an attention network). We have proposed that in addition to "attention deficit" disorder, the label "motivation deficit" disorder may be appropriate for the clinical condition of attention-deficit/hyperactivity disorder (ADHD). Data are from Volkow et al. (2009, Figure 2). E.S. = effect size.

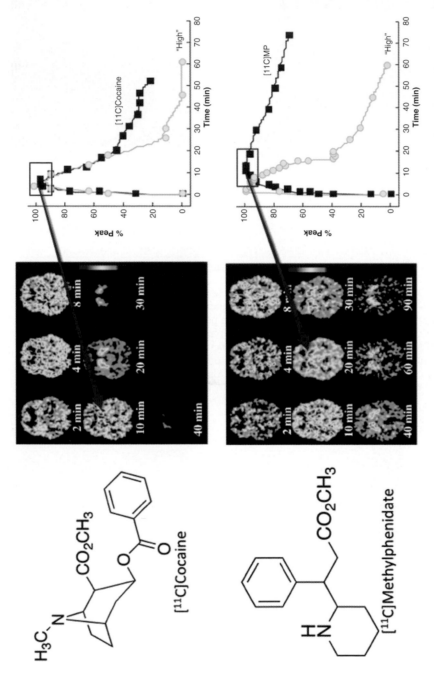

Color Plate 4. Time activity curves for carbon-11-labeled methylphenidate and cocaine in striatum (dark lines) and the subjective rating of the experience of "feeling high" (light lines).

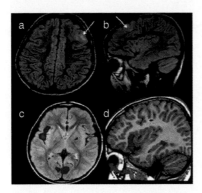
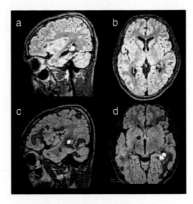

Color Plate 5. Usefulness of functional magnetic resonance imaging (fMRI) in selecting patients for surgery, tailoring surgical resection, and predicting postsurgical outcome. A young boy with a cavernoma in the left superior temporal gyrus underwent to know the hemispheric dominance and closeness of the lesion to Wernicke's area. The sagittal and axial fluid attenuation inversion recovery images (a, b) show the mixed-intensity lesion (arrows). Language fMRI done using the verb generation task shows left-hemisphere language dominance and lesion's closeness to Wernicke's area (c, d). Fortunately, seizures were well controlled on antiepileptic medication, and conservative management was used.

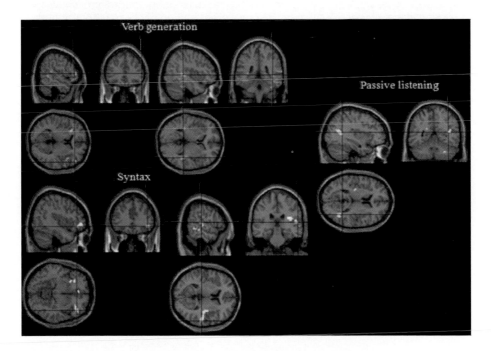

Color Plate 6. Activation patterns of various language paradigms.

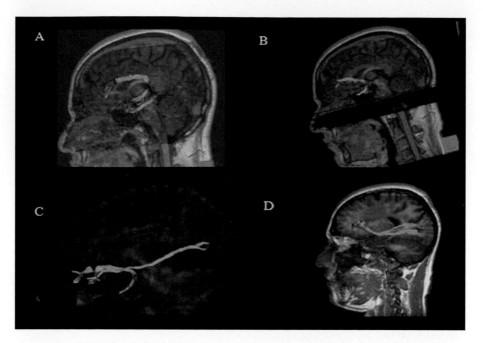

Color Plate 7. Fiber tractography of major white matter tracts involved in human language processing. Verb generation and syntactic language paradigms show activation in the inferior frontal gyrus (Broca's area) and posterior parietotemporal language area (Wernicke's area) in the left hemisphere. Passive listening produced activation in the posterior parietotemporal language area in the left hemisphere and no activation in the inferior frontal gyrus.

Several studies have revealed the existence of a developmental component in prerequisite learning skills such as sustained attention and joint attention during the preschool period (Sarid & Breznitz, 1997; Watt, Wetherby, & Shumway, 2006). Although the importance and the developmental component of the acquisition of these prerequisite skills have been recognized, quantification of these skills has not been done, and there is hardly any scientific documentation of the extent to which these skills are present in neurotypical children at different ages. Yet such quantification is important for targeting these skills in intervention. In a study on the efficacy of early intervention for children with ASDs (Karanth, Shaista, & Srikanth, 2010), for instance, parents reported that although the gains in developmental skills made by their children subsequent to intervention were considerable, concerns regarding the adequacy of the prerequisite learning skills still remained. These skill deficits were in fact seen as the main obstacles to the children being enrolled and retained in regular schools.

In a previous study, Archana S (2009) analyzed parent–child interactions to explore baseline data on joint attention, sustained attention, eye contact, eye gaze, sitting tolerance, and compliance in 22 typically developing children ages 1 to 3 years in a naturalistic setting (see Table 7.1). Significant differences were found between the younger children (12–24 months) and older children (25–36 months) in all the six prerequisite skills. Archana S concluded that significant age-related differences indicated the existence of a developmental trend from 1 to 3 years of age. Tentative age norms have been developed based on this sample (Archana S, 2009).

This area of study has important implications for the early identification and treatment of children with ASDs. Each of these skill areas represents an important target for early intervention programs that promote communicative competence and improved long-term outcomes for young children with autism. To document and quantify the difference in prerequisite learning skills between TD children and children with an ASD, in the current study we compared the findings on four children with ASDs with those on the TD children studied by Archana S (2009). In this chapter, we present the implications of these findings for our understanding of learning in young children and for the management of children with developmental disorders such as autism.

A STUDY OF PREREQUISITE LEARNING SKILLS IN YOUNG CHILDREN WITH ASDS

Four children diagnosed with ASDs, two in the age range of 12 to 24 months and two in the age range of 25 to 36 months, were chosen on the basis of the availability of children of that age group and the willingness

TABLE 7.1
Developmental Pattern of Prerequisite Learning Skills in Typically Developing Children

Prerequisite learning skill	Behaviors measured by frequency		Behaviors measured by duration	
P1. Joint attention	P1.1. Number of activities communicated for joint attention	+	P1.2. Attention-getting interval (s)	−
			P1.3. Attention-maintaining interval (min)	+
P2. Sustained attention	P2.1. Number of activities engaged in per observation session	+	P2.6. Average length of time the child attended to an activity (min)	+
	P2.3. Number of pauses during an activity	−		
	P2.4. Number of times the child returned to the activity previously engaged in after a pause	+		
	P2.5. Number of times the child terminated an activity and began a new one after a pause	−		
P3. Eye contact	P3.1. Number of times the child made eye contact with mother during interaction	+	—	
	P3.2. Number of times the child made eye contact with mother to get her attention	+		
P4. Eye gaze	P4.1. Number of correct[a] looks	+	P4.4 Duration of correct looking (s)	+
	P4.2. Number of incorrect[a] looks	−		
	P4.3. Frequency of looking	+		
P5. Sitting tolerance	P5.2. Number of pauses during an activity	−	P5.1. Average length of time the child attended to all activities (min) by sitting in one place	+
	P5.5. Number of activities engaged in per observation session	+		
			P5.3. Duration of pauses (s)	−
P6. Compliance	P6.1. Number of activities changed per observation session	−	—	
	P6.2. Number of activities for which the child cooperated	+		
	P6.3. Number of activities the child completed	+		
	P6.4. Number of times the child protested when changing an activity	−		

Note. Skills P2.2 and P5.4 were assessed in activities that parents carried out during interaction with their child (e.g., puzzles, stacking blocks) and were not included in the statistical analysis and quantification.
+ = value increases as age increases; − = value decreases as age increases; — = not applicable.
[a]*Correct looks* were instances in which the child looked across to see what the adult was pointing at; *incorrect looks* were instances in which the child looked at anything other than where the mother was pointing at, just looked down, or did not look.

of their mothers to cooperate in data collection. The children of both age groups were all of the middle socioeconomic status. The method used to study the children with ASDs was the same as that used for the 22 TD children (Archana S, 2009); the same questionnaire and key for analysis of the data were used in this study. As in the previous study, a video recording of parent–child interaction lasting 30 minutes, was used to observe each child's prerequisite learning skills and communication skills.

The questionnaire was administered to the mothers of the four children diagnosed with ASDs who were selected for the study. A video recording of parent–child interaction along with free play for 30 minutes was done in a naturalistic setting. To ensure that each child's behavior during the video recording was not incidental, the investigator later sought clarification from the mothers regarding the difference between the child's usual behavior and his or her behavior during the video recording. All mothers reported that their child's behavior was more or less typical during the video recording. Hence, another recording was not attempted. After obtaining the data, the mothers' responses to the questionnaire and the video recordings of the children were analyzed. For the video recording analysis, the children's responses were coded in terms of number of occurrences and average duration of occurrence as applicable for different behaviors.

The data from the children with ASDs showed a marked difference in all six prerequisite learning skills in both age groups (12–24 months and 25–36 months) compared with the 22 TD children (see Table 7.2). In comparison with the TD children, the children with ASDs participated in fewer activities involving joint attention, sought attention less frequently, and sustained it for briefer durations. They also used fewer verbal or gestural signals to draw the adult's attention to an event or to obtain an object. The TD child brought objects (toys) over to show an adult, whereas the children with ASDs did not. The children with ASDs, compared with the TD children, made eye contact with the mother less frequently and less meaningfully. They made far fewer attempts at making eye contact with the mother in order to get her attention and maintained eye contact for briefer durations. Whereas the TD children looked across to see what the adult was pointing at, the children with ASDs did not, nor did they point to desired objects. The children with ASDs were less able to tolerate sitting compared with the TD children, and consequently the attending time for activities in one place was far lower for the children with ASDs. The children with ASDs showed greater numbers and durations of pauses in attention. The number of activities the children with ASDs cooperated on and completed was far lower than for the typical children.

TABLE 7.2
Comparison of Data on Children With Autism Spectrum Disorders (ASDs) and Typically Developing (TD) Children

Behavior	Average values for children 12–24 months old		Average values for children 25–36 months old	
	TD children	Children with ASDs	TD children	Children with ASDs
P1. Joint attention				
P1.1. Number of activities communicated for joint attention	5	2	7	2
P1.2. Attention-getting interval	4.80 s	20 s	0.91 s	8 s
P1.3. Attention-maintaining interval	1.74 min	0.62 min	2.89 min	0.72 min
P2. Sustained attention				
P2.1. Number of activities engaged in per observation session	6	2	9	4
P2.3. Number of pauses during an activity	20	34	8	31
P2.4. Number of times the child returned to the activity previously engaged in after a pause	4	1	6	2
P2.5. Number of times the child terminated an activity and began a new one after a pause	14	25	4	20
P2.6. Average length of time the child attended to an activity	1.74 min	0.62 min	2.89 min	0.72 min
P3. Eye contact				
P3.1. Number of times the child made eye contact with mother during interaction	45	9	58	26
P3.2. Number of times the child made eye contact with mother to get her attention	9	3	15	7

(*continues*)

TABLE 7.2
Comparison of Data on Children With Autism Spectrum Disorders (ASDs)
and Typically Developing (TD) Children   (*Continued*)

Behavior	Average values for children 12–24 months old		Average values for children 25–36 months old	
	TD children	Children with ASDs	TD children	Children with ASDs
P4. Eye gaze				
P4.1. Number of correct looks[a]	19	7	38	9
P4.2. Number of incorrect looks[a]	3	9	2	7
P4.3. Frequency of looking	16	1	36	5
P4.4. Duration of correct looking	24.4 s	5.75 s	35 s	4.65 s
P5. Sitting tolerance				
P5.1. Average length of time the child attended to all activities by sitting in one place	3.54 min	1.28 min	5.74 min	1.31 min
P5.2. Number of pauses during an activity	20	34	8	31
P5.3. Duration of pauses	26.87 s	70 s	17.54 s	44 s
P5.5. Number of activities engaged in per observation session	6	2	9	4
P6. Compliance				
P6.1. Number of activities changed per observation session	9	14	6	9
P6.2. Number of activities for which the child cooperated	5	3	7	3
P6.3. Number of activities the child completed	2	1	3	2
P6.4. Number of times the child protested when changing an activity	2	9	1	14

Note. Skills P2.2 and P5.4 were assessed in activities that parents carried out during interaction with their child (e.g., puzzles, stacking blocks) and were not included in the statistical analysis and quantification.
[a]*Correct looks* were instances in which the child looked across to see what the adult was pointing at; *incorrect looks* were instances in which the child looked at anything other than where the mother was pointing at, just looked down, or did not look. Adapted from Archana S (2009).

DISCUSSION

The analyses of the data for children with ASDs revealed differences from TD children in the entire range of prerequisite learning skills. However, it must be emphasized that the current data were arrived at on the basis of only four children with ASDs and need to be verified on a much larger sample. When confirmed with larger numbers of children with ASDs, these data can serve as guidelines for both early identification and early intervention, as well as measurement of the adequacy of intervention, for children with ASDs.

Of the group of prerequisite skills we reported above, measures such as gaze following, seen as a prerequisite for establishing joint attention and language development, have been used to monitor younger siblings of children with ASDs for detection of early identifiers of ASD (Presmanes, Walden, Stone, & Yoder, 2007; Yirmiya et al., 2006; Yirmiya & Ozonoff, 2007). The findings of these studies suggest that children with ASDs and those at risk for ASD are impaired in both gaze following and language development by their 2nd year. However, a longitudinal study by Young, Merin, Rogers, and Ozonoff (2009) on gaze behaviors in infants as young as 6 months did not support their usefulness as an early marker for autism, at least at this very early age. Instead, they suggested that gaze directed to the mother's mouth by 6-month-old infants may be useful in predicting difficulties in language development.

Children diagnosed with an ASD and those at risk for an ASD are being trained in gaze following in order to improve overall skills (Isaksen & Holth, 2009; Klein, Macdonald, Vaillancourt, Ahearn, & Dube, 2009). Longitudinal studies of young children with autism suggest that when the children are provided with support for joint attention through shared objects and language, differences can be seen in both receptive and expressive language (Adamson et al., 2009). At the same time, caution against the assumption of a causal link between difficulties in gaze following and language acquisition is also being voiced, as is the necessity to go beyond merely quantifying these behaviors for improving intervention outcomes with children with ASDs (Gliga et al., 2012).

CONCLUSION

It is important to further delineate patterns of functioning in these prerequisite skills in children with ASDs and PDDs as compared with those with other developmental language disorders. Some comparative studies have been carried out on groups of children with ASDs and children with

Down syndrome. It is perhaps even more important to investigate the nature of these prerequisite learning skills in children with developmental language disorders (e.g., specific language impairment, pragmatic language impairment) compared with those diagnosed with ASDs, given the overlap between these diagnostic categories and the theoretical debates that surround them. In conclusion, the importance of these early learning skills should be emphasized in programs for early identification, differential diagnosis, and early intervention for better long-term outcomes for language and communication and for schooling.

REFERENCES

Adamson, L. B., Bakeman, R., Deckner, D. F., & Romski, M. A. (2009). Joint engagement and the emergence of language in children with autism and Down syndrome. *Journal of Autism and Developmental Disorders*, *39*, 84–96. doi:10.1007/s10803-008-0601-7

Archana S. (2009). *Pre-requisite learning skills: Baselines for communication intervention.* (Unpublished master's thesis). Bangalore University, Bangalore, India.

Bacon, A. L., Fein, D., Morris, R., Waterhouse, L., & Allen, D. (1998). The responses of autistic children to the distress of others. *Journal of Autism and Developmental Disorders*, *28*, 129–142. doi:10.1023/A:1026040615628

Brooks, R., & Meltzoff, A. N. (2008). Infant gaze following and pointing predict accelerated vocabulary growth through two years of age: A longitudinal, growth curve modeling study. *Journal of Child Language*, *35*, 207–220. doi:10.1017/S030500090700829X

Charman, T. (1997). The relationship between joint attention and pretend play in autism. *Development and Psychopathology*, *9*, 1–16. doi:10.1017/S095457949700103X

Charman, T. (1998). Specifying the nature and course of the joint attention impairment in autism in the preschool years: Implications for diagnosis and intervention. *Autism*, *2*, 61–79. doi:10.1177/1362361398021006

Dawson, G., Meltzoff, A., Osterling, J., & Rinaldi, J. (1998). Neuropsychological correlates of early autistic symptoms. *Child Development*, *69*, 1276–1285. doi:10.2307/1132265

Dawson, G., Munson, J., Estes, A., Osterling, J., McPartland, J., Toth, K., . . . Abbott, R. (2002). Neurocognitive function and joint attention ability in young children with autism spectrum disorder versus developmental delay. *Child Development*, *73*, 345–358. doi:10.1111/1467-8624.00411

Dawson, G., Toth, K., Abbott, R., Osterling, J., Munson, J., Estes, A., & Liaw, J. (2004). Early social attention impairments in autism: Social orienting, joint attention, and attention to distress. *Developmental Psychology*, *40*, 271–283. doi:10.1037/0012-1649.40.2.271

Gliga, T., Elsabbagh, M., Hudry, K., Charman, T., Johnson, M. H., & the BASIS team. (2012). Gaze following, gaze reading, and word learning in children at risk for autism. *Child Development, 83*, 926–938.

Isaksen, J., & Holth, P. (2009). An operant approach to teaching joint attention skills to children with autism. *Behavioral Interventions, 24*, 215–236. doi:10.1002/bin.292

Karanth, P., Shaista, S., & Srikanth, N. (2010). Efficacy of Communication DEALL—An indigenous early intervention program for children with autism spectrum disorders. *Indian Journal of Pediatrics, 77*, 957–962. doi:10.1007/s12098-010-0144-8

Klein, J. L., Macdonald, R. F., Vaillancourt, G., Ahearn, W. H., & Dube, W. V. (2009). Teaching discrimination of adult gaze direction to children with autism. *Research in Autism Spectrum Disorders, 3*, 42–49. doi:10.1016/j.rasd.2008.03.006

Presmanes, A. G., Walden, T. A., Stone, W. L., & Yoder, P. J. (2007). Effects of different attentional cues on responding to joint attention in younger siblings of children with autism spectrum disorders. *Journal of Autism and Developmental Disorders, 37*, 133–144. doi:10.1007/s10803-006-0338-0

Sarid, M., & Breznitz, Z. (1997). Developmental aspects of sustained attention among 2- to 6-year-old children. *International Journal of Behavioral Development, 21*, 303–312. doi:10.1080/016502597384884

Watt, N., Wetherby, A., & Shumway, S. (2006). Prelinguistic predictors of language outcome at 3 years of age. *Journal of Speech, Language, and Hearing Research, 49*, 1224–1237. doi:10.1044/1092-4388(2006/088)

Yirmiya, N., Gamliel, I., Pilowsky, T., Feldman, R., Baron-Cohen, S., & Sigman, M. (2006). The development of siblings of children with autism at 4 and 14 months: Social engagement, communication, and cognition. *Journal of Child Psychology and Psychiatry, 47*, 511–523. doi:10.1111/j.1469-7610.2005.01528.x

Yirmiya, N., & Ozonoff, S. (2007). The very early phenotype of autism. *Journal of Autism and Developmental Disorders, 37*, 1–11. doi:10.1007/s10803-006-0329-1

Young, G. S., Merin, N., Rogers, S. J., & Ozonoff, S. (2009). Gaze behavior and affect at 6 months: Predicting clinical outcomes and language development in typically developing infants and infants at risk for autism. *Developmental Science, 12*, 798–814. doi:10.1111/j.1467-7687.2009.00833.x

III

ORIGIN OF SELF, CULTURE, AND SOCIAL COGNITION

8

SELF-CONSCIOUSNESS AND THE ORIGINS OF AN ETHICAL STANCE

PHILIPPE ROCHAT

In this chapter, I discuss self-consciousness as a unique feature of our species. As a student of early childhood, my goal is to provide some developmental light on the origins and consequences of this feature that arguably shapes human experience. At the core of my argument is the idea that self-consciousness is inseparable from the human propensity to take an ethical stance toward others, but also toward the self in terms of reputation and the construction of a moral identity. I therefore consider the ontogenetic emergence of self-consciousness and its relation to the emergence of an ethical stance in children.

HUMAN PROSOCIAL PREDISPOSITIONS

Much comparative and developmental research demonstrates that humans have a propensity toward prosocial actions that might be unique among other animals. Our social life revolves around the perception of shared intentions leading to unique collaboration, cooperation, and helpful behaviors

DOI: 10.1037/14043-009
Cognition and Brain Development: Converging Evidence From Various Methodologies, B. R. Kar (Editor)
Copyright © 2013 by the American Psychological Association. All rights reserved.

(Tomasello, 2008). Recent evidence shows that clear signs of such a propensity probably emerge by the 2nd year in human ontogeny (Hamann, Warneken, Greenberg, & Tomasello, 2011). In general, it is safe to say that humans are potentially more inclined to cooperate than any other primates Yet, because other primate species and maybe other nonprimate animals (e.g., elephants) also show signs of cooperation and other prosocial behaviors, the theoretical debate continues to be lively, and divergences on the issue persist. However, it is hard to argue against the fact that human cooperation is linked to particularly exacerbated proclivities that are spontaneously expressed and correspond to what amount to strong and sophisticated prosocial predispositions, including other-regarding preferences, collaboration, and behaviors that are driven by a concern for the welfare of others.

If the evolutionary roots of humans' "unique" prosocial predispositions remain largely unknown, their developmental origins and the way such predispositions might emerge in ontogeny can be captured empirically and therefore provide a better ground for theoretical speculations. Here I want to treat and further speculate on the question of the origins of such predispositions in development.

The background intuition guiding my speculation is that if humans are a uniquely self-conscious species, this uniqueness translates into a unique care for reputation. We are indeed a self-conscious species that has the particular proclivity to care about reputation. The questions are, how do such specifically human prosocial proclivities (e.g., exacerbated care for reputation, self-consciousness, explicit moral sense) emerge in development, and how do they eventually determine our strong sense of what is right and what is wrong and provide the foundation of a unique sense of explicit justice (rules, norms, and regulations)?

Humans are indeed the only species that has evolved institutions or codes of law governing social affairs, particularly those pertaining to possessions, retribution, and the rightful distribution of resources. I suggest that human moral and prosocial ways, and hence also the inverse (human antimoral and antisocial ways), rest primarily on the capacity (or lack thereof) for *self-consciousness*: the ability to represent the self as represented and evaluated by others. I will show that this unique ability emerges from approximately the middle of the 2nd year. In this chapter, I try to give readers a sense of its emergence, its roots, and its development in the first 3 to 5 years of life.

HUMAN SELF-CONSCIOUSNESS

Unlike any other species, humans care about their public appearance, and we are the only species that spends energy and effort adorning ourselves with makeup and other beautifying accessories. But such effort is not only geared toward surface appearance and mere social seduction or conquest; it is also about *reputation*, or the calculation of how others construe us in terms of enduring qualities such as intelligence, power, wealth, charm, attractiveness, or moral integrity. Etymologically, the word *reputation* derives from the Latin verb *putare*, to compute or calculate. As humans, we work hard on appearance to signal deeper qualities regarding who we are as persons.

Overall, in human affairs, we gauge the incomparable secure feeling of social affiliation or closeness or the fragile sense of belonging to a social niche by having agency and a place among others. In general, we gauge our social affiliation via the attention, respect, and admiration of others—namely, our "good" reputation. In human affairs, the equation is simple: good reputation = good affiliation. The struggle for recognition and the maintenance of a good reputation shape the development of human social cognition. It is a major drive behind it (see Rochat, 2009).

CARDINAL IMPORTANCE OF OTHERS' GAZE

In the human struggle for recognition, the gaze of others gains, figuratively and literally, a particular status (Rochat, in press). In comparison with other primates, humans evolved a new function and meaning of others' gaze as a social signal, the main marker of intimacy and affiliation (Emery, 2000). Humans are uniquely endowed with eyes that have a clear sclera with a highly contrasted pupil, enhancing directionality and dispositional cues including the relative attention and engagement of others toward the self. This is evident, for example, in the particularly marked tendency toward gaze grooming in humans, a sign of affiliation and relational intimacy not found in other primate species, with maybe the exception of bonobo chimpanzees (Kobayashi, & Hashiya, 2011; Kobayashi & Kohshima, 1997).

EVOLUTIONARY CONTEXT

Compared with other primate species, humans are born both precociously (too soon) and highly *altricial* (dependent on others to survive; see Gould, 1977). This state is due to a combination of the proportionally larger brain we evolved as a species, together with the narrowing of the female's birth canal associated with bipedal locomotion, a posture uniquely evolved by our species and linked to protracted external gestation (Konner, 2010; Montagu, 1961; Trevathan, 1987). We start standing and roaming the world on our own by only 12 months, and it takes many, many long childhood years to separate from one's own original nurturing niche to become autonomous in order to reproduce this cycle of development with new progenies.

The premature human birth leads to a state of protracted dependence during approximately one fifth of our life. This remarkable dependence shapes our psychology from the outset. It is a simple, straightforward fact, yet it is probably the major determinant of what makes us psychologically unique in the animal kingdom: the self-conscious and ethical species we are. This basic evolutionary context leads to specific developmental problems.

HUMAN EXISTENTIAL CONUNDRUM

The prolonged immaturity and dependence that characterize human childhood also give rise to the unique existential conundrum: maintaining proximity with those dispensing the indispensable care while responding to the insatiable curiosity instinct that pushes all healthy infants to roam and explore the world. The problem is that this instinct pushes the child away from the secure base of the mother that he or she needs. All healthy children are faced with this basic conundrum from around 8 months of age on average—the typical onset of *independent locomotion*, operationally defined as the child's ability to creep or crawl a distance of 4 feet in 1 minute (Benson, 1993; Bertenthal & Campos, 1990). Coincidentally, it is also at this precise juncture in development that infants are known to show signs of strangers' presence and separation anxiety (the 8th-month "anguish" described by Spitz, 1965). More intriguing is the fact that it is also at this exact developmental juncture that infants begin to engage in *joint attention* with others—that is, secondary intersubjectivity or explicit triangulation between self and others in relation to objects in the world (Scaife & Bruner, 1975; Tomasello, 1995; Trevarthen, 1980).

One way to look at the developmental emergence of joint attention and secondary intersubjective triangulation is that children are pushed by the drive to engage others in their object exploration, checking back and forth whether the gaze of others is attuned to and aligned with their own object of interest. In this view, joint attention is the basic process by which children can resolve the basic human conundrum. In joint attention, children manage de facto to incorporate others (whom they need for their own survival and to whom they are opportunistically attached) into their own free roaming and object exploration. Stated differently, with joint attention, children begin to control others' attention onto the self from a distance. Via the control of others' gaze oriented toward the self, young children manage to maintain psychological proximity, but at a distance. It allows them to be physically separated while continuing to be recognized and enjoying others' undivided attention (the "alone but together" or "together alone" conundrum). Via joint attention, children thus gain "telecontrol" (control at a distance) of others' attention toward the self. In this development, the gaze of others now conveys new, evaluative meanings about the self. It leads children to become increasingly *self-conscious*: explicitly aware of the self through the valued and evaluative eyes of others. I also suggest that this could represent the ontogenetic root of the human moral sense: the proclivity to be principled and take an ethical stance toward others.

SELF-CONSCIOUSNESS IN DEVELOPMENT

For decades now, the mirror mark test has been used as an acid test of conceptualized self-awareness from both a developmental and a comparative perspective (Amsterdam, 1968, 1972; Gallup, 1970). Self-directed behaviors toward a mark surreptitiously put on the face and discovered in the mirror attest to *self-concept*—in other words, an objectified sense of the self (see also Mitchell, 1993, for more nuanced views on the mirror mark test). What the individual sees in the mirror is "me," not another person, a feat that is not unique to humans because chimpanzees, orangutans, dolphins (Parker, Mitchell, & Boccia, 1995), and now magpies as well as elephants have also been reported to pass the test (Plotnik & de Waal, 2006; Prior, Schwarz, & Güntürkün, 2008).

The majority of children pass the mirror mark test by 21 months, touching the mark on their face rather than the mirror, thus indicating that the perceived specular image is self-referred (Bertenthal & Fisher, 1978). Note, however, that the onset and manifestation of such behavior in front of the mirror depends on culture (Broesch, Callaghan, Henrich, Murphy, & Rochat, 2011). But beyond the mirror mark test and what its passing might actually mean in terms of emerging self-concept, there is an early and universal reaction to mirrors that, in my view, is most revealing of human psychology. This reaction is the typical expression of an apparent uneasiness and social discomfort associated with *mirror self-experience*. The same is true for seeing photographs of oneself or hearing a recording of one's own voice. Across cultures, mirror self-experience is uncanny, an expression of deep puzzlement. This is evident even in adults who grew up with no mirrors and who manifest "terror" when confronted for the first time with their own specular image (see Carpenter, 1976). Looking at the self in a mirror puts people, young and old, in some sort of arrested attention and puzzlement. Mirror self-experience is indeed an uncanny experience (Rochat & Zahavi, 2011).

In general, aside from the landmark passing by a majority of children of the mirror mark test from around the second birthday, mirror self-experience develops to become incrementally troubling and unsettling for the healthy child. Such a development is not observed in young autistic children, who are impaired in their reading of others' mind (Baron-Cohen, 1995) but pass the mirror mark test (Neuman & Hill, 1978). Autistic children remove the mark from their faces when they perceive it but do not show the signs of coyness and embarrassment—the troubled or unsettling reactions that are so typical of nonautistic children when discovering themselves in the mirror with a mark on their face (Hobson, 2002, p. 89). It appears that for autistic children, there is a different meaning attached to the mark they discover on their faces that they eventually touch and remove. This meaning would not entail the same kind of self-evaluation or self-critical stance in reference to the evaluative gaze of others expressed in typical children via self-conscious emotions. Autistic children's passing of the mirror test is not self-consciousness proper and does not appear to entail any sense of reputation as defined earlier.

In her pioneering research examining children's reactions to mirrors and establishing (in parallel with Gallup, 1970) the mirror mark test, Amsterdam (1968, 1972) described four main developmental periods unfolding between 3 and 24 months of age:

1. The first period is of mainly sociable behaviors toward the specular image. Infants between 3 and 12 months tend to treat their own image as a playmate.
2. A second period is accounted for by the end of the 1st year; infants appear to show enhanced curiosity regarding the nature of the specular image, touching the mirror or looking behind it.
3. By 13 months, a third period starts in which infants show a marked increase in withdrawal behaviors, with the infant crying and hiding from or avoiding looking at the mirror.
4. Finally, Amsterdam accounted for a fourth period starting at around 14 months but peaking by 20 months in which the majority of tested children demonstrated embarrassment and coy glances toward the specular image, as well as clowning.

These changes index the self-reflective and ultimately the unique self-conscious psychology unfolding in human ontogeny. Such psychology is the product of a complex interplay of cognitive and affective progress that takes place during this early period of child development (Amsterdam & Levitt, 1980), something that Darwin already inferred observing his own child long before the recent wave of experimental work around the mirror mark test.

In his book *The Expression of the Emotions in Man and Animals*, Darwin (1872/1965) described being struck by the unique and selective human crimsoning of the face, a region of the body that is most conspicuous to others. He wrote, "Blushing is the most peculiar and the most human of all expressions" (p. 309). Observing blushing in his son from approximately 3 years of age, and not before, Darwin highlighted the mental states that seem to induce human blushing:

> It is not the simple act of reflecting on our own appearance, but the thinking what others think of us, which excites a blush. In absolute solitude the most sensitive person would be quite indifferent about his appearance. We feel blame or disapprobation more acutely than approbation; and consequently depreciatory remarks or ridicule, whether of our appearance or conduct, causes us to blush much more readily than does praise. (p. 325)

These observations capture something fundamental and distinctive about humans, a unique motivation behind their social cognition: the exacerbated quest for approbation and affiliation with others and the unmatched fear of being rejected by others (see Rochat, 2009).

The expression of embarrassment in front of mirrors by 2- to 3-year-olds is associated with the child's growing metacognitive abilities, in particular, the child's growing ability to hold multiple representations and perspectives on the same thing, including the self. For the child, the recognition of the self in the mirror is also the recognition of how the self is publicly perceived. When recognizing themselves in the mirror and discovering that they have a mark on their face, children tend to touch the mark but will leave the mark if they notice that other people around them also wear the same mark. Such observations show that from 20 months on, passing the mirror mark test seems to be inseparable from social awareness. From the outset, when children pass the test, research shows that they do so with the norm of others in mind (Rochat, Broesch, & Jayne, in press).

From the point of view of neurophysiology, there is an apparent link between the emergence of metacognitive abilities around 2 to 3 years of age and the documented orderly maturation of the rostrolateral region of the prefrontal cortex. The growth of this prefrontal cortical region would correlate with the development of new levels of consciousness, in particular, the transition from minimal to metacognitive levels of self-consciousness (Bunge & Zelazo, 2006; Zelazo, Gao, & Todd, 2007).

Elsewhere (Rochat, 2009), I interpreted the negative affective connotation of mirror self-experience (e.g., embarrassment and self-conscious emotions as opposed to positive jubilation) as the expression of a universal tendency to hold an overestimated representation about the self that is at odds with what is actually seen by others, the latter "truly" revealed in the mirror. The first-person (private) perspective on the self is generally overestimated compared with the third-person (public) perspective. This interpretation is supported by the well-documented illusory superiority phenomenon found in adults (Ames & Kammrath, 2004; Beer & Hughes, 2010; Hoorens, 1993). I speculated that mirrors would bring about the experience of a generalized gap between private (first-person) and public (third-person) self-representations, a gap that is the source of basic psychic tension and anxiety, the expression of a generalized social phobia and universal syndrome expressed from the age of 2 to 3 years (Rochat, 2009).

An alternative interpretation would be that young children shy away from their reflection in the mirror not because they are self-conscious but because they wrongly construe the presence of another child staring at them with a persistent, still face as something to be avoided. But this is doubtful considering, as we have noted, that very early on infants discriminate between seeing themselves and seeing someone else in a video (Bahrick, Moss, & Fadil, 1996; Rochat & Striano, 2002).

By showing embarrassment and other so-called secondary emotions (Lewis, 1992), young children demonstrate a propensity toward an evaluation of the self in relation to the social world (the "looking glass self" first proposed by Cooley in his 1902 book). They begin to have others in mind, existing *through* in addition to *with* others.

Children begin to express secondary emotions such as shame or pride by 2 to 3 years in parallel with, and probably linked to, the emergence of symbolic and pretend play. Such play entails, if not at the beginning but by at least ages 3 to 4 years, some ability to simulate events and roles and to take and elaborate on the perspective of others (Harris, 1991; Striano, Tomasello, & Rochat, 2001; Tomasello, 1999; Tomasello, Striano, & Rochat, 1999).

The process of imagining what others might perceive or judge about the self, whether this imagination is implicitly or explicitly expressed, is linked to the cognitive ability of running a simulation of others' minds as they encounter the self. There are fantasies and phantasms involved, the stuff that feeds the self-conscious mind and characterizes a metacognitive level of self-awareness (i.e., the construal and projection of what others might see and evaluate in us).

POSSESSION AND SELF-CONSCIOUSNESS IN DEVELOPMENT

By 21 months, children's mouths are full of personal pronouns and adjectives like *I*, *me*, and *mine* (Bates, 1990; Tomasello, 1998). Not only do children recognize themselves in mirrors as the author of their own actions (objectified self-agency), but they also begin to recognize themselves as the proprietor of particular things. By the end of the 2nd year, children become explicit about what belongs to the self and, de facto, to nobody else (the explicit ownership stance). When the child begins to claim, "that is mine!" it is also to say, "that is not yours!" and not just to bring attention to the object or just the forceful ostentation of a request for it (Tomasello, 1998). The first claim of possession is an assertion of power over objects in relation to others. It is an ostentatious act of self-incorporation whereby the *mine* (the object of possession) becomes *me*, henceforth giving it solidity, as suggested years ago by John Dewey (1922).

The claim of possession emerging by 21 months does indeed give solidity to the embodied self in relation to others. It is primarily an expression of social self-assertiveness (Rochat, 2009, 2011), being first and foremost self-elevating and self-magnifying in relation to others. There is an absolutist connotation in the first identification of young children with objects and their forceful claims as proprietor, a typical trait of the "terrible 2s." In stating "it is *mine*," children are saying that it is nobody else's, that it is absolutely nonalienable. But this first inclination changes rapidly in the context of social exchanges and reciprocation. Learning to live with others (i.e., the process of socialization) appears to constrain young children to realize that there are advantages in terms of gains in social power and ascendance over others in becoming more reciprocal by letting go of exclusive possessions through bartering transactions and giving and receiving in social exchanges (Rochat, 2011).

EMERGENCE OF AN ETHICAL STANCE

By 2 to 3 years of age, children eventually learn the central notion that objects that are possessed by the self do not have to be exclusive and nonalienable but can also be alienable, brought into a space of exchange governed by principles of fairness and reciprocity. Research on sharing in children from various cultures and socioeconomic backgrounds has shown that this development appears to occur universally between 3 and 5 years of age (see Rochat et al., 2009), despite the well-documented variability in children's developmental niche and sociocultural circumstances (Whiting, 1963; Whiting & Edwards, 1988). The degree of young children's fairness in sharing (i.e., the relative equitable distribution of valuable resources using a dictator game paradigm with children as either recipients or not recipients of the exchange) does vary across cultures, but there is a tendency to become more equitable and avert inequity as a function of age in children regardless of culture (Rochat et al., 2009).

The notion of possession, from being primarily a claim of unalienability and self-edification (by the end of the 2nd year and in parallel with the development of self-consciousness, as discussed previously), becomes alienable or shareable. From this point on, children discover the social power of property in the context of exchanges (Faigenbaum, 2005). Even if they show an original trend for self-maximizing gains, consistent with an absolutist unalienable sense of property, research shows that from 36 months on, children begin to develop a complex sense of equity and fairness in sharing, developing a sense of justice that tends to favor protagonists on the basis of ethical principles (e.g., first possession principle, Friedman & Neary, 2008; relative wealth, Rochat, 2009).

During the preschool years (3–5 years old), children develop the ability to apply rules of equity in sharing desirable goods with others, particularly ingroup others, overriding the strong self-maximizing propensities (i.e., self-assertiveness in relation to others) that prevail in 2-year-olds. Preschoolers develop an ethical stance in relation to possession, a notion now defined by its alienability in the context of balanced social exchanges increasingly guided by principles of reciprocity and aversion to inequality, the basic ingredients of human sociality (Fehr, Bernhard, & Rockenbach, 2008; Olson & Spelke, 2008; Rochat, 2009). By 5 years of age, for example, North American middle-class children develop the principled propensity to share equitably and to enforce equity by punishing other, nonabiding protagonists, even if it is at their own cost (i.e., costly punishment; see Robbins & Rochat, 2011). There are indeed emerging signs of strong and principled reciprocity between 3 and 5 years of age, with some evidence of cross-cultural variations, however, that need further empirical scrutiny (Robbins & Rochat, 2011).

Reciprocity requires a concept of self that is enduring in a moral space made of consensual values and norms, a space in which the child becomes accountable and in which reputation starts to play a central role. Self-consciousness, in particular, the valued (ethical) sense of self in relation to others, does appear to develop in parallel to the early development of reciprocal exchanges, although much more empirical work is needed to document this developmental link (Rochat, 2009). Changes in self-concept, in an objectified sense of the embodied self, would accompany the development of reciprocal exchanges and presumably an alienable sense of possession in development. Reciprocal exchanges constrain children to project themselves, as well as what they perceive of others, in the context of ongoing social transactions. Exchanges based on reciprocation require that the protagonists keep track of and agree on who owns what and when at all times. Engaging in such exchanges, starting at approximately 3 years of age (preschool age), forces children to objectify themselves as embodied entities not only in the here and now of perception and action but also in past and future social situations (Povinelli, 2001). There is an intriguing synchronicity between the developmental emergence of the notion of alienable possession brought into a space of reciprocal exchanges with others and the notion of an embodied, physical self that is permanent and enduring over time. Much more research is needed to document this synchrony, in particular, the mechanisms of cross-fertilization and mutual determination of the *me* (objectified sense of the embodied self) and of the *mine* (objectified sense of what belongs to the embodied self) starting at 2 years of age.

CONCLUSION

In this chapter, I have presented what I view as cardinal features of human development: the emergence of self-consciousness and the putative origins of an ethical stance toward others that would be the foundation of unique human potentials for collaboration, cooperation, and other-regarding attitudes. Such ethical or prosocial attitudes are explicitly manifested from at least 5 years of age, with precursor signs already evident by the 2nd year (see Tomasello, 2008). I have tried to show that the development of an ethical stance in children is inseparable from the development of an objectified sense of the self as perceived and evaluated by others (i.e., self-consciousness). This development parallels developmental changes in the meaning of others' gaze that infants learn to use and coopt to explore the world independently while maintaining contact with others, controlling others' attention onto the self at a distance, and mobilizing others into their own activities. I have suggested that this developmental script could represent the seminal context and fertile soil for self-consciousness to develop: the objectified sense of self as perceived, attended, and ultimately evaluated by others. It is a context that favors the particular care about reputation, literally the accounting of others' evaluative gaze onto the self (reputation = computing, etymologically).

I also have tried to show that as self-consciousness becomes increasingly evident in children, equally evident is children's inclination to claim possession over physical objects in the environment. From being in essence unalienable possession at first, children quickly learn that there are great social advantages in bringing such possessions into a zone of exchange with others (Rochat, 2011). It is in this developmental transition that children learn the social advantages of exchanging properties that are alienable and are constrained to learn about what is fair and what is not. This is a crucial developmental gain that I tried to account for in its putative origins.

As emphasized by the philosopher Charles Taylor (1989),

> being a self is inseparable from existing in a space of moral issues, to do with identity and how one ought to be. It is being able to find one's standpoint in this space, being able to occupy a perspective in it. (p. 112)

Much more empirical research is needed to further specify the mechanisms by which children develop their own compass to navigate the moral space that is, in many ways, unique to humans.

REFERENCES

Ames, D. R., & Kammrath, L. K. (2004). Mind-reading and metacognition: Narcissism, not actual competence, predicts self-estimated ability. *Journal of Nonverbal Behavior*, 28, 187–209. doi:10.1023/B:JONB.0000039649.20015.0e

Amsterdam, B. (1972). Mirror self-image reactions before age two. *Developmental Psychobiology*, 5, 297–305. doi:10.1002/dev.420050403

Amsterdam, B. K. (1968). *Mirror behavior in children under two years of age* (Doctoral dissertation, University of North Carolina, Chapel Hill; University Microfilms No. 6901569).

Amsterdam, B. K., & Levitt, M. (1980). Consciousness of self and painful self consciousness. *Psychoanalytic Study of the Child*, 35, 67–83.

Bahrick, L., Moss, L., & Fadil, C. (1996). Development of visual self-recognition in infancy. *Ecological Psychology*, 8, 189–208. doi:10.1207/s15326969eco0803_1

Baron-Cohen, S. (1995). *Mind blindness*. Cambridge, MA: MIT Press.

Bates, E. (1990). Language about me and you: Pronominal reference and the emerging concept of self. In D. Cicchetti & M. Beeghly (Eds.), *The self in transition: Infancy to childhood* (pp. 165–182). Chicago, IL: University of Chicago Press.

Beer, J. S., & Hughes, B. L. (2010). Neural systems of social comparison and the "above-average" effect. *NeuroImage*, 49, 2671–2679. doi:10.1016/j.neuroimage.2009.10.075

Benson, J. B. (1993). Season of birth and onset of locomotion: Theoretical and methodological implications. *Infant Behavior & Development*, 16, 69–81. doi:10.1016/0163-6383(93)80029-8

Bertenthal, B., & Campos, J. J. (1990). A systems approach to the organizing effects of self-produced locomotion during infancy. In C. Rovee-Collier & L. P. Lipsitt (Eds.), *Advances in infancy research* (Vol. 6, pp. 1–60). Norwood, NJ: Ablex.

Bertenthal, B., & Fisher, K. (1978). Development of self-recognition in the infant. *Developmental Psychology*, 14, 44–50. doi:10.1037/0012-1649.14.1.44

Broesch, T., Callaghan, T., Henrich, J., Murphy, C., & Rochat, P. (2011). Cultural variations in children's mirror self-recognition. *Journal of Cross-Cultural Psychology*, 42, 1018–1029.

Bunge, S. A., & Zelazo, P. D. (2006). A brain-based account of the development of rule use in childhood. *Current Directions in Psychological Science*, 15, 118–121. doi:10.1111/j.0963-7214.2006.00419.x

Carpenter, E. (1976). The tribal terror of self-awareness. In P. Hockings (Ed.), *Principles of visual anthropology* (pp. 451–461). Berlin, Germany: Walter de Gruyter.

Cooley, C. O. (1902). *Human nature and the social order*. New York, NY: Scribner's.

Darwin, C. (1965). *The expression of the emotions in man and animals*. Chicago, IL: Chicago University Press. (Original work published 1872)

Dewey, J. (1922). *Human nature and conduct: An introduction to social psychology*. New York, NY: Carlton House.

Emery, N. J. (2000). The eyes have it: The neuroethology, function and evolution of social gaze. *Neuroscience and Biobehavioral Reviews, 24,* 581–604. doi:10.1016/S0149-7634(00)00025-7

Faigenbaum, G. (2005). *Children's economic experience: Exchange, reciprocity, and value.* Buenos Aires, Argentina: Libros En Red.

Fehr, E., Bernhard, H., & Rockenbach, B. (2008, August 28). Egalitarianism in young children. *Nature, 454,* 1079–1083. doi:10.1038/nature07155

Friedman, O., & Neary, K. R. (2008). Determining who owns what: Do children infer ownership from first possession? *Cognition, 107,* 829–849. doi:10.1016/j.cognition.2007.12.002

Gallup, G. G. (1970, January 2). Chimpanzees: Self-recognition. *Science, 167,* 86–87. doi:10.1126/science.167.3914.86

Gould, S. J. (1977). *Ontogeny and phylogeny.* Cambridge, MA: Harvard University Press.

Hamann, K., Warneken, F., Greenberg, J. R., & Tomasello, M. (2011, August 18). Collaboration encourages equal sharing in children but not in chimpanzees [Letter]. *Nature, 476,* 328–331. doi:10.1038/nature10278

Harris, P. (1991). The work of the imagination. In A. Whiten (Ed.), *Natural theories of mind* (pp. 283–304). Oxford, England: Blackwell.

Hobson, R. P. (2002). *The cradle of thought.* London, England: Pan Macmillan.

Hoorens, V. (1993). Self-enhancement and superiority biases in social comparison. *European Review of Social Psychology, 4,* 113–139. doi:10.1080/14792779343000040

Kobayashi, H., & Hashiya, K. (2011). The gaze that grooms: Contribution of social factors to the evolution of primate eye morphology. *Evolution and Human Behavior, 32,* 157–165.

Kobayashi, H., & Kohshima, S. (1997, June 19). Unique morphology of the human eye. *Nature, 387,* 767–768. doi:10.1038/42842

Konner, M. (2010). *The evolution of childhood.* Cambridge, MA: Harvard University Press.

Lewis, M. (1992). *Shame: The exposed self.* New York, NY: Free Press.

Mitchell, R. W. (1993). Mental models of mirror-self-recognition: Two theories. *New Ideas in Psychology, 11,* 295–325. doi:10.1016/0732-118X(93)90002-U

Montagu, A. (1961). Neonatal and infant immaturity in man. *JAMA, 178,* 56–57. doi:10.1001/jama.1961.73040400014011

Neuman, C. J., & Hill, S. D. (1978). Self-recognition and stimulus preference in autistic children. *Developmental Psychobiology, 11,* 571–578. doi:10.1002/dev.420110606

Olson, K. R., & Spelke, E. S. (2008). Foundations of cooperation in young children. *Cognition, 108,* 222–231. doi:10.1016/j.cognition.2007.12.003

Parker, S. T., Mitchell, R. W., & Boccia, M. L. (1995). *Self-awareness in animals and humans: Developmental perspectives.* Cambridge, MA: Cambridge University Press.

Plotnik, J. M., & de Waal, F. B. M. (2006). Self-recognition in an Asian elephant. *Proceedings of the National Academy of Sciences of the United States of America, 103*, 17053–17057. doi:10.1073/pnas.0608062103

Povinelli, D. J. (2001). The self: Elevated in consciousness and extended in time. In C. Moore & K. Lemmon (Eds.), *The self in time: Developmental perspectives* (pp. 75–95). Mahwah, NJ: Erlbaum.

Prior, H., Schwarz, A., & Güntürkün, O. (2008). Mirror-induced behavior in the magpie *(Pica pica)*: Evidence of self-recognition. *PLoS Biology, 6*, e202. doi:10.1371/journal.pbio.0060202

Robbins, E., & Rochat, P. (2011). Emerging signs of strong reciprocity in human ontogeny. *Frontiers in Developmental Psychology, 353* (2), 1–14. doi:10.3389/fpsyg.2011.00353

Rochat, P. (2009). *Others in mind: Social origins of self-consciousness*. New York, NY: Cambridge University Press.

Rochat, P. (2011). Possession and morality in early development. *New Directions in Child and Adolescent Development, 2011*, 23–38.

Rochat, P. (in press). The gaze of others. In M. Banaji & S. Gelman (Eds.), *The development of social cognition*. New York, NY: Oxford University Press.

Rochat, P., Broesch, T., & Jayne, K. (in press). Social awareness and early mirror self-recognition. *Consciousness and Cognition*.

Rochat, P., Dias, M. D. G., Guo, L., MacGillivray, T., Passos-Ferreira, C., Winning, A., & Berg, B. (2009). Fairness in distributive justice by 3- and 5-year-olds across 7 cultures. *Journal of Cross-Cultural Psychology, 40*, 416–442. doi:10.1177/0022022109332844

Rochat, P., & Striano, T. (2002). Who is in the mirror? Self–other discrimination in specular images by 4- and 9-month-old infants. *Child Development, 73*, 35–46. doi:10.1111/1467-8624.00390

Rochat, P., & Zahavi, D. (2011). The uncanny mirror: A re-framing of mirror self-experience. *Cognition and Consciousness, 20*, 204–213.

Scaife, M., & Bruner, J. S. (1975, January 24). The capacity for joint visual attention in the infant [Letter]. *Nature, 253*, 265–266. doi:10.1038/253265a0

Spitz, R. A. (1965). *The first year of life: A psychoanalytic study of normal and deviant development of object relations*. New York, NY: Basic Books.

Striano, T., Tomasello, M., & Rochat, P. (2001). Social and object support for early symbolic play. *Developmental Science, 4*, 442–455.

Taylor, C. (1989). *Sources of the self: The making of modern identity*. Cambridge, MA: Harvard University Press.

Tomasello, M. (1995). Joint attention as social cognition. In C. J. Moore & P. Dunham (Eds.), *Joint attention: Its origins and role in development* (pp. 103–130). Hillsdale, NJ: Erlbaum.

Tomasello, M. (1998). One child's early talk about possession. In J. Newman (Ed.), *The linguistics of giving* (pp. 349–374). Amsterdam, the Netherlands: John Benjamins.

Tomasello, M. (1999). *Cultural origins of human cognition*. Cambridge, MA: Harvard University Press.

Tomasello, M. (2008). *Origins of human communication*. Cambridge, MA: MIT Press.

Tomasello, M., Striano, T., & Rochat, P. (1999). Do young children use objects as symbols? *British Journal of Developmental Psychology, 17,* 563–584. doi:10.1348/026151099165483

Trevarthen, C. (1980). The foundations of intersubjectivity: Developments of interpersonal and cooperative understanding in infants. In D. R. Olson (Ed.), *The social foundations of language and thought: Essays in honor of Jerome S. Bruner* (pp. 382–403). New York, NY: Norton.

Trevathan, W. R. (1987). *Human birth: An evolutionary perspective*. Hawthorne, NY: Aldine de Gruyter.

Whiting, B. B. (1963). *Six cultures: Studies of child rearing*. Cambridge, MA: Harvard University Press.

Whiting, B. B., & Edwards, C. (1988). *Children of different worlds: The formation of social behavior*. Cambridge, MA: Harvard University Press.

Zelazo, P. D., Gao, H. H., & Todd, R. (2007). The development of consciousness. In P. D. Zelazo, M. Moscovitch, & E. Thompson (Eds.), *The Cambridge handbook of consciousness* (pp. 405–432). Cambridge, England: Cambridge University Press. doi:10.1017/CBO9780511816789

9

LEARNING TO SHARE: THE EMERGENCE OF JOINT ATTENTION IN HUMAN INFANCY

GEDEON O. DEÁK, JOCHEN TRIESCH, ANNA KRASNO, KAYA DE BARBARO, AND MARYBEL ROBLEDO

The social sciences are struggling to understand the dynamics of social groups as complex systems (Strogatz, 2001). How do individuals adapt their behaviors in the presence of others? How do they learn patterns of social information? Answering such questions requires theoretical frameworks and predictive models that are closely fitted to empirical behavioral, ethnographic, and physiological data. A major topic is how humans develop social behaviors and social knowledge during infancy. There is evidence that the foundations of social behaviors are laid in infant–caregiver interactions (Sroufe, 1996). What remains to be established is how the structure of infants' social and physical environment interacts with changes in their neural, sensorimotor, and body structures to yield new social knowledge and behavior.

Support for the research reported in this chapter was provided by the National Science Foundation (Contracts SES-0527756 and BCS-0827040); the M.I.N.D. Institute at the University of California, Davis; and the National Alliance for Autism Research. The authors thank numerous colleagues and former students, including Andrea Chiba, Jordan Danly, Kaya de Barbaro, Ian Fasel, Joanne Jao, Hector Jasso, Anna Krasno, Josh Lewis, Yu Liao, Javier Movellan, Cindy Nam, Jackie Overton, Yuri You, and Corrine Zavala.

DOI: 10.1037/14043-010
Cognition and Brain Development: Converging Evidence From Various Methodologies, B. R. Kar (Editor)

The infant–caregiver dyadic system has intricate dynamic properties. Infants' brains and bodies rapidly develop as they acquire vast, varied experience in the family socioecosystem. Parents are themselves complex systems that select from a large behavioral repertoire while interacting with and in the presence of infants. New infant social skills emerge within this complex metasystem. These emerging skills are, despite the high-dimensional complexity of the metasystem, stochastically predictable within some broad parameters of variance. These parameters have been partly outlined by vigorous research efforts spanning the past 4 decades.

In spite of these efforts, we still lack a viable framework that can integrate existing descriptive findings. Such a framework should address questions like the following: How do parents' behaviors contribute to specific infants' social skills? What learning processes does the infant's developing brain bring to bear? How do affect and arousal systems modulate the expression of social behaviors? There is, to be sure, a lot of descriptive evidence that can be brought to bear and a growing if vague acknowledgment that explanations must be framed in terms of dynamic physical systems. What we lack is a powerful theoretical model or, better yet, alternative models that are biologically plausible, ecologically plausible, and capable of generating specific predictions. However, new research incorporating more rigorous, high-dimensional behavioral and physiological experiments, microethnographic studies, insights from computational and basic neuroscience, and computational simulations have begun to yield plausible models of how infant social skills develop.

In this chapter, we describe one such effort: the MESA (Modeling the Emergence of Shared Attention) Project, an interdisciplinary collaboration begun at the University of California, San Diego, by Jochen Triesch, Javier Movellan, and Gedeon Deák. The guiding framework of the project is a theory of the development of attention sharing and other social behaviors. The PLeASES theory starts with the assumption that complex behaviors like gaze following could emerge from the complex interplay of infants' early phenotypes—Perceptual routines, Learning mechanisms, and Affective traits—and their environment, or Social Ecology Structures.

In the following pages, we summarize some MESA research that was done to test and refine the PLeASES theory. First, we summarize descriptive findings on the development of social attention in the first 2 years. This selective review focuses on phenomena that are relatively challenging to integrate within a plausible theory. Next, we outline our approach to formulating the theory. This approach has general implications: It can serve as a template for formulating a viable theory of any developing system of behavior. Next, we explain some of the main assumptions, claims, and predictions of the PLeASES theory. We then describe several empirical efforts to test and refine the PLeASES theory. The first is a naturalistic videoethnographic study that shows how infants can learn to follow gaze as an incidental by-product of their own reward systems and attention shifting and of their parents' visual and manual actions. The second is a series of computational simulations showing that even a very simple adaptive agent with biologically inspired learning mechanisms and input that replicates real parents' actions can acquire many of the attention-shifting behaviors that we identified as challenging to integrate. The last is a series of results from experiments on infants' looking patterns and affective responses to social and nonsocial stimuli. All three strands of research speak to claims of the PLeASES theory and suggest aspects of the theory that can be refined or expanded.

INFANT ATTENTION SHARING: WHAT PHENOMENA SHOULD A THEORY EXPLAIN?

Attention sharing is deliberately shifting attention to the focus of another individual's attention because of seeing the individual seemingly attending to that focal stimulus. Social activities—like people watching at a café, visiting a museum or zoo, playing cards, or discussing a blueprint—all require shared attention. Yet, attention sharing is no mere social lubricant. It facilitates entire categories of interactions that are critical to humans, notably teaching and learning. Monitoring others' attention can provide useful information about uncertain, novel, and even dangerous environments. It is a key element for learning difficult or complex procedures.

Attention sharing is a critical skill for infants and children (Bakeman & Adamson, 1984). It is part of the behavioral system by which infants forge socioemotional bonds (Stern, 2000). It helps infants learn what is important in a complex environment and will eventually help children infer what information they do or do not share with another person (O'Neill, 1996). Attention sharing also facilitates language learning (Baldwin, 1993; Tomasello, 1999). By early childhood, attention-sharing skills are presumed in all educational settings (Rogoff, 1990).

Yet, attention-sharing skills vary widely across infants and even children. At one extreme, attention-sharing deficits are predictors of social and language deficits in autism (Mundy, Sigman, & Kasari, 1990). A plausible theory, then, should account for both typical variability and atypical developmental paths. Within this developmental path, gaze following and point following are typically the first behaviors to emerge during infancy. *Gaze following* is shifting visual attention to match another person's gaze target as a result of encoding and reacting to that person's looking behaviors. *Point following* is shifting attention to the distal target of another person's outstretched arm and (typically) finger or fingers.

Gaze following, point following, and other attention-sharing skills emerge in a semipredicable sequence from 3 to 24 months of age (Butterworth & Cochran, 1980; Butterworth & Itakura, 2000; Butterworth & Jarrett, 1991; Deák, Flom, & Pick, 2000; Flom, Deák, Phill, & Pick, 2004). At 4 or 5 months of age, infants do not respond to parents' looking or pointing bids to redirect attention (Robledo, Danly, Acuña, Ramundo, & Deák, 2009); some 9-month-olds occasionally, in stripped-down laboratory settings, follow gaze to targets already in their visual fields (Flom et al., 2004). A few 6-month-olds rarely show this response, again, in impoverished laboratory settings (Butterworth & Jarrett, 1991; Morales, Mundy, & Rojas, 1998). When 6- to 9-month-olds do turn in the direction of the adult's gaze, they tend to focus on the first thing they see, even if it is not the adult's focus of attention (e.g., Butterworth & Cochran, 1980). This "premature capture" declines from 9 to 12 months (Deák et al., 2000).

There have been claims that infants follow gaze by 3 months or younger (Hood, Willen, & Driver, 1998). However, those studies show limited, weak effects that are attributable to directional motion cueing (Farroni, Johnson, Brockbank, & Simion, 2000; Farroni, Massaccesi, Pividori, & Johnson, 2004). Recently, Robledo et al. (2009) followed infants from 4 to 12 months, testing gaze and point following monthly. In a critical test, infants learned that six monitors spaced around a room would sometimes play reinforcing videos. Infants received more immediate video rewards if they followed the adult's cue (gaze, point, or both) to the specified target. The conditional reinforcement design rules out the possibility that young infants do not follow gaze or point because they are simply unmotivated (see Deák et al., 2000). Motivational factors are a confound in virtually all previous experimental studies of infant attention sharing. Preliminary results are shown in Figure 9.1: Even 6-month-old infants did not follow gaze, even to front targets. Not until 9 to 10 months did some infants reliably follow gaze to targets in the periphery. Even at 12 months, infants rarely followed gaze to targets behind them. This is strong evidence that gaze following per se (i.e., not just motion cuing) emerges around 9 to 10 months.

The development of point following is in some ways similar, emerging around 9 to 12 months. From this period forward, infants are more likely to follow points than gaze shifts (Deák et al., 2000; Deák, Walden, Yale, & Lewis, 2008; Desrochers, Morissette, & Ricard, 1995). Point following is affected by some of the same variables as gaze following: For example, infants are more likely to follow points to targets in front of them than behind them (Deák et al., 2000; Flom et al., 2004). This finding suggests that some common factors underlie these behaviors—there might not be, for example, a narrowly specialized system that mediates gaze following behaviors.

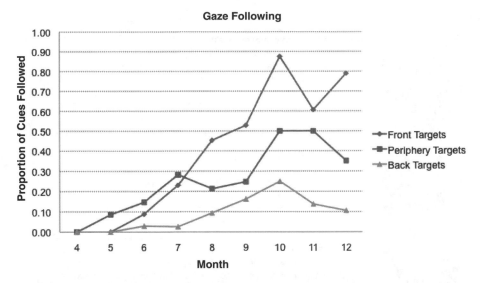

Figure 9.1. Proportion of gaze following responses to an 8-s cue (i.e., an adult turning head and eyes to one of six video targets), from the MESA longitudinal study (preliminary results; *n* = 32).

Figure 9.2 shows some major developmental changes in infancy that we postulated might relate to the emergence of attention-sharing skills in the first 16 months. These changes include learning, perceptual, and traits; we return to these below in our description of the PLeASES theory. However, what remains unanswered by this list of traits, or by the phenomena described above, is why infants eventually follow gaze and pointing. These skills follow months of social experience, maturation, and learning, but we do not know how the experiences of those weeks and months cause change. A possible partial explanation is that parents' gaze and pointing actions help infants predict the location of future rewards—that is, the actions serve as basic reward cues (Schultz, Dayan, & Montague, 1997). If this was so, and if gaze and point perfectly predicted high-value stimulus locations, infants might quickly learn to use them. But adults' gaze shifts and pointing gestures are not perfect predictors of reward locations: For example, adults occasionally look at things that are boring for infants (e.g., rectangles of paper, small handheld blocks). They also roll their eyes, stare at the wall, blink, look at the infant, and otherwise produce uninformative or confusing fixations. Similarly, parents sometimes outstretch their arm or extend their finger to point out things to other adults, or gesticulate, or stretch their arms. All such behaviors are confusing "noise" for the infant who is learning which gestures are informative. Moreover, even if infants reliably attained a desirable outcome whenever they looked in the direction of adults' cues, the infant's

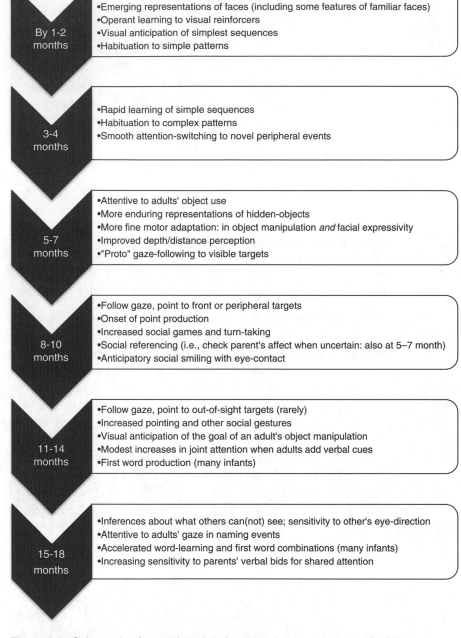

By 1-2 months
- Prefer faces/voices to comparison stimuli
- Emerging representations of faces (including some features of familiar faces)
- Operant learning to visual reinforcers
- Visual anticipation of simplest sequences
- Habituation to simple patterns

3-4 months
- Rapid learning of simple sequences
- Habituation to complex patterns
- Smooth attention-switching to novel peripheral events

5-7 months
- Attentive to adults' object use
- More enduring representations of hidden-objects
- More fine motor adaptation: in object manipulation *and* facial expressivity
- Improved depth/distance perception
- "Proto" gaze-following to visible targets

8-10 months
- Follow gaze, point to front or peripheral targets
- Onset of point production
- Increased social games and turn-taking
- Social referencing (i.e., check parent's affect when uncertain: also at 5–7 month)
- Anticipatory social smiling with eye-contact

11-14 months
- Follow gaze, point to out-of-sight targets (rarely)
- Increased pointing and other social gestures
- Visual anticipation of the goal of an adult's object manipulation
- Modest increases in joint attention when adults add verbal cues
- First word production (many infants)

15-18 months
- Inferences about what others can(not) see; sensitivity to other's eye-direction
- Attentive to adults' gaze in naming events
- Accelerated word-learning and first word combinations (many infants)
- Increasing sensitivity to parents' verbal bids for shared attention

Figure 9.2. Schematic of some key developmental changes in, and related to, the development of gaze and point following skills in infants during the first 18 months of life. Some of the traits are key elements of the PLeASES theory.

learning task would not be trivial. First, to use adults' attention-specifying actions as predictive cues, infants must parse relevant events from a stream of highly variable social actions. Yet adults are often in continuous motion when interacting with infants (Deák, Wakabayashi, Jasso, & Triesch, 2004), and there is no guarantee that infants will notice, much less segment, the adults' critical head turn or eye or arm movement as a unit of significance. Even if they do, the infants must still induce what aspect of the action (e.g., final vector of the index finger) predicts the rewarding outcome. This is not inevitable. Also, the adult's actions are executed in variable contexts, and infants cannot be expected to know which contextual factors matter and to what extent. For example, the direction of light falling on the adult's face generally does not matter. However, the adult's head angle must be calculated relative to the infant's own heading, the triangulated distance and angle of various possible target objects, and the configuration of the shared space—for example, the location of opaque barriers between the adult and various objects. The infant must learn which of these things matter and which do not. The variability of all of these factors, across all environments where the infant interacts with adults, complicates the learning problem. In sum, any theory must consider the high dimensionality and continuousness of adults' actions, the nonobvious association between social actions and outcomes, and the many differences across shared environments.

Despite the challenges posed by these considerations, Deák and Triesch (2006) and Triesch, Teuscher, Deák, and Carlson (2006) proposed that reinforcement learning is an important element of infants' acquisition of attention-following behaviors. Naturally, although instrumental functions are critical aspects of social learning, they are the only critical elements (as we explain later). Also, learning attention-sharing policies is not a discrete goal for the infant; it is a category of states that sometimes occur in the context of various other motivated actions and motivating events. During social interactions, for example, infants babble, attempt to prolong games, point to things, seek proximity with parents, or try to separate and explore. They watch people use tools, watch the family pet, watch TV, and watch other children playing games. The reward function of attention sharing is dynamically nested within an extensive, ever-growing, and dynamically changing hierarchy of costly and rewarding responses to an often-unpredictable environment. At any moment, the status of this cost–reward hierarchy is unknown. Moreover, what infants learn from any given instance of attention sharing is unknown. Finally, caregivers simultaneously have their own range of predicted costs and benefits and related motivations. Parents work to bond with their infants, teach them, elicit smiles and chuckles, show off their infant to peers, or quickly finish a feeding or diaper change and get back to work (or sleep). In sum, attention-sharing episodes emerge within a fluid panorama of concurrent motivational states, goals (convergent and conflicting), affective changes, and learned expectancies and responses. All of these states, changes, and so forth will have been shaped in a rich history of social experiences. Our challenge as researchers is to infer how these factors interact to generate, extend, and terminate episodes of shared attention. Indeed it is, mutatis mutandi, the challenge of understanding any emergent category of social behavior in infants.

IF IT PLeASES: AN APPROACH TO FORMULATING THEORIES OF EMERGENT BEHAVIORAL SYSTEMS

What experiences and changes in the first 6 to 12 months after birth lead to gaze following and related skills? To answer this, we should consider neural, behavioral, and ecological factors that might contribute to social behaviors. In addition, the answer should include a model of how those factors cause change. When the MESA Project began in 2001, there were no alternative theories and few, if any, examples of developmental theories that synthesized detailed behavioral, biological, and ecological factors in an explanatory model. For that reason, some of our early discussions focused on the basic question of how to generate a developmental theory (see Fasel, Deák, Triesch, & Movellan, 2002). Thus, although the strategy outlined here came from formulating a theory of attention-sharing development, the approach can be used to generate a theory of any class or system of social behavior. In broad sketches, the approach is as follows:

- Specify an age range when the behavioral system does not yet occur. Ideally, this is far enough back to allow enough time for input and growth processes but not so early that the explanatory problem is intractable (e.g., do not start at the blastula stage).
- Do a task analysis or "reverse engineering" of the behavioral system at some later, more mature state. Ideally, the behavioral phenotypes at this period are well documented and robust across population samples and context (however, that is not always known).
- Hypothesize a minimal set of established precursor phenotypes that would be necessary to acquire that phenotype. The set must be constrained by biological facts not only about age-specific brain physiology and anatomy but also about age-specific peripheral physiology (i.e., sympathetic and parasympathetic systems), sensory development, and body and motor maturation. Precursor phenotypes should be documented and observable (e.g.,

contrast acuity developmental curves), not speculative (e.g., shared attention module).

- Propose a process by which neural plasticity/learning mechanisms and biological maturation processes cause the more mature phenotype to emerge from the minimal set. All of the elements in this explanatory model should be grounded in biological evidence, not purely hypothetical.
- Document pertinent events, objects, and human actions in the infant's environment. This often requires exploratory ethnographic documentation, especially of patterns of events that tend to occur soon before, during, and after the behaviors of interest. From this and other evidence, hypothesize an ecological model of the information/experience patterns that are relevant to the emergent behavior.

The initial model will therefore specify the processes by which some minimal set of observable phenotypes, embodied in an organism that experiences a history of events-in-settings, will develop new phenotypes. The model can then be tested in the following ways:

- *Formal tests of the sufficiency of the precursor set, learning model, and ecological model.* Deák, Bartlett, and Jebara (2007) referred to the process of modeling both the agent's encoding and learning processes and the information in the environment as a *dual modeling problem*. That is, if we construct an artificial agent with the proposed precursor set of phenotypes and an environment with naturalistic patterns of available experiences, and we simulate the proposed learning processes, we can observe whether the agent develops new responses that resemble the emerging behaviors of human infants. If it does, we can claim that the model was not falsified. If it does not develop the expected behaviors, then the theory is falsified—although we do not know whether the problem is in our model of the precursor set, in the critical ecological information structures, in the learning process, or in more than one of these elements. Note that simulation experiments are only proofs of plausibility, and the strength of any simulation outcomes rests on the number and range of natural phenomena—especially odd or noninevitable phenomena—that are replicated (Simmering, Spencer, Deák, & Triesch, 2010). For example, a model derives greater plausibility if it predicts how changing a particular parameter will evoke different patterns of disordered or disabled behavioral development (Richardson & Thomas, 2006; Triesch et al., 2006). Also, if natural development shows discontinuities rather than constant, gradual improvement (which can be predicted by many models), then simulation tests become more informative: The discontinuities are critical tests that will not emerge inevitably from "any old" learning model. In general, then, the more phenomena (i.e., infant behaviors) simulated without "hand wiring" (i.e., overspecifying the agent), the more support (i.e., plausibility) is accorded the model.

- *Experimental longitudinal studies.* A powerful model should support predictions about how variability in precursor phenotypes and in ecological patterns will influence the emergence of new behaviors. For example, if a proposed precursor trait (e.g., speed of habituation) is truly important in the processing model, then individual differences in that trait should relate to later individual differences in the emergent behavior (e.g., its age of onset, efficiency, or benefit).

- *Naturalistic microbehavioral ethnographies and quantitative measures of infants' environments.* This type of study can specify the event and information structures that permit and promote new behavioral phenotypes. Such studies are seldom available, however, and require laborious efforts. Fortunately, technological advances are allowing researchers to more easily collect, code, and analyze naturalistic data sets that are larger, richer, and more objective than ever before (see Spink et al., 2010). Without these studies, though, any theory or model is predicated on guesses or assumptions about what information might be available to infants and what information they naturally notice.

For related discussions, see Cangelosi et al. (2010), Deák et al. (2007), Goldstein et al. (2010), Grossberg and Vladusich (2010), and Roy et al. (2006). Examples of empirical work that tests biologically and ecologically viable theories include Messinger, Ruvolo, Ekas, and Fogel (2010), Yu and Ballard (2007), and Cameron et al. (2005). In the remaining pages of this chapter, we describe the PLeASES theory of infant attention-sharing and our efforts to test the theory.

PLeASES: A THEORY OF THE EMERGENCE
OF ATTENTION-SHARING SKILLS

The PLeASES theory rests on the idea that infants' attention-shifting decisions can become influenced by specific adult actions if those actions serve as predictive cues to the locations of relatively interesting things. It assumes that infants have no prior expectations that other people's eye, head, or arm actions are correlated with structures in the environment, or with their own behaviors, or with any internal state (e.g., intention) of the actor. PLeASES is therefore a nonnativist, instrumentalist, mechanistic theory (Deák, Fasel, & Movellan, 2001; Deák & Triesch, 2006; Fasel et al., 2002; Krasno, Deák, Triesch, & Jasso, 2007; Teuscher & Triesch, 2007; Triesch et al., 2006; Triesch, Jasso, & Deák, 2007). It is also biologically grounded: All processes of infant cue perception, attention, action selection, reward calculation, and so forth are to be specified, at least roughly, by neurobiological evidence. Finally, it is ecologically grounded because infants cannot learn skills like gaze following unless the adult cue actions systematically correlate with locations of stimuli that infants find relatively rewarding and unless the timing, form, and frequency of those cues make them detectable and learnable to infants.

The main postulate of PLeASES is that infants learn to follow adults' gaze, pointing, or other actions because those cues can predict the locations of relatively interesting sights (C. Moore, 1996) in infants' everyday environments. A second postulate is that infants' interest is modulated by habituation and arousal. An ancillary assumption is that infants' relative levels of interest in various stimuli are correlated with adults' relative interest in the same stimuli. Thus, whatever grabs adults' attention has a fair shot at getting infants' attention. A third postulate is that the timing constraints on infants' looking decisions (i.e., fixating and shifting) are close enough to adults' looking and acting timing parameters that infants can follow parents' action cues fast enough to yield some episodes of shared attention.

The PLeASES theory emerged from discussions among researchers across several disciplines, taking into consideration modern learning theory and neuroscience; research on infants' perception, action, and physiology; and ethnographies of infant–parent social patterns in natural settings. As noted earlier, PLeASES is an acronym for Perceptual routines, Learning mechanisms, Affective traits, and Social Ecological Structures. Keeping with the strategy outlined previously, we attempted to define the minimum set of infant traits that are functioning before gaze or point following emerged and that would seem to be necessary for attention-sharing skills to emerge in their documented sequence. Traits were deemed necessary on the basis of a task analysis of the first attention-sharing skills to emerge. The theory eschews hypothetical special-purpose mechanisms (e.g., the shared attention mechanism; Baron-Cohen, 1995) under the philosophy that one should first prove that established, general mechanisms cannot explain some specific effect (e.g., gaze following) before postulating narrowly specialized mechanisms. This strategy indicated a starting age of 2 to 3 months. By that age, infants have all of the general precursor traits and ecological structures proposed (from the task analysis) to be sufficient and needed to yield later, specific attention-following skills. The starting set includes the elements of the PLeASE acronym: perceptual routines, learning mechanisms, affective dispositions, and social ecology structures. (Note that this list is not comprehensive; many general phenotypes such as center-surround visual receptive fields, retinal heterogeneity of contrast and motion acuity, and audition attention traits are left implicit in the theory. However, we judged these phenotypes to be more distantly related to the phenotypes of interest.)

Perceptual Routines

Several visual processes are hypothesized to be critical for attention sharing. Speed of attention shifting to a new target improves around 2 to 3 months (Butcher, Kalverboer, & Geuze, 2000; Johnson, Posner, & Rothbart, 1994) as recurrent connections from frontal eye fields (FEF) to superior parietal networks mature. This allows for top-down saccade planning that will be constrained by new (learned) factors, such as multidimensional salience maps (Itti & Koch, 2001) and experience-influenced autonomic neuromodulation (e.g., Aston-Jones & Cohen, 2005). These emergent changes in attention-shifting dynamics can have effects on infants' social attention (e.g., de Barbaro, Chiba, & Deák, 2011; Field, 1981). They also can be simulated in simple computational implementations (e.g., Nagai & Rohlfing, 2009; Triesch et al., 2006).

The model also presumes that spatial mappings from the environment to retinal fields become mapped to sensorimotor loops (e.g., neck, torso, orbital muscles) within the first 4 to 6 months. These developments involve maturation of area V5/MT+ (higher level visual cortical regions), caudal FEF, and cerebellar networks (Rosander, 2007). Critically, they permit fast, smooth shifts of attention by coordination of multiple motor systems. Our simulations show that if infants' shifting is too slow, infants lose opportunities to use adults' gaze cues. Thus, we identified this aspect of visual maturation as a precursor of gaze following.

Another critical perceptual skill is discriminating adults' head poses (i.e., angles), which older infants use to estimate gaze direction (C. Moore, Angelopoulos, & Bennett, 1997). By 1 month of age, infants can discriminate frontal from profile head poses (Sai & Bushnell, 1988). Discrimination of head poses increases in acuity from 6 to 12 months (Butterworth & Jarrett, 1991), but little is known about this; for example, there are no data on acuity growth curves or on head features that infants use to discriminate head angles. Yet age limitations in infants' gaze following, especially to targets behind them, seem to be partly due to limited sensitivity to changes in head pose, durability of head pose representations, or both (Deák et al., 2000). Also, the development of head pose sensitivity could plausibly explain premature capture errors in 6- to 9-month-olds (Butterworth & Jarrett, 1991). Younger infants sometimes follow gaze by turning to the correct hemifield but stop at the incorrect target (i.e., whichever is closer to midline), perhaps due to an imprecise encoding of the adult's head angle. Notably, in simulations of the PLeASES model (Triesch et al., 2006), infant-agents gained more rewards if they more accurately encoded caregivers' head pose. Thus, although young infants discriminated grossly dissimilar head poses, acuity improved with age. This could be a contributor to gaze following, a consequence of successful gaze following, or both.

The model also presumes that by 2 to 4 months of age, infants can, in optimal cases, discriminate different rotational positions of the eyes in the orbits—that is, eye direction. This presumption has empirical support (Farroni, Johnson, & Csibra, 2004; Symons, Hains, & Muir, 1998). However, there is no good evidence that infants under 12 to 18 months use eye direction, as opposed to head angle, to follow gaze (e.g., Butler, Caron, & Brooks, 2000; Doherty, 2006; C. Moore et al., 1997). Thus, young infants can detect eye direction but require many months to learn to associate it with adults' direction of attention, consistent with PLeASES: Infants would have to be able to perceive eye direction, but they require extensive input to learn that eye direction, which is subtler than but highly correlated with head angle, is uniquely predictive of adults' locus of attention. Thus, perceptual sensitivity alone is inadequate: We must also consider learning processes.

Learning Mechanisms

The critical mechanisms of change proposed in PLeASES are temporal difference reinforcement learning (TD-RL) and habituation. Reinforcement learning is an established approach to machine learning (Sutton & Barto, 1998) with attractive features for modeling infant learning.[1] An insight of TD-RL is that adaptive behavior can be represented as learned policies of stochastic action selection based on a matrix of previously experienced situations and the outcomes (immediate and longer term) of actions previously taken in those situations. Outcomes are valued in terms of hedonic, material, or uncertainty-reducing outcomes, and immediate rewards are valued higher than delayed rewards. This model can be used to formalize a wide range of

[1]TD-RL functions can be captured by other learning approaches (e.g., partially observable Markov models, optimal control theory; Singh, Jaakkola, & Jordan, 1994; Wolpert, Ghahramani, & Flanagan, 2001). However, a TD-RL algorithm can capture some important and realistic ecological and cognitive constraints (e.g., partial feedback). The learning model was chosen on the basis of biological and cognitive plausibility: Infants are *not* optimal systems, and our goal is to replicate their errors and difficulties.

infant behaviors. For example, 2-month-olds can learn, after viewing alternating lights for a short time, to look at where the next light will be (Haith, Hazan, & Goodman, 1988). In this situation, if a light is more interesting than nothing and infants make different looking actions in the different event states (i.e., left on, right on, both off), then a TD-RL process can explain how infants' looking decision policy is shaped to yield such early and fast contingency learning.

There has been great progress in detailing some neural mechanisms of TD-RL (Schultz et al., 1997). Although we cannot experimentally test those mechanisms in human infants, we can test behavioral predictions in human or artificial infants (de Barbaro et al., 2011; Schlesinger & Parisi, 2001). For example, gaze following requires infants to notice a state of the environment (e.g., parent turned 90° to the left) and to choose either to keep looking or to look somewhere else, and if so, where. If, when the infant shifts gaze to the same target as the adult (after encoding his or her head or eye direction), and if that shared target is more interesting than other targets, the infant might strengthen the expected reward for selecting a similar attention shift in similar situations. That is not inevitable, as we shall explain below. First, however, we note several features of TD-RL models that are suited to problems of social prediction. One is that the models incorporate exploration (i.e., not always repeating the most-rewarded action) and stochastic action selection; this can explain the high variability of infants' responses to social cues. Another is that action policies can shift dynamically in response to changing environments (e.g., adapting to a new caregiver who is less demonstrative). Also, the models represent probabilistic memories for action outcomes, especially the most recent ones. This captures effects of personal history with a caregiver, as well as recency effects.

TD-RL models are complex enough that a full evaluation requires several distinct tests. First, it must be established how the agent classifies and differentiates states of the environment (e.g., head poses, regions of the environment), which over time can be associated with different actions. This requires psychophysical tests. Second, it is necessary to specify a priori reward values for different outcomes. This requires behavioral data such as looking time tests and facial expression coding. Third, it is necessary to show that previous actions affect future actions. These are significant challenges, but they are in fact challenges to all theories (e.g., How does a laboratory task generalize to everyday situations? Does praise carry the same value for every child in a sample?). The advantage of TD-RL models is that the assumptions are explicit, and researchers must be explicit about how they set the corresponding parameters or algorithms.

Habituation is another necessary learning mechanism. When an infant looks at a caregiver's face or a toy, habituation begins, and over time the probability of a gaze shift gradually increases. This is necessary for infants to look away from parents, to seek out new and interesting sights, and to alternate gaze between caregivers and objects—a behavior taken as evidence that infants represent other people's attention (Tomasello, 1995). Habituation is often used as a methodological tool for infant studies but is mostly overlooked as a key learning mechanism in itself (Sirois & Mareschal, 2002). Yet, even neonates habituate to complex visual patterns (Slater, Earle, Morison, & Rose, 1985) and faces (Colombo, Mitchell, O'Brien, & Horowitz, 1987). Also, individual differences in habituation (e.g., rate) correlate with qualities of infant–parent interactions (Saxon, Frick, & Colombo, 1997; Tamis-LeMonda & Bornstein, 1989). It is possible that infants who habituate too fast or too slow relative to a caregiver's schedule of attention shifting miss opportunities to follow his or her cues to shift to interesting sights. In simulations, we parameterized habituation rate and found that very fast or very slow habituators were slower to learn gaze following (Triesch et al., 2006). This prediction is currently being tested in a longitudinal study (Ellis, Robledo, & Deák, 2012).

Affective Traits

Reinforcement learning depends on the prior value of different outcomes. In social situations, shaping of action policies depends partly on what events or stimuli are interesting, fun, and so forth or are uncomfortable or stressful. Infants enjoy faces and voices, particularly those of caregivers (DeCasper & Fifer, 1980; Field, Cohen, Garcia, & Greenberg, 1984), and they enjoy participating in reciprocal, synchronized social interactions (Bigelow & Birch, 1999; G. A. Moore & Calkins, 2004). For example, 8- to 10-month-olds smile in anticipation of adults' next reaction (Venezia, Messinger, Thorp, & Mundy, 2004). Yet infants also show interest in complex objects such as toys (e.g., Rochat, 1989), and this can introduce conflict between the reward value of people and of objects (Bakeman & Adamson, 1984). The resulting dynamics can be modeled in simulations of the PLeASES model. For example, changing the relative values of faces and toys will, at extremes, yield patterns of disordered attention sharing: face avoidance that resembles autistic behaviors or hypersociability that resembles Williams syndrome (see Triesch et al., 2006). However, it is unknown how less extreme individual differences in these preferences affect the acquisition of attention sharing. It is also unknown what infants enjoy looking at in natural social settings, which must be known to test whether the PLeASES model can explain the acquisition of gaze and point following behaviors.

Social Ecology Structures

Caregivers produce nonrandom social behavior patterns when interacting with infants (e.g., Cohn, Matias, Tronick, Connell, & Lyons-Ruth, 1986; Field, Healy, Goldstein, & Guthertz, 1990; Watson & Ramey, 1972), and infants learn these patterns (Kaye, 1982). For example, Nagai and Rohlfing (2009) and Zukow-Goldring and Arbib (2007) described how adults alter object manipulations to play with infants. Yu and Smith and their colleagues have described how parents' actions when sharing objects with toddlers, together with the toddlers' own activity and perception, jointly support toddlers' exploration and learning about the objects and even about object labels (Richert, Yu, & Favata, 2010; Smith, Yu, & Pereira, 2011; Yu & Smith, 2011). Parents also modify speech and gestures when interacting with infants (Brand, Baldwin, & Ashburn, 2002; Fernald & Kuhl, 1987). However, individual parents modify their behaviors with infants to varying degrees: Parents suffering from depression, for example, tend to be less reactive, and their infants learn different response policies than infants of nondepressed parents (Field et al., 1990; G. A. Moore & Calkins, 2004). Such findings must be accounted for by any theory. In initial simulations of the PLeASES model, Teuscher and Triesch (2007) varied the actions of virtual caregivers, making them, for example, very predictable, or neglectful, or chaotic and unpredictable. Infant-agents learned gaze following more or less quickly as a function of these styles, providing more evidence for the plausibility of the PLeASES theory.

However, little is known about how healthy, typical caregivers' social behavior patterns and individual or cultural differences affect infants' attention-sharing skills. To test whether PLeASES can explain the effects of these social structures, we must document what actual parents do while interacting with real infants and what infants do in response. Without this information, we cannot say what input infants have the opportunity to learn. Such information requires large videoethnographic data sets from which a wide range of caregiver actions are coded at high temporal resolution. Such data are costly to collect, however, so we are typically ignorant of infants' social information structures. Thus, our hypotheses about social input are often based on scant information from unnatural contexts, plus intuition and folk hypotheses. Yet these data sets are needed: They sometimes yield results (e.g., Smith et al., 2011) that are undetectable by other methods and at odds with conventional beliefs or inconsistent with results from the socially bizarre settings of laboratory experiments.

Putting Together the Pieces

PLeASES predicts the following process: Infants in their first weeks develop a preference (i.e., reward) for the parent's face—frontal poses above profiles—and for colorful objects. By 3 months, they smoothly shift gaze and habituate to static patterns on the same time scale as adults' fixation times. Parents often look at their infant when the infant is attentive, but they also look at other targets. Infants enjoy (i.e., are rewarded by) parents' direct gaze, but they often look away. In our model, this is because (a) other targets are also interesting; (b) habituation gradually reduces the value of the parent's face; and (c) in every time step, there is a possibility that the infant will explore—that is, look around to see if there happens to be something interesting. For these reasons, the cumulative likelihood of looking away from the parent gradually increases whenever the infant does look at the parent. Also, when the parent looks away, the infant sees a profile face, and instantaneous reward is reduced. Thus, the dynamics of TD-RL ensure that infants will eventually turn away. When they do, their next fixation target will not be random relative to the parent's gaze direction. Given the structure of the environment and similarities of the infant's and parent's visual systems, there is a relatively high probability that both will fixate on a nearby salient (e.g., colorful, moving, high-contrast) target. This requires the *Affective* and *Social Ecology* aspects of PLeASES. Sometimes, then, infant and parent will end up looking at the same target after the infant encoded the parent's head direction. Eventually, the infant will learn to expect higher accumulated reward by relating the parent's head poses (and later eye directions) to specific action commands (i.e., head turns) toward corresponding regions of the environment. This sequence involves *Perceptual* elements of PLeASES as well as TD-RL processes.

Testing the PLeASES theory required filling in unknown parameters. It was unknown what infants like to look at (i.e., find rewarding) in natural environments and whether these objects overlap with the things adults look at. It was also unknown how regularly infants see adults looking toward these objects or whether infants look toward these objects soon after they see the adult's head direction. One goal was to start to document these parameters in order to sharpen the predictions of PLeASES. Another goal was to sharpen and evaluate the model by formalizing and testing it in computational simulations using the above parameters to improve realism. A third goal has been to test behavioral predictions of PLeASES in a longitudinal study of infants. A fourth goal, more recently, has been to approach the mechanisms predicted by the PLeASES model using physiological studies of infants engaged in social interactions.

Summary

PLeASES explains the emergence of attention-sharing skills in terms of dynamically interacting biological, sensorimotor, and ecological factors.

It has undergone initial testing through behavioral and physiological experiments, dense ethnographic studies, and computational simulations. Some preliminary findings are summarized next.

TESTING THE PLeASES MODEL: INITIAL RESULTS

Learning: What Do Infants Value?

One goal is to replace assumptions about what infants find rewarding with empirical evidence. Without knowing what infants enjoy in social events, we cannot falsify TD-RL models. Our first test was a cross-sectional microethnographic study of 32 infants ages 3 to 11 months playing at home with caregivers (Deák, Krasno, Triesch, Lewis, & Sepeda, 2012). Initially, we expected infants to mostly fixate on caregivers' faces (it was commonly assumed that infants' favorite sight is their mother's face!). Then, when parents looked away, infants would eventually become bored and look elsewhere—fairly often, this would match where the parent was looking and would bring another fairly interesting target (e.g., toy) into view. Such sequences would gradually yield gaze following.

This neat story was not completely correct, but the real story is intriguing and provocative. First, although parents' faces are somewhat interesting to infants, they are not nearly as interesting as parents' hands manipulating objects. When parents were holding and moving things, infants of every age spent over 60% of total looking time, on average, watching adults' object handling. Considering the range of things that infants might look at when playing at home, this is a remarkably strong preference.

Figure 9.3 shows the proportion of total time infants spent looking at three sights: the parent's face, objects held by parents, or nonheld (static) objects. This graph includes the times when parents held nothing, so it underrepresents the robustness of infants' interest in watching object manipulation. These data belie the common assumption that infants most enjoy watching a parent's face (see also Smith et al., 2011). What, then, about the parents? Quite unlike infants, they spent most of the time looking at the infant's face. These facts, taken together, raise a puzzling question: If infants mostly watch objects, and parents mostly watch infants, how do infants ever learn gaze following?

What Is the Learning Signal?

The answer lies in the margins—that is, in moments when infants do look at the parent and the parent happens to be looking away from the infant.

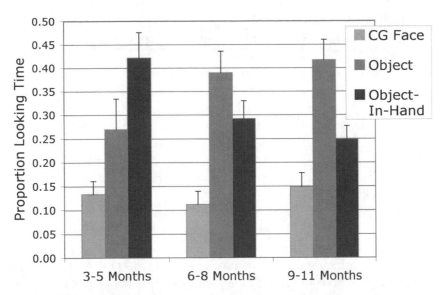

Figure 9.3. Infants' preferences for the caregiver's (CG's) face, objects held by the CG, and objects not held by the CG (e.g., sitting on highchair tray). Data are taken from a study of 35 infants ages 3 to 11 months, videotaped with their parents during a casual object play episode. Videos were coded frame by frame for gaze directions, manual actions, object kinds and locations, and speech and nonspeech sounds.

At those times, parents tend to look at their hands (Land, Mennie, & Rusted, 1999), and infants have an opportunity to see a parent looking toward their favorite sight (i.e., manipulating an object). If they do then turn from the parent's face to that sight, they receive a reward signal that would be temporally linked to a state of the environment that includes the adult's head pose. However, infants might instead see the parent's head (pointed to their hands), then look in another direction where they could see another, moderately rewarding stimulus, such as another toy (Krasno et al., 2007). This would provide misleading input for gaze following, because the infant would receive a reward signal for associating the parent's head pose with an unrelated location. Yet the scenario is plausible, especially in cluttered environments like homes. Critically, if such sequences occur as often as valid training sequences (i.e., seeing the parent's face, then high-value targets where the parent is also looking), then the learning component of the PLeASES would be disconfirmed. Thus, it was critical to determine where infants look just after they see the parent looking somewhere.

By virtue of having a large corpus of data coded frame by frame for gaze direction and gaze targets of mothers and infants, as well as manual actions of parents, we could verify that infants experience more of the former, teaching events than the latter, misleading events. This is true even with 3- to

5-month-olds, who cannot yet follow gaze, which means that infants receive a necessary training signal for RL in the form of structured events that are contingent on their actions. These results are captured in Figure 9.4: The left bar shows the mean rate of occurrences when infants turned from the mother's face to fixate in the same location where she was looking and manipulating an object. The right bar shows the mean rate of misleading events, when infants turned to a different location than the parent but nonetheless saw a toy (i.e., visual reward) there. This shows that infants were rewarded more often by looking in the same direction as an adult than by looking in another direction. This proves a necessary condition for a reinforcement learning process to yield gaze following.

These data also illustrate how social ecological data can establish the operating conditions for the development of a skill. Here, showing that infants like to look at adults' object handling not only disproved a common assumption (i.e., that infants most enjoy looking at faces) but also established what sort of events would serve as rewarding sights. Further, showing that

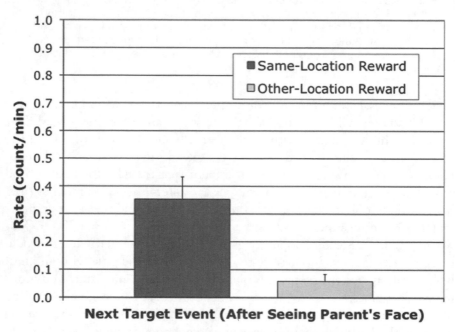

Next Target Event (After Seeing Parent's Face)

Figure 9.4. In the cross-sectional study, after (uncommon instances of) looking at the parent's face, infants were more likely to turn in the same direction as the parent's gaze and see a preferred (i.e., rewarded) sight than to turn in a different direction and see a rewarding sight in that other location. Typically the same-location "reward" was the parent manipulating an object (while looking at it), and the other-location reward was a static object. Thus, infants obtained a larger reward for turning in the same direction as the parent's gaze more often than they obtained a smaller reward for turning in a different direction.

infants are more likely to look toward their favorite sight after seeing the parent turned in that direction illustrates, for the first time in the infancy literature, that in the margins of everyday events, the social environment provides a statistically reliable, if weak, teaching signal.

As converging evidence that gaze following is an incidentally learned policy that has a modest profile, we queried the database for "pure" gaze following events—that is, when the infant saw the parent looking toward the region of a stationary toy and then turned to that same region. These events were quite rare, even among the oldest infants. This finding extends Deák et al.'s (2008) experimental finding that "pure" gaze following rarely occurs in face-to-face interactions within cluttered or distracting environments. Of course, older infants can follow gaze in stark experimental settings (Butterworth & Jarrett, 1991; Deák et al., 2000). This paradox has a possible solution in the previous results: Even if infants gradually learn gaze following via reinforcement learning, gaze following might almost never occur in situ because it is not needed. Parents do not usually sit on their hands, so to speak: They do things and often look at what they are doing. Infants might passively learn associations between parents' head poses and locations but respond to stronger cues and preferences in everyday settings. However, in the bizarre, stark laboratory setting, with none of the cues or rewards of an adult's manual actions or interesting toys, the most salient remaining source of information is the parent's head. In this low-stakes, low-conflict setting, infants can use their implicitly learned associations between head poses and location to select actions and look toward anything of marginal interest. In support of this explanation, Deák et al. (2008) found that infants in a stripped-down testing setting were more likely to follow gaze to interesting, distinctive targets than to boring, repetitive targets. One explanation is that when the few available targets were marginally more rewarding, the adult's gaze cue was marginally more valid, and infants learned to expect more reward for gaze following.

How Does the Social Environment Structure Attention Sharing?

A final analysis of the naturalistic data set stems from the question, If gaze following is nearly absent in naturalistic infant–parent interactions, how do attention-sharing episodes emerge? To determine this, we did a transitional state space analysis of dyadic states. These states include three characterized by coordinated attention: mutual gaze (State 1), shared attention (infant following parent; State 2), shared attention (parent following infant; State 3); they also include three states of uncoordinated attention: parent looking at infant but infant looking away (State 4), infant looking at parent but parent looking away (State 5), and each looking at different things (State 6).

Figure 9.5 schematizes the one-back transitions among these states. The frequency of each state is proportional to circle size. Line thickness is proportional to the number of transitions between states. Deviations from expected frequencies (based on marginal frequencies) are indicated by arrowheads (i.e., more than expected) or inhibition markers (i.e., fewer than expected). The results were surprising: We had expected that attention-sharing states would follow a canonical sequence: After a period of mutual gaze (State 1), one partner would turn away (State 4 or 5), and eventually the other part-

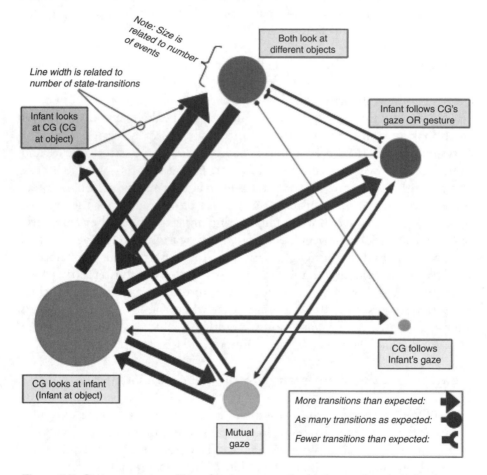

Figure 9.5. State-space transitions from cross-sectional observational study of 35 infants. Arrow thickness is proportional to frequency of successive state transitions. Note that states in which the caregiver (CG) is looking at the infant and the infant is looking at something else is a common "pivot" state leading either to shared attention (usually by infant looking at something the CG is manipulating or gesturing toward) or to both looking at different objects. Arrowheads indicate more transitions than expected given marginal expected frequencies; inhibition symbols indicate fewer transitions than expected.

ner would turn to explore the same location, thereby establishing shared attention (State 2 or 3). However, as can be seen in Figure 9.5, mutual gaze (State 1) was uncommon and seldom proceeded in the expected sequence; in fact, only 0.7% of all three-step sequences followed that template. Rather, usually the infant looked away, and the parent kept watching the infant.

More commonly, shared attention was preceded by the parent's manual bid for the infant's attention: The parent kept watching the infant, primarily, and picked up a toy to play with. (It was in these moments when the parent sometimes looked to the object and the infant was set up to receive face-pose input, as explained previously.) Somewhat less often, infant and parent were looking at different things, then the infant shifted directly to the parent's target (usually because the parent was manipulating it). No one, including us, had predicted that these are the event sequences that set the stage for infant–parent attention sharing. However, two other data sets have shown some consistent phenomena (Amano, Kezuka, & Yamamoto, 2004; Smith et al., 2011).

Can the PLeASES Theory Explain These Results?

In our early computational experiments, we did not know about infants' propensity to watch parents' object handling, and the simulations were not designed to test whether such patterns would emerge from a theoretical test of PLeASES. More recently, however, Lewis, Deák, Jasso, and Triesch (2010) used a 3D environment with a physics model in which a virtual infant-agent learned from a simulated parent. The parent was embodied as an anthropomorphic avatar (see Figure 9.6A), and targets were digitized images of multiple well-rendered toys in a furnished room, so the input was more visually realistic than in prior simulations. The infant-agent had TD-RL/habituation learning processes and biologically inspired visual processes (from the OpenCV computer vision library) that simulated a visual field with salience maps for contrast, color, and motion (see Itti & Koch, 2001). The visual field was converted to a multidimensional probability map, which tended to feature regions of salience around the caregiver and objects (Figure 9.6B). However, the presence of multiple toys and furnishings added clutter, or competing regions of salience, to simulate the effects of clutter on infants' attention following (Deák et al., 2008). The visual routines allowed rough discrimination of the parent-avatar's head poses, but specific knowledge of gaze direction was not given. Head poses might define different representational states in the infant-agent, but the infant-agent might not learn to associate the poses with locations in space.

A great advantage of this testing environment is that the parent-avatar could behave more realistically. Lewis et al. (2010) had the parent-avatar

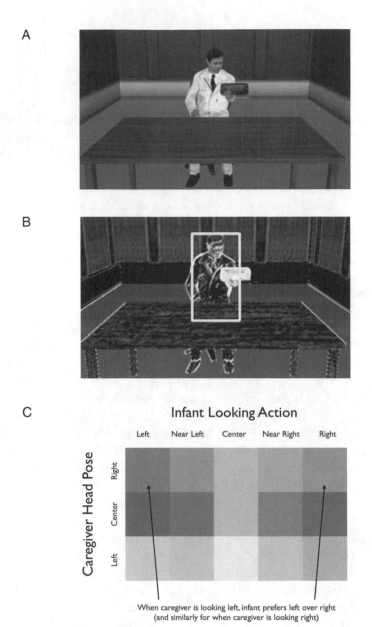

Figure 9.6. Scenes and results from the MESA (Modeling the Emergence of Shared Attention) Project stage simulation environment. The caregiver replicates sequences of actions by "real" caregivers in naturalistic play with their infants. An infant learning agent carries out PLeASES (*P*erceptual routines, *Le*arning mechanisms, *A*ffective traits, *S*ocial *E*cology *S*tructures) temporal difference reinforcement learning (TD-RL) and habituation learning on the dynamic scene. A: Full-vision snapshot of the infant's visual field, with caregiver holding a high-contrast object. B: Weighted multidimensional saliency map calculated by the infant from that frame. C: Results from a pilot simulation (see text). Note that the original animations were in color, and color contrast was included in the OpenCV generated salience maps.

produce series of actions from our frame-by-frame records of real parents' actions during the naturalistic home play sessions (Krasno et al., 2007). Although the parent-avatar did not respond to the infant-agent, it produced strings of simplified actions—looking at things and picking up, moving, and putting down toys—with the same timing, order, and locations as real parents. Of course, real parents produce many more, and much richer, actions, and the simulation leaves out many potentially important details. Nonetheless, it was a first step toward an ecologically nonarbitrary test of theory-driven predictions about infants' social learning and behaviors.

Initial results were promising: Within a reasonable number of time steps, the infant-agent learned to "predict" greater future reward for looking left when the parent-avatar looked left and for looking right when the parent-avatar looked right. This is shown in Figure 9.6C, in which lighter squares indicate a stronger reward prediction. It also generated a high expected value of locations at the center of the visual field, where the parent-avatar was located, as well as of objects held by the parent-avatar. Thus, the infant-agent learned first that its parent was interesting to look at and later learned that the parent's head angle was predictive of the location (at least, left or right) of other interesting sights.

This result supports, broadly, the plausibility of the PLeASES model. An agent with no prior knowledge about head poses acquired rudimentary differentiation of, and responsiveness to, head and eye angles given a fairly sparse and weak set of very general perceptual, learning, and affective traits within an adult-structured, cluttered environment.

IMPLICATIONS OF A NEUROCONSTRUCTIVIST ACCOUNT

Microbehavioral ethnographic studies might give us insight into the social happenings of the real world, and computational simulations might establish the plausibility of a process model. However, PLeASES must also be biologically plausible. The facts of developmental neurobiology and systems neuroscience, as far as they are known, must constrain all predictions concerning infants' processes of learning, perception, action, and affect in social settings.

What sorts of neural computations and representations might be required for gaze following? We know that humans represent both head angles and eye directions (Hooker et al., 2003). We know that locations in space become associated with one's own actions, including head turns (e.g., Brotchie, Anderson, Snyder, & Goodman, 1995). We also can infer that vectors of perceived gaze direction in space are used to generate corresponding gaze shifting actions that will create an intersection of gaze. However, this mapping cannot be represented simply as a "look-up table" (i.e., simple matrix) that relates each (observed) head angle to some "setting" for one's own neck and eye muscles. The intersection of gaze vectors depends on the distances, locations, and relative headings of the infant and the adult. Gaze following thus requires the integration of information about the other person's head (and eye) angles, the infant's own visual and proprioceptive information, the infant's representation of his or her own and others' relative locations in an allocentric space, and possibly the layout and contents of the environment. Any theory must provide a plausible and detailed neurological account of how these spatial and perceptual–motor representations and routines can be learned so that they are reliably generated during social interactions. What, then, is known about the neural bases of these neural representations?

In most studies of adults' hemodynamic responses to head and eye direction, activation is observed in several regions: posterior superior temporal sulcus (pSTS; e.g., Hooker et al., 2003), bilateral fusiform gyrus (FFG; George, Driver, & Dolan, 2001), and—especially in encoding direct versus averted gaze—amygdala (e.g., George et al., 2001). The converging evidence on activation of these areas might indicate a cortical and subcortical system that develops fairly efficient encoding of gaze and head direction cues (and perhaps other directional social cues like pointing; Macaluso, Driver, & Frith, 2003), even within a broader, multipurpose face processing network.

There is also evidence that the network that processes gaze information interacts with reward-computing networks: Kampe, Frith, Dolan, and Frith (2001) found that bilateral striatal responses to direct versus averted gaze were modulated by attractiveness of the stimulus face (see also Calder et al., 2002). Thus, perceived gaze direction impacts the reward values of outcomes (Schultz et al., 1997), which is consistent with PLeASES.

It is also noteworthy that encoded gaze direction activates not just the pSTS and FFG but also parts of intraparietal sulcus (IPS; e.g., Hoffman & Haxby, 2000). This finding is deemphasized, possibly due to a methodological artifact: Functional magnetic resonance imaging (fMRI) studies have almost always used disembodied, 2D face images that are static, canonical, repetitive, and cue invalid (e.g., there is no gaze target). Such stimuli and contexts are least likely to activate spatial maps. Yet even in these unnatural fMRI environments, Pelphrey, Singerman, Allison, and McCarthy (2003) found that IPS activation varied with whether or not a floating visual target matched a disembodied head's eye direction. It was also modulated by the latency of the perceived gaze shift: Perhaps, as subjects' attention to the target declined—that is, as they habituated—activation of that region of spatial maps also declined. This is what PLeASES would predict. Furthermore, and also consistent with the theory, one function of the FEF–IPS loop is to relate spatial cues to spatial maps for purposes of action planning (e.g., Andersen & Cui, 2009).

Interestingly, the parietal-prefrontal network that does saccade planning using, among other information, directional social cues also is subject to reinforcement learning. Campos, Breznen, Bernheim, and Andersen (2005) found that regions within the supplemental motor area compute expected reward related to gaze shifts. In light of the evidence reviewed above, this suggests that as adults, we have learned to relate social cues (e.g., direct vs. averted gaze) to gaze-shifting actions and to expect temporally discounted reward outcomes for those actions. This is exactly the prediction of PLeASES. Triesch et al. (2007) further explored the prediction in another simulation of gaze following acquisition and yielded a striking result: Through training, motor-planning units came to "mirror" location-specific units that corresponded to the eye and head direction input. That is, as the infant-agent learned to map caregiver head and eye angles to locations in allocentric space, location-sensitive processing units became coactivated by motor commands that shifted attention toward those same locations.

Such coactivated units fit the definition of mirror neurons (Rizzolatti & Craighero, 2004). Thus, the model predicts the existence of cells tuned for gaze following with mirror neuron properties (Triesch et al., 2007). Although at that time there was no evidence relevant to this prediction, Shepherd, Klein, Deaner, and Platt (2009) subsequently found cells that respond to both perceived gaze direction and saccade planning cells in macaque lateral intraparietal cortex. These are putative mirror cells for gaze direction. Although we cannot generalize from adult captive macaques to human infants, the converging evidence suggests a biologically plausible mechanism for the emergence of gaze following. The simulation result has a broader implication: The recent abundance of research and theory on the mirror neuron system has barely addressed how mirroring properties develop. Triesch et al.'s (2007) simulation, and the PLeASES theoretical framework, suggest one account. An expansive model by Grossberg and Vladusich (2010) offers another account. Both models share the goal of going beyond describing how mirror systems work to explain how they come to be.

FURTHER TESTS OF BEHAVIOR, PHYSIOLOGY, AND ECOLOGY OF ATTENTION SHARING

In a neuroconstructivist, embodied model like PLeASES, some early parameters will affect the trajectory of later-emerging behavioral phenotypes. For example, in any system that uses reinforcement learning, the prior values of various outcomes can affect learning and action selection. For example, preferred (i.e., higher valued) stimuli are more likely to be foci of attention. If those stimuli are related to some selective action, the preference can affect skill learning. For example, in simulations, we varied the prior reward values of various stimuli for different infant-agents: The stimuli included the caregiver's face and objects. At the extremes, unbalanced values led to disordered joint attention. That is, autistic-looking gaze patterns were obtained by making the caregiver's face unrewarding; conversely, making faces too rewarding caused hypersociable gaze patterns reminiscent of Williams syndrome (Triesch et al., 2006, 2007). These results are evocative, but they point to just one possible phenotype among a range of phenotypic variations within each of these diverse disorders. A more theoretically powerful question is whether individual infants' preferences (i.e., comparative reward values) for different stimuli could affect their acquisition of joint attention skills. However, we found surprisingly little evidence on the stability and variability of infants' preferences for, for example, faces and toys. Do these preferences vary across individual infants? Do these preferences modulate the emergence of social routines such as gaze following? Perhaps, for example, infants who are less attracted to faces require more time to learn to map observed gaze directions onto their own saccades. We had hints that infants might show large individual differences in preferences for faces and objects: Infants in our ethnographic study (Krasno et al., 2007) spent an average of 12.8% of their time looking at their mother's face; however, across infants this ranged from 3% to 36% of time. Might these preferences predict how quickly an infant learns to discriminate gaze directions?

To address this, Robledo, Deák, and Kolling (2010) examined infants' sustained interest in photographs of faces and in colorful toys. This was tested every month and related to later gaze following skill. Interest in novel faces (i.e., total looking time) was moderately stable from 6 to 9 months (mean intermonth association $r_{mean} = .39$). By contrast, attentiveness to toys was not stable. Also, infants' sustained interest in faces was weakly related to later gaze following: Recovery of interest in a novel face at 6, 8, and 9 months was correlated with gaze following from a controlled laboratory task at 9 months of age ($rs_{partials}$ .30–.46), even with looking time to novel toys partialled out (to control for attentiveness or processing speed). Thus, interest in faces seems to be a modest predictor of gaze following in typically developing infants.

AFFECTIVE DISPOSITIONS

The PLeASES model implies that the tendency to shift gaze at any moment is influenced by visual salience, the results of past action outcomes, and related predictive cues within structured environments. However, in reinforcement learning models, a parameter called *temperature* also matters. This refers to an agent's disposition to exploit actions that previously yielded high rewards in similar situations versus exploring actions that yielded lower (or no) rewards in the past. Typically, machine-learning simulations have implemented temperature as a static variable. However, biological systems implement temperature as a dynamic variable. In particular, the locus coeruleus (LC), responding to signals from outcome- and expectancy-encoding networks, modulates norepinephrine (NE) expression. In the central nervous system, NE has widespread effects on cortical, cerebellar, and hippocampal targets (see Aston-Jones & Cohen, 2005). Some of these are effects on attention and arousal. LC output can shift between phasic and tonic states. During phasic LC output states, an animal's attention and learning are focused on a specific task or goal, and arousal (i.e., preparedness for action) is moderate. This can be construed as a bias toward *exploitation*. In tonic output states, attention and arousal are more distributed and less focused on a specific task or goal; this is overtly manifested in vigilant behavior and can be construed as a bias toward *exploration*. Notably, tonic (vigilance-biasing) LC states are negatively related to social affiliation, even in infants (Fortunato, Dribin, Granger, & Buss, 2008). Thus, we expect infants to shift gaze frequently and broadly instead of focusing on an adult social partner. In TD-RL models, this increase in "gain" to external stimuli can be represented as an increase in temperature, or a reduction in top-down guidance of attention. The model would therefore predict less cue following when infants are in high LC/NE-tonic states.

De Barbaro et al. (2011) reported evidence from human infants that fits this prediction: Infants in the MESA longitudinal study were, at 6 to 7 months of age, coded frame by frame for four visual behaviors, all related to NE-modulated vigilance in nonhuman mammals and in adult humans. The four behaviors were tightly correlated, indicating that individual infants showed coherent patterns of vigilant behavior. Notably, more-vigilant infants were less attentive to the adult experimenter, who periodically used pointing cues to indicate a distal target. More-vigilant infants did shift attention to the targets but were more compelled by intrinsic properties of the targets than by social cues.

Currently Zavala, de Barbaro, Chiba, and Deák (2010) are examining relations between these vigilance behaviors, social responsiveness, and concentrations of α-amylase, a digestive molecule that is highly correlated with peripheral and central NE levels (Chatterton, Vogelsong, Lu, Ellman, & Hudgens, 1996). Saliva samples were collected from infants in the MESA longitudinal study at 6, 7, and 12 months of age. Levels of α-amylase were assayed from these samples. Preliminary results show that α-amylase levels were stable within sessions and somewhat stable across sessions. Moreover, the levels correlated with some, though not all, vigilance-related behaviors. We are currently analyzing the data to test for relations between joint attention behaviors and α-amylase levels. If so, it would suggest a link between LC-modulated attentiveness and arousal (temperature), and consequent changes in social actions including attention sharing.

CONCLUSION

By understanding the development of infant social attention, we might gain insight into the processes of social development more generally. We might also gain insight into the origins of individual differences including, at the extreme, developmental disabilities (Karmiloff-Smith, 1998). We might even generate ideas for new interventions for the social-behavioral symptoms of disabilities. Only limited progress can be made from within a single discipline. Real progress will depend on integrating disciplines including psychology, neuroscience, artificial intelligence, anthropology and sociology, and others (e.g., linguistics). This is true whether or not the PLeASES theory continues to garner confirmatory data. To be sure, the current version of PLeASES lacks the means to explain later attention sharing outcomes, such as learning verbs of perception (e.g., *see*) or inferring another's visual perspective. These are elements we hope to develop in future work (e.g., Jao, Robledo, & Deák, 2010).

Our efforts so far have used computational simulations for proofs of the sufficiency of a theory and for greater specification of the theory. We stress that simulations are useful only insofar as they are biologically valid and insofar as the input structure is true to a "real" learning environment. Our efforts also make extensive use of microbehavioral and naturalistic behavioral evidence. Without that, we cannot know whether the behavioral output of the system is similar to real infants. Theory building and theory testing must be grounded in the structures and exigencies of real behavior in real environments. Qualitative, rough-coded ethnographic records are good sources of ideas but are inadequate for process models. Social actions occur within temporal intervals as short as 10 ms, so naturalistic social interactions should be coded at sampling rates that approach that granularity.

The goal of the PLeASES theory is to use the most relevant biological, cognitive, ecological, and microbehavioral information to explain how infants acquire new attention-sharing skills. It starts with a set of precursor phenotypes that we proposed as the minimum necessary for attention sharing behaviors to emerge, given a regimen of parent-provided social ecological structures. The precursor phenotypes are clearly demonstrable in young infants; no further special-purpose modules are proposed.

In tests of the PLeASES theory so far, we have discovered unknown phenomena. These include, for example, the fact that infants prefer to watch adults manipulate objects and the role of this preference in indirect learning of gaze following responses. We also found that individual infants' sustained attentiveness to faces is a modest predictor of gaze following skills. Both of these findings are supported by simulations that implement the PLeASES model in an infant-agent. We have also extended the reinforcement learning aspect of the model to examine the temperature parameter, operationalized as the behavioral consequences of LC modulation of NE levels. Our results underscore the importance of this mechanism and its relevance to infants' attentiveness to social cues. Finally, our simulations have made novel predictions, such as the emergence of gaze following mirror neurons. Ongoing research is testing other predictions of the PLeASES model and exploring new questions that will flesh out the details of PLeASES. We believe that our approach is a model of the application of interdisciplinary concepts and methods to generate and test 21st-century theories of behavioral and cognitive development.

REFERENCES

Amano, S., Kezuka, E., & Yamamoto, A. (2004). Infant shifting attention from an adult's face to an adult's hand: A precursor of joint attention. *Infant Behavior & Development, 27*, 64–80. doi:10.1016/j.infbeh.2003.06.005

Andersen, R. A., & Cui, H. (2009). Intention, action planning, and decision making in parietal-frontal circuits. *Neuron, 63*, 568–583. doi:10.1016/j.neuron.2009.08.028

Aston-Jones, G., & Cohen, J. D. (2005). An integrative theory of locus coeruleus–norepinephrine function: Adaptive gain and optimal performance. *Annual Review of Neuroscience, 28*, 403–450. doi:10.1146/annurev.neuro.28.061604.135709

Bakeman, R., & Adamson, L. B. (1984). Coordinating attention to people and objects in mother–infant and peer–infant interaction. *Child Development, 55*, 1278–1289. doi:10.2307/1129997

Baldwin, D. A. (1993). Infants' ability to consult the speaker for clues to word reference. *Journal of Child Language, 20*, 395–418. doi:10.1017/S0305000900008345

Baron-Cohen, S. (1995). The eye direction detector (EDD) and the shared attention mechanism (SAM): Two cases for evolutionary psychology. In C. Moore & P. Dunham (Eds.), *Joint attention: Its origins and role in development* (pp. 41–59). Hillsdale, NJ: Erlbaum.

Bigelow, A. E., & Birch, S. A. (1999). The effects of contingency in previous interactions on infants' preference for social partners. *Infant Behavior & Development, 22*, 367–382. doi:10.1016/S0163-6383(99)00016-8

Brand, R., Baldwin, D., & Ashburn, L. (2002). Evidence for "motionese": Modifications in mothers' infant-directed action. *Developmental Science, 5*, 72–83. doi:10.1111/1467-7687.00211

Brotchie, P. R., Anderson, R. A., Snyder, L. H., & Goodman, S. J. (1995, May 18). Head position signals used by parietal neurons to encode locations of visual stimuli. *Nature, 375,* 232–235. doi:10.1038/375232a0

Butcher, P. R., Kalverboer, A. f., & Geuze, R. H. (2000). Infants' shifts of gaze from a central to a peripheral stimulus: A longitudinal study of development between 6 and 26 weeks. *Infant Behavior & Development, 23,* 3–21. doi:10.1016/S0163-6383(00)00031-X

Butler, S. C., Caron, A. J., & Brooks, R. (2000). Infant understanding of the referential nature of looking. *Journal of Cognition and Development, 1,* 359–377. doi:10.1207/S15327647JCD0104_01

Butterworth, G., & Itakura, S. (2000). How the eyes, head and hand serve definite reference. *British Journal of Developmental Psychology, 18,* 25–50. doi:10.1348/026151000165553

Butterworth, G. E., & Cochran, E. (1980). Towards a mechanism of joint visual attention in human infancy. *International Journal of Behavioral Development, 3,* 253–272.

Butterworth, G. E., & Jarrett, N. L. (1991). What minds have in common is space: Spatial mechanisms serving joint visual attention in infancy. *British Journal of Developmental Psychology, 9,* 55–72. doi:10.1111/j.2044-835X.1991.tb00862.x

Calder, A. J., Lawrence, A. D., Keane, J., Scott, S. K., Owen, A. M., Christoffels, I., & Young, A. W. (2002). Reading the mind from eye gaze. *Neuropsychologia, 40,* 1129–1138. doi:10.1016/S0028-3932(02)00008-8

Cameron, N. M., Champagne, F. A., Parent, C., Fish, E. W., Ozaki-Kuroda, K., & Meaney, M. J. (2005). The programming of individual differences in defensive responses and reproductive strategies in the rat through variations in maternal care. *Neuroscience and Biobehavioral Reviews, 29,* 843–865. doi:10.1016/j.neubiorev.2005.03.022

Campos, M., Breznen, B., Bernheim, K., & Andersen, R. A. (2005). The supplementary motor area encodes reward expectancy in eye movement tasks. *Journal of Neurophysiology, 94,* 1325–1335. doi:10.1152/jn.00022.2005

Cangelosi, A., Metta, G., Sagerer, G., Nehaniv, C., Fischer, K., Tani, J., . . . Zeschel, A. (2010). Integration of action and language knowledge: A roadmap for developmental robotics. *IEEE Transactions on Autonomous Mental Development, 2,* 167–195. doi:10.1109/TAMD.2010.2053034

Chatterton, R. T., Jr., Vogelsong, K. M., Lu, Y. C., Ellman, A. B., & Hudgens, G. A. (1996). Salivary alpha-amylase as a measure of endogenous adrenergic activity. *Clinical Physiology, 16,* 433–448. doi:10.1111/j.1475-097X.1996.tb00731.x

Cohn, J. F., Matias, R., Tronick, E. Z., Connell, D., & Lyons-Ruth, K. (1986). Face-to-face interactions of depressed mothers and their infants. *New Directions for Child and Adolescent Development, 1986,* 31–45. doi:10.1002/cd.23219863405

Colombo, J., Mitchell, D. W., O'Brien, M., & Horowitz, F. D. (1987). The stability of visual habituation during the first year of life. *Child Development, 58,* 474–487. doi:10.2307/1130524

Deák, G. O., Bartlett, M. S., & Jebara, T. (2007). How social agents develop: New trends in integrative theory-building. *Neurocomputing, 70*, 2139–2147.

Deák, G. O., Fasel, I., & Movellan, J. R. (2001). The emergence of shared attention: Using robots to test developmental theories. In C. Balkenius, J. Zlatev, H. Kozima, K. Dautenhahn, & C. Breazeal (Eds.), *Proceedings of the 1st International Workshop on Epigenetic Robotics: Modeling cognitive development in robotic systems* (Lund University Cognitive Studies Vol. 85, pp. 95–104). Lund, Sweden: Lund University Cognitive Science.

Deák, G. O., Flom, R., & Pick, A. D. (2000). Effects of gesture and target on 12- and 18-month-olds' joint visual attention to objects in front of or behind them. *Developmental Psychology, 36*, 511–523. doi:10.1037/0012-1649.36.4.511

Deák, G. O., Krasno, A., Triesch, J., Lewis, J., & Sepeda, L. (2012). *Watch the hands: Human infants can learn gaze-following by watching their parents handle objects.* Manuscript submitted for publication.

Deák, G. O., & Triesch, J. (2006). The emergence of attention-sharing skills in human infants. In K. Fujita & S. Itakura (Eds.), *Diversity of cognition* (pp. 331–363). Kyoto, Japan: University of Kyoto Press.

Deák, G., Wakabayashi, Y., Jasso, H., & Triesch, J. (2004, October). *Attention-sharing in human infants from 3 to 11 months of age in naturalistic conditions.* Paper presented at the 3rd International Conference on Development and Learning, La Jolla, CA.

Deák, G. O., Walden, T. A., Yale, M., & Lewis, A. (2008). Driven from distraction: How infants respond to parents' attempts to elicit and re-direct their attention. *Infant Behavior & Development, 31*, 34–50. doi:10.1016/j.infbeh.2007.06.004

de Barbaro, K., Chiba, A., & Deák, G. O. (2011). Micro-analysis of infant looking in a naturalistic social setting: Insights from biologically based models of attention. *Developmental Science, 14*, 1150–1160. doi:10.1111/j.1467-7687.2011.01066.x

DeCasper, A. J., & Fifer, W. P. (1980, June 6). Of human bonding: Newborns prefer their mothers' voices. *Science, 208*, 1174–1176. doi:10.1126/science.7375928

Desrochers, S., Morissette, P., & Ricard, M. (1995). Two perspectives on pointing in infancy. In C. Moore & P. Dunham (Eds.), *Joint attention: Its origins and role in development* (pp. 85–101). Hillsdale, NJ: Erlbaum.

Doherty, M. J. (2006). The development of mentalistic gaze understanding. *Infant and Child Development, 15*, 179–186. doi:10.1002/icd.434

Ellis, E., Robledo, M., & Deák, G. O. (2012). *Visual prediction in infancy: Does it predict later vocabulary?* Manuscript submitted for publication.

Farroni, T., Johnson, M. H., Brockbank, M., & Simion, F. (2000). Infants' use of gaze direction to cue attention: The importance of perceived motion. *Visual Cognition, 7*, 705–718. doi:10.1080/13506280050144399

Farroni, T., Johnson, M. H., & Csibra, G. (2004). Mechanisms of eye gaze perception during infancy. *Journal of Cognitive Neuroscience, 16*, 1320–1326. doi:10.1162/0898929042304787

Farroni, T., Massaccesi, S., Pividori, D., & Johnson, M. (2004). Gaze following in newborns. *Infancy, 5,* 39–60. doi:10.1207/s15327078in0501_2

Fasel, I., Deák, G. O., Triesch, J., & Movellan, J. (2002). Combining embodied models and empirical research for understanding the development of shared attention. *Proceedings of the International Conference on Development and Learning, 2,* 21–27.

Fernald, A., & Kuhl, P. K. (1987). Acoustic determinants of infant preference for motherese speech. *Infant Behavior & Development, 10,* 279–293. doi:10.1016/0163-6383(87)90017-8

Field, T., Healy, B., Goldstein, S., & Guthertz, M. (1990). Behavior-state matching and synchrony in infant–mother interactions of nondepressed versus depressed dyads. *Developmental Psychology, 26,* 7–14. doi:10.1037/0012-1649.26.1.7

Field, T. M. (1981). Infant gaze aversion and heart rate during face-to-face interaction. *Infant Behavior & Development, 4,* 307–315. doi:10.1016/S0163-6383(81)80032-X

Field, T. M., Cohen, D., Garcia, R., & Greenberg, R. (1984). Mother–stranger face discrimination by the newborn. *Infant Behavior & Development, 7,* 19–25. doi:10.1016/S0163-6383(84)80019-3

Flom, R., Deák, G. O., Phill, C., & Pick, A. D. (2004). Nine-month-olds' shared visual attention as a function of gesture and object location. *Infant Behavior & Development, 27,* 181–194. doi:10.1016/j.infbeh.2003.09.007

Fortunato, C. K., Dribin, A. E., Granger, D. A., & Buss, K. A. (2008). Salivary alpha-amylase and cortisol in toddlers: Differential relations to affective behavior. *Developmental Psychobiology, 50,* 807–818. doi:10.1002/dev.20326

George, N., Driver, J., & Dolan, R. J. (2001). Seen gaze-direction modulates fusiform activity and its coupling with other brain areas during face processing. *NeuroImage, 13,* 1102–1112. doi:10.1006/nimg.2001.0769

Goldstein, M. H., Waterfall, H. R., Lotem, A., Halpern, J. Y., Schwade, J. A., Onnis, L., & Edelman, S. (2010). General cognitive principles for learning structure in time and space. *Trends in Cognitive Sciences, 14,* 249–258. doi:10.1016/j.tics.2010.02.004

Grossberg, S., & Vladusich, T. (2010). How do children learn to follow gaze, share joint attention, imitate their teachers, and use tools during social interactions? *Neural Networks, 23,* 940–965. doi:10.1016/j.neunet.2010.07.011

Haith, M. M., Hazan, C., & Goodman, G. S. (1988). Expectation and anticipation of dynamic visual events by 3.5-month-old babies. *Child Development, 59,* 467–479. doi:10.2307/1130325

Hoffman, E. A., & Haxby, J. V. (2000). Distinct representations of eye gaze and identity in the distributed human neural system for face perception. *Nature Neuroscience, 3,* 80–84. doi:10.1038/71152

Hood, B. M., Willen, J. D., & Driver, J. (1998). Adult's eyes trigger shifts of visual attention in human infants. *Psychological Science, 9,* 131–134. doi:10.1111/1467-9280.00024

Hooker, C. I., Paller, K. A., Gitelman, D. R., Parrish, T. B., Mesulam, M. M., & Reber, P. J. (2003). Brain networks for analyzing eye gaze. *Cognitive Brain Research, 17*, 406–418. doi:10.1016/S0926-6410(03)00143-5

Itti, L., & Koch, C. (2001). Computational modeling of visual attention. *Nature Reviews Neuroscience, 2*, 194–203. doi:10.1038/35058500

Jao, R. J., Robledo, M., & Deák, G. O. (2010). The emergence of referential gaze and perspective-taking in infants. In *Proceedings of the 32nd Annual Conference of the Cognitive Science Society* (pp. 284–289). Austin, TX: Cognitive Science Society.

Johnson, M. K., Posner, M. I., & Rothbart, M. K. (1994). Facilitation of saccades toward a covertly attended location in early infancy. *Psychological Science, 5*, 90–93. doi:10.1111/j.1467-9280.1994.tb00636.x

Kampe, K. K. W., Frith, C. D., Dolan, R. J., & Frith, U. (2001, October 11). Reward value of attractiveness and gaze. *Nature, 413*, 589–590. doi:10.1038/35098149

Karmiloff-Smith, A. (1998). Development itself is the key to understanding developmental disorders. *Trends in Cognitive Sciences, 2*, 389–398. doi:10.1016/S1364-6613(98)01230-3

Kaye, K. (1982). *The mental and social life of babies.* Chicago, IL: University of Chicago Press.

Krasno, A., Deák, G., Triesch, J., & Jasso, H. (2007, April). *Watch the hands: Do infants learn gaze-following from parents' object manipulation?* Paper presented at the meeting of the Society for Research in Child Development, Boston, MA.

Land, M., Mennie, N., & Rusted, J. (1999). Eye movements and the roles of vision in activities of daily living: Making a cup of tea. *Perception, 28*, 1311–1328. doi:10.1068/p2935

Lewis, J., Deák, G. O., Jasso, H., & Triesch, J. (2010). Building a model of infant social interaction. In S. Ohlsson & R. Catrambone (Eds.), *Proceedings of the 32nd Annual Conference of the Cognitive Science Society* (pp. 278–283). Austin, TX: Cognitive Science Society.

Macaluso, E., Driver, J., & Frith, C. D. (2003). Multimodal spatial representations engaged in human parietal cortex during both saccadic and manual spatial orienting. *Current Biology, 13*, 990–999. doi:10.1016/S0960-9822(03)00377-4

Messinger, D. M., Ruvolo, P., Ekas, N. V., & Fogel, A. (2010). Applying machine learning to infant interaction: The development is in the details. *Neural Networks, 23*, 1004–1016. doi:10.1016/j.neunet.2010.08.008

Moore, C. (1996). Theories of mind in infancy. *British Journal of Developmental Psychology, 14*, 19–40. doi:10.1111/j.2044-835X.1996.tb00691.x

Moore, C., Angelopoulos, M., & Bennett, P. (1997). The role of movement in the development of joint visual attention. *Infant Behavior and Development, 20*, 83–92. doi:10.1016/S0163-6383(97)90063-1

Moore, G. A., & Calkins, S. (2004). Infants' vagal regulation in the still-face paradigm is related to dyadic coordination of mother–infant interaction. *Developmental Psychology, 40*, 1068–1080. doi:10.1037/0012-1649.40.6.1068

Morales, M., Mundy, P., & Rojas, J. (1998). Following the direction of gaze and language development in 6-month-olds. *Infant Behavior and Development, 21*, 373–377. doi:10.1016/S0163-6383(98)90014-5

Mundy, P., Sigman, M., & Kasari, C. (1990). A longitudinal study of joint attention and language development in autistic children. *Journal of Autism and Developmental Disorders, 20*, 115–128. doi:10.1007/BF02206861

Nagai, Y., & Rohlfing, K. J. (2009). Computational analysis of motionese toward scaffolding robot action learning. *IEEE Transactions on Autonomous Mental Development, 1*, 44–54. doi:10.1109/TAMD.2009.2021090

O'Neill, D. K. (1996). Two-year-old children's sensitivity to a parent's knowledge state when making requests. *Child Development, 67*, 659–677. doi:10.2307/1131839

Pelphrey, K. A., Singerman, J. D., Allison, T., & McCarthy, G. (2003). Brain activation evoked by perception of gaze shifts: The influence of context. *Neuropsychologia, 41*, 156–170. doi:10.1016/S0028-3932(02)00146-X

Richardson, F., & Thomas, M. S. C. (2006). The benefits of computational modelling for the study of developmental disorders: Extending the Triesch et al. model to ADHD. *Developmental Science, 9*, 151–155. doi:10.1111/j.1467-7687.2006.00473.x

Richert, M., Yu, C., & Favata, A. (2010). Joint attention through the hands: Investigating the timing of object labeling in dyadic social interaction. In *Proceedings of the IEEE 10th International Conference in Development and Learning* (pp. 114–119). Washington, DC: IEEE.

Rizzolatti, G., & Craighero, L. (2004). The mirror-neuron system. *Annual Review of Neuroscience, 27*, 169–192. doi:10.1146/annurev.neuro.27.070203.144230

Robledo, M., Danly, J. D., Acuña, J., Ramundo, A. A., & Deák, G. O. (2009, April). *A longitudinal study of the emergence of attention-sharing in different contexts.* Paper presented at the meeting of the Society for Research in Child Development, Denver, CO.

Robledo, M., Deák, G. O., & Kolling, T. (2010). Infants' visual processing of faces and objects: Age-related changes in interest, and stability of individual differences. In *Proceedings of the 32nd Annual Conference of the Cognitive Science Society* (pp. 2482–2487). Austin, TX: Cognitive Science Society.

Rochat, P. (1989). Object manipulation and exploration in 2- to 5-month-old infants. *Developmental Psychology, 25*, 871–884. doi:10.1037/0012-1649.25.6.871

Rogoff, B. (1990). *Apprenticeship in thinking: Cognitive development in social context.* New York, NY: Oxford University Press.

Rosander, K. (2007). Visual tracking and its relationship to cortical development. *Progress in Brain Research, 164*, 105–123. doi:10.1016/S0079-6123(07)64006-0

Roy, D., Patel, R., DeCamp, P., Kubat, R., Fleischman, M., Roy, B., . . . Gorniak, P. (2006). The Human Speechome project. In *Proceedings of the 28th Annual Meeting of the Cognitive Science Society* (pp. 2059–2064). Wheat Ridge, CO: Cognitive Science Society.

Sai, F., & Bushnell, W. R. (1988). The perception of faces in different poses by 1-month-olds. *British Journal of Developmental Psychology, 6*, 35–41. doi:10.1111/j.2044-835X.1988.tb01078.x

Saxon, T. F., Frick, J. E., & Colombo, J. (1997). A longitudinal study of maternal interactional styles and infant visual attention. *Merrill-Palmer Quarterly, 43*, 48–66.

Schlesinger, M., & Parisi, D. (2001). The agent-based approach: A new direction for computational models of development. *Developmental Review, 21*, 121–146. doi:10.1006/drev.2000.0520

Schultz, W., Dayan, P., & Montague, P. R. (1997, March 14). A neural substrate of prediction and reward. *Science, 275*, 1593–1599. doi:10.1126/science.275.5306.1593

Shepherd, S. V., Klein, J. T., Deaner, R. O., & Platt, M. L. (2009). Mirroring of attention by neurons in macaque parietal cortex. *Proceedings of the National Academy of Sciences of the United States of America, 106*, 9489–9494. doi:10.1073/pnas.0900419106

Simmering, V. R., Spencer, J., Deák, G., & Triesch, J. (2010). To model or not to model? A dialogue on the role of computational modeling in developmental science. *Child Development Perspectives, 4*, 152–158. doi:10.1111/j.1750-8606.2010.00134.x

Singh, S., Jaakkola, T., & Jordan, M. I. (1994). Learning without state-estimation in partially observable Markovian decision processes. In W. W. Cohen & H. Hirsch (Eds.), *Proceedings of the 11th International Conference on Machine Learning*. San Francisco, CA: Morgan Kauffman.

Sirois, S., & Mareschal, D. (2002). Models of habituation in infancy. *Trends in Cognitive Sciences, 6*, 293–298. doi:10.1016/S1364-6613(02)01926-5

Slater, A., Earle, D. C., Morison, V., & Rose, D. (1985). Pattern preferences at birth and their interaction with habituation-induced novelty preferences. *Journal of Experimental Child Psychology, 39*, 37–54. doi:10.1016/0022-0965(85)90028-1

Smith, L. B., Yu, C., & Pereira, A. F. (2011). Not your mother's view: The dynamics of toddler visual experience. *Developmental Science, 14*, 9–17. doi:10.1111/j.1467-7687.2009.00947.x

Spink, A. Grieco, F. Krips, O. Loijens, L. Noldus, L., & Zimmerman, P. (Eds.). (2010). *Proceedings of the 7th International Conference on Methods and Techniques in Behavioral Research*. Eindhoven, the Netherlands: Association for Computing Machinery.

Sroufe, L. A. (1996). *Emotional development: The organization of emotional life in the early years*. Cambridge, England: Cambridge University Press. doi:10.1017/CBO9780511527661

Stern, D. N. (2000). *The interpersonal world of the infant* (rev. ed.). New York, NY: Basic Books.

Strogatz, S. H. (2001). Exploring complex networks. *Nature, 410*, 268–276. doi:10.1038/35065725

Sutton, R. S., & Barto, A. G. (1998). *Reinforcement learning*. Cambridge, MA: MIT Press.

Symons, L. A., Hains, S. M., & Muir, D. W. (1998). Look at me: Five-month-old infants' sensitivity to very small deviations in eye-gaze during social interactions. *Infant Behavior & Development, 21,* 531–536. doi:10.1016/S0163-6383(98)90026-1

Tamis-LeMonda, C. S., & Bornstein, M. H. (1989). Habituation and maternal encouragement of attention in infancy as predictors of toddler language, play, and representational competence. *Child Development, 60,* 738–751. doi:10.2307/1130739

Teuscher, C., & Triesch, J. (2007). To each his own: The caregiver's role in a computational model of gaze following. *Neurocomputing, 70,* 2166–2180. doi:10.1016/j.neucom.2006.02.023

Tomasello, M. (1995). Joint attention as social cognition. In C. Moore & P. Dunham (Eds.), *Joint attention: Its origins and role in development* (pp. 103–130). Mahwah, NJ: Erlbaum.

Tomasello, M. (1999). *The cultural origins of human cognition*. Cambridge, MA: Harvard University Press.

Triesch, J., Jasso, H., & Deák, G. O. (2007). Emergence of mirror neurons in a model of gaze following. *Adaptive Behavior, 15,* 149–165. doi:10.1177/1059712307078654

Triesch, J., Teuscher, C., Deák, G., & Carlson, E. (2006). Gaze-following: Why (not) learn it? *Developmental Science, 9,* 125–147. doi:10.1111/j.1467-7687.2006.00470.x

Venezia, M., Messinger, D. S., Thorp, D., & Mundy, P. (2004). The development of anticipatory smiling. *Infancy, 6,* 397–406. doi:10.1207/s15327078in0603_5

Watson, J. S., & Ramey, C. T. (1972). Reactions to response-contingent stimulation in early infancy. *Merrill-Palmer Quarterly, 18,* 218–227

Wolpert, D. M., Ghahramani, Z., & Flanagan, J. R. (2001). Perspectives and problems in motor learning. *Trends in Cognitive Sciences, 5,* 487–494. doi:10.1016/S1364-6613(00)01773-3

Yu, C., & Ballard, D. H. (2007). A unified model of early word learning: Integrating statistical and social cues. *Neurocomputing, 70,* 2149–2165. doi:10.1016/j.neucom.2006.01.034

Yu, C., & Smith, L. B. (2011). What you learn is what you see: Using eye movements to study infant cross-situational word learning. *Developmental Science, 14,* 165–180.

Zavala, C., de Barbaro, K., Chiba, A., & Deák, G. O. (2010, January). *Does stress influence infant attention patterns over time?* Paper presented at the Temporal Dynamics of Learning Center Meeting, San Diego, CA.

Zukow-Goldring, P., & Arbib, M. A. (2007). Affordances, effectivities, and assisted imitation: Caregivers and the directing of attention. *Neurocomputing, 70,* 2181–2193. doi:10.1016/j.neucom.2006.02.029

10

CULTURE AND COGNITIVE DEVELOPMENT: THE DEVELOPMENT OF GEOCENTRIC LANGUAGE AND COGNITION

RAMESH C. MISHRA AND PIERRE R. DASEN

In this chapter, we examine the role of culture in cognitive development. The focus is on the development of geocentric spatial cognition. We also examine the linkage between language and cognition, a theme that has been fairly controversial in research carried out during past decades. The research presented here is rooted in non-Western cultures, which are not much studied and hence not represented in theories of cognitive development. We summarize the findings of a major research study (see Dasen & Mishra, 2010) that focused on the development of the geocentric spatial frame of reference (FoR). A *geocentric FoR* means using a wide-range orientation system for localizing objects in small-scale space, such as a tabletop, and inside a room as well as outside. Constantly updating one's position in the environment (dead reckoning) and describing a display independently of one's position are some other features of a geocentric FoR.

Developmental studies of spatial cognition have been carried out mainly in the Piagetian tradition, which holds that children build up spatial

DOI: 10.1037/14043-011
Cognition and Brain Development: Converging Evidence From Various Methodologies, B. R. Kar (Editor)

concepts in relation to their own body following the sequence of topological, projective, and Euclidean space (Piaget & Inhelder, 1956). The distinction between these spatial concepts is similar to the distinction established at the linguistic level between object-centered (or intrinsic), viewer-centered (relative or egocentric), and extrinsic or environment-centered (absolute or geocentric) spatial terms. In an *intrinsic* frame, objects' locations are described in relation to each other. In the *relative* frame, objects are described in relation to a viewer's left, right, front, and back (LRFB). In the *absolute* frame, objects are located according to a coordinate system that is external to the scene; knowledge of the viewer's position and orientation in space is not required in this case. Research indicates that different language communities preferentially use different reference frames (Levinson, 1996, 2003).

Although the ability to use geocentric spatial representations varies with age, Western research generally suggests that it occurs only when the child has built up body-related spatial representations. There is some indication that both of these abilities may evolve together and that the choice of a reference frame may be situation dependent rather than a developmental feature (Allen, 2007). However, there is no evidence to suggest a reversal from the sequence originally described by Piaget. Much of the evidence (e.g., Taylor & Tversky, 1996; Werner & Hubel, 1999) supports the theory that spatial representation is basically built up from the point of view of the human body.

Studies on spatial concept development have been carried out largely with Western samples (Mishra, 1997). Researchers have never questioned whether the same sequence of stages of development can be found in other cultures. That individuals construct space on the basis of their body could be a theoretical conceptualization biased by Western individualism. In some cross-cultural studies, the issue has been addressed from the emic and etic points of view (Segall, Dasen, Berry, & Poortinga, 1999). On the emic side are anthropological descriptions that tell us how space is organized in different cultures (e.g., Gladwin, 1970; Hutchins, 1983), but they convey little about developmental aspects. On the etic side is the cross-cultural replication of Piaget's theory using classical Piagetian tasks, research that suggests neither any reversals in the sequence of stages nor indeed any culturally specific cognitive processes (Mishra, 1997). Greenfield (1976) indicated that there could be different developmental pathways, and hence different developmental end stages, but this proposition has never been empirically established. Wassmann and Dasen (1998) noted a reversal in the development of spatial concepts in Bali, a finding that has motivated some of our research in this domain (Dasen & Mishra, 2010; Dasen, Mishra, & Niraula, 2004; Mishra, Dasen, & Niraula, 2003; Niraula, Mishra, & Dasen, 2004).

LINGUISTIC RELATIVISM

Does language determine the way one thinks? Whorf's (1956) hypothesis of linguistic relativity has been revisited in some recent cognitive research (Gumperz & Levinson, 1996; Levinson, 1996, 2003; Lucy, 1997). Cross-cultural research shows not only that basic cognitive processes are universal (Mishra, 1997; Segall et al., 1999), but also that languages themselves seem to follow many universal principles (Holenstein, 1993). A widely held assumption is that the coding of spatial arrays for memory is determined by general properties of visual perception, and hence it should also be natural and universal to conceptualize space from an egocentric or "relative" point of view. Research also indicates that speakers of European languages habitually use egocentric encoding. Thus, it is not surprising that the egocentric conception of space is considered universal and "more natural and primitive" (Miller & Johnson-Laird, 1976, p. 34).

Some researchers (e.g., Wassmann, 1994; Wassmann & Dasen, 1998) have questioned these basic assumptions. In the English language, we generally describe the position of an object or person with respect to another by using the projective notions of right and left in reference to the speaker's body, but there are languages that do not use body-centered spatial notions of right, left, front, and back; they use environment-centered or geocentric frames of reference. Although in a relative frame, the description of an object or person changes depending on one's body position (e.g., left may become right and vice versa); in the geocentric frame, the description does not necessarily change with the change in viewer's position (e.g., north remains north even if the viewer's body position is changed).

This kind of (geocentric) linguistic coding of spatial objects raises a fundamental question regarding the correspondence between linguistic and conceptual differences. We may assume that spatial representations are influenced either by sensory information (which is egocentric) or by language (which may or may not be egocentric). In European languages, which are egocentric, the two are confounded, but there are other languages that use either intrinsic or absolute (geocentric) or mixed frames of reference. It is possible to dissociate these influences by carrying out studies with speakers of these languages.

Working mainly with adults, cognitive anthropologists (e.g., Danziger, 1993; Levinson, 1996, 2003; Pederson, 1993; Pederson et al., 1998) have carried out research in several locations. In language development studies, de León (1994, 1995) found an overall developmental trend that seemed to go from intrinsic terms to locally geocentric and, in some cases, to abstract geocentric terms. Because the populations de León studied did not at all use relative terms (e.g., left and right), this research does not tell us much about the relationship between the egocentric and the geocentric systems. However, this work clearly brings out the need for research in locations where an egocentric system exists in the language but is not the predominant one. These studies also deal only with the development of language; they do not allow us to conclude that cognitive development necessarily has to follow the same sequence of development.

A STUDY OF GEOCENTRIC LANGUAGE AND COGNITION

The study described in this chapter is part of a larger project Dasen and Mishra (2010) carried out at several locations in India, Indonesia, Nepal, and Switzerland. The major research questions addressed are as follows: How does the geocentric FoR develop with age? Is there a link between language and encoding at the individual level? What is the role of culture (e.g., religion, type of schooling, socioeconomic features of groups) in spatial language and cognition?

Our previous research in India and Nepal (Dasen et al., 2004; Mishra et al., 2003; Niraula et al., 2004) provided us with some interesting indications. For example, we found that the geocentric FoR in both language and cognition was used more systematically in rural than in urban settings, and in all samples, it increased with age. Schooling had only a limited impact on its development; for example, in rural Nepal, unschooled children tended to use the geocentric FoR with two sectors (up and down, which is appropriate in a mountain setting), whereas schooled children learned to use the cardinal directions (i.e., north, south, east, and west [NSEW]).

Method

Design and Sample

Children were studied using a combination of observation, interview, testing, and experimentation. In this chapter, we summarize the findings obtained at Varanasi (India) and Kathmandu (Nepal). The details of the samples are given in Table 10.1. At Kathmandu, we had the opportunity to sample 4- to 12-year-old children from English and Nepali medium schools (i.e., where the medium of instruction is English or Nepali). At Varanasi, we sampled slightly older children (10–15 years) from Sanskrit (traditional) and Hindi (modern) medium schools.

An ethnographic survey of the populations in Varanasi indicated that children from Sanskrit schools described space and spatial relationships mainly in geocentric (NSEW) terms, whereas those from Hindi schools used both geocentric and egocentric (LRFB) terms. On the basis of the impact

TABLE 10.1
Sample Characteristics

Location	School type	Age (years)	Gender Boys	Girls	Total
Varanasi	Hindi school	11	9	30	39
(N = 376)		12	26	59	85
		13	9	46	55
		14	5	31	36
		15	0	6	6
		Total	49	172	221
	Sanskrit school	10	2	0	2
		11	6	3	9
		12	35	5	40
		13	49	6	55
		14	30	7	37
		15	3	9	12
		Total	125	30	155
Kathmandu	English school	4	11	11	22
(N = 400)		5	11	11	22
		6	11	11	22
		7	11	11	22
		8	11	10	21
		9	11	12	23
		10	12	11	23
		11	10	13	23
		12	11	11	22
		Total	99	101	200
	Nepali school	4	10	11	21
		5	11	11	22
		6	11	12	23
		7	11	11	22
		8	11	11	22
		9	11	11	22
		10	11	11	22
		11	12	12	24
		12	11	11	22
		Total	99	101	200

of bilingualism we found in Bali (cf. Chapter 11, this volume), we initially expected more use of geocentric terms by Kathmandu children in Nepali medium schools, whereas in English medium schools we expected egocentric terms to be more common. This led to the expectation that children's socialization in a traditional cultural context (e.g., in Sanskrit or Nepali medium schools) would encourage the use of a geocentric FoR, whereas in a relatively nontraditional context (e.g., in English or Hindi medium schools), the use of an egocentric frame would be encouraged.

Tasks

The tasks used in this study were divided into three main categories: language elicitation tasks, encoding tasks, and spatial cognitive tasks. These tasks are described in detail in Dasen and Mishra (2010). Here we introduce them briefly.

Language Elicitation Tasks

Language elicitation tasks are designed to produce spatial language systematically. One is called the *perspectives task*, in which the child describes a very simple display of three objects from different positions. Another is the *road task*, in which a car is moved along a path model that has several right-angle turns and one diagonal turn. At every turning point, the child describes the direction in which the car should be moved. The third one is a set of three encoding tasks (described below); the language used on two items of each task is recorded to allow researchers to study more closely the correspondence between nonverbal behavior and how it is justified verbally. These tasks were generally used in the local language except in the English medium school of Kathmandu, where much of the testing took place in English.

Language Coding Scheme. The language produced on the three tasks was coded using a scheme adapted from Pederson (1993) shown in Table 10.2. The terms are grouped into the three broad categories of topological, projective, and Euclidean space according to Piagetian theory. The scores on each task are the number of items classified into each language category (out of nine for perspectives, eight for road, and six for encoding tasks). We computed for each task a geocentric language score, subtracting E (egocentric) from G (geocentric) items. The assumption is that if a person scores as many E items as G items, there is no evidence that this person uses a geocentric or an egocentric FoR.

Nonverbal Spatial Encoding Tasks. These tasks were initially devised by the Cognitive Anthropology Research Group (CARG) at the Max Planck Institute for Psycholinguistics in Nijmegen, the Netherlands. Hence, they are sometimes called the *Nijmegen tasks*. Precise procedures are provided in *Cognition and Space Kit, Version 1.0* by Danziger (1993; see also Levinson, 2003; Senft, 2007). We used three of these tasks in our study.

One is "animals in a row" task. This task presents the child with four familiar animals, three aligned along a table (only two in the case of 4- to 6-year-olds), all facing in one direction, and a fourth animal at a right angle.

TABLE 10.2
Language Coding Scheme

Spatial concept category	Language code	Meaning	Explanation and examples
Topological	I	Intrinsic	Next to, near, before, etc.
Projective	E	Egocentric (relative)	Left, right, in front, in back (LRFB) in relation to speaker
Intermediate	SL	Situationally specific landmarks	Toward the window, the door (landmarks within the room)
	CL	Conventional landmarks	Toward the temple, the hospital, a locality (land-marks outside the room)
Euclidean	G	Geocentric (absolute)	Cardinal directions: north, south, east, west (NSEW)
		Up, down	*Up* represents the north and east sectors; *down* the south and west in Dolakha, Nepal
		Kaja, kelod, kangin, kauh (KKKK)	North, south, east, west in Bali
Other	D	Deictic	"This way, that way" (usually accompanied with the gesture of a finger or the whole hand or arm)

The child is asked to remember this display and to move on to another table after a 180° rotation (90° rotation on the last two trials) to align another set of the same animals the way they were shown before. Another is the "chips task," in which two-dimensional shapes with small or large, red or blue squares are drawn on cards. After a series of practice trials, the child is presented one of these cards in a particular orientation. The child moves on to another table (after a 180° rotation) to identify a similar card from a set of four arranged in a cross pattern. Two items with a 90° rotation are also used. The third task, called "Steve's maze" (also called the "scout game"; Senft, 2007, p. 239), consists of six pictures of landscapes that depict a house, rice fields, trees, and an incomplete pathway. The child is presented with a picture showing the route visually and is told a story with a verbal description of the route that one can take from the end of the drawn path back to the house. The child is asked to remember this route while moving on to another table (with a 180° rotation) where three cards are displayed showing three different path segments. One of these represents an egocentric encoding, another is a geocentric solution, and the third one is an irrelevant choice (distractor). One item is used for demonstration; another five items constitute the test series.

We computed for each task a geocentric encoding score, for which E-encoded items are subtracted from G items. These scores (with a constant added) were then submitted to a Princals data reduction procedure, producing a summary object score (Dimension 1) of geocentric nonverbal spatial encoding.

Knowledge of Orientation System and Egocentric References. This procedure was used to check the actual knowledge of spatial vocabulary in relation to the egocentric and geocentric FoR. Children were asked to indicate their left, right, front, and back. They were also asked about the four directions of the local orientation system ("Show me where north is"). We did this first outside in the schoolyard, where cues such as the sun's position were available, and then again inside the room used for testing.

Additional Cognitive Tasks

Block Designs Test (BDT). This test, which is a standard of psychological testing (also called the *Kohs block test*), involves the construction of pictorially presented designs of increasing difficulty with the help of four, nine, and 16 blocks within specified periods of time. A short version of the test (10 designs; Mishra, Sinha, & Berry, 1996) was used. Both time and accuracy of performance were recorded; in our data analysis, we reported only the number of correct items (but we checked that similar results were obtained when using the timed measure).

Story-Pictorial Embedded Figures Test (SPEFT). The SPEFT (Sinha, 1984) comprises 11 sets of pictures. Each set consists of a simple and a complex card. On the simple card, objects and animals are depicted that are embedded in a larger scene depicted on the complex card (e.g., snakes in the forest). The child has to locate in the complex card, within a maximum of 90 s, the objects or animals of the simple card described in the background of a story that is narrated with each card to encourage the child to locate the embedded items. Time taken and number of objects correctly located by the child were recorded, but in the analysis of results, only the number of correct items was reported. In this study we used only seven sets of pictures, two for practice and five for testing.

Hemispheric Lateralization Tests. For hemispheric lateralization, we used a peripheral measure (called *handedness*) adapted from Mandal, Pandey, Singh, and Asthana (1992) and a central measure. The peripheral measure consisted of a number of tasks that the child could do with a hand, foot, eye, or ear. Children were first asked about their preference to do the task with the left or right limb or organ and whether they would do it "always" or "sometimes" with that one. Then they were asked to perform tasks with a hand, foot, eye, or ear (there were separate tasks for each). The use of the limb or organ was recorded.

The central measure consisted of a brain lateralization task administered with the help of a laptop computer using a program developed by M. K. Mandal (personal communication, November 2002). This task used the split-field technique, in which the child was asked to concentrate on a black spot that appeared in the center of the computer screen. Then an arrow appeared that pointed to either the left or the right in random order. The child was asked to look at the object or the word that appeared in the direction the arrow pointed to. The child's hand was placed on a key that was to be pressed soon after the stimulus pointed to by the arrow was correctly recognized. The presentation time of each stimulus was 180 ms. The child's reaction time to stimuli presented to left and right was assessed with the help of the computer program. Accuracy of response was recorded manually on a sheet developed for that purpose. In one sequence of trials, the child responded to words for objects and animals. In another sequence, responses for male and female faces were obtained. Before conducting the test, the children were given practice trials to make sure their responses were not made randomly; the eligibility criterion was eight correct responses out of 12 presentations during practice trials.

Procedure

In Kathmandu, all tasks were given to all children; in Varanasi, the brain lateralization measure was administered to children who were classified as using either a geocentric or an egocentric frame of reference, called the G and E groups. In this classification, consistency in correct language use and encoding were considered together. Of 376 children, only 88 could be placed in the G and E groups; others tended to use the frames inconsistently. A child questionnaire and a home questionnaire were also administered to children and their parents to assess a number of socioenvironmental variables that might be linked to the G or E frame of reference.

Results

Language

The mean scores of the groups at various age levels were computed. The G and E scores were also scored for accuracy (called G+ and E+) of language use. An obvious feature of the finding at Varanasi is that G language was used most frequently and systematically in both school groups. The gap between the use of G and G+ in the Sanskrit school was very small, which was not true for the Hindi school. This finding indicates that although children in the Hindi school also tended to use the normative geocentric language, they were less perfect in getting the directions right than the Sanskrit schoolchildren. Some egocentric language did occur, mainly in the Hindi school group and on the road task.

Use of the other language categories—deictic, situational landmarks, conventional landmarks, and intrinsic—was negligible. In Kathmandu, language in the younger age groups (ages 4–6) was strongly characterized by the use of deictic ("this way") language, usually accompanied by a gesture. In this age group, situational landmarks also were used, but this use diminished with age. Egocentric language occurred to a small extent throughout the age groups (4–12 years). Some intrinsic (i.e., "next to," "near") references occurred in the middle age group (7–10 years), whereas conventional landmarks were almost never used. Geocentric language clearly replaced deictic language by age 7, and it continued to increase with age to dominate all other language categories. The difference between G and G+ shows that although using cardinal directions was the norm, it was not easy to do it correctly. Even in the older age groups, a gap remained.

For each of the language elicitation tasks, a summary score was computed by subtracting E from G, and these scores, treated as ordinal, were submitted to a Princals optimal scaling procedure. The object scores obtained on Dimension 1 were used as the summary measure for the language variable.

Knowledge of NSEW and LRFB

In the Sanskrit school group at Varanasi, the knowledge of NSEW was almost perfect; the knowledge of LRFB was also better than that of the Hindi school group, $F(2, 218) = 92.20$, $p < .001$, for NSEW; $F(2, 152) = 19.97$, $p < .001$, for LRFB. In the Hindi school group, the knowledge of relative directions was fairly high and accurate, but the correct knowledge of cardinal direction was far from perfect. There was no difference between performance inside and outside the building in either school group.

In Kathmandu, almost no child 4 to 6 years of age knew the cardinal directions; starting with ages 7 to 8 in the English group and 9 to 10 in the Nepali group, about half of the children could tell these directions. Although the NSEW system is the cultural norm for children in both types of schools, it was not acquired by many children even by ages 11 to 12. Analysis of variance (ANOVA) indicated a significant effect of age and a significant difference between the school groups in favor of the English school group, $F(1, 195) = 4.83$, $p < .05$.

With respect to the use of LRFB, English schooling had some impact. In the English school group, all four egocentric references were known perfectly at age 5, whereas in the Nepali school group, some children younger than 8 years knew only left and right. ANOVA indicated a significant difference between the school groups, $F(1, 195) = 9.173$, $p < .01$, in favor of the English group.

Nonverbal Encoding

We computed encoding for the animals in rows, chips, and Steve's maze tasks. Higher geocentric encoding was found on the animals in rows task, followed by the chips task. On the Steve's maze task, geocentric encoding was very low. The pattern was almost the same in the Varanasi and Kathmandu samples. In order to discover a structural relationship among the three tasks, we used the Princals procedure, which resulted in a two-factor solution. Dimension 1 was used as a summary measure for nonverbal encoding at both locations.

In Varanasi, the mean object scores on correct geocentric language and geocentric encoding (both derived from Princals) were higher in the Sanskrit school group than the Hindi school group, $F(1, 371) = 117.27$, $p < .001$, for language; $F(1, 371) = 21.07$, $p < .001$, for encoding. There was a significant effect of age for encoding, $F(2, 371) = 4.38$, $p < .05$, but not for language. In Kathmandu, the mean object scores on correct geocentric language showed only the significant effect of age, $F(3, 195) = 10.88$, $p < .001$. On the encoding summary score, ANOVA showed a significant difference between the English and Nepali groups, $F(1, 195) = 5.115$, $p < .05$, with more geocentric encoding in the English group. A significant school type by age interaction, $F(3, 195) = 3.548$, $p < .01$, showed more geocentric encoding in the English group and a stronger increase with age in that group, a finding that goes against our prediction: In Kathmandu, bilingualism with English did not seem to foster more egocentric encoding.

The findings also reveal that the choice of a FoR for encoding is not homogeneous across different tasks. In particular, the Steve's maze task always fosters more egocentric encoding than the animals in rows and chips tasks.

Language and Encoding

Pearson correlation between geocentric language and geocentric encoding in the Varanasi sample was found to be moderate ($r = .39$, $p < .01$). Controlling for age and school type, the partial correlation was still significant (age-controlled $r = .33$, $p < .01$; school type–controlled $r = .25$, $p < .01$). Controlling for grade or years of schooling did not change the value of this correlation.

For the Kathmandu school group, we found a statistically nonsignificant correlation ($r = .11$, $p > .05$) between geocentric language and geocentric encoding. If these correlations are computed separately for the two school groups, it is somewhat higher for the English school group ($r = .22$, $p < .05$) but very low ($r = .002$, $p > .05$) for the Nepali school group. These results allow us to argue against a strong link between language use and encoding.

A Summary Model for Varanasi

Amos modeling was used to derive a summary model showing the relationships among the variables of the study. The modeling was carried out with a subsample of 80 children because most of the background variables were available only for this group. The model is illustrated in Figure 10.1. Fit statistics are satisfactory. The graph does not include error terms.

The main variable is school type, Hindi versus Sanskrit. This variable covers a large array of sociocultural aspects (e.g., language spoken in the home, SES), as well as migration history and contact with the village, two aspects that were linked to using geospatial language in separate analyses. The age range of the sample was more reduced (11–15 years), so age does not come into the model as a significant variable.

The interesting aspect of the model is the contribution of a virtual variable, spatial ability, which is strongly linked to knowledge of the NSEW orientation system and geospatial encoding and weakly linked to geospatial

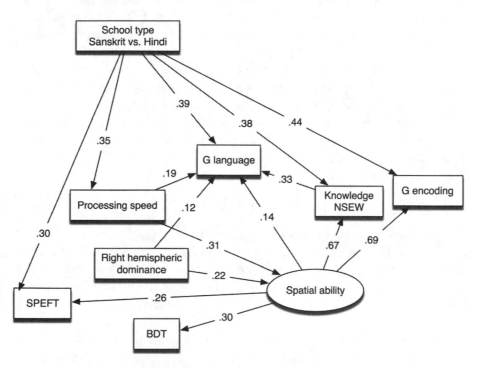

Figure 10.1. Amos structural equation model for Varanasi. Likelihood ratio chi-square = 7.300, *df* = 12, *p* = .837; root-mean-square error of approximation = 0; goodness of fit index = .978; comparative fit index = 1; Tucker–Lewis index = 1.058. BDT = block designs test; G = geospatial; NSEW = north, south, east, west; SPEFT = story-pictorial embedded figures test.

language. This variable is assessed through the SPEFT and BDT. Performance on the SPEFT is itself linked to school type, indicating that the Sanskrit school pupils seemed to have overall better spatial skills.

Spatial ability is also influenced by other cognitive process measures, notably overall processing speed (mean reaction time on the lateralization task) and right hemispheric dominance (on the same test). These measures also show a direct link to geospatial language, which could indicate that those who have a faster processing capacity, especially in the right hemisphere, are better able to deal with the complex aspects of geocentric language independently of or in addition to the link through spatial ability, which is itself more strongly linked to knowledge of the orientation system and encoding than to language.

A striking feature of the model is the absence of a direct relationship between spatial language and encoding; introducing a link reduces the fit statistics. However, the model shows that geocentric language itself is part of a pattern that includes sociocultural variables, subsumed under school type, and other psychological and neurophysiological characteristics of children.

A Summary Model for Kathmandu

We had information about several contextual variables through our child and family questionnaires, including variables like child's mobility, activities outside of school, contact with the village, language spoken in the home, socioeconomic status, migration history, and parents' language. Component scores were derived using Princals. We present here a summary model in which the relationships of these variables with each other as well as with geocentric language and encoding can be easily visualized.

Because the age range of the children in Kathmandu was large (4–12 years), it was difficult to find an Amos model suitable for the whole sample. The model discussed here (see Figure 10.2) was produced with the 7-to-12 age group. The same model shows reasonable fit when applied separately to 7- to 9- and 10- to 12-year-olds. In contrast, it does not fit well for the youngest group, perhaps because of low reliability of the psychometric test scores. For the sake of clarity, age as a variable is not shown in the graph; it has a −.30 link with English in home, .21 with passive mobility, .19 with independent mobility, .57 with spatial ability, and .16 with geospatial language.

In Kathmandu, the traditional culture variable (a virtual variable) is linked to school type (there were more traditional families in the Nepali schools), contact maintained with the village, and whether English is used in the home (−.72). Contrary to what we found in Bali (cf. Chapter 11, this volume), traditional culture is not linked with a higher use of the geocentric FoR; the links with geocentric language and encoding are negative,

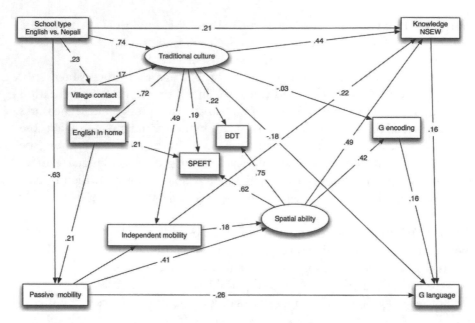

Figure 10.2. Amos structural equation model for Kathmandu. Likelihood ratio chi-square = 20.0, *df* = 32, *p* = .952; root-mean-square error of approximation = 0; goodness of fit index = .986; comparative fit index = 1; Tucker–Lewis index = 1.025. BDT = block designs test; G = geospatial; NSEW = north, south, east, west; SPEFT = story-pictorial embedded figures test.

even though they are quite small (−.18 and −.03). This finding is congruent with what other data analyses indicated, namely that the pupils of the English school showed not less but more geocentric encoding than the Nepali school group.

In contrast, we found a positive link to knowledge of the NSEW system, which dissociates the traditional culture variable somewhat from geocentric language and encoding, even though it is itself linked positively to geocentric language. A variable reflecting the foreign (and egocentric) language spoken in the home is part of the model. It is linked to passive mobility (English-speaking children lived further away from school and were driven there).

The link between the variable English in the home and SPEFT reflects some higher test sophistication in the upper-class children speaking English. In contrast, there is also a positive (.19) input from traditional culture, which could be due to the fact that this test has been adapted, in terms of content, to make it more appropriate to the Indian children than the BDT.

The second virtual variable is spatial ability, measured through the BDT and SPEFT and influenced by both mobility variables, showing that both passive and independent mobility are linked to increased spatial ability. Spatial ability, in this model, is directly linked to knowledge of cardinal directions and geocentric encoding, but the link to geocentric language occurs only through knowledge. Passive mobility has a separate negative direct link to geocentric language, indicating that being driven through the city may foster an egocentric rather than a geocentric FoR.

In this model, contrary to Varanasi, geocentric encoding is linked to geocentric language, although not very strongly (.16). Reversing the arrow (from language to encoding) would diminish the statistical fit of the model.

These models bring out not only the complexity of experiences embedded in the ecocultural system but also the role of different elements of this system in the organization of spatial language and cognition. The message is clear: Spatial cognitive processes cannot be attributed to a single cultural variable called *language*; a number of other variables that constitute the textured context of children's development need to be considered in order to understand the relationship between language and cognition.

DISCUSSION

The findings from Varanasi indicate that geocentric spatial cognition is significantly linked to fundamental spatial cognitive ability as measured by the SPEFT and BDT. The dominant use of geocentric language and geocentric encoding in Sanskrit compared with Hindi schoolchildren suggests that the use of the ability can be sharpened by its practice and actualization in day-to-day life. Vajpayee, Dasen, and Mishra (2008) noted how Sanskrit schoolchildren are exposed in daily activities to a variety of experiences that predispose them to organize space in a geocentric manner. Their previous learning of geocentric references in the village environment gets reinforced in the city with Sanskrit medium schooling.

The geocentric orientation also exists in the environment of the Hindi medium schoolchildren, but it is not strongly emphasized in their daily routines except in the matters of eating, sleeping, and a few other activities. It may be noted that all children in Varanasi learn the distinction between the right and left hands from a very early age. However, Sanskrit schoolchildren learn this distinction in a more active manner because of their participation in certain rituals that require habitual switching from the left to the right hand and vice versa.

The picture of spatial cognitive development noted in Kathmandu is somewhat different than that found at Varanasi. One significant feature of the findings is the dominant occurrence of geocentric over egocentric encoding only on one task (i.e., animals in rows) and in the older age groups only. This presents us with evidence of discrepancy between the use of language (which is geocentric) and the nature of encoding (which is egocentric). This discrepancy is obvious in the very low correlation coefficients between language and encoding and also in our comparisons of encoding and the language used to explain it on the three encoding tasks. This discrepancy shows that the choice of one system or the other becomes more unpredictable in an urban environment such as Kathmandu when the egocentric and the geocentric systems are both available, with the geocentric one emphasized more by the cultural environment (even in the school curriculum) and the egocentric one more functional in daily city life.

The most unexpected result comes from the comparison between the English and Nepali school groups. Research comparing bilingual with monolingual individuals has generally pointed to the importance of bilingualism in modifying cognitive outcomes across the life span (Bialystok, 2011). Bilingual individuals have been found to consistently outperform their counterpart monolinguals on tasks involving cognitive organization and executive control (Bialystok, 2010). In our study, on the basis of results of research in Bali (see Chapter 11, this volume), we expected an influence of bilingualism on the choice of an egocentric versus geocentric cognitive style. Learning English, and spending the whole day in this language environment, should strongly encourage children toward using egocentric language and encoding. But this was not the case. Although we found significantly greater use of geocentric language in the higher age groups of the Nepali school, there was greater geocentric encoding in the English, not in the Nepali, school group. In other words, bilingualism with English did *not* seem to foster more egocentric encoding in the Kathmandu situation.

This lack of effect of bilingualism with English is further confirmed by a microanalysis of the impact of actually choosing English on the road task. There is a small but statistically significant correlation ($r = .14, p < .01$) between choosing English and geocentric encoding (on the animals in rows and chips tasks), and this finding is confirmed by a significant correlation ($r = .11, p < .05$) between using English in the home and geocentric encoding.

Thus, we seem to have a coherent set of data to show that in this case, bilingualism with English does not have the same effect as was found with Indonesian in Bali (Dasen & Mishra, 2010; see also Chapter 11, this volume). The finding warrants discussion of some possible explanations, such as other differences between the English and Nepali school groups that could provide alternative explanations (or, at least, post hoc hypotheses). The link of religious practices to SES is one of these.

The English school group in Kathmandu was clearly composed of families with higher SES, higher contact with the media, and less contact with the rural area. In our results (based on home interviews with a subsample of 70 families), we found that high-SES children indeed used less geocentric language ($r = -.24, p < .05$), but there was no relationship with encoding. In other words, SES does not "explain" the finding by itself. In fact, SES as a "packaged" variable itself is a composite of many possible variables.

One of these variables could be religious practices. Our observational data indicate that the English school families (largely Brahmin) spent more time on Hindu rituals in the home, in which cardinal directions are very important. From our study in Varanasi, we know how important Hindu religious rituals can be in fostering a geocentric FoR. This emphasis on the symbolic aspects of geocentric spatial orientation could therefore explain why geocentric encoding is as important in this group as it is in the Nepali school group. It would be interesting to collect more detailed information on these practices to appreciate their role in the development of a geocentric FoR more precisely.

It may also be noted that in Nepal, the geocentric system of cardinal directions is taught explicitly in Grade 2 of all schools, including the English medium schools. All teachers were Nepali with English as their second language, so it is quite likely that they tended to use the locally predominant spatial system when they spoke about space, even in English, and even for small-scale space inside the classroom. It would be interesting to document this further through behavior observations in the schools.

Coming back to the Varanasi study, we noticed that although Sanskrit schoolchildren used the geocentric FoR almost exclusively in both language and cognition, they also had the egocentric FoR at their disposal (and even managed it very accurately). The Hindi schoolchildren also had both frames at their disposal, but they tended to choose the egocentric FoR more often. For both groups, it can be said that the "choice" of a frame of spatial reference is a matter of cognitive style: The cognitive processes for both frames are available to all, but which one is chosen in any particular situation depends on a variety of ecocultural variables (see Chapter 11, this volume).

CONCLUSION

How does the geocentric FoR develop with age? In fact, this question has been addressed specifically in much of our research (cf. Dasen & Mishra, 2010) in which we included children with a full developmental range, from ages 4 to 15 years. Generally speaking, we found that the use of a geocentric FoR, in both language and cognition, tended to increase with age in all locations where such a frame is culturally appropriate in adulthood. Mishra et al. (2003) showed that in rural settings of India and Nepal, the geocentric FoR was established by ages 6 to 8 but somewhat later in urban settings such as Kathmandu or Varanasi. Nevertheless, from the data at hand, we can conclude that, at the level of language use, there is no developmental change after age 10, but there is still an increase of geocentric encoding in both locations.

This difference in developmental trends between language and encoding reflects the more general finding that the relationship between the two domains is only moderate. This finding does not go well with the position of strong linguistic relativism taken by Levinson (2003), for whom it was only language that determines cognition. That there is a link is obvious at the group level: In societies in which geocentric language is used predominantly, there is also a tendency to prefer a geocentric FoR in cognition. But this link is far from deterministic. Depending on the features of the task at hand (e.g., animals in rows and chips tasks vs. Steve's maze task), and depending on various ecocultural variables, individuals may choose one frame or the other, and they may even choose one for speaking and the other for encoding. Indeed, when the relationships between all of the available variables are analyzed through structural equation modeling, the best fit at Varanasi is obtained with a model showing no direct link between geocentric language and encoding. In Kathmandu, the best fit is achieved in a model in which the path is drawn from geospatial encoding to geospatial language, not from geospatial language to geospatial encoding.

We strongly feel that research focusing on other ecocultural variables is necessary. In this particular research, we looked at the role of Hindu religious practices, but a geocentric orientation system is also important in other religions, such as Islam and Buddhism. Several hunter-gatherer populations, who display extremely accurate dead reckoning skills (e.g., pointing to faraway landmarks), also use this system (Levinson, 2003), and it would be interesting to follow up on this research with other religious and relevant Adivasi groups (e.g., Asur, Birhor) who still live in India on hunting and gathering. The relationship between the use of a geocentric FoR and dead reckoning skills (see Dasen & Mishra, 2010; Mishra, Singh, & Dasen, 2009) and other cognitive tasks (e.g., Mishra et al., 2003) begs the question of relationships to other cognitive processes. We take these findings as an indication that the geocentric FoR is indeed linked to wider aspects of cognition, but much more research is needed on this issue.

REFERENCES

Allen, G. L. (Ed.). (2007). *Applied spatial cognition: From research to cognitive technology*. Mahwah, NJ: Erlbaum.

Bialystok, E. (2010). Global-local and trail-making tasks by monolingual and bilingual children: Beyond inhibition. *Developmental Psychology, 46*, 93–105. doi:10.1037/a0015466

Bialystok, E. (2011). Reshaping the mind: The benefits of bilingualism. *Canadian Journal of Experimental Psychology, 65*, 229–235. doi:10.1037/a0025406

Danziger, E. (Ed.). (1993). *Cognition and space kit, version 1.0*. Nijmegen, the Netherlands: Cognitive Anthropology Research Group, Max Planck Institute for Psycholinguistics.

Dasen, P. R., & Mishra, R. C. (2010). *Development of geocentric spatial language and cognition: An eco-cultural perspective*. Cambridge, England: Cambridge University Press. doi:10.1017/CBO9780511761058

Dasen, P. R., Mishra, R. C., & Niraula, S. (2004). The influence of schooling on cognitive development: Spatial language, encoding and concept development in India and Nepal. In B. N. Setiadi, A. Supratiknya, W. J. Lonner, & Y. H. Poortinga (Eds.), *Ongoing themes in psychology and culture* (pp. 223–237). Yogyakarta, Indonesia: Kanisius.

de León, L. (1994). Exploration in the acquisition of geocentric location by Tzotzil children. *Linguistics, 32*, 857–884. doi:10.1515/ling.1994.32.4-5.857

de León, L. (1995). *The development of geocentric location in young speakers of Guugu Yimithirr* (CARG Working Paper No. 32). Nijmegen, the Netherlands: Cognitive Anthropology Research Group, Max Planck Institute for Psycholinguistics.

Gladwin, T. (1970). *East is a big bird: Navigation and logic on Puluwat Atoll*. Cambridge, MA: Harvard University Press.

Greenfield, P. M. (1976). Cross-cultural research and Piagetian theory: Paradox and progress. In K. F. Riegel & J. A. Meacham (Eds.), *The developing individual in a changing world* (Vol. 1, pp. 322–333). The Hague, the Netherlands: Mouton.

Gumperz, J. J., & Levinson, S. C. (1996). *Rethinking linguistic relativity*. Cambridge, England: Cambridge University Press.

Holenstein, E. (1993). Menschliche Vorstellungen und maschinelle Repräsentationen [Human conception and machine representation]. In J. Wassmann & P. R. Dasen (Eds.), *Alltagswissen—Les savoirs quotidiens* (pp. 277–294). Fribourg, Switzerland: Universitätsverlag.

Hutchins, E. (1983). Understanding Micronesian navigation. In D. Gentner & A. Stevens (Eds.), *Mental models* (pp. 191–225). Hillsdale, NJ: Erlbaum.

Levinson, S. C. (1996). Frames of reference and Molyneux's question: Cross-linguistic evidence. In P. Bloom, M. Peterson, L. Nadel, & M. Garrett (Eds.), *Language and space* (pp. 109–169). Cambridge, MA: MIT Press.

Levinson, S. C. (2003). *Space in language and cognition*. Cambridge, England: Cambridge University Press. doi:10.1017/CBO9780511613609

Lucy, J. A. (1997). Linguistic relativity. *Annual Review of Anthropology, 26*, 291–312. doi:10.1146/annurev.anthro.26.1.291

Mandal, M. K., Pandey, G., Singh, S. K., & Asthana, H. S. (1992). Degree of asymmetry in lateral preferences: Eye, foot, ear. *Journal of Psychology: Interdisciplinary and Applied, 126*, 155–162.

Miller, G., & Johnson-Laird, P. (1976). *Language and perception*. Cambridge, England: Cambridge University Press.

Mishra, R. C. (1997). Cognition and cognitive development. In J. W. Berry, P. R. Dasen, & T. S. Saraswathi (Eds.), *Handbook of cross-cultural psychology: Vol. 2*.

Basic processes and human development (2nd ed., pp. 143–176). Boston, MA: Allyn & Bacon.

Mishra, R. C., Dasen, P. R., & Niraula, S. (2003). Ecology, language, and performance on spatial cognitive tasks. *International Journal of Psychology, 38,* 366–383. doi:10.1080/00207590344000187

Mishra, R. C., Singh, S., & Dasen, P. R. (2009). Geocentric dead reckoning in Sanskrit- and Hindi-medium school children. *Culture & Psychology, 15,* 386–408. doi:10.1177/1354067X09343330

Mishra, R. C., Sinha, D., & Berry, J. W. (1996). *Ecology, acculturation and psychological adaptation: A study of Adivasis in Bihar.* New Delhi, India: Sage.

Niraula, S., Mishra, R. C., & Dasen, P. R. (2004). Linguistic relativity and spatial concept development in Nepal. *Psychology and Developing Societies, 16,* 99–124. doi:10.1177/097133360401600202

Pederson, E. (1993). Geographic and manipulable space in two Tamil linguistic systems. In A. U. Frank & I. Campari (Eds.), *Spatial information theory* (pp. 294–311). Berlin, Germany: Springer Verlag.

Pederson, E., Danziger, E., Levinson, S., Kita, S., Senft, G., & Wilkins, D. (1998). Semantic typology and spatial conceptualization. *Language, 74,* 557–589. doi:10.2307/417793

Piaget, J., & Inhelder, B. (1956). *The child's conception of space.* London, England: Routledge & Kegan Paul.

Segall, M. H., Dasen, P. R., Berry, J. W., & Poortinga, Y. H. (1999). *Human behavior in global perspective: An introduction to cross-cultural psychology* (rev. 2nd ed.). Boston, MA: Allyn & Bacon.

Senft, G. (2007). The Nijmegen space games: Studying the interrelationship between language, culture and cognition. In J. Wassmann & K. Stockhaus (Eds.), *Experiencing new worlds* (pp. 224–244). Oxford, England: Berghahn.

Sinha, D. (1984). *Manual for Story-Pictorial EFT and Indo-African EFT.* Varanasi, India: Rupa.

Taylor, H. A., & Tversky, B. (1996). Perspective in spatial descriptions. *Journal of Memory and Language, 35,* 371–391. doi:10.1006/jmla.1996.0021

Vajpayee, A., Dasen, P. R., & Mishra, R. C. (2008). Spatial encoding: A comparison of Sanskrit- and Hindi-medium schools. In N. Srinivasan, A. K. Gupta, & J. Pandey (Eds.), *Advances in cognitive science* (Vol. 1, pp. 255–265). New Delhi, India: Sage.

Wassmann, J. (1994). The Yupno as post-Newtonian scientists: The question of what is "natural" in spatial description. *Man, 29,* 645–666. doi:10.2307/2804347

Wassmann, J., & Dasen, P. R. (1998). Balinese spatial orientation: Some empirical evidence for moderate linguistic relativity. *Journal of the Royal Anthropological Institute, 4,* 689–711.

Werner, S., & Hubel, C. (1999). Spatial reference systems. *Spatial Cognition and Computation, 1*(4), iii–vii.

Whorf, B. (1956). *Language, thought and reality.* Cambridge, MA: MIT Press.

11

CULTURAL DIFFERENCES IN COGNITIVE STYLES

PIERRE R. DASEN AND RAMESH C. MISHRA

This chapter is a continuation of Chapter 10 of this volume, and in it we set the study of geocentric spatial language and cognition into a broader theoretical framework, as well as provide additional data from field work in Bali and Geneva. Our main conclusion is that the choice of a geocentric frame of reference (FoR), as opposed to an egocentric FoR, is best viewed as a cognitive style. This means that both cognitive processes are potentially available to all individuals but that various ecocultural, social, and individual variables determine which of the two styles is likely to be favored in any given situation. In view of this theoretical interpretation, we first present an integrated theoretical framework that allows us to view human development in an ecocultural perspective, and we then review cross-cultural research on cognitive development (in particular, in the Piagetian tradition, but also from other perspectives). We conclude that cultural differences reside in cognitive styles more than in the presence or absence of basic cognitive processes.

DOI: 10.1037/14043-012
Cognition and Brain Development: Converging Evidence From Various Methodologies, B. R. Kar (Editor)

AN INTEGRATED THEORETICAL FRAMEWORK FOR THE CROSS-CULTURAL STUDY OF HUMAN DEVELOPMENT

As part of the goal of developing a more universal developmental psychology, Dasen (2003, 2008) has attempted to combine various theoretical frameworks encountered over the years and found useful in a variety of contexts. An updated version of this framework is presented in Figure 11.1.

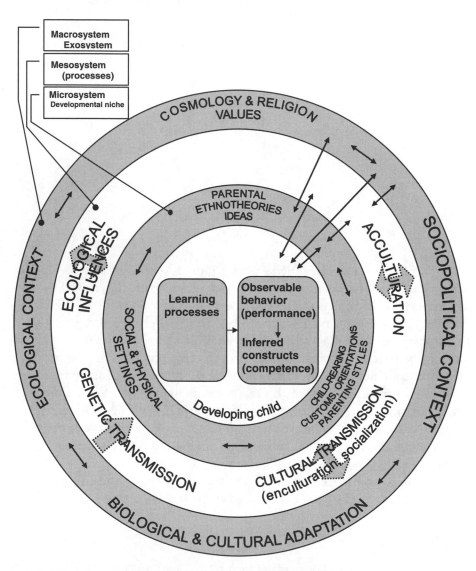

Figure 11.1. An integrated theoretical framework for cross-cultural human development.

At the center of the framework is the individual child, with his or her particular set of inherited and acquired dispositions. Surrounding the child is the microcontext in which development occurs, also called the *developmental niche* (a framework first formulated by Super & Harkness, 1997), which has three components:

1. the settings, or physical and social contexts in which the child lives;
2. the customs, or culturally determined rearing and educational practices; and
3. the psychological characteristics of the caretakers, including the (explicit and implicit) parental ethnotheories of child development.

The developmental niche is a system in which the component parts interact and function in a coordinated fashion. Typically there is consonance among the elements of the niche, especially under conditions of stability in the society, but sometimes there are also inconsistencies, especially under the impact of social change and acculturation. Moreover, it is an open system in which each component is linked with other aspects of the more general environment. The latter is represented in the outer circle of the macrosystem, which includes the ecological and sociohistorical contexts to which each society adapts both biologically and culturally. This part of the framework comes from the ecocultural model Berry has developed over the years, used for textbooks of cross-cultural psychology (Berry, Poortinga, Segall, & Dasen, 2002; Segall, Dasen, Berry, & Poortinga, 1999). It is also akin to Bronfenbrenner's (1979) ecological systems theory. Note that interactions are postulated between every level of the framework, not only between adjacent sectors.

The processes that link the phenomena at the group level to those at the individual level are shown in the mesosystem. Among these, as educators, we are most interested in the processes of cultural transmission, notably enculturation and socialization. In fact, this is how we define *education*, not only as schooling but as the totality of cultural transmission (Dasen, 2008). However, all societies are now in contact with each other in a globalized world (Akkari & Dasen, 2008), so processes of acculturation are also important.

Note that Sinha (1982) presented an "ecological map of the child," which is entirely compatible with this framework. In the macrocontext, Sinha included institutional settings, such as caste and class, and general services and amenities that no doubt reflect the particularities of Indian society.

The integrated framework shows a direct link between parental ethnotheories at the level of the developmental niche and, in the macrosystem, cosmology and cultural belief systems—in particular, religious practices. There is a hierarchical system, starting from isolated parental ideas and extending to more integrated ethnotheories and then to the overarching elements of culture. Most of the time, there is coherence in this system, as stated above, and these cultural belief systems have interesting implications for educational practices (see, e.g., Harkness & Super, 1996; Super & Harkness, 1997).

CULTURE AND COGNITIVE DEVELOPMENT: TOWARD COGNITIVE STYLES

An extensive research program on culture and cognition based mainly on adapting laboratory experiments to make them culturally more appropriate was carried out by Cole, Gay, Glick, and Sharp (1971) in Liberia, Mexico, and the United States (for a review, see Segall et al., 1999). The authors came to the following conclusion: "Cultural differences in cognition reside more in the situations to which particular cognitive processes are applied than in the existence of a process in one cultural group and its absence in another" (Cole et al., 1971, p. 233). This conclusion came as a surprise to many, the common understanding being that illiterate people, for example, lacked some of the cognitive processes promoted by schooling or literacy (see the section Cognitive Styles in Cross-Cultural Research, this chapter).

We agree fully with this conclusion, although in a slight reformulation: "Cultural differences in cognition reside more in cognitive styles than in the existence of a process in one cultural group and its absence in another" (Dasen & Mishra, 2010, pp. 13–14). We speak of a *cognitive style* when a set of cognitive processes are all potentially available, but some are preferentially used rather than others. An important aspect of cognitive styles is that there is no value judgment attached; that is, it is not inherently "better" to choose one style rather than another. This "choice" may of course be unconscious and is influenced by many individual and ecocultural variables.

COGNITIVE STYLES

Cognitive styles can be defined as "an individual's preferred and habitual modes of perceiving, remembering, organizing, processing, and representing information" (Dörnyei, 2005, p. 125) or even more generally as "one's preferred way of processing information and dealing with tasks" (Zhang & Sternberg, 2006, p. 3). We are in the presence of a cognitive style when different individuals (or different groups) react differently to a cognitive problem (e.g., task, test, experiment) in some systematic way even though they have the same underlying cognitive capacity or competence. They "choose" to react in this particular way under the influence of a variety of factors, such as their age, gender, previous experience, and socialization. Of course, this is not necessarily a conscious choice; it is in fact more likely to be unconscious, linked to habits, customs, or preferred values—in other words, to culture. An important aspect of cognitive styles is that there is no judgmental aspect to this choice. It is not inherently "better" or "more advanced" to react one way or another.

Riding (2002) analyzed a series of cognitive style theories as reflecting a contrast between *wholists* and *analytics*. The former see a situation as a whole and appreciate the total context; the latter see a situation as a collection of parts. This typology includes what is probably the best-known cognitive style, field dependence or independence (FDI), also called *psychological differentiation* on the basis of Witkin's (1978) theory. Field-independent individuals tend to be more analytic and produce judgments independently of their visual or social surroundings; field-dependent individuals are more influenced by the latter and more global in their perception. This is a dimension on which people can be positioned anywhere, but there is evidence for coherence, so that people who tend to be on the field-independent side will show analytical cognitive functioning and will not be easily influenced by social opinion and those who are field dependent function globally and show social empathy. Analytical cognition is marked, for example, by the ability to quickly pick a single element out of a complex figure. Witkin's theory also links psychological differentiation to child-rearing patterns and to differential brain functioning.

Psychological differentiation is the only cognitive style that has led to extensive cross-cultural research, notably by Berry (1976) and his colleagues. Some of the early findings were reviewed by Witkin and Berry (1975) and some of the more recent research by R. C. Mishra, Sinha, and Berry (1996). Berry (1976) found a strong ecocultural factor when studying FDI cross-culturally across a wide range of societies: members of nomadic hunting-gathering societies tend to be more field independent than members of sedentary societies living from subsistence agriculture. However, FDI was also found to be influenced by acculturation, probably because of test-taking familiarity linked to education or employment in the "modern" sector.

R. C. Mishra et al. (1996) studied parents and children of the Birhor (a nomadic hunter-gatherer group), Asur (recent settlers pursuing a mixed economy of hunting-gathering and agriculture), and Oraon (long-standing agriculturists) tribal cultural groups in the state of Bihar (now Jharkhand) in India. In each group, both low and highly acculturated individuals were included. Parents' emphases on compliance or self-assertion during socialization were assessed through a combination of observation, interview, and testing. The results provided evidence for the existence of cognitive styles that could be reliably related to ecological, cultural, and acculturation characteristics of the groups. It was also possible to predict the cognitive style of children and adults on the basis of variables like parental helping and feedback. Similar results were obtained in another study carried out with children of hunting-gathering, agricultural, and wage-earning samples of the Tharu culture in the Himalayan region of India (K. Mishra, 1998).

Dasen, Berry, and Witkin (1979) argued for a value-free interpretation of cognitive styles (and even cognitive development more generally) in the context of cross-cultural studies. To be field independent is not inherently better than being field dependent, although it tends to be valued in many situations. Field independence also increases with age, which may unavoidably give it the connotation of being more advanced. However, someone who is more field dependent has more empathy and more social skills and can fit in better with a group and see things in a more holistic fashion. Note the similarities to Nisbett's (2003) Asian mode of thinking or to collectivism as opposed to individualism (Kagitçibasi, 1997).

Although there are similarities between cognitive styles and learning styles, the two areas of research are somewhat different. Dörnyei (2005) defined *learning styles* as "an individual's natural, habitual, and preferred way(s) of absorbing, processing, and retaining new information and skills" (p. 121). There has been much debate in educational research on the subject, the assumption being that the way information is being presented to learners should match their learning styles. However, a recent review of the literature has not revealed any sound scientific demonstration of this relationship (Pashler, McDaniel, Rohrer, & Bjork, 2008). Dörnyei remarked,

> Although the theoretical basis of cognitive styles is more solid than that of learning styles, even cognitive styles have been subject to a lot of criticism, which never allowed for the concept to take a substantial place in mainstream cognitive psychology. (p. 126)

Although these problems cannot be denied, we still think that the concept is useful in the interpretation of cross-cultural data on cognition.

Dörnyei (2005) made a further distinction between *styles* and *strategies*. The former are considered to be fairly fixed for an individual and may even have a physiological basis, whereas the latter are learned and less stable across time and situations. Also, styles operate without individual awareness, whereas strategies involve a conscious choice of alternatives (Dörnyei, 2005; Sternberg & Grigorenko, 2001).

COGNITIVE STYLES IN CROSS-CULTURAL RESEARCH

Beyond cross-cultural research on Witkin's (1978) psychological differentiation, the concept of cognitive style is beginning to take root in cross-cultural cognitive psychology. Berteaux (2010), for example, used it to interpret his findings on modes of classification in the French-speaking islands in the Indian Ocean. He found that the (French-inspired) school system considered only taxonomic classification, whereas the local cognitive style favored functional classification schemes. Troadec (2011) used the concept explicitly in his review of research on culture and cognition.

There are also many findings in cross-cultural research on cognition that can be reinterpreted as reflecting cognitive styles, even if the authors themselves did not use this concept explicitly. Nisbett's (2003) typology of holistic Asian versus analytic Western thought is a good example. Another example comes from Tapé's (1994) research in Côte d'Ivoire. He started with analyzing the African traditional cosmology, in which mankind is part of nature, as opposed to the Western conception (exemplified by the Christian religion but also by Islam), in which mankind is above nature and is thus allowed to conquer and control it. This leads to two types of reasoning: global, symbolic, and experiential, on one hand, and analytical and experimental, on the other.

Tapé (1994) presented schooled and unschooled informants with a number of Piaget's tasks of formal operational reasoning. In one of these tasks, the person has to determine which variables (e.g., length, section, thickness, material, weight put at the end) influence the flexibility of rods. To carry out a proper experiment, one has to test one factor at a time, keeping all others constant. Although about a third of the 14- to 16-year-old schoolchildren could perform the task, illiterate adults basically refused to deal with it or gave answers based on past experience. Tapé formulated this finding in terms of a plural model of intelligence. According to this model, each individual in every culture has at his or her disposal at least two ways of dealing with information with the help of two forms of intelligence: the analogical mode for global, immediate processing, which is economical but lacks precision, and the conceptual mode for an analytically precise but costly processing. Culture, through the impact of schooling and the contexts of learning, can value one mode rather than the other.

Most relevant is the research carried out by Scribner (1979) in Liberia on syllogistic reasoning. What she found was that illiterate adults could use this form of logic perfectly well but would apply it only to premises in line with their social reality; if the premises were unfamiliar, they would either change them to fit reality or refuse to answer. Scribner called this the *empirical mode*, as opposed to the so-called theoretical mode of schooled informants, who accept a request to reason with any, even unfamiliar, premises. In school, pupils get a lot of practice in dealing with unfamiliar and even hypothetical situations. Schooling does not produce new cognitive processes but provides the training to generalize (transfer) existing processes to a wide range of situations. In other words, it produces a theoretical cognitive style. A preference for the theoretical mode may be brought about by schooling, because most activities in school are decontextualized, or possibly by literacy, because writing and reading imply a double abstraction from reality (Goody & Watt, 1963). However, there are indications that it is Western-type schooling, and not literacy per se, that is effective (Berry & Bennett, 1991; Scribner & Cole, 1981).

This empirical cognitive style was also found by Schliemann and Acioly (1989) among adult lottery ticket sellers in Recife, Brazil. Although they could all deal very efficiently with probabilities linked to a combination of numbers as part of their job, those who were illiterate or had little schooling absolutely refused to answer a transfer task in which they were requested to say in how many ways one could combine letters such as C, A, S, and A. They would say, "I cannot do this, since I cannot read." They stuck to this refusal even when prompted to replace the letters by numbers.

We are now also ready to reinterpret some of our own previous research findings in terms of cognitive styles. For example, research on sensorimotor intelligence in West Africa (Dasen, Inhelder, Lavallée, & Retschitzki, 1978) found that the sequence of substages in early cognitive development was indeed universal, but some babies did show what we would now call a different style. The babies, sitting on their mother's lap, were presented with an interesting object set on the table in front of them, too far to be reached directly. The babies' cognitive stage was determined by the way they were able to use a tool, such as a plastic rake or a ruler, to reach for the object and slide it toward them.

The children in the Baoulé sample were able to do this very well, and on average several weeks in advance compared with French norms. However, some babies, instead of using one of the instruments offered, pushed their mother's arm toward the object. This use of a social object is akin to what Greenfield, Keller, Fuligni, and Maynard (2003) called an *interdependent developmental path*.

In subjects in middle childhood in Côte d'Ivoire and in Kenya, Dasen and his team studied another aspect of Piaget's theory: the development of concrete operations. In one study among the Baoulé with 47 children ages 8 and 9 years, 19 Piagetian tasks were used in three domains of thinking: conservation, elementary logic, and space (Dasen, 1984). The contents of the tasks were partly adapted so as to be familiar to village children, and the testing was performed in the local language. A principal component factor analysis showed a three-factor structure in accordance with Piaget's theory, clearly differentiating spatial reasoning and conservation, with the tasks of elementary logic loading mainly on a third factor but also partly on the two others in accordance with task demands. This indication of structural equivalence (cf. Fischer & Fontaine, 2011) supports the universality of the structure of concrete operational thinking.

Together with research in Australia and Canada, the results in Côte d'Ivoire and Kenya also showed variations in the rate of development of different conceptual areas according to which concepts are more valued in any given environment. For example, nomadic hunter-gatherers valued spatial concepts more than quantification, whereas agriculture, because goods are stored, exchanged, and sold, seems to be linked to a more rapid development of concepts of conservation (Dasen, 1975a; see also Segall et al., 1999). In an ecocultural perspective, these results are not surprising. Obviously, people value and foster those concepts and skills that are adaptive, and this is reflected in child development.

Several studies using so-called operational training techniques were also carried out (Inhelder, Sinclair, & Bovet, 1974). Children were given the opportunity to discover a concept through handling objects (similar to test materials) and interacting with the experimenter. Of course, they were never told the "right" answer, which would be uninteresting, but they were challenged in their preoperational thinking and induced to discover the various dimensions of a task. Ten- to 14-year-old Inuit children were trained in the conservation of liquids (Dasen, 1975b), and training procedures for conservation, class inclusion, and horizontality were used with 7- to 14-year-old Baoulé children in Côte d'Ivoire (Dasen, Lavallée, & Retschitzki, 1979; Lavallée & Dasen, 1980) and with 12- to 14-year-old Kikuyu children in Kenya (Dasen, Ngini, & Lavallée, 1979). The results showed a statistically significant training effect in each training group for each concept. In most cases where there was initially a time lag (an apparently slow development of a particular concept), training was sufficient to reduce or completely eliminate these lags. We found that training in one concept would generalize to other concepts, either in the same domain (e.g., training in conservation of liquids to conservation of number or substance) or across domains (conservation to class inclusion and vice versa but not to horizontality).

In some cases, training was very fast with the older children (12–14 years), leading to the conclusion that these children must have had the competence for the concept being tested but were initially unable to display this in their performance on the task. The training situation helped them actualize their underlying competence.

We conclude from this very brief summary of some of our own results (but we know of no other research, in Africa or elsewhere, that contradicts this) that Piaget's theory of sensorimotor intelligence and concrete operations is indeed universal at the structural level.[1] What we mean by this is that the substages described by Piaget, and the type of reasoning these represent,

---

[1]The conclusions about Piaget's stage of formal operations are controversial. Most research shows that formal schooling at the secondary level is necessary (but not sufficient) for this type of reasoning to develop; however, there may be an artifact insofar as the assessment tasks are very school-like. There are a few studies that found formal operations in out-of-school situations (but see Nunes, Schliemann, & Carraher, 1993; Retschitzki, 1989). Tapé's (1994) research is also relevant.

are found everywhere and in the same succession. However, there are cultural differences in the speed of development of particular concepts depending on whether these are valued and fostered or not in any particular setting. These differences can be compensated by appropriate operational training procedures, which shows that they are not permanent but are in fact quite malleable. In some cases, children have the underlying competence for a particular concept but cannot display it without some help.

These conclusions have important implications for teachers. They can assume that all children[2] have the possibility to acquire all basic cognitive processes, even though some children, depending on their sociocultural background and previous experiences, may not necessarily be able to use them spontaneously in school tasks. The challenge for teachers and caretakers is to find the appropriate ways to help these children either actualize their underlying competence or discover and acquire the relevant concepts through interactions with their physical and social surroundings.

Other research on everyday cognition (reviewed in Segall et al., 1999; see also Schliemann, Carraher, & Ceci, 1997), particularly on ethnomathematics (Dasen, Gajardo, & Ngeng, 2005; Nunes, Schliemann, & Carraher, 1993; Saxe, 1991), shows that mathematical procedures acquired outside of school can be quite sophisticated, but they tend to be restricted to specific contexts; that is, transfer to unfamiliar situations may be limited. Implications for teachers are that they should not only look for the knowledge children bring to school and value this knowledge even if it is different from what is usually taught at school, but also actively train pupils to apply their knowledge to a large set of contents.

We think that the general conclusion of cultural differences residing in cognitive styles is also true for the processes of spatial cognition, and in particular for the "choice" of a spatial frame of reference between the egocentric and the geocentric frames. This is the topic of the second part of this chapter.

GEOCENTRIC SPATIAL LANGUAGE AND COGNITION

The design and methods of the extensive research project that we have been carrying out over the past decade (Dasen & Mishra, 2010) were summarized in Chapter 10 of this volume. In this part of this chapter, we mention results from our research in Bali and Geneva, which illustrate both theoretical backgrounds presented so far: the integrated theoretical framework of human development and cognitive styles.

---

[2]This, of course, means all "normal" children; in every population there are individual differences, and there are some children with disabilities to whom this conclusion may not apply.

In Bali, a geocentric orientation system is used when speaking the local language, Balinese, which has two orthogonal axes, one opposing upstream to downstream ("to the mountain"or "to the sea"), *kaja* and *kelod,* and the transverse, *kauh* and *kangin,* which are notoriously difficult to translate (cf. Wassmann & Dasen, 1998). Much of Balinese culture is linked to this orientation system, which is also prominent in many aspects of daily life. In Bali, however, schooling occurs in the official Bahasa Indonesian, which favors egocentric spatial references (left, right, front, back) and uses cardinal directions as an orientation system.

Figure 11.2 presents the average number of items on one of the language elicitation tasks, perspectives, in which geocentric(G), egocentric (E)

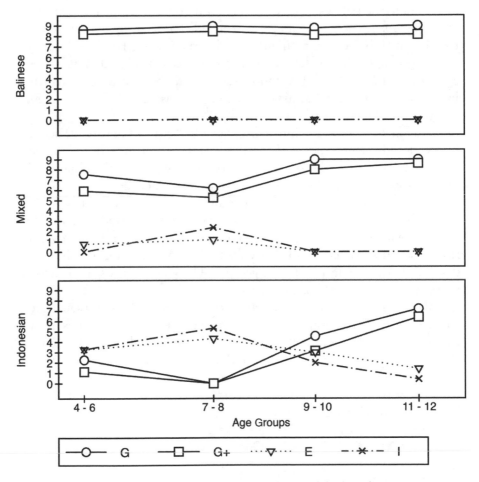

Figure 11.2. Spontaneous language on perspectives task in three language groups in Bali. G = geocentric; E = egocentric; I = intrinsic.

or intrinsic[3] (I) language is used, as well as how many of the geocentric items are correct (G+), in three language groups. In Bali, it so happened that while being tested in Balinese, some (18%) of the children preferred to speak Indonesian systematically, others (28%) used a mix of Balinese and Indonesian, and the third group used only Balinese; this was the case for 71% of the children in the village and 29% of those in the city. Note that all Balinese children are bilingual because teaching occurs only in Indonesian; the difference between the language groups is one of preference.

Figure 11.2 illustrates the impact of bilingualism with Indonesian. Whereas geocentric language is the only one used by children who speak Balinese, even as young as age 4, those speaking Indonesian use more egocentric and intrinsic language up to age 8 and start switching to geocentric language only after that age. The results of the mixed group are intermediate but closer to the Balinese-speaking group. It therefore seems that bilingualism with a language that favors an egocentric FoR has a strong impact, reducing the choice of the geocentric frame in children up to age 10, after which they all conform to the local adult norm even when they speak Indonesian. Before age 10, the children preferring Indonesian used more egocentric and intrinsic language, whereas the Balinese speakers never used any of these language categories, even at an early age.

In our study in Bali, bilingualism occurred as a sort of (useful) accident in our design, which means that this variable is not pure but is linked to other sociocultural and ecological variables. For example, the children who prefer to speak Indonesian tend to be from the higher socioeconomic status (SES) families in the city. In the structural equation model (see Figure 11.3), preferring to speak Balinese defines a virtual variable, traditional culture, together with the knowledge of the Balinese orientation system, a variable that is also linked to ecology (village vs. city) and to SES. It is this cluster that determines the likelihood of using geospatial language or geospatial encoding rather than the separate components.

Our results in Bali contrast those of another study of bilingualism we carried out in Kathmandu, Nepal, where the sampling was purposely organized to contrast children schooled in Nepali or in English (see Chapter 10, this volume). A similar conformity to the adult norm was found in the older age group, but not the impact of bilingualism at younger ages. The structural equation model also contains a traditional culture virtual variable, but its impact on geospatial language and encoding is very different (i.e., nonexistent or even negative). The reasons for this discrepancy are discussed by Dasen and Mishra (2010) and in Chapter 10 of this volume.

---

[3]*Intrinsic language* is defined for the purposes of this research as referring one object to another, with terms such as *near, next to, before*, and so forth. It relates to what Piaget called *topological space*.

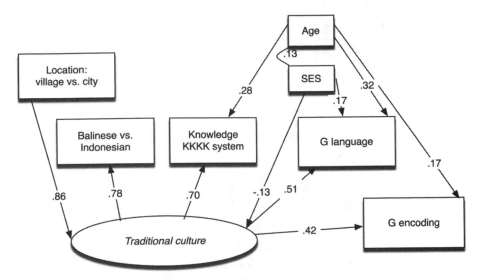

Figure 11.3. Amos structural equation model for Bali. Fit statistics: likelihood ratio chi-square = 6.114, *df* = 10, *p* = .806; root-mean-square error of approximation = 0; goodness-of-fit index = .99; comparative fit index = 1; Tucker–Lewis index = 1.025. Knowledge = knowledge of Balinese orientation system inside; Balinese vs. Indonesian = language spoken at home and on our tests; G (geocentric) language and G encoding = Princals summary object scores; KKKK = north, south, east, west in Bali; SES = socioeconomic status.

Figure 11.4 presents the proportion of geocentric encoding on the non-verbal encoding tasks in the two main locations of our study in Bali (a small city in the north of the island and a village nearby). The figure shows the impact of ecology, with more geocentric encoding in the rural locations. This is, of course, an ecocultural variable reflecting closeness to Balinese traditional culture or, one might say, the opposite of acculturation to outside influences. The figure also shows that results can be quite different with different task situations; notably, in all of our studies, we found that one task, called *Steve's maze*, produces systematically more egocentric encoding. In this task, children are asked to remember the shape of a path, which is much easier to encode iconically than linguistically. Task specificity is an argument in favor of cognitive style: Individuals choose to apply one type of frame in one situation but another type in another situation, even though these were designed to be structurally similar.

Task specificity is also illustrated through a change in procedures on the same task. For example, on the animals in rows task, the format initially used in most studies was to align three animals in a row in a sequence of five items. We then added a fourth animal placed at a right angle from the

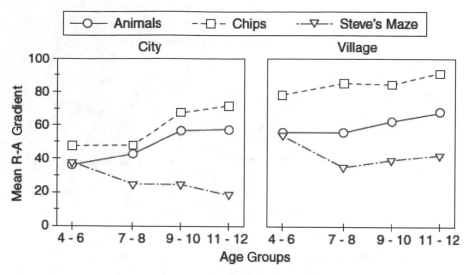

Figure 11.4. R-A (relative to absolute) gradients (i.e., proportion of geocentric encoding) on three tasks by location in Bali, Indonesia.

three, and we added two items with a 90° instead of a 180° rotation (cf. Chapter 10, this volume). The new procedure obviously represents a much more stringent measure of geocentric encoding, eliminating, in particular, the possible confusion between intrinsic (e.g., three animals aligned with the table's edge) and geocentric encoding. The impact of such a change of procedure is illustrated in Figure 11.5 for the Geneva sample. When only three

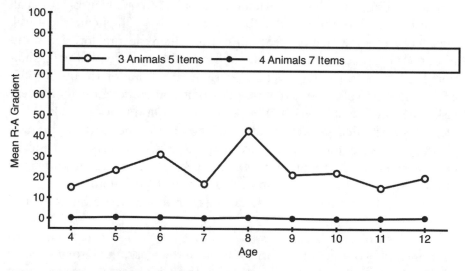

Figure 11.5. Geocentric encoding on animals in rows task, with change in procedures (five and seven items), in Geneva, Switzerland. R-A = relative to absolute.

animals were used, there seemed to be an average of about 20% of geocentric encoding, about one item out of five. Contrary to what we found in the other locations of our study, in Geneva there was no age trend (the variations are nonsignificant). When the more stringent procedure was used, the percent of geocentric encoding becomes zero. In other words, in Geneva, there was no geocentric encoding (just as there was no geocentric language being used at any age).

This complete absence of a geocentric FoR is a challenge to our interpretation in terms of cognitive styles: In Geneva, there seems to be a complete absence of a particular cognitive process. Nevertheless, we argue that even in Geneva, this frame can be used, albeit in a different context, in particular when traveling for longer distances. But in Geneva, geocentric references are never carried inside and used for table space. Also, recent research by Troadec (2009) with French children showed that these can be trained to use larger outside references such as landmarks.

CONCLUSION

Although we chose for this chapter only a few examples out of the complete project (Dasen & Mishra, 2010; see also Chapter 10, this volume), they illustrate our overarching theoretical frameworks: that of the ecocultural framework and that of cultural differences in cognitive styles. As to the latter, it is obvious that the children in Bali possessed both frames of spatial reference—the egocentric and the geocentric—and, for the latter, two forms of it—the traditional Balinese frame and the cardinal directions linked to Bahasa Indonesian. The overall preference in this context is obviously the geocentric frame, but depending on various ecocultural variables, the egocentric frame also comes into play. For example, children who live in the city rather than in the village and those who prefer to speak Bahasa Indonesian chose egocentric language and egocentric encoding up to half the time until age 9, whereas village children preferred geocentric language exclusively as early as age 4. The latter also preferred geocentric encoding from early on, at least on one of the tasks, chips (cf. Chapter 10, this volume); task specificity is in itself an illustration of the functioning of a cognitive style.

The limits of a cognitive style interpretation are illustrated with the results from Geneva, where geocentric language and encoding were absent in daily behavior, and on the tasks used in this research. We keep the interpretation of cognitive style on the assumption that even Western children could, in the right circumstances, and certainly when given the necessary training, switch to a geocentric frame.

The results also illustrate the framework presented in Figure 11.1. The developing child in Bali, for example, is surrounded by a developmental niche that, through enculturation and socialization, fosters the choice of a geocentric frame through language and various cultural practices, some of which are linked to religion and hence have a strong ideological aspect. This is also illustrated in the results in Varanasi reported in Chapter 10 of this volume. Hence, this development obviously occurs within a wider ecocultural context. Acculturation, or culture change, is illustrated through the impact of bilingualism and in the urban–rural contrast. Language is an important part of cultural transmission, but contrary to Levinson's (2003) affirmation of strong linguistic relativism, it is only one aspect of the overall ecocultural framework.

REFERENCES

Akkari, A., & Dasen, P. R. (2008). The globalization of schooling: Major trends and issues in the South and the North. In P. R. Dasen & A. Akkari (Eds.), *Educational theories and practices from the majority world* (pp. 367–392). New Delhi, India: Sage.

Berry, J. W. (1976). *Human ecology and cognitive style*. New York, NY: Sage/Halsted/Wiley.

Berry, J. W., & Bennett, J. A. (1991). *Cree syllabic literacy: Cultural context and psychological consequences*. Tilburg, the Netherlands: Tilburg University Press.

Berry, J. W., Poortinga, Y. H., Segall, M. H., & Dasen, P. R. (2002). *Cross-cultural psychology; Research and applications* (2nd ed., rev.). Cambridge, England: Cambridge University Press.

Berteaux, P. (2010). Influence des modes d'enculturation scolaire sur les styles cognitifs: L'exemple des écoles coranique et laïque à La Réunion et aux Comores [The influence of school enculturation modes on cognitive styles: The example of Koranic and government schools in Réunion and the Comoros]. *Carrefours de l'éducation, 29*, 215–237.

Bronfenbrenner, U. (1979). *The ecology of human development*. Cambridge, MA: Harvard University Press.

Cole, M., Gay, J., Glick, J. A., & Sharp, D. W. (1971). *The cultural context of learning and thinking: An exploration in experimental anthropology*. New York, NY: Basic Books.

Dasen, P. R. (1975a). Concrete operational development in three cultures. *Journal of Cross-Cultural Psychology, 6*, 156–172. doi:10.1177/002202217562002

Dasen, P. R. (1975b). Le développement des operations concrètes chez les esquimaux canadiens [The development of concrete operations in Canadian Inuit children]. *International Journal of Psychology, 10*, 165–180. doi:10.1080/00207597508247330

Dasen, P. R. (1984). The cross-cultural study of intelligence: Piaget and the Baoulé. *International Journal of Psychology, 19*, 407–434. doi:10.1080/00207598408247539

Dasen, P. R. (2003). Theoretical frameworks in cross-cultural developmental psychology: An attempt at integration. In T. S. Saraswathi (Ed.), *Cross-cultural perspectives in human development: Theory, research, and applications* (pp. 128–165). New Delhi, India: Sage.

Dasen, P. R. (2008). Informal education and learning processes. In P. R. Dasen & A. Akkari (Eds.), *Educational theories and practices from the majority world* (pp. 25–48). New Delhi, India: Sage.

Dasen, P. R., Berry, J. W., & Witkin, H. A. (1979). The use of developmental theories cross-culturally. In L. Eckensberger, Y. Poortinga, & W. Lonner (Eds.), *Cross-cultural contributions to psychology* (pp. 69–82). Amsterdam, the Netherlands: Swets & Zeitlinger.

Dasen, P. R., Gajardo, A., & Ngeng, L. (2005). Education informelle, ethnomathématiques et processus d'apprentissage [Informal education, ethnomathematics and learning processes]. In O. Maulini & C. Montandon (Eds.), *Formel? Informel? Les formes de l'éducation* (pp. 39–63). Brussels, Belgium: DeBoeck Université.

Dasen, P. R., Inhelder, B., Lavallée, M., & Retschitzki, J. (1978). *Naissance de l'intelligence chez l'enfant Baoulé de Côte d'Ivoire* [The birth of intelligence in Baoulé children of Côte d'Ivoire]. Berne, Switzerland: Hans Huber.

Dasen, P. R., Lavallée, M., & Retschitzki, J. (1979). Training conservation of quantity (liquids) in West African (Baoulé) children. *International Journal of Psychology, 14*, 57–68. doi:10.1080/00207597908246712

Dasen, P. R., & Mishra, R. C. (2010). *Development of geocentric spatial language and cognition: An eco-cultural perspective.* Cambridge, England, and New Delhi, India: Cambridge University Press. doi:10.1017/CBO9780511761058

Dasen, P. R., Ngini, L., & Lavallée, M. (1979). Cross-cultural training studies of concrete operations. In L. Eckensberger, Y. Poortinga, & W. Lonner (Eds.), *Cross-cultural contributions to psychology* (pp. 94–104). Amsterdam, the Netherlands: Swets & Zeitlinger.

Dörnyei, Z. (2005). *The psychology of the language learner.* Mahwah, NJ: Erlbaum.

Fischer, R., & Fontaine, J. R. J. (2011). Methods for investigating structural equivalence. In D. Matsumoto & F. J. R. van de Vijver (Eds.), *Cross–cultural research methods in psychology* (pp. 179–215). Cambridge, England: Cambridge University Press.

Goody, J., & Watt, I. (1963). The consequences of literacy. *Comparative Studies in Society and History, 5*, 304–345. doi:10.1017/S0010417500001730

Greenfield, P. M., Keller, H., Fuligni, A., & Maynard, A. (2003). Cultural pathways through universal development. *Annual Review of Psychology, 54*, 461–490. doi:10.1146/annurev.psych.54.101601.145221

Harkness, S., & Super, C. M. (Eds.). (1996). *Parents' cultural belief systems: Their origins, expressions, and consequences.* New York, NY: Guilford Press.

Inhelder, B., Sinclair, H., & Bovet, M. (1974). *Learning and the development of cognition*. London, England: Routledge & Kegan Paul.

Kagitçibasi, C. (1997). Individualism and collectivism. In J. W. Berry, M. H. Segall, & C. Kagitçibasi (Eds.), *Handbook of cross-cultural psychology: Vol. 3. Social psychology* (2nd ed., pp. 1–49). Boston, MA: Allyn & Bacon.

Lavallée, M., & Dasen, P. R. (1980). L'apprentissage de la notion d'inclusion de classes chez de jeunes enfants Baoulés (Côte d'Ivoire) [The learning of class inclusion by young Baoulé children (Côte d'Ivoire)]. *Journal of Instructional Psychology, 15*, 27–41.

Levinson, S. C. (2003). *Space in language and cognition*. Cambridge, England: Cambridge University Press. doi:10.1017/CBO9780511613609

Mishra, K. (1998). *Cognitive style of Tharu children in relation to daily life activities and experiences of schooling* (Unpublished doctoral dissertation). Banaras Hindu University, Varanasi, India.

Mishra, R. C., Sinha, D., & Berry, J. W. (1996). *Ecology, acculturation and psychological adaptation: A study of Adivasis in Bihar*. New Delhi, India: Sage.

Nisbett, R. E. (2003). *The geography of thought: How Asians and Westerners think differently . . . and why*. New York, NY: Free Press.

Nunes, T., Schliemann, A. S., & Carraher, D. W. (1993). *Street mathematics and school mathematics*. Cambridge, England: Cambridge University Press.

Pashler, H., McDaniel, M., Rohrer, D., & Bjork, R. (2008). Learning styles: Concepts and evidence. *Psychological Science in the Public Interest, 9*, 105–119.

Retschitzki, J. (1989). Evidence of formal thinking in Baoulé awele players. In D. M. Keats, D. Munro, & L. Mann (Eds.), *Heterogeneity in cross-cultural psychology* (pp. 234–243). Amsterdam, the Netherlands: Swets & Zeitlinger.

Riding, R. (2002). Cognitive style: A review. In R. Riding & S. G. Rayner (Eds.), *Interpersonal perspectives on individual differences: Vol. 1. Cognitive styles* (pp. 315–344). Stamford, CT: Ablex.

Saxe, G. B. (1991). *Culture and cognitive development: Studies in mathematical understanding*. Hillsdale, NJ: Erlbaum.

Schliemann, A., Carraher, D., & Ceci, S. (1997). Everyday cognition. In J. W. Berry, P. R. Dasen, & T. S. Saraswathi (Eds.), *Handbook of cross-cultural psychology: Vol. 2. Basic processes and human development* (2nd ed., pp. 177–216). Boston, MA: Allyn & Bacon.

Schliemann, A. D., & Acioly, N. M. (1989). Mathematical knowledge developed at work: The contribution of practice versus the contribution of schooling. *Cognition and Instruction, 6*, 185–221. doi:10.1207/s1532690xci0603_1

Scribner, S. (1979). Modes of thinking and ways of speaking: Culture and logic reconsidered. In R. O. Freedle (Ed.), *New directions in discourse processing* (pp. 223–243). Norwood, NJ: Ablex.

Scribner, S., & Cole, M. (1981). *The psychology of literacy*. Cambridge, MA: Harvard University Press.

Segall, M. H., Dasen, P. R., Berry, J. W., & Poortinga, Y. H. (1999). *Human behavior in global perspective: An introduction to cross-cultural psychology* (2nd ed., rev.). Boston, MA: Allyn & Bacon.

Sinha, D. (1982). Sociocultural factors and the development of perceptual and cognitive skills. In W. W. Hartup, I. M. Ahammer, & H. L. J. Pick (Eds.), *Review of child development research* (Vol. 6, pp. 441–472). Chicago, IL: University of Chicago Press.

Sternberg, R. J., & Grigorenko, E. L. (2001). A capsule history of theory and research on styles. In R. J. Sternberg & L.-F. Zhang (Eds.), *Perspectives on thinking, learning, and cognitive styles* (pp. 1–21). Mahwah, NJ: Erlbaum.

Super, C. M., & Harkness, S. (1997). The cultural structuring of child development. In J. W. Berry, P. R. Dasen, & T. S. Saraswathi (Eds.), *Handbook of cross-cultural psychology: Vol. 2. Basic processes and human development* (2nd ed., pp. 1–39). Boston, MA: Allyn & Bacon.

Tapé, G. (1994). *L'intelligence en Afrique: Une étude du raisonnement experimental* [Intelligence in Africa: A study of experimental reasoning]. Paris, France: L'Harmattan.

Troadec, B. (2009). *Genèse des connaissances et contexts écologiques et culturels: Les exemples de l'espace et du temps* [The genesis of knowledge and ecological and cultural contexts: The examples of space and time]. Bordeaux, France: Université Victor Segalen.

Troadec, B. (2011). Cognition et culture: Le rôle de la transmission sociale et culturelle [Cognition and culture: The role of social and cultural transmission]. In B. Troadec & T. Bellaj (Eds.), *Psychologies et cultures* (pp. 25–62). Paris, France: L'Harmattan.

Wassmann, J., & Dasen, P. R. (1998). Balinese spatial orientation: Some empirical evidence for moderate linguistic relativity. *Journal of the Royal Anthropological Institute, 4,* 689–711.

Witkin, H. A. (1978). *Cognitive style in personal and cultural adaptation.* Worcester, MA: Clark University Press.

Witkin, H. A., & Berry, J. W. (1975). Psychological differentiation in cross-cultural perspective. *Journal of Cross–Cultural Psychology, 6,* 4–87.

Zhang, L.-F., & Sternberg, R. J. (2006). *The nature of intellectual styles.* Mahwah, NJ: Erlbaum.

IV

LANGUAGE AND READING DEVELOPMENT

12

CHILDREN'S READING DEVELOPMENT: LEARNING ABOUT SOUNDS, SYMBOLS, AND CROSS-MODAL MAPPINGS

SONALI NAG AND MARGARET J. SNOWLING

Reading draws on multiple cognitive and linguistic domains in complex ways. Research in the last half century or so has begun to clarify how children learn about the script of a language. A comprehensive theoretical account about reading development, however, remains elusive, and it is not immediately apparent how theories that have evolved in the context of one language or script can account for phenomena seen in other writing systems. A mature science of reading should explain how learning occurs across languages and across scripts. Moreover, because languages and scripts vary in multiple ways, it follows that the models of reading need to factor in different developmental pathways into proficiency.

Ziegler and Goswami (2005) drew together cross-linguistic findings to explain reading development across languages, proposing three contributing

This chapter was written while Sonali Nag was a Newton International Fellow at the University of York. Sections of the research reported here were funded by a British Academy grant to Margaret J. Snowling. The authors acknowledge with gratitude the participation of children and their families and schools in the studies reported in the chapter.

DOI: 10.1037/14043-013
Cognition and Brain Development: Converging Evidence From Various Methodologies, B. R. Kar (Editor)

factors. The first factor was the *availability* of different sound units prior to reading. The second factor was the degree of *consistency* seen in the associations between the sounds and the symbols of the language. The third factor was *granularity*, which refers to the level of mappings between the sounds and symbols in the language, whether they were smaller or larger sized units. The authors also argued that the nature of instruction is important for understanding reading development. This framework, known as the *psycholinguistic grain size theory*, considers reading development to depend on the abstraction of optimal mappings between orthographic units and the sounds of the language.

The factors of availability, consistency, and granularity are each seen to aid in the process of learning. Thus, if the sound units represented by the writing system are phonological structures that are already established in everyday speech, that availability should make learning to read easier. If the correspondences between sounds and symbols are consistent and hence predictable, then learning the associations becomes easier. Granularity is perhaps the least specified factor in the proposal. Granularity refers to whether a writing system represents sounds at one particular sublexical level or if there are multiple mappings (as in English, to large and small units simultaneously); the concept thus embodies the "grain size" of the phonological units to which the symbols map (large vs. small) and whether the mappings are fine or coarse grained. Within this view, scripts that contain predominantly one size of unit (e.g., Finnish with phoneme-level units) should be easier to learn than languages in which mappings to symbol units are at more than one unit size. English is often given as an example of a language with such multisized mappings, in which minimal sound units (e.g., the phoneme /ai/) may be represented by single letters (e.g., *I*) and also by letter strings (e.g., *igh*). Such multiple mappings are seen as presenting a challenge to learners. It is notable, however, that the psycholinguistic grain size framework is silent about scripts outside the alphabetic writing systems, and although there is an implicit assumption that the formulation is language-general (e.g., Yang, McCandliss, Shu, & Zevin, 2009), it is as yet unclear how universal the constructs in the framework are.

In this chapter, we begin by discussing some of the ways in which scripts differ and why it is important to attend to these differences in order to understand children's reading development. We then go on to examine one particular script, the alphasyllabary of Kannada, a language spoken in South India. The Kannada orthography (and, more generally, alphasyllabic writing systems) is understudied and is a good test case for current theories of reading development. Taking the psycholinguistic grain size model as a framework, we first specify the processes involved in learning about the sounds and symbols in the Kannada writing system and then examine the predictors of individual differences in reading attainment. We end this chapter by discussing the commonalities in reading development using findings from the alphasyllabic, logographic, and alphabetic scripts. Specifically, we consider the cognitive universals that underpin reading acquisition across writing systems.

The ground that this chapter covers is specific to the sound–symbol learning processes involved in learning to read. We acknowledge that the purpose of reading is for understanding, and hence knowledge of morphology and syntax is also important to reading development. Moreover, methods of instruction can change the developmental pathways into literacy. However, our focus is on reading accuracy and reading fluency and the skills for learning the symbols of a writing system and the sounds they represent.

DIVERSITY IN SCRIPTS

Scripts differ in appearance, or the visual form of its symbol set. They also differ in the ways in which the symbols map onto units in the speech stream. A perceptually salient unit of the speech stream is the *syllable*, which in turn is made up of perceptually less stable units called *phonemes*. A combination of the phonemes /m/ and /ai/, for example, makes the syllable unit/ mai/. The alphasyllabic scripts of South Asian languages like Bengali, Hindi, and Tamil have code spoken speech at two levels. Symbol units, called *akshara*, represent sounds at the level of a syllable and a phoneme (Salomon, 2000). In contrast, the alphabetic scripts of languages like English, Czech, and Italian represent sounds at the level of the phoneme. Returning to the example of /m/ + /ai/, English captures the two phonemes in a spelling with two symbols (the pronoun *my*), whereas in an alphasyllabary, this one-syllable word is spelled with one symbol (representation at the level of syllable), but there are distinct visual features within the symbol linked to /m/ + /ai/ (representation at the level of the phonemes). In the case of both alphasyllabic and alphabetic scripts, the symbol units are sublexical representations. These symbol units map onto spoken language at a level that is not meaning bearing in itself. In other scripts, such as Japanese Kanji, symbol units called *characters* typically encode lexical information. Each character maps onto a morpheme, making the symbol units lexical or meaning-representations of spoken language. The difference between a meaning-bearing and a non-meaning-bearing symbol system implies that scripts differ in their representational characteristics.

Given the differing characteristics of writing systems, it is natural to expect that script-specific typological features will influence learning to read. For example, we know that the pace of learning depends on the size of the symbol set; the contained orthographies of Latin-derived scripts comprise between 20 and 40 letters, and the names and sounds of these letters are typically learned by the end of first year in school (Seymour, 2005). The more extensive symbol sets of the Indian alphasyllabaries, with 200 to 500 symbols, take longer, with less frequent symbols not yet fully mastered by children in Grades 3 and 4 (Nag, 2007; Sircar & Nag, in press; Tiwari, Nair, & Krishnan, 2011). In Chinese, the number of characters runs into the thousands, and surveys show that learning of new character symbols continues into Grade 6 and beyond (Shu, Chen, Anderson, Wu, & Xuan, 2003). Because learning to read depends on establishing mappings between phonology and orthography, statistical learning principles underpin reading acquisition across languages (Seidenberg, 2007). The influence of statistical learning mechanisms in organizing the reading system has been demonstrated in studies of symbol learning (Yang, et al., 2009) and reading (Zevin & Seidenberg, 2004). Notwithstanding this language-general learning mechanism, a comprehensive account of reading development needs to explain variations in component processes in different writing systems. Examples of components are symbol learning, phonology or sound processing, and cross-modal mappings between sounds and symbols. Such features of diversity in scripts have been examined from various points of view (see Exhibit 12.1).

SCRIPT-SPECIFIC ASPECTS OF LEARNING TO READ

To begin our examination of the script-specific processes that are involved in learning to read, we turn to Kannada, an alphasyllabic writing system. Table 12.1 gives a quick overview of how the Kannada writing system is distinct from the alphabet system of English. Kannada belongs to the South Dravidian group of languages and is a language of South India. The Kannada symbol unit, called akshara, is derived from the ancient Indian script called the Brahmi script, and this lineage makes Kannada closely related to the several other Brahmi-derived alphasyllabaries of South and Southeast Asia. Thus, like the Bengali, Hindi, and Tamil scripts, the Kannada writing system comprises four types of symbol sets: primary vowels (/V/), consonants with the vowel /a/ (/Ca/), consonants with vowels other than /a/ (/CV/), and consonant clusters (/CCV/).[1] The vowel /a/ in the orthographic syllable /Ca/ is unmarked, and this has led to the use of the term *inherent vowel* to describe these symbols.

A second feature of the akshara system is the stacking together (i.e., arranging together) of two or more phonemic markers to form the /CV/ and /CCV/ symbols. The inherent vowels and stacked phonemic markers have together been considered as defining features of the akshara writing system

---

[1]The phonemic consonant /C/ is the fifth akshara type; these are similar to the /Ca/ akshara, with markers to suppress the inherent vowel /a/.

EXHIBIT 12.1
Three Perspectives on Writing Systems

A *typological perspective* is essentially a nonhistorical approach that focuses on script characteristics rather than the context in which the script has emerged and is used. A typology of writing systems that has been popular for several decades is the threefold classification of logographic, syllabic, and alphabetic scripts. A problem with this narrow classification is that many of the world's scripts do not neatly fit into these categories. There are scripts that have mixed characteristics, such as the Indian *akshara* (a symbol unit that represents sounds at the level of a syllable and a phoneme) writing systems, which have both alphabetic and syllabic features. In addition, the classification system undervalues the ways in which scripts, particularly those referred to as logographic, represent sublexical phonetic information.

In a *cultural enterprise perspective,* different types of writing systems are seen as particular solutions that emerged within different cultures for the common aim of coding spoken language. This perspective acknowledges that all writing systems are a motivated solution (see, e.g., Seidenberg, 2011) and essentially disagrees with the notion of alphabetic solutions being the best solution.

An *evolutionary perspective* is essentially a sociopolitically driven approach that judges one script or set of scripts as higher in level than another. Thus, the alphabetic scripts may be presented as more advanced than the logographic and syllabic scripts. Historically, the most strident manifestations of this perspective have been the mass-scale destruction of nonalphabetic texts—the Mayan texts during the Spanish inquisition, for example. In recent years the perspective is less visible and often couched within arguments that the differing pace of learning in different scripts is problematic. A faster rate of learning is argued to make one script better than the other. For example, the shift from the Arabic script to the Latin script for the Turkish language came to be seen as a "positive change" because the Latin script was seen as being simple and allowing for a more transparent and easy-to-learn writing system (Davis, 2005, p. 10). The politics of placing one script over another has far-reaching implications for policy and practice and for how theorizing will account for differences.

(Nag, 2011; Salomon, 2000). Both of these typological features have an impact on children's symbol learning and sound processing and the mapping of sounds to symbols in Kannada. Most of the current research in Kannada is on the impact of the stacked phonemes on learning to read, and even though the inherent feature of the vowel /a/ is one of the first aspects of the writing system that children encounter, we do not as yet understand how this null marker is learned or what the influences of this feature may be on emergent understanding of mappings between sound and symbol (Sircar & Nag, in press).

LEARNING ABOUT SYMBOLS

Children learning to read in Kannada have to master a set of about 400 akshara. For each akshara, they have to learn the association between the symbol and the constituent sounds and the rules that govern the making of

TABLE 12.1

A Comparison of the Kannada Writing System With English

Area	Kannada	English
Name of symbol unit	Akshara	Letter
Phonological representation of symbol units	Level of both syllables and phonemes	Level of only phonemes
Orthographic representation for consonants or vowels	Two representations, a primary form and a secondary form	Single representation; may be written in upper- or lowercase
Choice of symbol for any given consonant or vowel	Governed by phonological context—for example, use of secondary form if unit follows a consonant	Governed by writing conventions—for example, use of uppercase to begin a sentence
Distinctive feature	Use of phonemic markers and stacking of phonemes to make symbol blocks	Use of individual symbols for each phoneme and lined up in a linear fashion rather than in blocks
Symbol set	Extensive (400+ symbols)	Contained (26 symbols)

Note. Akshara = a symbol unit that represents sounds at the level of a syllable and a phoneme.

symbol sequences in the system. Because information in much of the 400-plus symbol set is redundant, learning the combinatorial rules for stacking of phonemes to form /CV/ and /CCV/ akshara allows for a more economical route to mastery. In addition, the frequency of encounters with the akshara shapes the learning process. In this section, we examine each of these aspects of learning the akshara symbols.

The influential orthographic depth framework categorizes writing systems according to the extent to which symbols reliably and consistently represent sounds. The more consistent systems are called *shallow* or *transparent* orthographies and the more unpredictable ones *deep* or *opaque* orthographies (Bentin & Frost, 1987). Within the orthographic depth framework, Kannada would feature as a transparent orthography, and research with other consistent but alphabetic writing systems would suggest that this consistency aids the process of learning to read (Seymour, 2005; Ziegler et al., 2010).

There are no published studies that have investigated systematically the consistency effect in Kannada. One study in the Hindi alphasyllabary, however, confirmed that the consistency of the akshara writing system aids reading (Rao, Vaid, Srinivasan, & Chen, 2011). Hindi-Urdu words can be closely matched on morphological and semantic parameters because of the sociohistorical processes that have shaped these languages. It is therefore possible to compile lists of words that differ only in the script used to write the items. In this way it is possible to contrast the consistency in an akshara script,

Hindi, with the more opaque Arabic-derived alphabetic script of Urdu. Rao et al. (2011) exploited this aspect of the Hindi–Urdu language pair to study the impact of consistency on adult word recognition. They showed that the orthographic depth of Urdu attracted greater processing costs during visual word recognition than the more consistent Hindi. In Kannada, too, similar advantages of consistency can be expected during visual word recognition. But given the sheer number of symbols that must be learned, the advantages of consistency are overshadowed by the extensiveness of the symbol set, at least in the initial phases of akshara learning (Nag, 2007).

Graphotactics can be defined as rules for the use of specific symbols, individually and in combination with other symbols (Coulmas, 1999). These rules define what is legal in a writing system. In linear writing systems such as French and English, graphotactic conventions define what sequences of letters are allowed in spelling. In the visually complex Chinese, spatial conventions define how the characters must be written out. In Kannada, the role of graphotactic conventions in symbol learning flows out of the availability of two symbol representations for all sounds. All consonants and vowels have two symbol representations—a full symbol, called the *primary form*, and a diacritic symbol, referred to as the *secondary form* (see Figure 12.1 for examples). Each pair of primary and secondary forms maps onto the same sound on every occasion, and it is this regularity of mapping that makes Kannada a consistent orthography. Among consonants, the primary form is used to represent the consonant in the /Ca/ and /CV/ syllables, and the diacritic form is used to represent the second and third consonant in consonant clusters. Among vowels, the diacritic form is used when the vowel follows a consonant. For vowels in word-initial positions or representing a separate morpheme, the primary form is used. These rules for choosing the appropriate symbols on the basis of the phonological context of a sound add a layer to symbol learning in Kannada (and indeed all akshara languages) that is not seen in many writing systems.

A further detail about the akshara system is that some akshara in the middle of words are representations of sound units from two syllables. These medial akshara represent the coda of the preceding syllable and the onset or full syllable of the next. Thus, the second akshara /nnu/ in the word /ka-nnu/ (eye) comprises the coda in /kan/ and the final syllable /nu/. Although not much is known about how akshara that straddle two syllables are learned in Kannada, there is evidence from Bengali that these sorts of akshara–syllable relationships are particularly difficult for children to learn (Sircar & Nag, in press).

Individual differences in learning the details of the symbol set can be seen early in development. In a longitudinal study, differences in akshara knowledge were seen right through primary school (Nag, 2007). When these

	Primary Symbol Form	Secondary Symbol Form
	Kannada	
/o/	**M**	**ÉÆ**
/m/	**ªÀïï**	**ä**
/p/	**¥ï**	**à**
	Bengali	
/o/	৩	(ⵔ)T
/n/	**XË**	**O**
/b/	**[Ë**	**'**

Figure 12.1. A selection of primary and secondary forms in two akshara systems. An *akshara* is a symbol unit that represents sounds at the level of a syllable and a phoneme.

children were in middle school, we investigated the profile of the poor readers in the group. Children who fell in the bottom 15% of reading attainment had difficulties in multiple domains: phonological processing, speed of processing, vocabulary and knowledge of inflections, and visual processing. Importantly, poor readers almost always showed very poor knowledge of the akshara (Nag & Snowling, 2011). Their knowledge of consonant clusters and less often encountered akshara was particularly low. One reason for consonant clusters (/CCV/, /CCCV/) being difficult could be because these clusters represent a larger set of phonemes and thus require recall of more visual features to construct the akshara. In addition, limited encounters with certain /Ca/ and /CV/ akshara in day-to-day reading and writing tasks probably account for the time taken to become fluent. Although all children take longer to learn these infrequently encountered akshara, acquisition is particularly slow for poor readers.

LEARNING ABOUT SOUNDS

Children's phonological awareness is influenced by the characteristics of their ambient language. In a comparison of Czech and German, which share several cognates, ambient language shaped the extent of explicit awareness that children had about word onsets (Caravolas & Landerl, 2010). Czech, unlike German, has a high frequency of consonant clusters in the word-initial position, and phonemic awareness for word-initial sounds had developed to a greater extent among the Czech children when compared with the German children in the study. These were children who had not yet received any reading instruction, making the finding particularly important because the main debate in research with alphabetic scripts has been the nature of the relationship between growth of phonemic awareness and reading instruction.

In this section, we examine the factors that influence the growth of syllable- and phoneme-level processing based on a study of 95 Grades 4 and 5 children studying Kannada as their first school language. In Kannada, as in the few other akshara languages that have been documented, children show high levels of syllable awareness, but growth of phonemic skills is relatively slow. We first developed a set of 73 nonsense words by taking a list of common bisyllabic words and interchanging one syllable between word pairs. We did this iteratively until all the obtained items were meaningless in the language. We chose to study how children would perform at the syllable and phoneme level on tasks that were matched for task demands—a substitution task in which a target had to be replaced with another supplied syllable/ phoneme and a deletion task in which the target had to be dropped. We were also interested to see how the position of a phonological unit would influence performance.

Overall, children found tasks requiring syllable processing easier than those requiring processing of phonemes. Table 12.2 shows the means for performance in two positions (initial, final) for the two types of task (substitution, deletion). The top row is the results for syllable manipulations and the bottom row for phoneme manipulations. On syllables, children's performance was significantly better when the target sound was in the initial position. Moreover, manipulations requiring initial syllable deletions were

TABLE 12.2
Means (Standard Deviations) of Proportion of Correct Responses
for Syllable- and Phoneme-Level Manipulations According to
Type of Task and Position of Manipulation ($N = 95$)

Symbol unit	Deletion task		Substitution task	
	Initial	Final	Initial	Final
Syllable	.84 (.20)	.43 (.20)	.74 (.28)	.48 (.22)
Phoneme	.18 (.26)	.19 (.24)	.12 (.19)	.19 (.28)

easier than initial syllable substitutions. There was a significant main effect of position (initial, final), $F(1, 94) = 317.26$, $p < .001$, $\eta^2 = .5$, but not task (substitution, deletion), and there was an interaction between task and position, $F(1, 94) = 21.77$, $p < .001$, $\eta^2 = .04$.

It is also clear from Table 12.2 that the children had significant difficulty in all conditions requiring the manipulation of phonemes (second row). Of the 95 children, 74 performed above chance level on both tasks in both positions; the rest were unable to be accurate even on one trial (floor effect). When compared to syllable manipulations, the trends were reversed for phonemes; the final position was easier than the initial position on the phoneme substitution task.

We also examined the role of syllable complexity on performance. We studied manipulation of simple /CV/ syllables and the more complex /CCV/ syllables in the word-final position. For the deletion task, the mean proportion score was .72 ($SD = .26$) on simple syllables and .13 ($SD = .26$) on complex syllables, and for the substitution task the mean proportion score was .67 ($SD = .32$) for simple and .30 ($SD = .24$) for complex syllables. Next, we analyzed the mean success rate on the four conditions of syllable substitution and syllable deletion for simple and complex syllables. There was a significant main effect of syllable complexity (simple, complex), $F(1, 94) = 304.46$, $p < .001$, $\eta^2 = .6$, but not task (substitution, deletion), and a significant Syllable Complexity × Task interaction, $F(1, 94) = 25.08$, $p < .001$, $\eta^2 = .03$. Our findings therefore show that complex syllables were significantly more difficult to manipulate than simple syllables. Moreover, syllable complexity affected performance in deletion more than in substitution, and the effect of task was significant on /CCV/ but not /CV/ structures. The analysis did not include the comparable phoneme tasks because too few children had shown a degree of skill for phoneme-level processing.

In summary, in a sample of Kannada readers, performance on syllable-processing tasks was better than on phoneme-processing tasks, and performance was modulated by the position of the phonological unit and its complexity. This detailed examination gives us insights into the factors that account for the pattern of phonological development among native speakers of Kannada.

LEARNING ABOUT CROSS-MODAL MAPPINGS

We turn next to the connections or mappings that emerge between the symbols of the writing system and the sounds of the language. The associative learning of symbols to sounds and sounds to symbols occurs across sensory modalities and is therefore a cross-modal process. Efficient mapping requires a fine-grained representation of the phonological details as well as the symbol system of the language. In the visually complex symbols of the Chinese writing system, linear and nonlinear arrangements of individual strokes combine to make functional symbol units called *radicals*. These units may be further organized into characters that, in part, indicate the sound or sounds they represent. Because individual strokes and radicals may not always carry phonetic information, this introduces a level of surface ambiguity to sound representation, particularly if the Latin-centric logic of a linear mapping of sound strings onto symbol strings is applied. Despite the seemingly arbitrary nature of sound–symbol associations and debates about the architecture of the orthography–phonology connections in the language (Perfetti, Liu, & Tan, 2005; Yang et al., 2009), there is evidence that fine-grained cross-modal mappings are an important learning requirement for Chinese literacy (Tong & McBride-Chang, 2010; Tong et al., 2011).

An indication of the possible cross-modal associations occurring in the Kannada alphasyllabary was first reported by Nag (2007). In a 3-year longitudinal survey that began when children were in Grades 1 through 3, the associations between type of akshara knowledge and level of phonological awareness were seen across grades. In Grade 1, knowledge about the akshara was limited to the /Ca/ symbols (i.e., akshara without phoneme markers), performance on phoneme tasks was at floor, and among the areas assessed the association of symbol–sound knowledge was circumscribed to the syllable. In Grade 4, knowledge of the akshara with phoneme markers (/CV/, /CCV/) had developed; performance on phoneme tasks, although still low, had emerged for many children; and association of phonological awareness and symbol–sound knowledge was strongest at the level of the phoneme. Further, children's knowledge of the akshara with phonemic markers was a predictor of phoneme-processing skills 15 months later. It would appear that those children who have better knowledge of cross-modal mappings between sound and symbol are more advanced in reading, and reciprocally, better reading helps further improve cross-modal mappings.

We tested this proposal in a cross-sectional analysis of the same 95 middle school children reported in the Learning About Sounds section of this chapter. We divided the children into three levels of reading fluency according to their speed and accuracy. Figure 12.2 summarizes the level of akshara knowledge and syllable and phoneme processing of the three reading fluency groups. Better readers had better akshara knowledge and better syllable and phoneme processing. But more important, there were differences in the intercorrelations between the measures. Among Level 1 readers, the association between akshara knowledge and syllable processing was significant ($r = .51$), but this was not the case among children in the more advanced reading fluency groups (Level 2, $r = .35$; Level 3, $r = .27$). At the level of the phoneme, a stepwise pattern was seen; Level 3 readers showed the strongest associations between akshara knowledge and phoneme processing ($r = .68$), followed by Level 2 ($r = .48$) and Level 1 ($r = .33$).

Together, these findings suggest there is a reciprocal relationship between learning about symbols and cross-modal mappings, phonological processing, and reading development. We suggest that the better knowledge of the akshara seen among fluent readers was accompanied by an awareness of the intrasymbol visual features that constitute the phonemes in the akshara. We propose that increasing knowledge about mappings of specific markers to phonemic units

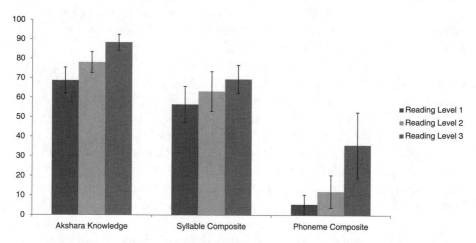

Figure 12.2. Percentage of correct responses among children in three reading levels on measures of akshara knowledge, syllable processing, and phoneme processing (error bars are at the 95% confidence interval). An *akshara* is a symbol unit that represents sounds at the level of a syllable and a phoneme. From "Reading in an Alphasyllabary: Implications for a Language Universal Theory of Learning to Read," by S. Nag and M. J. Snowling, 2012, *Scientific Studies of Reading, 16,* p. 415. Copyright 2012 by the Society for the Scientific Studies of Reading. Reprinted with permission of Taylor & Francis.

provides a boost to phonemic processing. This, then, is an important script-specific phenomenon, tied entirely to the type of sublexical representations embodied in the akshara writing system. The akshara has an alphasyllabic system of symbolic representation at the level of both syllables and phonemes. Children who infer this alphasyllabic principle are better readers.

The concurrent predictors of individual differences in this sample of readers further confirm the role of symbol and sound learning (akshara knowledge, phonological processing) and cross-modal mappings (which, we argue, is captured by the rapid automatized naming [RAN] task) in Kannada reading (Nag & Snowling, 2012). As might be predicted from our foregoing discussion, Kannada reading accuracy was strongly predicted by akshara knowledge, syllable awareness, and phoneme awareness. However, Kannada reading fluency was predicted by akshara knowledge, phoneme awareness, and RAN. Thus, similar to other writing systems, symbol knowledge was an important predictor for reading (Lin et al., 2010; Muter, Hulme, Snowling, & Stevenson, 2004; Puolakanaho et al., 2008). But akshara-specific factors also emerged as important. Recall that akshara knowledge is quite different from letter knowledge and character knowledge because of the way in which phonemic markers within a syllable are either parsed or stacked in nonlinear arrangements. At the level of sounds, we found that syllable and phoneme awareness were independent predictors of alphasyllabic reading. Whereas most studies with other writing systems have found one particular unit as being the best predictor of reading accuracy, this study with the alphasyllabic writing system suggests a dual representation at the level of the syllable and the phoneme. Thus, for logographic Chinese, syllables are important (Tong et al., 2011), and for alphabetic languages, phonemes are important (Ziegler et al., 2010); against this backdrop, our finding of a dual syllable–phoneme pattern of predictors makes this another script-specific finding.

Even though English and Kannada can be characterized as representing phonological details at both small and large grain sizes, there is a fundamental difference in the consistency of the sound–symbol mappings in the two writing systems. In English, the multiple types of sound–symbol mappings cause ambiguity (hence the mappings in /ai/—*igh, I, eye, ai*). In contrast, mappings in Kannada are regular and consistent; the small grain size representations of phonemic markers are not confusable with the large grain size representation of an orthographic syllable.

THE PSYCHOLINGUISTIC GRAIN SIZE FRAMEWORK REVISITED

We next consider the implications of our findings from an alphasyllabic writing system for psycholinguistic grain size theory (Ziegler & Goswami, 2005). We review three main predictions emerging from the theory: first, that the ease of learning to read is determined by the availability of the phonological units in the spoken language; second, that the consistency of the mappings between phonological and orthographic units should ease learning to read; and third, that the granularity of the mappings when fixed to one grain size should better support learning to read.

As we have seen, the Kannada alphasyllabary is an example of a writing system that is high in availability (of the sounds) and consistency (of the mappings). The akshara represents syllables, a phonological unit prominently available in ambient speech. Learning these large grain size representations enables reading to begin, leaving the task of learning the more ambiguous (less available) phoneme level units for later. Our findings confirmed that children were better at syllable than phoneme awareness, and in line with this, better readers had better-developed awareness of phonemes. Next, the framework's definition of consistency has to be refined from one-to-one correspondences, a construct that has grown out of alphabetic systems, to a description that includes mappings of one phoneme to two symbols. Within this broadened definition of consistency, the number of symbols increases, and the straightforward prediction that consistency implies ease of reading acquisition needs modification. Although Kannada is a consistent akshara language, both reading and spelling of words with low-frequency symbols remains hard well into middle school (Nag, 2007; Nag, Treiman, & Snowling, 2010).

However, it is in the third construct of granularity—the size of symbol units that can reliably map phonology in a language—that the framework is most clearly limited by conceptions that are based on linearized alphabetic writing systems. In alphabetic scripts, *grain size* refers to single letters (small grain size) or letter strings (chunks of large grain size). In this formulation, a writing system supports efficient reading more easily when the mappings are representations of a single grain size than when mappings are to both small and large grain size units. Kannada, with its consistent but dual representation at large and small unit sizes (syllable and phoneme), challenges this conception of granularity. Our findings suggest that akshara knowledge among the skilled readers of Kannada is characterized by knowledge of both the small and large unit sizes embedded in each symbol. Thus, our findings run contrary to the predictions made by the psycholinguistic grain size theory because this mixed representation did not appear to have an adverse effect on the rate of reading acquisition. Rather than multiple grain sizes increasing processing costs, better akshara knowledge predicted greater reading fluency. Put differently, alphasyllabic strategies that draw on mappings to phonemes and syllables (small and large grain size units) reduce rather than increase processing demands.

SCRIPT-INDEPENDENT ASPECTS OF LEARNING TO READ

A remaining question is whether some aspects of reading development are universal. A quick task analysis of the skills involved in learning about symbols, sounds, and the mappings between the two offers insights into script-independent processes.

There is strong evidence that children focus on visual features when learning to read. They are sensitive to feature position and their internal details (e.g. Nag et al., 2010; Tong et al., 2011) and the distributed information associated with neighboring visual features (Yang et al., 2009). This is irrespective of whether the features are embedded within Chinese characters, Kannada akshara, or Latin letters. Moreover, there appears to be a developmental progression in symbol processing for visually complex scripts, beginning with the processing of symbols as wholes and proceeding to attention to their internal details. In Chinese, for example, this would entail knowledge at the subcharacter level about semantic and phonetic information-bearing radicals (Tong & McBride-Chang, 2010); in the akshara languages, this would entail knowledge that phonemic markers reveal sound sequences (Nag, 2011). The level of task complexity involved, however, is much reduced in Latin-based scripts because of the simplicity of the visual arrangements in the writing system (Seidenberg, 2011). It seems therefore that such analytic processing of the underlying design of a script may be a universal process at the foundation of reading development.

Moving to knowledge about sounds for learning to read, Perfetti and Tan (1998) proposed the universal phonological hypothesis whereby, irrespective of the writing system, recognition of written words entails activation of the phonological domain. Strong evidence for this cognitive universal comes from the European orthographies (Ziegler et al., 2010), Chinese (Lin et al., 2010; Tong et al., 2011), and our own study with the Kannada alphasyllabary (Nag & Snowling, 2012). The strength of association of phonological awareness across the different component skills of reading differs and is moderated by the nature of the script. Among alphabetic scripts, phoneme awareness is a significant predictor for fluency in transparent orthographies but also for accuracy in opaque orthographies (Ziegler et al., 2010). Similarly, although the unit of significance may be different in different scripts—syllable for Chinese, phoneme for English, syllable-phoneme for Kannada—the processing skills for phonological units are unequivocally involved in learning to read.

Another general aspect of learning to read has to do with making efficient linkages between the sounds and symbols in a language. A prerequisite for establishing efficient mappings between sounds and symbols is fine-tuned knowledge about these two layers of representation; we propose that precision mappings are important for skilled reading in all languages. Indirect evidence of the role of precision mappings comes from the robust finding that rapid naming is a predictor for reading across languages (Ding, Richman, Yang, & Guo, 2010; Nag & Snowling, 2012; Puolakanaho et al., 2008; Ziegler et al., 2010). Rapid naming undeniably captures multiple parallel processes, including speed of processing, visual processing, and phonological processing. But the consistent finding that performance on the task predicts individual differences in reading skill across writing systems suggests that the associations are with the component in RAN associated with cross-modal mappings—a language-general phenomenon. Moreover, there is growing evidence that individuals who have difficulties in rapid naming are at high risk of reading failure (Puolakanaho et al., 2008).

CONCLUSION

In this chapter, we have examined many of the processes that are critical in order to "crack the code" of a writing system. We have argued that there are both language-specific and language-universal cognitive demands of learning to read and that different scripts pose differing challenges to the learner. Two key issues that remain understudied are how children acquire knowledge of the symbols of the language and what places constraints on this process. More generally, models of reading and its development need to take account of the diversity across writing systems if they are to inform not only theory but also practice in the field of reading and its disorders.

REFERENCES

Bentin, S., & Frost, R. (1987). Processing lexical ambiguity and visual word recognition in a deep orthography. *Memory & Cognition, 15,* 13–23. doi:10.3758/BF03197708

Caravolas, M., & Landerl, K. (2010). The influences of syllable structure and reading ability on the development of phoneme awareness: A longitudinal, cross-linguistic study. *Scientific Studies of Reading, 14,* 464–484. doi:10.1080/10888430903034804

Coulmas, F. (1999). *The Blackwell encyclopaedia of writing systems.* Oxford, England: Blackwell. doi:10.1111/b.9780631214816.1999.x

Davis, C. (2005). *Shallow vs non-shallow orthographies and learning to read workshop.* Paris, France: Organisation for Economic Co-operation and Development, Centre for Educational Research and Innovation.

Ding, Y., Richman, L. C., Yang, L., & Guo, J. (2010). Rapid automatized naming and immediate memory functions in Chinese Mandarin–speaking elementary readers. *Journal of Learning Disabilities, 43,* 48–61. doi:10.1177/0022219409345016

Lin, D., McBride-Chang, C., Shu, H., Zhang, Y. P., Li, H., Zhang, J., . . . Levin, I. (2010). Small wins big: Analytic Pinyin skills promote Chinese word reading. *Psychological Science, 21*, 1117–1122. doi:10.1177/0956797610375447

Muter, V., Hulme, C., Snowling, M. J., & Stevenson, J. (2004). Phonemes, rimes, vocabulary, and grammatical skills as foundations of early reading development: Evidence from a longitudinal study. *Developmental Psychology, 40*, 665–681. doi:10.1037/0012-1649.40.5.665

Nag, S. (2007). Early reading in Kannada: The pace of acquisition of orthographic knowledge and phonemic awareness. *Journal of Research in Reading, 30*, 7–22. doi:10.1111/j.1467-9817.2006.00329.x

Nag, S. (2011). The akshara languages: What do they tell us about children's literacy learning? In R. Mishra & N. Srinivasan (Eds.), *Language-cognition: State of the art* (pp. 272–290). Berlin, Germany: Lincom.

Nag, S., & Snowling, M. J. (2011). Cognitive profiles of poor readers of Kannada. *Reading and Writing, 24*, 657–676. doi:10.1007/s11145-010-9258-7

Nag, S., & Snowling, M. J. (2012). Reading in an alphasyllabary: Implications for a language universal theory of learning to read. *Scientific Studies of Reading, 16*, 404–423. doi:10.1080/10888438.2011.576352

Nag, S., Treiman, R., & Snowling, M. J. (2010). Learning to spell in an alphasyllabary: The case of Kannada. *Writing Systems Research, 2*, 41–52. doi:10.1093/wsr/wsq001

Perfetti, C. A., Liu, Y., & Tan, L. H. (2005). The lexical constituency model: Some implications of research on Chinese for general theories of reading. *Psychological Review, 112*, 43–59. doi:10.1037/0033-295X.112.1.43

Perfetti, C. A., & Tan, L. H. (1998). The time course of graphic, phonological, and semantic activation in Chinese character identification. *Journal of Experimental Psychology: Learning, Memory, and Cognition, 24*, 101–118. doi:10.1037/0278-7393.24.1.101

Puolakanaho, A., Ahonen, T., Aro, M., Eklund, K., Leppänen, P. H. T., Poikkeus, A.-M., . . . Lyytinen, H. (2008). Developmental links of very early phonological and language skills to second grade reading outcomes: Strong to accuracy but only minor to fluency. *Journal of Learning Disabilities, 41*, 353–370.

Rao, C., Vaid, J., Srinivasan, N., & Chen, H. (2011). Orthographic characteristics speed Hindi word naming but slow Urdu naming: Evidence from Hindi/Urdu biliterates. *Reading and Writing, 24*, 679–695. doi:10.1007/s11145-010-9256-9

Salomon, R. (2000). Typological observations on the Indic script group and its relationship to other alphasyllabaries. *Studies in the Linguistic Sciences, 30*, 87–104.

Seidenberg, M. S. (2007). Connectionist models of word reading. In G. Gaskell (Ed.), *Oxford handbook of psycholinguistics* (pp. 235–250). Oxford, England: Oxford University Press.

Seidenberg, M. S. (2011). Reading in different writing systems: One architecture, multiple solutions. In P. McCardle, J. Ren, O. Tzeng, & B. Miller (Eds.), *Dyslexia across languages: Orthography and the gene–brain–behavior link* (pp. 146–168). Baltimore, MD: Brookes.

Seymour, P. H. K. (2005). Early reading development in European orthographies. In M. J. Snowling & C. Hulme (Eds.), *The science of reading: A handbook* (pp. 296–315). Boston, MA: Blackwell. doi:10.1002/9780470757642.ch16

Shu, H., Chen, X., Anderson, R. C., Wu, N., & Xuan, Y. (2003). Properties of school Chinese: Implications for learning to read. *Child Development, 74,* 27–47. doi:10.1111/1467-8624.00519

Sircar, S., & Nag, S. (in press). Akshara-syllable mappings in Bengali: A language-specific skill for reading. In H. Winskel & P. Padakannaya (Eds.), *South and Southeast Asian psycholinguistics.* Cambridge, England: Cambridge University Press.

Tiwari, S., Nair, R., & Krishnan, G. (2011). A preliminary investigation of akshara knowledge in the Malayalam alphasyllabary: Extension of Nag's (2007) study. *Writing Systems Research, 3,* 145–151. doi:10.1093/wsr/wsr013

Tong, X., & McBride-Chang, C. (2010). Developmental models of learning to read Chinese words. *Developmental Psychology, 46,* 1662–1676. doi:10.1037/a0020611

Tong, X., McBride-Chang, C., Wong, A. M. Y., Shu, H., Reitsma, P., & Rispens, J. (2011). Longitudinal predictors of very early Chinese literacy acquisition. *Journal of Research in Reading, 34,* 315–332. doi:10.1111/j.1467-9817.2009.01426.x

Yang, J., McCandliss, B. D., Shu, H., & Zevin, J. (2009). Simulating language-specific and language-general effects in a statistical learning model of Chinese reading. *Journal of Memory and Language, 61,* 238–257. doi:10.1016/j.jml.2009.05.001

Zevin, J. D., & Seidenberg, M. S. (2004). Age of acquisition effects in reading aloud: Tests of cumulative frequency and frequency trajectory. *Memory & Cognition, 32,* 31–38.

Ziegler, J. C., Bertrand, D., Tóth, D., Csépe, V., Reis, A., Faísca, L., Saine, N., . . . Blomert, L. (2010). Orthographic depth and its impact on universal predictors of reading: A cross-language investigation. *Psychological Science, 21,* 551–559. doi:10.1177/0956797610363406

Ziegler, J. C., & Goswami, U. (2005). Reading acquisition, developmental dyslexia, and skilled reading across languages: A psycholinguistic grain size theory. *Psychological Bulletin, 131,* 3–29. doi:10.1037/0033-2909.131.1.3

13

YOUNG CHILDREN'S USE OF COLOR INFORMATION DURING LANGUAGE–VISION MAPPING

FALK HUETTIG

Color vision is the "capacity to discriminate among stimuli that differ in wavelength composition, on the basis of the difference in wavelength composition alone" (Teller, 1998, p. 3281). There is plenty of evidence that 2-month-old infants can respond to high-contrast red/green chromatic differences (e.g., Peeles & Teller, 1975). Four-month-olds habituate after viewing a color for some time and look away, and then look again when shown a color from a different universal category, but not when shown a new color from the same category (Özgen, 2004). Thus, color discrimination abilities appear to be present very early in infancy.

Reports about children's apparent difficulty in naming colors, however, are abundant in the developmental literature. Wolfe (1890) found that there was no color word among the first 300 to 500 words that infants possess. Modreski and Goss (1969) found that 3- to 5-year-old children

DOI: 10.1037/14043-014
Cognition and Brain Development: Converging Evidence From Various Methodologies, B. R. Kar (Editor)
Copyright © 2013 by the American Psychological Association. All rights reserved.

have a better knowledge of form names than of color names. According to Bornstein (1985b), Darwin reported,

> I carefully followed the mental development of my small children, and I was astonished to observe in two or, as I rather think, three of these children, soon after they had reached the age in which they knew the names of all the ordinary things that they appeared to be entirely incapable of giving the right names to the colors of a color etching. They could not name the colors, although I tried repeatedly to teach them the names of the colors. I remember quite clearly to have stated that they are color blind. But afterwards this turned out to be an ungrounded apprehension. (p. 74)

Consistent with Darwin's anecdotal reports, Davidoff and Mitchell (1993) found that 3- and 4-year-olds performed very poorly if asked to point to the correctly colored object when shown an appropriately colored option and an inappropriately colored one. Davidoff and Mitchell reported that one of the children they tested commented on Father Christmas when coloring: "This is Father Christmas, he wears a red coat" and then proceeded to color the line drawing in green (p. 135). Nagel (1906) even coined the term *Farbendummheit* ("color stupidity") for early childhood. Bornstein (1985a) found that in a shape name and color name association study in which 3-year-olds were asked to learn paired associates of arbitrary proper names, the children performed much better for shape name pairs than color name pairs.

Bornstein (1985b) summarized the literature as revealing that

> (i) even young infants perceive colors accurately, that is, discriminate, match, and categorize colors; (ii) young children recognize that color is a separate domain of experience and readily identify it as such, and so the question, "what color is this?", regularly elicits a color term (though infrequently not among the very youngest children); and, (iii) children know different color words. However, (iv) children's color identification is immature in that they reply with incorrect names to colors they see or pick incorrect colors for names they hear; (v) there seems to be a lower age bound for mature color naming that hovers around 4 years. (p. 78)

Bornstein concluded that "early in life, sensory and linguistic color knowledge seem to coexist, but a proper map connecting names and perception is late in developing" (p. 78).

In the present chapter, I describe some recent eye-tracking studies that contradict this conclusion. This more recent research reveals that although (at least some) young children struggle with explicit color knowledge, their implicit object color knowledge in fact is fairly advanced. This research shows that even young children's mapping between linguistic and visual representations is mediated by color knowledge. Perceptual–conceptual knowledge about typical object color can determine toddlers' language-mediated eye gaze behavior even before they have mastered the ability to link color words with the appropriate colors.

Understanding how young children use color information during online word–object mapping is important for our larger understanding of the development of cognition. It reveals how developing higher order cognitive (e.g., linguistic) representations interact with the developing mechanisms underlying visual attention and perceptual processing, something we know surprisingly little about. Before describing the relevant developmental studies, I review related research on language–vision mapping with adult participants.

BACKGROUND: PAST RESEARCH ON ADULT LANGUAGE–VISION MAPPING

How mature language users integrate lexical information retrieved during spoken language processing (e.g., knowledge about semantic and visual properties of a word's referent) with information retrieved from the visual environment (e.g., the semantic and visual properties of copresent visual objects) to guide their eye gaze has recently attracted great interest. In an early study, Cooper (1974) observed that there is a tight link between spoken language processing and eye gaze to objects in the concurrent visual environment (see also Tanenhaus, Spivey-Knowlton, Eberhard, & Sedivy, 1995). His participants listened to short narratives (e.g., a story about a safari in Africa) while their eye movements were monitored on an array of spatially distinct line drawings of common objects, some of which were referred to in the spoken sentences. Cooper observed that his participants very quickly shifted their eye gaze to objects that were referred to, often already during the acoustic duration of the respective word (e.g., halfway during the acoustic unfolding of the word *lion*, participants started to shift their overt attention to the line drawing of the lion). Cooper also noticed that semantically related objects attracted increased overt attention (e.g., on hearing *Africa*, participants were more likely to look at a snake, a lion, and a zebra than semantically unrelated objects). Although Cooper recognized the potential of the new experimental technique "for the real-time investigation of perceptual and cognitive processes" (p. 84), he did not use the method to explore these issues any further. Only recently has the mapping of language-derived and vision-derived representations begun to be explored in a systematic manner. To understand how (e.g., color) representations are mapped (by both adults and children), it is necessary to determine what and when different types of representations are retrieved from both systems.

Research with adult participants has shown that individuals establish matches at phonological (Allopenna, Magnuson, & Tanenhaus, 1998), semantic (Huettig & Altmann 2005; Yee & Sedivy, 2006), and visual (shape: Dahan & Tanenhaus, 2005; Huettig & Altmann, 2004, 2007; color: Huettig & Altmann, 2004, 2011) levels of processing between information retrieved from the spoken words and from the visual surroundings (see Huettig, Rommers, & Meyer, 2011, for a review).

Shifts in eye gaze based on a (partial) phonological match between spoken word (e.g., "beaker") and visual object (e.g., a beaver; both *beaker* and *beaver* are phonologically similar at word onset) depend crucially on the amount of time participants have to inspect the visual scene. If participants have sufficient time to inspect the scene (e.g., 2 or 3 seconds for a simple display of four objects), they appear to be able to make use of a match between the phonological information retrieved from the speech signal and the phonological information retrieved from the object (i.e., the object's name; Huettig & McQueen, 2007, Experiment 1). If participants have insufficient time (e.g., 200 ms; Huettig & McQueen, 2007, Experiment 2) to retrieve the name of the visual object (e.g., the beaver) before the spoken target word (e.g., "beaker") starts to unfold, no increased overt attention to phonological competitors is observed.

Shifts in eye gaze based on semantic information appear to be due to semantic similarity rather than all-or-none categorical knowledge. Huettig and Altmann (2005) found that the probability of fixating a semantic competitor (e.g., a trumpet on hearing "piano") correlated significantly with the semantic similarity between target (e.g., piano) and competitor (e.g., trumpet) as derived from semantic feature production norms (Cree & McRae, 2003). Similarly, Huettig, Quinlan, McDonald, and Altmann (2006) showed that semantic similarity between target and competitor as derived from corpus-based measures such as latent semantic analysis (Landauer & Dumais, 1997) and contextual similarity (McDonald, 2000) predicted fixation behavior.

Shifts in eye gaze based on visual information (the type of mapping I focus on in the present chapter) could reflect a match between visual information accessed from hearing the spoken word (e.g., the prototypical shape of a snake on hearing "snake") and the visual features accessed from viewing the objects in the display (the particular properties of a displayed cable) or the stored knowledge about the prototypical shapes of the concurrent visual objects (the stored knowledge about the typical shape of cables). In the first case the match of the language-derived information is with the perceptual properties of the visual input, but in the second case the match is with the stored knowledge about the depicted objects. This question is difficult to address experimentally for shape-related items (e.g., shape-cable) because objects tend to retain their shape. Color, in contrast, allows experimental exploration of this issue because conceptual color attributes (e.g., the knowledge that frogs tend to be green in Northern Europe) can be dissociated from perceptual attributes (the perceptual properties, or the greenness of the copresent frog) because surface color and prototypical color can be different (e.g., a yellow frog or the picture of a frog presented in black and white).

Huettig and Altmann (2011), to investigate this issue, presented participants with spoken sentences that included a critical target word whose concepts were associated with a prototypical color (e.g., "spinach"; spinach is typically green) while their eye gaze was monitored to displays of (a) black-and-white line drawings of objects associated with a prototypical color (e.g., a black-and-white line drawing of a frog), (b) photographs of objects associated with a prototypical color (e.g., a color photograph of a yellow frog), and (c) objects not associated with a prototypical color (e.g., a blouse) but presented in the prototypical color of the target concept (i.e., a green blouse). Participants were asked to look at the screen and to listen carefully to the sentences (a look and listen task; cf. Huettig & Altmann, 2005). Look and listen tasks allow researchers to evaluate whether particular (e.g., competition) effects are a more general feature of language–vision interactions or whether they are limited to certain specific goal-directed task demands.

These studies revealed that adults' color-mediated shifts in eye gaze are mostly due to the surface colors of the objects in the visual surroundings rather than stored color knowledge accessed from viewing the objects. Effects of surface object color were large and immediate (at least when no competing representational matches were present between the spoken target word and the visual objects), but effects of stored object color knowledge were very small and occurred late.

Other studies have shown that the timing of shifts in eye gaze mediated by phonological, visual, and semantic levels of processing is codetermined by the type of information in the visual environment (see Huettig & McQueen, 2011), the timing of cascaded processing in the word and object recognition systems, and the temporal unfolding of the speech signal (see Huettig & McQueen, 2007).

In sum, the study of language–vision mapping in mature language users has revealed that it is a complex behavior involving a tight coupling between visual and linguistic processing systems. There are, however, still many unknowns about how language affects visual orienting. One unanswered set of questions concerns the development of such language–vision interactions. Are children's linguistic representations structured in such a way that leads them to behave in a similar manner as adults during online language processing? It is conceivable that rapid online activation of specific conceptual attributes (e.g., the prototypical color of objects) coupled with efficient online visual processing emerges only with accrued experience. Alternatively, it is possible that a tight language–vision mapping is foundational to human cognition and thus evident very early in development.

BACKGROUND: RELEVANT DEVELOPMENTAL RESEARCH

One may ask how likely it is that young children's conceptual processing and language–vision mapping differ from adultlike behavior. Results of recent studies suggest that young children's semantic/conceptual knowledge is quite advanced. Styles and Plunkett (2009), for instance, presented 18- and 24-month-olds with noun pairs in quick succession. The nouns were either related (e.g., " . . . cat dog") or unrelated (e.g., " . . . plate dog"). Target and distractor pictures (e.g., a dog and a ship) were presented 200 or 400 ms after target word onset. Styles and Plunkett found that 24-month-olds fixated targets (e.g., the dog) longer when the target was preceded by a related word (e.g., "cat"). The authors argued that this priming effect reflects that "infants integrate each word they learn into a complex, adult-like semantic system which encodes relatedness between words" (p. 20). Similarly, Torkildsen, Syversen, Simonsen, Moen, and Lindgren (2007) found that 24-month-olds displayed event-related potentials (ERP) N400 negativity for target words preceded by a semantically unrelated word compared with target words that were preceded by a semantically related word. The N400 ERP component reflects a response to a semantic anomaly in the preceding context (Kutas & Hillyard, 1980). Torkildsen et al. (2007) concluded that the N400 in their study reflected "processing of semantic relationships, although influence of associative relations cannot be excluded" (p. 348). Other, earlier studies demonstrated that young children have some knowledge of prototypical examples of familiar objects. Macario (1991), for instance, found that they performed above chance in a forced choice test in which they were required to indicate the color of well-known foods (see also Meints, Plunkett, & Harris, 1999). Finally, young children have been found to recognize taxonomic relationships between words (Bauer & Mandler, 1989; Markman & Hutchinson, 1984).

For the present research on children's language–vision mapping, past investigations of children's eye gaze behavior are particularly relevant. Developmental psychologists have been studying children's cognitive processing by means of eye gaze for over 20 years using the preferential looking paradigm (Golinkoff, Hirsh-Pasek, Cauley, & Gordon, 1987). In this method, children typically view two side-by-side screens while listening to some auditory input. Their eye gaze is recorded and later analyzed. Children's looking preferences are taken as an indicator of processing.

Using this task, Naigles and Gelman (1995) asked toddlers to find a referent that matched a given label (e.g., "dog"). When the specified referent was present (e.g., as one of two puppets), toddlers consistently chose the matching screen over the mismatching one (see also Hollich, Hirsh-Pasek, & Golinkoff, 2000). When the specified referent was not present, toddlers' looking behavior was far less determinant. This finding suggests that toddlers also know when a referent is not present. Thus, on hearing a spoken word, toddlers appear to access conceptual information associated with that word and then search for the referent in the visual displays.

Many developmental studies have investigated comprehension and production of absent reference (e.g., Greenfield, 1982; Huttenlocher, 1974; Huttenlocher & Smiley, 1987; Veneziano & Sinclair, 1995). Saylor (2004) presented 12- and 16-month-olds with simple color panels (red, blue, yellow, green) matching the color and spatial location of a mentioned absent object (e.g., a blue car) or matching the color and spatial location of a nonmentioned absent object. The infants showed comprehension of absent reference by directing more looks and gestures to the display matching the absent object than the display matching the nonmentioned absent object.

Ganea, Shutts, Spelke, and DeLoache (2007) taught 19- and 22-month-olds the name for a toy. Later they removed the toy and told them that it had become wet (i.e., a change of state). The 22-month-olds (but not the 19-month-olds) could subsequently identify the toy on the basis of this information. Thus, 22-month-olds, given the right circumstances, are able to update mental representations of absent objects on the basis of what other people tell them.

Note, however, that except for the Naigles and Gelman (1995) and Saylor (2004) studies, missing-referent studies investigating conceptual development have presented children with either fully matching or fully mismatching named target objects. Such studies therefore do not tell us whether young children represent individual properties of concepts or objects such as prototypical color in such a manner that they are readily accessed and used during online language-mediated visual orienting.

Young children, for instance, may know that bananas are yellow and not blue, but they may not be able to abstract the yellowness away from the concept of bananas rapidly when hearing "banana" (cf. Bornstein, 1985b). Or, early in development, there may be an increased focus on certain object attributes (e.g., object shape). Shape, for instance, tends to be a more reliable diagnostic property of objects than color. Human-made objects tend to vary in their color but have a distinct shape. Most theories of object recognition (e.g., Biederman, 1987; Marr & Nishihara, 1978) therefore have emphasized the role of edge-based information rather than surface information. Indeed, many developmental studies have found that young children treat shape (e.g., Graham & Diesendruck, 2010) but not color as a defining attribute of new words (e.g., Graham & Poulin-Dubois, 1999; Landau, Smith, & Jones, 1988; see also Bornstein, 1985a).

COLOR-MEDIATED LANGUAGE–VISION MAPPING IN YOUNG CHILDREN

In a series of eye-tracking studies (Johnson & Huettig, 2011; Johnson, McQueen, & Huettig, 2011; Mani, Johnson, McQueen, & Huettig, in press), researchers have recently begun to investigate the development of language-mediated visual orienting systematically. Johnson and Huettig (2011) used 16 words typically known by Dutch 36-month-olds as search targets. Twelve of these words referred to objects associated with a prototypical color: *aardbei* (strawberry), *sinaasappel* (orange), *kikker* (frog), *wortel* (carrot), *banaan* (banana), *brandweerauto* (fire truck), *peer* (pear), *olifant* (elephant), *varken* (pig), *tomaat* (tomato), *komkommer* (cucumber), and *zon* (sun). The remaining four words referred to objects that are not associated with a prototypical color: *lamp* (lamp), *huis* (house), *tafel* (table), and *bed* (bed).

Forty-two Dutch-learning 36-month-olds were presented with three types of trials. During target-present trials, participants were presented with two familiar objects (e.g., a sock and a fire truck) on a screen and asked to find one of the objects (e.g., "Can you find the fire truck?"). During color-matched distractor trials and unrelated distractor trials, participants were presented with two objects that were identical except for color (e.g., a ball colored red and the same one in green) and asked to find an object that was not present (e.g., a frog). Critically, during color-matched distractor trials, there was a match in color between the prototypical color of the concept referred to by the spoken target word (e.g., "frog") and one of the colored objects in the display (e.g., the green ball but not the red ball). The prediction was that the 36-month-olds would look longer at the color-matched distractors than the color-mismatched distractors if they had stored prototypical color knowledge and used it during online language–vision mapping (e.g., when hearing "frog," they should look longer at the green ball than the red ball). The unrelated distractor trials served as a control condition. In these trials, children also saw two objects that were identical except for color (e.g., a chair colored red and the same one in gray), but there was no match in color between the spoken target word (e.g., "lamp") and either of the colored objects in the display (e.g., the red chair and the gray chair).

Children sat on a caregiver's lap in a dimly lit room about 1 m from a large television screen on which the test trials were presented. The caregivers were listening to masking music over headphones. After the experiment, a flip book was used by the experimenter to test the children's color knowledge. The children were asked to point to one of four differently colored objects (e.g., "Where is the red one?"). The colors tested were red, blue, green, yellow, orange, pink, and gray. Children pointed to the correct object on 74% of these color test trials. Thus, the 36-month-olds' color label knowledge was well above chance.

Johnson and Huettig (2011) found that during the experimental trials, targets (e.g., the fire truck) were fixated significantly more than the control objects (e.g., the sock) from 300 ms after the onset of the spoken target word (e.g., "fire truck"). Importantly, color-matched distractors (e.g., the green ball) were also fixated significantly more than the control objects (e.g., the red ball). This effect, however, was slightly delayed, reaching significance during 1,300 to 1,800 ms after the onset of the spoken target word (e.g., "frog"). There was no corresponding bias in fixations to the target in the unrelated distractor trials. Thus, the children readily retrieved prototypical color knowledge on hearing the spoken target words (e.g., "frog") and fixated more on an object that had the same surface color (e.g., a green ball) than a different one (e.g., a red ball).

The proportion of time spent looking away from the screen supports this conclusion. Initially, on hearing the critical target word (1,000 to 2,500 ms after target onset), the 36-month-olds looked away from the screen less often during both target-present trials and color-matched distractor trials than during unrelated distractor trials, suggesting that for both target and color-matched distractor trials, something interesting captured the children's attention. During the 2,500 to 4,000 ms time window, however, the pattern was reversed. During this late time region, children's fixation in color-matched distractor trials patterned more like their fixations in unrelated distractor trials. In other words, the color-related distractors could not hold the 36-month-olds' attention as much as the targets could.

The difference between these findings and past missing referent studies is that the Johnson and Huettig (2011) study demonstrates that 36-month-olds are sensitive to the overlap in specific conceptual features retrieved on hearing spoken words and specific features of objects in the concurrent visual environment. They rapidly extract the greenness from their stored knowledge of frogs, recognize this same trait in other (concurrent) objects, and use this knowledge online to direct eye gaze. This finding demonstrates that there is a strong link between overt eye gaze and lexical processing in 3-year-olds. It is also noteworthy that this effect occurred for conceptual features that are not the most predictable indicator of object identity, namely color (cf. Davidoff & Mitchell, 1993).

The question that arises, therefore, is whether the color effect in Johnson and Huettig (2011) was mediated by stored verbal color labels or more visual knowledge. When listeners hear the word "frog," do they access an associated stored color label (green), which makes them more likely to look at green things in their visual surroundings? Or, alternatively, do listeners, on hearing "frog," access a target template, a sort of veridical description of the target (see Huettig, Olivers, & Hartsuiker, 2011, for further discussion), which then leads to a match with items matching this "perceptual" template? Davidoff and Mitchell (1993), for instance, argued that "3-year-olds have more difficulty matching object colors with mental templates than they do with color naming" (p. 133) on the basis of the finding that their 3-year-old participants tended to successfully judge that a banana is colored yellow in a verbal task but failed to choose the yellow banana as the correct one from differently colored bananas.

To examine this issue, Johnson et al. (2011) tested 48 Dutch-learning toddlers (average age, 751 days) who lacked reliable color term knowledge. Sixteen Dutch words commonly known to 2-year-olds were selected as spoken target words. Six of those words referred to foods with a prototypical color (e.g., strawberry), another six referred to animals with a prototypical color (e.g., frog), and four referred to objects not associated with a prototypical color (e.g., table). During the target trials, the 2-year-olds were asked to find one of the two objects presented on a screen (e.g., "Can you find the banana?" when a bike and a banana were displayed). During related distractor trials, they were asked to look for an absent object (e.g., a frog) while being presented with two objects, with one of them sharing either a color (a green truck and a yellow plane) or a semantic relationship (a bird and a red plane) with the target word. During unrelated distractor trials, toddlers were asked to look for an absent object (e.g., a house) while being presented with two completely unrelated objects (e.g., a sandwich and a toothbrush). Note that the items were counterbalanced across toddlers (i.e., no toddler saw the same image twice) and that images shown during related distractor trials were identical to the images shown during unrelated distractor trials (i.e., only the spoken target words differed). This design allowed assessment of how toddlers' fixation during related distractor trials and unrelated distractor trials were influenced by the (color or semantic) relationships between target word and concurrent pictures.

During color label trials, presented at the end of the experiment, toddlers were asked to look at one of two smiley faces (e.g., "Look at the blue one"), which were identical except for their color. These trials testing for color label knowledge were unlike most previous studies of color label knowledge because they did not require toddlers to produce a motor response (e.g., pointing; Davidoff & Mitchell, 1993; Gleason, Fiske, & Chan, 2004) or a verbal response (e.g., Johnson, 1977).

Johnson et al. (2011) found that on hearing the spoken target words, toddlers looked immediately at the targets (e.g., on hearing "banana," they shifted their eye gaze immediately toward the banana). Importantly, during the time region from 1 to 2 s after word onset, they also looked significantly more at the objects that were either color related or semantically related to the named absent target (e.g., on hearing "frog," they were more likely to look at a green truck and a bird than completely unrelated objects). Thus, 2-year-olds recognize partial perceptual–conceptual matches between heard words and seen objects—that is, they naturally map mental representations accessed on hearing words and mental representations accessed from viewing visual objects. Importantly, Johnson et al. (2011) tested 2-year-olds who lacked reliable color term knowledge to examine whether language–vision mapping is mediated by stored verbal labels (i.e., the lexicalized label *green*). Such a possibility is supported by responses of adult participants in free word association tasks. Participants in such tasks typically produce the answer "green" when asked to write down the first word that comes to mind when reading the word *frog* (Nelson, McEvoy, & Schreiber, 1998). In other words, Johnson et al. (2011) tested whether language–vision mapping can be driven via a direct route (e.g., via accessing some sort of "perceptual template") or whether such mapping is more indirect (e.g., that mediation by color label knowledge is necessary and thus proficient mapping develops late; cf. Bornstein, 1985b).

The findings of Johnson et al. (2011) strongly suggest that language-mediated shifts in visual orienting are independent of knowing color labels—that is, such shifts are not mediated by stored lexicalized color labels. How sure can we be that the toddlers in Johnson et al. did not use any color label knowledge for their visual orienting? Caregivers of the toddlers were asked to indicate whether their child knew any color labels and how accurately those color labels were used. These parental report data suggest that only 12 of the 48 toddlers knew more than one color term correctly at least "most of the time." "Most of the time," of course, does not indicate that the child has necessarily full and reliable comprehension of color labels. Moreover, parental report may overestimate or underestimate toddler knowledge (e.g., Tomasello & Mervis, 1994). For instance, a child may say that blue is his or her favorite color but pick up a ball of a different color when asked to pick up a blue ball. Or a child may memorize a phrase such as "blue ball" without understanding what *blue* means. Preferential looking data, in contrast, appear to be more reliable (e.g., Houston-Price, Mather, & Sakkalou, 2007). Johnson et al. excluded all trials from the data set for which caregivers had reported that the children knew some color labels and observed the same overall pattern of results.

In any case, the primary data in the Johnson et al. (2011) study come from the preferential looking task, and thus the most appropriate test of whether toddlers' color label knowledge influenced performance in the experiment should also be based on preferential looking. The analysis of the color label trials (e.g., "Look at the blue one," with a red and blue smiley presented) revealed that the toddlers comprehended appropriately, at most, two colors. The experimental results showed the same overall pattern when all trials involving these two colors were taken out. Thus, there was a clear within-toddler dissociation in the preferential looking task that gets around the issue of precisely which few color labels some of the toddlers may have known and how well they did so. Words such as *strawberry* resulted in shifts in eye gaze to red things, but color words such as "red" did not. Two-year-olds look to color-matched competitors even if they do not know the label for that color. The Johnson et al. results do not rule out that adults have both direct and indirect routes linking color knowledge of words such as *strawberry* to color concepts such as *red*. What the Johnson et al. results show, however, is that the direct routes exist before the indirect route (i.e., mediation via lexicalized color labels) has a chance to develop.

Finally, Mani et al. (in press) recently investigated whether these results can be replicated using a referent-present experimental design. The Johnson and Huettig (2011) and Johnson et al. (2011) studies strongly suggest that toddlers rapidly extract color attributes on hearing spoken words referring to objects with a typical color, recognize this same trait in other (visually con-current) objects, and use this knowledge online to direct eye gaze. In both studies, however, the children were asked to find objects not present on the screens—that is, the studies used referent-absent tasks. The understanding of absent reference is a crucial ability during the development of language processing (cf. Saylor, 2004) as often spoken language is about things that are not physically present. It is, however, conceivable that asking children to find objects not present on the screen leads them to search for additional informa-tion that might help them integrate information arriving through visual and speech channels. In other words, referent-absent tasks may encourage toddlers to extract information that is not routinely retrieved during language–vision mapping.

Mani et al. (in press) used a primed intermodal preferential looking task (see also Arias-Trejo & Plunkett, 2009, and Styles & Plunkett, 2011, for similar tasks investigating semantic priming). Toddlers were presented with a prime label followed by the label for one of the images presented on screen— for example, children heard, "I saw a strawberry . . . cup" while looking at a red cup and a blue chair. The same stimuli as in Johnson et al. (2011) were used. Thus, the only difference from the Johnson et al. study is that after being pre-sented with the prime label (e.g., "strawberry"), toddlers also heard the label for the target on the screen (e.g., "cup"). If the effects of color in the previous studies were driven by children struggling to find a match between the spoken instruction (e.g., "strawberry") and the mismatching objects (e.g., the red cup) presented to them, there should be a reduced preference for color matching objects in the current experimental task. If, in contrast, toddlers readily activate stored color knowledge during spoken word processing, they should show a robust preference for the target in color-matching trials but not in unrelated trials. Mani et al. found that despite being presented with the spoken target (e.g., "cup")—that is, facilitating an easy match between auditory and visual stimuli—toddlers showed a robust preference for the color-matching object (the red cup) when primed by a color-matching label (e.g., "strawberry"). The results of the Mani et al. study thus provide strong evidence for the retrieval of color knowledge in both referent-present and referent-absent designs and for its rapid use during language–vision mapping in toddlers.

CONCLUSION

In this chapter, I have discussed the results of three preferential looking experiments that investigated young children's use of color during the mapping between language-derived and vision-derived representations. The findings are clear: Toddlers readily retrieve stored knowledge about typical color and use this knowledge online to direct eye gaze to objects in the visual environment that match on the same trait. They do so even if they have plenty of time to recognize the objects for what they are (e.g., red planes and not strawberries). Even 24-month-olds who lacked color label knowledge exhibited the same behavior. This demonstrates that language-mediated shifts in visual attention are not necessarily mediated by stored lexicalized (color) labels. Although adults may have both direct and indirect routes linking color attributes of words such as *frog* to color concepts such as green, the results demonstrate that the direct route exists before the indirect route has had a chance to develop. The findings thus cast doubt on the claims in the literature that (older) children tend to rely on verbal encoding to remember how familiar objects are typically colored (e.g., Davidoff & Mitchell, 1993; Gleason et al., 2004). Moreover, claims that "a proper map connecting names and perception is late in developing" (Bornstein, 1985b, p. 78) appear to be unfounded. In other words, young children are not *farbendumm* (Nagel, 1906) but rather *farbenclever*.

REFERENCES

Allopenna, P. D., Magnuson, J. S., & Tanenhaus, M. K. (1998). Tracking the time course of spoken word recognition using eye movements: Evidence for continuous mapping models. *Journal of Memory and Language, 38,* 419–439. doi:10.1006/jmla.1997.2558

Arias-Trejo, N., & Plunkett, K. (2009). Lexical priming effects during infancy. *Philosophical Transaction of the Royal Society of London. Series B, Biological Sciences, 364,* 3633–3647. doi:10.1098/rstb.2009.0146

Bauer, P. J., & Mandler, J. M. (1989). Taxonomies and triads: Conceptual organization in one- and two-year-olds. *Cognitive Psychology, 21,* 156–184. doi:10.1016/0010-0285(89)90006-6

Biederman, I. (1987). Recognition-by-components: A theory of human image understanding. *Psychological Review, 94,* 115–147. doi:10.1037/0033-295X.94.2.115

Bornstein, M. H. (1985a). Color-name versus shape-name learning in young children. *Journal of Child Language, 12,* 387–393. doi:10.1017/S0305000900006498

Bornstein, M. H. (1985b). On the development of color naming in young children: Data and theory. *Brain and Language, 26,* 72–93. doi:10.1016/0093-934X(85)90029-X

Cooper, R. M. (1974). The control of eye fixation by the meaning of spoken language: A new methodology for the real-time investigation of speech perception, memory, and language processing. *Cognitive Psychology, 6,* 84–107. doi:10.1016/0010-0285(74)90005-X

Cree, G. S., & McRae, K. (2003). Analyzing the factors underlying the structure and computation of the meaning of chipmunk, cherry, chisel, cheese, and cello (and many other such concrete nouns). *Journal of Experimental Psychology: General, 132,* 163–201. doi:10.1037/0096-3445.132.2.163

Dahan, D., & Tanenhaus, M. (2005). Looking at the rope when looking for the snake: Conceptually mediated eye movements during spoken-word recognition. *Psychonomic Bulletin & Review, 12,* 453–459. doi:10.3758/BF03193787

Davidoff, J., & Mitchell, D. (1993). The color cognition of children. *Cognition, 48,* 121–137. doi:10.1016/0010-0277(93)90027-S

Ganea, P. A., Shutts, K., Spelke, E. S., & DeLoache, J. S. (2007). Thinking of things unseen: Infants' use of language to update mental representations. *Psychological Science, 18,* 734–739. doi:10.1111/j.1467-9280.2007.01968.x

Gleason, T. R., Fiske, K. E., & Chan, R. K. (2004). The verbal nature of representations of the canonical colors of objects. *Cognitive Development, 19,* 1–14. doi:10.1016/S0885-2014(03)00044-3

Golinkoff, R. M., Hirsh-Pasek, K., Cauley, K. M., & Gordon, L. (1987). The eyes have it: Lexical and syntactic comprehension in a new paradigm. *Journal of Child Language, 14,* 23–45. doi:10.1017/S030500090001271X

Graham, S. A., & Diesendruck, G. (2010). Fifteen-month-olds attend to shape over other perceptual properties in an induction task. *Cognitive Development, 25,* 111–123. doi:10.1016/j.cogdev.2009.06.002

Graham, S. A., & Poulin-Dubois, D. (1999). Infants' reliance on shape to generalize novel labels to animate and inanimate objects. *Journal of Child Language, 26,* 295–320. doi:10.1017/S0305000999003815

Greenfield, P. M. (1982). The role of perceived variability in the transition to language. *Journal of Child Language, 9,* 1–12. doi:10.1017/S0305000900003561

Hollich, G., Hirsh-Pasek, K., & Golinkoff, R. (2000). Breaking the language barrier: An emergentist coalition model of word learning. *Monographs for the Society for Research in Child Development, 65* (3, Serial No. 262).

Houston-Price, C., Mather, E., & Sakkalou, E. (2007). Discrepancy between parental reports of infants' receptive vocabulary and infants' behavior in a preferential looking task. *Journal of Child Language, 34,* 701–724. doi:10.1017/S0305000907008124

Huettig, F., & Altmann, G. T. M. (2004). The online processing of ambiguous and unambiguous words in context: Evidence from head-mounted eye-tracking. In M. Carreiras & C. Clifton (Eds.), *The on-line study of sentence comprehension: Eyetracking, ERP and beyond* (pp. 187–207). New York, NY: Psychology Press.

Huettig, F., & Altmann, G. T. M. (2005). Word meaning and the control of eye fixation: Semantic competitor effects and the visual world paradigm. *Cognition, 96,* B23–B32. doi:10.1016/j.cognition.2004.10.003

Huettig, F., & Altmann, G. T. M. (2007). Visual-shape competition during language-mediated attention is based on lexical input and not modulated by contextual appropriateness. *Visual Cognition, 15,* 985–1018. doi:10.1080/13506280601130875

Huettig, F., & Altmann, G. T. M. (2011). Looking at everything that is green when hearing "frog"—How object surface color and stored object color knowledge influence language-mediated overt attention. *Quarterly Journal of Experimental Psychology, 64,* 122–145. doi:10.1080/17470218.2010.481474

Huettig, F., & McQueen, J. M. (2007). The tug of war between phonological, semantic, and shape information in language-mediated visual search. *Journal of Memory and Language, 57,* 460–482. doi:10.1016/j.jml.2007.02.001

Huettig, F., & McQueen, J. M. (2011). The nature of the visual environment induces implicit biases during language-mediated visual search. *Memory & Cognition, 39,* 1068–1084. doi:10.3758/s13421-011-0086-z

Huettig, F., Olivers, C. N. L., & Hartsuiker, R. J. (2011). Looking, language, and memory: Bridging research from the visual world and visual search paradigms. *Acta Psychologica, 137,* 138–150. doi:10.1016/j.actpsy.2010.07.013

Huettig, F., Quinlan, P. T., McDonald, S. A., & Altmann, G. T. M. (2006). Models of high-dimensional semantic space predict language-mediated eye movements in the visual world. *Acta Psychologica, 121,* 65–80. doi:10.1016/j.actpsy.2005.06.002

Huettig, F., Rommers, J., & Meyer, A. S. (2011). Using the visual world paradigm to study language processing: A review and critical evaluation. *Acta Psychologica, 137,* 151–171. doi:10.1016/j.actpsy.2010.11.003

Huttenlocher, J. (1974). The origins of language comprehension. In R. Solso (Ed.), *Theories in cognitive psychology* (pp. 331–368). Hillsdale, NJ: Erlbaum.

Huttenlocher, J., & Smiley, P. (1987). Early word meanings: The case of object names. *Cognitive Psychology, 19,* 63–89. doi:10.1016/0010-0285(87)90004-1

Johnson, E. (1977). The development of colour knowledge in preschool children. *Child Development, 48,* 308–311. doi:10.2307/1128918

Johnson, E. K., & Huettig, F. (2011). Eye movements during language-mediated visual search reveal a strong link between overt visual attention and lexical processing in 36-month-olds. *Psychological Research/Psychologische Forschung, 75*, 35–42. doi:10.1007/s00426-010-0285-4

Johnson, E. K., McQueen, J. M., & Huettig, F. (2011). Toddlers' language-mediated visual search: They need not have the words for it. *Quarterly Journal of Experimental Psychology, 64*, 1672–1682. doi:10.1080/17470218.2011.594165

Kutas, M., & Hillyard, S. A. (1980, January 11). Reading senseless sentences: Brain potentials reflect semantic incongruity. *Science, 207*, 203–205. doi:10.1126/science.7350657

Landau, B., Smith, L. B., & Jones, S. S. (1988). The importance of shape in early lexical learning. *Cognitive Development, 3*, 299–321. doi:10.1016/0885-2014(88)90014-7

Landauer, T. K., & Dumais, S. T. (1997). A solution to Plato's problem: The latent semantic analysis theory of acquisition, induction and representation of knowledge. *Psychological Review, 104*, 211–240. doi:10.1037/0033-295X.104.2.211

Macario, J. F. (1991). Young children's use of color in classification: Foods and canonically colored objects. *Cognitive Development, 6*, 17–46. doi:10.1016/0885-2014(91)90004-W

Mani, N., Johnson, E. K., McQueen, J. M., & Huettig, F. (in press). How yellow is your banana: Toddlers' language-mediated visual search in referent-present tasks. *Developmental Psychology*.

Markman, E. M., & Hutchinson, J. E. (1984). Children's sensitivity to constraints on word meaning: Taxonomic versus thematic roles. *Cognitive Psychology, 16*, 1–27. doi:10.1016/0010-0285(84)90002-1

Marr, D., & Nishihara, H. K. (1978). Representation and recognition of the spatial organization of three dimensional structure. *Proceedings of the Royal Society of London. Series B, Biological Sciences, 200*, 269294. doi:10.1098/rspb.1978.0020

McDonald, S. A. (2000). *Environmental determinants of lexical processing effort* (Unpublished doctoral dissertation). University of Edinburgh, Scotland. Retrieved December 10, 2004, from http://www.inf.ed.ac.uk/publications/thesis/online/IP000007.pdf

Meints, K., Plunkett, K., & Harris, P. (1999). When does an ostrich become a bird? The role of typicality in early word comprehension. *Developmental Psychology, 35*, 1072–1078. doi:10.1037/0012-1649.35.4.1072

Modreski, R. A., & Goss, A. E. (1969). Young children's initial and changed names for form–colour stimuli. *Journal of Experimental Child Psychology, 8*, 402–409. doi:10.1016/0022-0965(69)90112-X

Nagel, W. A. (1906). Observations on the color-sense of a child. *Journal of Comparative Neurology & Psychology, 16*, 217–230. doi:10.1002/cne.920160306

Naigles, L. G., & Gelman, S. A. (1995). Overextensions in comprehension and production revisited: Preferential looking study of dog, cat, and cow. *Journal of Child Language, 22*, 19–46. doi:10.1017/S0305000900009612

Nelson, D. L., McEvoy, C. L., & Schreiber, T. A. (1998). *The University of South Florida word association, rhyme, and word fragment norms*. Retrieved from http://www.usf.edu/FreeAssociation/

Özgen, E. (2004). Language, learning, and color perception. *Current Directions in Psychological Science, 13*, 95–98. doi:10.1111/j.0963-7214.2004.00282.x

Peeles, D. R., & Teller, D. Y. (1975, September 26). Color vision and brightness discrimination in two-month-old human infants. *Science, 189*, 1102–1103. doi:10.1126/science.1162362

Saylor, M. M. (2004). Twelve- and 16-month-old infants recognize properties of mentioned absent things. *Developmental Science, 7*, 599–611. doi:10.1111/j.1467-7687.2004.00383.x

Styles, S., & Plunkett, K. (2011). Early links in the early lexicon: Semantically related word-pairs prime picture looking in the second year. In G. Gaskell & P. Zwitzerlood (Eds.), *Lexical representation: A multi-disciplinary approach* (pp. 51–88). Berlin, Germany: Mouton de Gruyter. doi:10.1515/9783110224931.51

Styles, S. J., & Plunkett, K. (2009). How do infants build a semantic system? *Language and Cognition, 1*, 1–24. doi:10.1515/LANGCOG.2009.001

Tanenhaus, M. K., Spivey-Knowlton, M. J., Eberhard, K. M., & Sedivy, J. C. (1995, June 16). Integration of visual and linguistic information in spoken language comprehension. *Science, 268*, 1632–1634. doi:10.1126/science.7777863

Teller, D. Y. (1998). Spatial and temporal aspects of infant color vision. *Vision Research, 38*, 3275–3282. doi:10.1016/S0042-6989(97)00468-9

Tomasello, M., & Mervis, C. B. (1994). The instrument is great, but measuring comprehension is still a problem: Commentary on Fenson, Dale, Reznick, Bates, Thal, and Pethick, 1994. *Monographs of the Society for Research in Child Development, 59*, 174–179. doi:10.1111/j.1540-5834.1994.tb00186.x

Torkildsen, J. V. K., Syversen, G., Simonsen, H. G., Moen, I., & Lindgren, M. (2007). Electrophysiological correlates of auditory semantic priming in 24-month-olds. *Journal of Neurolinguistics, 20*, 332–351. doi:10.1016/j.jneuroling.2007.02.003

Veneziano, E., & Sinclair, H. (1995). Functional change in early child language: The appearance of references to the past of explanations. *Journal of Child Language, 22*, 557–581. doi:10.1017/S0305000900009958

Wolfe, H. K. (1890). On the vocabulary of children. *Nebraska University Studies, 1*, 205–234.

Yee, E., & Sedivy, J. C. (2006). Eye movements to pictures reveal transient semantic activation during spoken word recognition. *Journal of Experimental Psychology: Learning, Memory, and Cognition, 32*, 1–14. doi:10.1037/0278-7393.32.1.1

14

FUNCTIONAL MAGNETIC RESONANCE IMAGING OF LANGUAGE IN PATIENTS WITH EPILEPSY

JIJA S. JAMES AND CHANDRASEKHARAN KESAVADAS

This chapter focuses mainly on the role of functional magnetic resonance imaging (fMRI), a noninvasive advanced neuroimaging technique, for mapping language areas in patients with intractable epilepsy as a part of their presurgical workup. The identification of eloquent cortex with important language function may be necessary in patients with intractable partial or localization-related epilepsy being considered for surgery to minimize post-surgical cognitive deficits. fMRI, a technique with excellent spatial resolution, is also a hemodynamic indicator of neuronal activity and can map the frontal and temporal language-processing areas on the basis of the performance of specific language-related tasks (so called language paradigms).

The first part of this chapter emphasizes epileptic disorders, the different causes of epileptic seizures, and various presurgical evaluation techniques that are used. The next part discusses the organization of language areas in the human brain and their processing, the role of language fMRI in epilepsy,

DOI: 10.1037/14043-015
Cognition and Brain Development: Converging Evidence From Various Methodologies, B. R. Kar (Editor)
Copyright © 2013 by the American Psychological Association. All rights reserved.

and various language paradigms (with examples) being used. The final part focuses on the technical considerations of fMRI and some important challenges in performing this technique.

EPILEPSY

Epilepsy is one of the most common neurological conditions characterized by occasional, excessive, and disorderly discharge of nervous tissue that results in seizures. A seizure may appear as a brief stare, a change of awareness, or a convulsion. Temporal lobe epilepsy (TLE) due to hippocampal sclerosis is a common cause of medically refractory seizures. This condition has good outcome following anterior temporal lobe resection. TLE may be associated with disrupted lateralization and localization of language (Penfield & Jasper, 1954). Studies using fMRI have demonstrated a higher incidence of atypical language dominance in preoperative left TLE patients (Adcock, Wise, Oxbury, Oxbury, & Matthews, 2003; Thivard et al., 2005), suggesting that dominant hemisphere lesions can lead to functional reorganization of language to contralateral cortical regions. A wide range of imaging techniques is available for imaging the epileptogenic zone, including high-resolution T1 MRI, T2 signal quantitation, magnetic resonance spectroscopy, diffusion imaging, positron emission tomography (PET), single-photon emission computed tomography (SPECT), and simultaneous electroencephalography (EEG)–fMRI (Billingsley-Marshall, Simos, & Papanicolaou, 2004). The technique of fMRI of motor and cognitive tasks holds great importance for noninvasive functional brain mapping in patients needing epilepsy surgery.

EPILEPSY AND EPILEPSY SURGERY

Epilepsy can occur due to various reasons, such as brain injury to the fetus during pregnancy, birth trauma and hypoxic brain damage, aftermath of infection (e.g., meningitis), head trauma (e.g., motor accident, sports injury, shaken baby syndrome), substance abuse, alteration in blood as sugar (hypoglycemia), other metabolic illness (hypocalcaemia), brain tumor, and stroke. The International League Against Epilepsy (ILAE) standardized classification and terminology for epileptic seizures and syndromes provide a fundamental framework for organizing and differentiating the epilepsies (Engel, 2006). Epilepsy syndromes are divided into two broad categories: partial (focal, local) and generalized. Partial seizures are further divided into the following types.

- Simple partial seizures (focal), in which signs and symptoms may be motor, sensory, autonomic, or psychic, depending on the location of the electrical discharge.
- Complex partial seizures (temporal lobe or psychomotor), in which seizures may begin with no warning or with motor, sensory, autonomic, or psychic signs or symptoms. Consciousness is impaired. Automatisms (automatic acts of which the patient has no recollection) may occur, and seizure is often followed by a period of confusion.
- Secondarily generalized partial seizures (tonic–clonic, or grand mal) in which seizures may begin with motor, sensory, autonomic, or psychic signs or symptoms. Consciousness is lost, with tonic increase in muscle tone and subsequent rhythmic (clonic) jerks that subside slowly. The patient is comatose after the seizure and recovers slowly. Tongue biting, incontinence, or both may occur.

Generalized seizures are further divided into

- absence seizures (petit mal), in which the seizure begins rapidly, with a brief period of unresponsiveness (average 10 s) and rapid recovery and in which there may be increased or decreased muscle tone, automatisms, or mild clonic movements; and
- primary generalized tonic–clonic seizures (grand mal), in which loss of consciousness occurs without warning or is preceded by myoclonic jerks and clinical features are similar to those of a secondarily generalized partial seizure.

Epilepsy surgery is defined as a neurosurgical intervention performed to eliminate the epileptogenic tissue (the seizure onset zone) so as to maximize seizure relief, minimize side effects, and improve quality of life. Approximately 60% of all patients with epilepsy experience symptomatic focal epilepsy syndromes. Among them, about 20% are drug resistant, and more than one third are potential candidates for surgical treatment. Considering the severity of the epilepsy in the population operated on, epilepsy surgery can be accepted as a successful therapy (Rosenow & Luders, 2001). The main objective of epilepsy surgery (Engel, 1993) is a complete disconnection of the epileptogenic zone, and this has to be achieved by preserving eloquent cortex. *Eloquent cortex* are areas in the brain that subserve important and useful functions such as motor, sensory, visual, language, and memory functions. Anterior temporal lobe resection is a common and highly effective treatment for intractable epilepsy (Al-Otaibi, Baeesa, Parrent, Girvin, & Steven, 2012; Téllez-Zenteno, Dhar, & Wiebe, 2005; Wiebe, Blume, Girvin, & Eliasziw,

2001) but carries a 30% to 50% risk of decline in naming ability when performed on the left temporal lobe. Hence, it becomes essential in epilepsy surgery to understand the risks of intervention for possible neurological deficits.

PRESURGICAL EVALUATION IN EPILEPSY

The various methods for presurgical evaluation include the following:

- Neuropsychological testing helps to evaluate the functional deficit zone and predict postoperative cognitive outcome.
- Video EEG monitoring allows for precise localization of epileptiform activity.
- MRI is the imaging method of choice for the identification of anatomical details and detection of epileptogenic lesions.
- PET and SPECT allow detection of focal hypo- or hyperperfusion of the epileptogenic area depending on the moment of injection of radioactive material.
- Intracranial EEG monitoring directly records epileptiform activity using invasive electrodes.
- Intracarotid amobarbital procedure (IAP), also called the *Wada test*, is an invasive method to assess hemispheric language dominance by injecting amobarbital sodium into the hemisphere opposite to the seizure focus. A brief evaluation of receptive and expressive language functions is done by asking the patient to perform some cognitive tasks.
- fMRI has the potential to replace IAP in presurgical evaluation of epilepsy patients. It provides localization of the epileptogenic area through the identification of blood oxygen level–dependent (BOLD) signal changes associated with ictal or interictal epileptic activity.
- EEG-correlated functional MRI (EEG–fMRI) can be used as part of the presurgical workup. The specific timing of interictal events can be identified on the EEG at millisecond resolution and spatially localized with fMRI at millimeter resolution. Therefore, simultaneous EEG–fMRI provides the opportunity to better investigate the spatiotemporal mechanisms of the generation of epileptiform activity in the brain.
- Magnetoencephalography (MEG) maps interictal magnetic dipole sources onto MRI to produce a magnetic source image. MEG spike sources can be used to localize the epileptogenic zone and can be part of the workup of the patient for epilepsy surgery.

FUNCTIONAL ORGANIZATION OF LANGUAGE IN THE BRAIN

Language is a form of communication that is unique to humans. It involves interactive systems for the manipulation of internally stored words and word meanings. The essence of language is the capacity to retain, retrieve, and combine arbitrary symbols of a native language into an infinite number of potential expressions. Language processing occurs at different levels, such as verbal output, reading, writing, and hearing, as well as visuomotor forms (e.g., sign language). Language is lateralized in the left cerebral hemisphere for most humans (Brown, 1978). A small percentage of individuals exhibit *atypical* language lateralization, which means that language is represented either bilaterally or in the right hemisphere. Neurobiological substrates of language can be subdivided into different components (Damasio & Geschwind, 1984; Poeppel & Hickok, 2004; Price, 2000): phonology (sounds of words), orthography (spelling of words), semantics (knowledge of words), and syntax (grammatical relationship between words).

The Broca–Wernicke–Lichtheim–Geschwind model (the classic model) was the first large-scale functional anatomical proposal on language processing. It was the result of the cumulative efforts of Broca, Wernicke, and Lichtheim during the 19th century, together with a modern revival incorporating one major modification by Geschwind (1965). The classic model of language organization consists primarily of two cortical regions of the left hemisphere: Broca's area (inferior frontal gyrus), or expressive language area, which is meant for planning and execution of speech, and Wernicke's area (superior temporal gyrus), or temporoparietal receptive language area, which is meant for speech comprehension and identification of linguistic stimuli. Broca's area is classically located in the pars opercularis and the posterior portion of the pars triangularis of the inferior frontal gyrus (Brodmann area [BA] 44 and posterior part of BA 45). Wernicke's area involves parts of the supramarginal gyrus, the angular gyrus, the bases of the superior and middle temporal gyri, and the planum temporale (BAs 22, 37, 39, and 40). This model was proposed on the basis of postmortem studies of two brain-lesioned aphasic patients with severe neurological deficits and lesions in the frontal and temporal cortices by Paul Pierre Broca in 1861 and Carl Wernicke in 1874. According to this model, the two cortical language areas are interconnected by a white matter tract, the arcuate fasciculus. This model also includes the angular gyrus, which represents the perception of written language.

The classical model of language processing was revived by Norman Geschwind (1965), and the model is called Wernicke's Geschwind model. He also reported a third region of the brain associated with language and composed by an anterior segment connecting Broca's area with the inferior parietal lobe and a posterior segment connecting the inferior parietal lobe to Wernicke's area. This region was named *Geschwind's territory*. According to Geschwind, the most basic requirement for language is the ability to name, which requires the association of objects or concepts with language symbols, specifically words. He explained that humans possess extralimbic supra-modal association cortices, such as dominant perisylvian cortex, that have the capacity for representation of abstract entities such as words. Geschwind used comparative anatomy to help explain the organization of language functions in humans. Because the left posterior superior temporal lobe is dominant for language, Geschwind and Levitsky (1968) measured the size of the posterior portion of the superior temporal gyrus (planum temporale) and found that in the majority of patients, this area was larger on the left side than on the right side. These findings initiated the entire research area oriented toward analyzing structure–function relationships.

Over the years, it has been recognized that language organization in the brain is much more complex than previously thought (Hickok & Poeppel, 2007). Proposed language models based on neurolinguistics and functional imaging studies (Hickok & Poeppel, 2000) offer a more dynamic network view in which multiple cortical areas are interconnected by white matter networks in which each holds a specific language function. Hickok and Poeppel (2004) proposed a dual-stream model for auditory language processing (see Figure 14.1). In this model, the posterior superior temporal gyrus (pSTG),

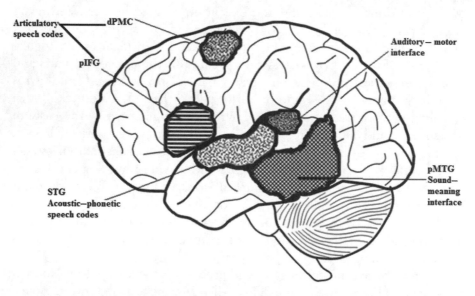

Figure 14.1. Dual-stream model for auditory language process. dPMC = dorsal pre-motor cortex; pIFG = posterior inferior frontal gyrus; pMTG = posterior middle temporal gyrus; STG = superior temporal gyrus.

which is engaged in early cortical stages of speech perception, diverges into two processing streams. The dorsal stream projects dorsally toward the inferior parietal lobule and the posterior frontal lobe (dorsolateral prefrontal cortex) and is involved in auditory motor integration by mapping acoustic speech sounds to articulator representations. The ventral stream projects ventrolaterally to the middle and inferior temporal cortices, and the ventrolateral prefrontal cortex serves as a sound–meaning interface by mapping sound-based representations of speech to widely distributed conceptual representations.

PRESURGICAL LANGUAGE LATERALIZATION IN EPILEPSY USING fMRI

The predominant neuroimaging technique for studying the neural basis of cognitive processes in humans is fMRI. Ogawa and colleagues at Bell Laboratories first noticed in 1990 that the functional relationships between brain regions can be measured using BOLD fMRI (Ogawa & Lee, 1990; Ogawa, Lee, Nayak, & Glynn, 1990).

Neuronal stimulation leads to a local increase in energy and oxygen consumption in functional areas. The subsequent local hemodynamic changes transmitted via neurovascular coupling are measured by fMRI. The BOLD technique (Faro & Mohamed, 2010) depends on the difference in the magnetic properties between oxygenated hemoglobin (oxy-Hb) and deoxygenated hemoglobin (deoxy-Hb). The paramagnetic deoxy-Hb produces local field inhomogeneities in the measurable range of MRI, resulting in signal decrease in susceptibility-weighted MRI sequences (T2*), whereas diamagnetic oxy-Hb does not interfere with the external magnetic field. When the neurons are stimulated, there is an increase in local oxygen consumption that results in an initial decrease of oxy-Hb and an increase in deoxy-Hb in the functional area. To provide the active neurons with oxygenated blood, perfusion in capillaries and draining veins is enhanced within several seconds. As a result of this process, the initial decrease of local oxy-Hb is equalized and then overcompensated. The deoxy-Hb is progressively washed out. This causes a reduction in local field inhomogeneity and an increase in the BOLD signal in T2*-weighted (T2*w) MRI images. Although the initial dip corresponds to the neuronal activity both temporally and spatially, this is more difficult to measure in clinical settings. Electrophysiologically, it is the local field potential that changes with an increase in the BOLD signal, and not the neuronal firing rate. Thus, fMRI with BOLD contrast provides indirect measurements of neuronal activity by monitoring local hemodynamic changes during performance of a task. This robust method is capable of imaging the whole brain with excellent

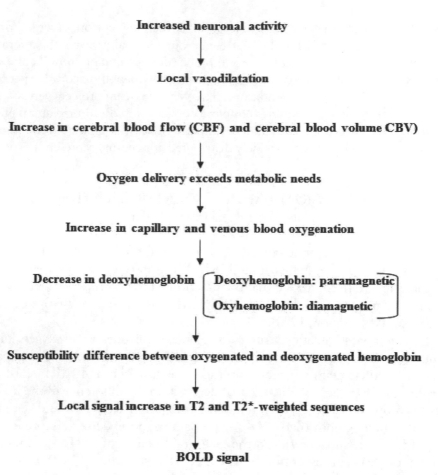

Increased neuronal activity

↓

Local vasodilatation

↓

Increase in cerebral blood flow (CBF) and cerebral blood volume CBV)

↓

Oxygen delivery exceeds metabolic needs

↓

Increase in capillary and venous blood oxygenation

↓

Decrease in deoxyhemoglobin   Deoxyhemoglobin: paramagnetic

                 Oxyhemoglobin: diamagnetic

↓

Susceptibility difference between oxygenated and deoxygenated hemoglobin

↓

Local signal increase in T2 and T2*-weighted sequences

↓

BOLD signal

Figure 14.2. Neuronal, physiological, and biophysical relationship between neuronal activity and the measured BOLD (blood oxygen level–dependent) signal changes.

coverage and higher spatial resolution. Figure 14.2 illustrates neuronal, physiological, and biophysical relationships connecting neuronal activity to measured signal changes using fMRI.

The most common imaging sequence used in fMRI studies is echo planar imaging (EPI). This is a very fast MRI imaging sequence that can collect whole-brain data within a few seconds. However, the spatial resolution is significantly lower than in anatomic MRI images. Also, EPI images are sensitive to field inhomogeneities, leading to geometric distortion of the images in certain brain regions. In a typical fMRI experiment, a large set of images is acquired very quickly while the patient or subject performs a task that shifts brain activity between two or more well-defined states.

fMRI experiments generate time series data that need to be analyzed in order to obtain the best activation results. For simple analysis, vendor-provided real-time fMRI processing helps. For event-related paradigms or more complex boxcar paradigms, extensive computation may be required using any of the free or commercial software such as Statistical Parametric Mapping (SPM; FIL Methods Group, 1994–2001; Friston, 1997, 2004; Penny, Friston, Ashburner, Kiebel, & Nichols, 2006; Stephan & Friston, 2010), Free Software Library (University of Oxford, 2008; see also Smith et al., 2004; Woolrich et al., 2009), or Brain Voyager (Goebel, 2012a, 2012b; Schuhmann, Schiller, Goebel, & Sack, 2009; van Atteveldt, Roebroeck, & Goebel, 2009). The basic idea of analysis of functional imaging data is to identify voxels that show signal changes that vary with the changes in the given cognitive or motor state of interest across the time course of the experiment.

LANGUAGE fMRI

Language fMRI plays an important role in presurgical evaluation of epilepsy because it noninvasively maps eloquent cortex (Binder, 1997) and thereby minimizes cognitive deficits after surgery. The main aims of presurgical language fMRI are to localize and lateralize language functions in cortical brain areas and also to determine intrahemispheric distribution of eloquent cortex. This method is noninvasive, cost-effective, and easy to implement. IAP or Wada testing has been the gold standard for identifying presurgical language lateralization, but this method is invasive and carries potential risks (Baxendale, Thompson, & Duncan, 2008; Lehéricy et al., 2000). fMRI offers a noninvasive and promising alternative approach, and there has been a good concordance between Wada testing and fMRI results (Binder et al., 1996).

In 1990, Petersen, Fox, Snyder, and Raichle first showed that functional neuroimaging has the potential to visualize active brain regions during language-processing stimuli. Later, in 1995, Desmond et al. showed that there was a strong correlation between Wada test and fMRI results based on his study on epilepsy patients. A number of investigators have established that fMRI has the potential to determine the lateralization of language functions (Bavelier et al., 1997; Binder et al., 1996, 1997; Cuenod et al., 1995; McCarthy, Blamire, Rothman, Gruetter, & Shulman, 1993). However, it has been demonstrated that the classic language model (Lichtheim 1885) is not sufficient to reflect the complexity of various language organizations.

Atypical language dominance, defined as right-handed or bilateral representation of language, is more common in patients with epilepsy than in the general population, supporting the hypothesis that insult to the brain in epilepsy induces language reorganization. Focal epilepsy is associated with disrupted localization and lateralization of language functions, and hence one would expect a higher possibility of abnormal language lateralization. Wada and Rasmussen (1960/2007) determined that over 93% of patients are left language dominant. The left-sided language dominance is more intrinsic for right-handers, but it can also be found in the majority of left-handers. Some patients also have bilateral representation of language. Several studies indicate that left temporal lobe pathology is often associated with atypical language lateralization. Patients with frontotemporal lesions in the dominant hemisphere are particularly prone to postsurgical motor or language deficits, so preservation of the functional areas and reduction of morbidity associated with the surgery are crucial. The functional lateralization of the cerebral cortex was first suggested by Geschwind and Levitsky (1968), who discovered that about 60% of human brains display anatomical differences between the two hemispheres in the posterior temporal lobe (the region that encompasses Wernicke's area). In line with these anatomical observations, language was the first function that was demonstrated to be lateralized in the human cerebral cortex. More recently, various other anatomical and functional differences have been documented between the two cerebral hemispheres.

The increased frequency of atypical language lateralization (right-sided or bilateral) in patients with focal epilepsy or lesions of the left hemisphere has been known for more than 30 years. Modern neuroimaging studies have shown that a considerable proportion of patients with early acquired or developmental left-sided perisylvian lesions show evidence of intrahemispheric reorganization of language (i.e., retain typical left-sided lateralization) often near the lesion (Swanson, Sabsevitz, Hammeke, & Binder, 2007). Furthermore, epilepsy patients with lesions in the remote language areas, more specifically in the mesial temporal cortex, often show atypical, often bilateral language representation. Binder et al. (1996) performed fMRI on 22 patients with epilepsy who also underwent a Wada test to determine language lateralization. For fMRI, they used different sets of language functions (e.g., object naming, semantic judgment task). A correlation analysis identified voxels significantly associated with task performance. On the basis of the number of voxels in each hemisphere that exceeded threshold, they calculated a laterality index. The authors reported that all patients showed concordant fMRI and Wada test results. Eighteen of 22 patients had strong left hemisphere dominance on both tests. The remaining four patients showed less strong or atypical language dominance on fMRI. In patients analyzed by Kesavadas et al. (2007), fMRI results matched those from intraoperative cortical stimulation for lesions in or close to eloquent cortex. For language hemispheric dominance, the fMRI results were concordant with Wada testing. Eloquent cortex mapping was performed in epilepsy patients with tumor, gliosis, or malformation of cortical development in or close to eloquent cortex. Our neurosurgeons found fMRI for eloquent cortex mapping most useful in patients with gliosis, in whom the distortion in anatomy makes prediction of eloquent cortex extremely difficult. Color Plate 5 illustrates the usefulness of fMRI in selecting patients for surgery, tailoring surgical resection, and predicting the postsurgical outcome.

For fMRI studies, the most common approach to quantifying hemispheric dominance is to calculate the laterality index (LI). The assessment of a meaningful LI measure depends on the nature of the quantification of left- and right-hemisphere contributions, localization of volumes of interest within each hemisphere, dependency on statistical threshold, choice of activation, and baseline conditions and reproducibility of LI values. The degree of lateralization is often quantified using the equation $LI = (L - R)/(L + R)$, where L and R represent the strength of activation for the left (L) and right (R) sides on the basis of the number of activated voxels for the whole hemisphere or using regions of interest targeted to known language areas. A positive value represents left language lateralization, and a negative value represents right-sided dominance. LI values close to zero are often classified as bilateral. This can be determined by counting the number of voxels exceeding a specified threshold of significance.

LANGUAGE PARADIGMS FOR FMRI STUDY

To visualize brain activity reliably in response to various cognitive tasks such as sensory, motor, or language, appropriate fMRI paradigms (experimental tasks) should be developed on the basis of neuropsychological principles. Identification of hemisphere dominance for language requires a language paradigm that best activates different language-processing streams. Most fMRI language paradigms are block design paradigms that rely on cognitive subtraction logic—that is, task blocks are subtracted from the rest of the blocks to show brain activity during any specific task. The advantage of block designs over event-related designs is that they are efficient in detecting differences between two conditions; however, they offer less flexibility in the experimental design required for studying complex cognitive functions. The extension of the cortex activated during the functional MRI experiment depends on the experimental task chosen to activate the function of interest. The choice of the baseline condition is also important because the brain processes occurring will be inevitably subtracted from the task condition. So the baseline condition will have to include all brain processes that are associated with the function of interest but are distinct from it. The most widely used experimental fMRI paradigms for presurgical assessment of language are verbal fluency tasks and language comprehension tasks.

Verbal fluency tasks include verb generation, word generation, and semantic and syntactic processing tasks. The verb generation task is the most commonly used fMRI language paradigm and probably the most reliable test in the clinical field (Schlösser, Hutchinson, & Joseffer, 1998). It is generally used to localize expressive and receptive language functions in the inferior frontal gyrus and superior temporal gyrus, respectively. In the verb generation task, the patient is instructed to generate verbs (e.g., "what to do with") that are semantically related to a presented noun (e.g., chair, pencil).

Word generation can also be used as a verbal phonological fluency task. In this task, the patient is instructed to generate words from a visually or aurally presented letter (e.g., "A" for *apple*) or in a given category (e.g., "birds" for *parrot*). Performance of this task results in the processing of mainly three linguistic components—syntax (the patient has to combine two word classes—e.g., a noun and a verb), semantics (the verb needs to be related to the noun), and phonology (i.e., phonemic encoding of the heard word and production of a phonemic string). The semantic language-processing task includes visual or auditory presentation of semantically related or unrelated sentences or words, and the subject is instructed to press the response button on seeing or hearing a semantically related word. This type of task produces predominant activation in posterior parietotemporal language areas in the dominant hemisphere (Binder et al., 1997). The syntactic language-processing task includes visual or auditory presentation of grammatically correct or incorrect sentences, and the subject is instructed to press the response button on seeing or hearing a grammatically correct sentence. This kind of task evokes the inferior frontal gyrus predominantly and produces a small amount of activation in parietotemporal language areas.

In language comprehension tasks, linguistically more complex sentences are presented rather than single words. Increased receptive area activation has been common among various language comprehension tasks and also produces a substantial amount of activation in several temporoparietal language processing areas, which are located outside Wernicke's area. It includes the superior temporal sulcus, the middle temporal gyrus, and some parts of the inferior temporal gyrus.

Passive listening is a common auditory paradigm of choice that includes listening to stories or phrases. This paradigm mainly produces activation in the temporal lobe language comprehensive areas (Wernicke's area) of the dominant hemisphere. The selection of a baseline condition is important in auditory paradigms; a series of tones, reverse speech, or an unfamiliar language may be used for the control condition for proper subtraction of auditory area activation.

All patients require proper training prior to fMRI scanning depending on the degree of epileptogenic lesion–associated language deficit. This training results in proper outcomes from the experiment and ensures robust functional localization. Color Plate 6 illustrates activation patterns of various language paradigms.

We studied 20 patients with intractable epilepsy (11 males, 9 females) and 10 normal healthy volunteers (seven males, three females) with no history of any disorder affecting brain function. Of 20 patients, 16 were right-handed and four were left-handed. The ages ranged from 15 years to 45 years. The origin of epilepsy was established on the basis of noninvasive data including medical history, standard EEG, video EEG recording, and a brain MRI. A neuropsychological evaluation was done to measure IQ. Table 14.1 presents the demographic and clinical details of the patients.

After proper training, the subjects were positioned on a 1.5 tesla MR Imager (Avanto SQ engine, Siemens, Erlangen, Germany). The auditory verb generation stimulus was delivered using MRI-compatible earphones, and visual stimulus was delivered using a projector and screen connected to a computer. Anatomical landmark images of the entire head were obtained with a 3D spoiled gradient-recalled acquisition in the steady state sequence (3-D FLASH; TR/TE 11/4.94 ms, flip angle 15°, FOV 256 mm, slice thickness

TABLE 14.1
Demographic and Clinical Details of Patients

Patient	Age	Gender	Type of epilepsy	Epilepsy duration (years)	Handedness	IQ
1	23	Male	TLE (LH)	20	Right	92
2	35	Male	FLE (RH)	32	Right	70
3	26	Male	FLE (RH)	16	Right	80
4	16	Male	FLE (RH)	10	Right	105
5	38	Male	TLE (LH)	38	Right	90
6	34	Female	PLE (LH)	7	Right	97
7	26	Female	TLE (LH)	20	Left	110
8	22	Female	FLE (LH)	12	Left	100
9	20	Female	TLE (RH)	18	Right	95
10	33	Male	TLE (LH)	23	Right	80
11	23	Male	FLE (LH)	9	Right	86
12	19	Female	PLE (RH)	11	Left	98
13	26	Female	TLE (RH)	30	Left	112
14	40	Male	FLE (LH)	2	Right	129
15	25	Female	TLE (LH)	13	Right	102
16	19	Female	TLE (LH)	16	Right	83
17	45	Male	FLE (LH)	25	Right	99
18	16	Male	TLE (LH)	10	Right	84
19	20	Female	FLE (LH)	15	Right	118
20	33	Male	FLE (LH)	5	Right	92

Note. FLE = frontal lobe epilepsy; LH = left hemisphere, PLE = parietal lobe epilepsy; RH = right hemisphere; TLE = temporal lobe epilepsy. IQ scores: < 50 = profound, 50–70 = moderate, 70–90 = dull normal, 90–109 = average, 110–119 = bright normal, 120–129 = superior, >130 = very superior.

1 mm, matrix 256 × 256), following the availability of 3D FLAIR (TR/TE/TI 5,000/405/1,800 ms, FOV 256 mm, slice thickness 1 mm, matrix 256 × 256). These sequences are used for final coregistration of the fMRI images to the anatomical images. For functional imaging, we used a gradient-echo echo planar sequence based on BOLD effects (TR/TE 3,580/50 ms, flip angle 90°, FOV 250 mm, matrix 64 × 64, slice thickness 3 mm) that was applied after the gradient field mapping to acquire T2*w functional images. To investigate language functions, we used three different language fMRI paradigms—visual verb generation, semantics, and syntax—to invoke various language-processing areas. The paradigms were presented as a block design consisting of alternating blocks of five active and five rest conditions, and each block consisted of 10 measurements. The baseline condition was the same for all the three visual tasks, during which a checkerboard was shown to the subjects. A total of 100 measurements were obtained in 6.02 minutes.

Offline fMRI data analysis was done using SPM5 implemented in MATLAB (Matlab 7.1). The fMRI data from each participant were slice acquisition corrected, motion corrected, and coregistered to the coplanar anatomical image from each participant and represented in a stereotaxic space, a standard brain space coordinate system for anatomical reference. The T1 images were normalized to the standard Montreal Neurologic Institute template with the transformation matrix applied to the coregistered functional images. The normalized functional images were spatially smoothed with a Gaussian filter (8 mm full width at half-maximum kernel) and interpolated to 3 mm isotropic voxel. Single-subject analysis was done by modeling the active and control conditions with a boxcar function convolved with the hemodynamic response function using the general linear model and applying a 128-s high-pass filter. This procedure generates statistical parametric maps of t statistics reflecting differences between active and rest states at each voxel location for each subject. For the description of differences between activation and control conditions in single-subject data, a probability threshold of $p < .001$ was chosen. The SPM results were also compared with vendor-provided real-time fMRI analysis results. There was significant concordance between the two techniques for the area of activation, amount of activation, and distance of the activated area from the lesion.

The fMRI results of most of the right-handed patients (14 patients) in our study showed a strong language lateralization to the left side (typical language dominance), and two of them showed symmetric or right-hemisphere dominance (atypical lateralization). Of the four left-handed patients, three showed lateralization on same side, and the remaining one showed bilateral representation of language. The fMRI results also revealed around 80% concordances with the results of Wada test in 17 patients in whom both techniques were performed. In four patients, lesions were located very close to eloquent cortex. Table 14.2 presents the summary of results.

TABLE 14.2

Summary of Results Based on Functional Magnetic Resonance Imaging (fMRI)
Using Language Paradigms for Patients With Epilepsy

Patients	Epileptogenic area	Paradigm used	fMRI activation results	Wada concordance[a]	fMRI information used for surgery?
1	Left hemisphere atophy with gliosis	VGEN, SY, SM	IFG, pSTG	80%	Yes
2	Right superior frontal gyrus lesion	VGEN, SY, SM	IFG, pSTG, PTJn	75%	Yes
3	Right frontal gliosis	VGEN, SY, SM	IFG, STG	90%	Yes
4	Right frontal FCD	VGEN, SY, SM	IFG, STG	—	No
5	Left posterior temporal mass lesion	VGEN, SY, SM	IFG, STG	92%	Yes
6	Right parieto-occipital FCD	VGEN, SY, SM	IFG, pSTG, PTJn	78%	Yes
7	Left hemisphere atophy	VGEN, SY, SM	IFG, pSTG	98%	Yes
8	Left frontal FCD	VGEN, SY, SM	IFG, pSTG	75%	Yes
9	Right temporal FCD	VGEN, SY, SM	IFG, pSTG	—	No
10	Left middle frontal gyrus mass lesion	VGEN, SY, SM	IFG, pSTG	82%	Yes
11	Left frontal FCD	VGEN, SY, SM	IFG, pSTG	99%	Yes
12	Right mesial occipital mass lesion	VGEN, SY, SM	IFG, pSTG, PTJn	88%	Yes
13	Right hemispheric encephalomalacia	VGEN, SY, SM	IFG, pSTG	64%	No
14	Left superior frontal gyrus FCD	VGEN, SY, SM	IFG, pSTG	74%	Yes
15	Left mesial temporal sclerosis	VGEN, SY, SM	IFG, pSTG	93%	Yes
16	Left hemisphere atophy with gliosis	VGEN, SY, SM	IFG, pSTG	94%	Yes
17	Encephalomalacia with gliosis left inferior frontal gyrus	VGEN, SY, SM	IFG, pSTG	82%	Yes
18	Left inferior temporal gyrus mass lesion	VGEN, SY, SM	IFG, pSTG, PTJn	—	No
19	Left frontal FCD	VGEN, SY, SM	IFG, pSTG	96%	Yes
20	Right frontal gliosis	VGEN, SY, SM	IFG, pSTG	99%	Yes

FCD = focal cortical dysplasia; IFG = inferior frontal gyrus; pSTG = posterior superior temporal gyrus; PTJn = parietotemporal junction; SM = semantics; SY = syntax; VGEN = verb generation.
[a]Dashes indicate that the Wada test was not done for this subject.

In general, the verb generation paradigm, involved in language expression and language comprehension, produced activation in the classic Broca's area (IFG) and often in Wernicke's area (pSTG) and parietotemporal language areas in the dominant hemisphere. The syntax paradigm produced activation in the classic Wernicke's area predominantly and also in the expressive speech areas in the inferior frontal gyrus in the dominant hemisphere. The semantic paradigm produced activation only in posterior language areas of the dominant hemisphere. We concluded that visual representation of language tasks works better and produces consistent results in both control and epilepsy groups, and there was no difference in language lateralization when gender is considered. Language lateralization did not differ among patients by seizure location within frontal, temporal, or parietal brain areas. Age at epilepsy onset and duration of epilepsy did not relate to language lateralization.

LANGUAGE fMRI TECHNICAL CONSIDERATIONS

The following characteristics of fMRI make it a potentially useful tool for language mapping:

- The relatively small size of fMRI voxels (typically 2–4 mm on an edge) ensures good image quality and spatial localization.
- Functional information can be coregistered onto high-resolution magnetic resonance images acquired at the same brain location, which enhances the ability to correlate functional with structural data.
- fMRI data processing can be performed repeatedly in the same subject within and across scanning sessions, providing improved statistical power, test–retest reliability, ability to monitor activation changes serially over time, and potential for exploring a range of cognitive processes.
- fMRI can be implemented on any clinical MRI scanner (1.5 tesla and above) with the addition of relatively inexpensive fast acquisition pulse sequences, ancillary hardware coils, and specialized stimulus delivery and response monitoring systems.

fMRI–DTI

Diffusion tensor imaging (DTI) maps the white matter tracts (Conturo et al., 1999; Mori, Crain, Chacko, & van Zijl, 1999). The combination of fMRI to identify cortical regions involved in language function with DTI helps visualize white matter pathways connecting these regions, offering an opportunity to study the relationship between structure and function in the language system. Studies (Adcock et al., 2003; Thivard et al., 2005) have revealed structural asymmetries in controls, with greater left-sided frontotemporal connections in the dominant hemisphere. Patients with left TLE had reduced left-sided and greater right-sided connections than both controls and right TLE patients, reflecting the altered functional lateralization seen in left TLE patients, and significant correlations were demonstrated between structure and function in controls and subjects, with subjects with more highly lateralized language function having a more lateralized pattern of connections. The combination of fMRI with information on the microstructural architecture of these normally and abnormally functioning areas offers the opportunity to improve understanding of the relationship between brain structure and function and may improve the planning of surgical resections to maximize the chance of seizure remission and to minimize the risks of cognitive impairment (Ramnani, Behrens, Penny, & Matthews, 2004). Color Plate 7 illustrates fiber tractography of major white matter tracts involved in human language processing.

CHALLENGES

- Patients with epilepsy on long-term antiepileptic medication and those who have frequent seizures can have low IQ. These patients may not cooperate for difficult tasks such as language and memory tasks.
- The effects of medication on the BOLD signal response have not been systematically studied. In a study by Jokeit, Okujava, and Woermann (2001), the extent of fMRI activation of the mesial temporal lobes induced by a task based on the retrieval of individual visuospatial knowledge was correlated with the serum carbamazepine level in 21 patients with refractory temporal lobe epilepsy (see also Jokeit & Ebner, 2002). The study showed that carbamazepine level can significantly influence the amount of fMRI activation.
- Ictal and interictal epileptic activity in a patient with epilepsy can influence the lateralization of mesiotemporal language functions.
- Signal intensity changes observed in fMRI images are small. These may be contaminated by gross head motion. Head motion during acquisition can be restricted by fixation of the head with straps. Also, stimulation paradigms that induce less patient head motion are preferred. Adequate training before imaging could increase familiarity with imaging process, especially in the case of pediatric fMRI studies.

- There is a concern that fMRI examinations at a field strength of 1.5 tesla does imaging of predominantly large, draining veins. Gao, Miller, Lai, Xiong, and Fox (1996) showed that fMRI images weighted toward the microcirculation may be obtained at 1.5 T by designing the pulse sequence for minimizing inflow effects and maximizing BOLD contribution. Maximizing the fMRI signal toward the site of neuronal activity can also be achieved by optimizing the mode of stimulation, as shown by the study of Le Rumeur, Allard, Poiseau, and Jannin (2000).
- Does the absence of a BOLD signal in a cortical area indicate with certainty a lack of electrical neuronal activity in that area? Different pathological conditions could weaken the hemo-dynamic response that is the source of the fMRI signal. Examples of this include peritumoral vasogenic edema producing mechanical vascular compression and drugs administered to the patient causing change in hemodynamic autoregulation.

CONCLUSION

fMRI offers a promising noninvasive approach for presurgical language mapping in epilepsy patients, and there exists a good concordance between Wada test and fMRI results. With the development and refinement of imaging techniques such as high-resolution structural MRI, fMRI, ictal SPECT with SPM, and fMRI combined with diffusion fiber tractography, a greater number of patients without a discrete lesion can be identified to improve seizure-free out-come to 50% to 60%. Several studies in this regard have shown improvement in quality of life, occupational outcome, and social and psychiatric outcome.

REFERENCES

Adcock, J. E., Wise, R. G., Oxbury, J. M., Oxbury, S. M., & Matthews, P. M. (2003). Quantitative fMRI assessment of the differences in lateralization of language-related brain activation in patients with temporal lobe epilepsy. *NeuroImage*, *18*, 423–438. doi:10.1016/S1053-8119(02)00013-7

Al-Otaibi, F., Baeesa, S. S., Parrent, A. G., Girvin, J. P., & Steven, D. (2012). Surgi-cal techniques for the treatment of temporal lobe epilepsy. *Epilepsy Research and Treatment*, *2012*, 1–13.

Bavelier, D., Corina, D., Jezzard, P., Padmanabhan, S., Clark, P., Karni, A., . . . Neville, H. (1997). Sentence reading: A functional MRI study at 4 tesla. *Journal of Cognitive Neuroscience*, *9*, 664–686. doi:10.1162/jocn.1997.9.5.664

Baxendale, S., Thompson, P. J., & Duncan, J. S. (2008). The role of the Wada test in the surgical treatment of temporal lobe epilepsy: An international survey. *Epilepsia, 49*, 715–720. doi:10.1111/j.1528-1167.2007.01515_1.x

Billingsley-Marshall, R. L., Simos, P. G., & Papanicolaou, A. C. (2004). Reliability and validity of functional neuroimaging techniques for identifying language critical areas in children and adults. *Developmental Neuropsychology, 26*, 541–563. doi:10.1207/s15326942dn2602_1

Binder, J. (1997). Functional magnetic resonance imaging: Language mapping. *Neurosurgery Clinics of North America, 8*, 383–392.

Binder, J. R., Frost, J. A., Hammeke, T. A., Cox, R. W., Rao, S. M., & Prieto, T. (1997). Human brain language areas identified by functional magnetic resonance imaging. *Journal of Neuroscience, 17*, 353–362.

Binder, J. R., Swanson, S. J., Hammeke, T. A., Morris, G. L., Mueller, W. M., Fischer, M., . . . Haughton, V. M. (1996). Determination of language dominance using functional MRI: A comparison with the Wada test. *Neurology, 46*, 978–984. doi:10.1212/WNL.46.4.978

Brown, J. W. (1978). Lateralization: A brain model. *Brain and Language, 5*, 258–261. doi:10.1016/0093-934X(78)90024-X

Conturo, T. E., Lori, N. F., Cull, T. S., Akbudak, E., Snyder, A. Z., Shimony, J. S., . . . Raichle, M. E. (1999). Tracking neuronal fiber pathways in the living human brain. *Proceedings of the National Academy of Sciences of the United States of America, 96*, 10422–10427. doi:10.1073/pnas.96.18.10422

Cuenod, C. A., Bookheimer, S. Y., Hertz-Pannier, L., Zeffiro, T. A., Theodor, W. H., & Le Bihan, D. (1995). Functional MRI during word generation using conventional equipment. *Neurology, 45*, 1821–1827. doi:10.1212/WNL.45.10.1821

Damasio, A. R., & Geschwind, N. (1984). The neural basis of language. *Annual Review of Neuroscience, 7*, 127–147. doi:10.1146/annurev.ne.07.030184.001015

Desmond, J. E., Sum, J. M., Wagner, A. D., Demb, J. B., Shear, P. K., Glover, G. H., . . . Morrell, M. J. (1995). Functional MRI measurement of language lateralization in Wada-tested patients. *Brain: A Journal of Neurology, 118*, 1411–1419. doi:10.1093/brain/118.6.1411

Engel, J., Jr. (1993). *Surgical treatment of the epilepsies* (2nd ed.). New York, NY: Raven Press.

Engel J., Jr. (2006). ILAE classification of epilepsy syndromes. *Epilepsy Research, 70*(Suppl.), S5–S10.

Faro, S. H., & Mohamed, F. B. (2010). *BOLD fMRI: A guide to functional imaging for neuroscientists.* New York, NY: Springer.

FIL Methods Group. (1994–2001). Statistical parametric mapping [Computer software]. Retrieved from http://www.fil.ion.ucl.ac.uk/spm

Friston, K. J. (1997). Analysing brain images: Principles and overview. In R. S. J. Frackowiak, K. J. Friston, C. D. Frith, R. J. Dolan, & J. C. Mazziotta (Eds.), *Human brain function* (pp. 25–41). San Diego, CA: Academic Press.

Friston, K. J. (2004). Experimental design and statistical parametric mapping. In R. S. J. Frackowiak (Ed.-in-Chief), *Human brain function* (2nd ed., pp. 599–634). San Diego, CA: Academic Press.

Gao, J. H., Miller, I., Lai, S., Xiong, J., & Fox, P. T. (1996). Quantitative assessment of blood inflow effects in functional MRI signals. *Magnetic Resonance in Medicine, 36,* 314–319. doi:10.1002/mrm.1910360219

Geschwind, N. (1965). Disconnexion syndromes in animals and man. *Brain: A Journal of Neurology, 88,* 237–294. doi:10.1093/brain/88.2.237

Geschwind, N., & Levitsky, W. (1968, July 12). Human brain: Left–right asymmetries in temporal speech regions. *Science, 161,* 186–187. doi:10.1126/science. 161.3837.186

Goebel, R. (2012a). Brain Voyager [Computer software]. Retrieved from http://www. brainvoyager.com/

Goebel, R. (2012b). BrainVoyager—Past, present, future. *NeuroImage, 62,* 748–756.

Hickok, G., & Poeppel, D. (2000). Towards a functional neuroanatomy of speech perception. *Trends in Cognitive Sciences, 4,* 131–138. doi:10.1016/S1364-6613(00)01463-7

Hickok, G., & Poeppel, D. (2004). Dorsal and ventral streams: A framework for understanding aspects of the functional anatomy of language. *Cognition, 92,* 67–99. doi:10.1016/j.cognition.2003.10.011

Hickok, G., & Poeppel, D. (2007). The cortical organization of speech processing. *Nature Reviews Neuroscience, 8,* 393–402. doi:10.1038/nrn2113

Jokeit, H., & Ebner, A. (2002). Effects of chronic epilepsy on intellectual functions. *Progress in Brain Research, 135,* 455–463. doi:10.1016/S0079-6123(02)35042-8

Jokeit, H., Okujava, M., & Woermann, F. G. (2001). Carbamazepine reduces memory induced activation of mesial temporal lobe structures: A pharmacological fMRI-study. *BMC Neurology, 1,* 6. doi:10.1186/1471-2377-1-6

Kesavadas, C., Thomas, B., Sujesh, S., Ashalata, R., Abraham, M., Gupta, A. K., & Radhakrishnan, K. (2007). Real time functional MR imaging (fMRI) for presurgical evaluation of pediatric epilepsy. *Pediatric Radiology, 37,* 964–974. doi:10.1007/s00247-007-0556-4

Lehéricy, S., Cohen, L., Bazin, B., Samson, S., Giacomini, E., Rougetet, R., . . . Baulac, M. (2000). Functional MR evaluation of temporal and frontal language dominance compared with the Wada test. *Neurology, 54,* 1625–1633. doi:10.1212/WNL.54.8.1625

Le Rumeur, E., Allard, M., Poiseau, E., & Jannin, P. (2000). Role of the mode of sensory stimulation in presurgical brain mapping in which functional magnetic resonance imaging is used. *Journal of Neurosurgery, 93,* 427–431. doi:10.3171/jns.2000.93.3.0427

Lichtheim, L. (1885). On aphasia. *Brain: A Journal of Neurology, 7,* 433–484.

McCarthy, G., Blamire, A., Rothman, D., Gruetter, R., & Shulman, R. G. (1993). Echo-planar magnetic resonance imaging studies of frontal cortex activation during word generation in humans. *Proceedings of the National Academy of Sciences of the United States of America, 90*, 4952–4956. doi:10.1073/pnas.90.11.4952

Mori, S., Crain, B. J., Chacko, V. P., & van Zijl, P. C. (1999). Three-dimensional tracking of axonal projections in the brain by magnetic resonance imaging. *Annals of Neurology, 45*, 265–269.

Ogawa, S., & Lee, T. M. (1990). Magnetic resonance imaging of blood vessels at high fields: In vivo and in vitro measurements and image simulation. *Magnetic Resonance in Medicine, 16*, 9–18. doi:10.1002/mrm.1910160103

Ogawa, S., Lee, T. M., Nayak, A. S., & Glynn, P. (1990). Oxygenation-sensitive contrast in magnetic resonance image of rodent brain at high magnetic fields. *Magnetic Resonance in Medicine, 14*, 68–78. doi:10.1002/mrm.1910140108

Penfield, W., & Jasper, H. H. (1954). *Epilepsy and the functional anatomy of the human brain*. Boston, MA: Little Brown.

Penny, W. D., Friston, K. J., Ashburner, J. T., Kiebel, S. J., & Nichols, T. E. (2006). *Statistical parametric mapping: The analysis of functional brain images*. London, England: Academic Press.

Petersen, S. E., Fox, P. T., Snyder, A. Z., & Raichle, M. E. (1990, August 31). Activation of extrastriate and frontal cortical areas by visual words and word-like stimuli. *Science, 249*, 1041–1044. doi:10.1126/science.2396097

Poeppel, D., & Hickok, G. (2004). Towards a new functional anatomy of language. *Cognition, 92*, 1–12. doi:10.1016/j.cognition.2003.11.001

Price, C. J. (2000). The anatomy of language: Contributions from functional neuroimaging. *Journal of Anatomy, 197*, 335–359. doi:10.1046/j.1469-7580.2000.19730335.x

Ramnani, N., Behrens, T. E. J., Penny, W., & Matthews, P. M. (2004). New approaches for exploring anatomical and functional connectivity in the human brain. *Biological Psychiatry, 56*, 613–619. doi:10.1016/j.biopsych.2004.02.004

Rosenow, F., & Luders, H. (2001). Presurgical evaluation of epilepsy. *Brain, 124*, 1683–1700. doi:10.1093/brain/124.9.1683

Schlösser, R., Hutchinson, M., & Joseffer, S. (1998). Functional magnetic resonance imaging of human brain activity in verbal fluency task. *Journal of Neurology, Neurosurgery, and Psychiatry, 64*, 492–498. doi:10.1136/jnnp.64.4.492

Schuhmann, T., Schiller, N. O., Goebel, R., & Sack, A. T. (2009). The temporal characteristics of functional activation in Broca's area during overt picture naming. *Cortex, 45*, 1111–1116.

Smith, S. M., Jenkinson, M., Woolrich, M. W., Beckmann, C. F., Behrens, T. E. J., Johansen-Berg, H., . . . Matthews, P. M. (2004). Advances in functional and structural MR image analysis and implementation as FSL. *NeuroImage, 23*(Suppl. 1), S208–S219.

Stephan, K. E., & Friston, K. J. (2010). Analyzing effective connectivity with functional magnetic resonance imaging. *Cognitive Science, 1*, 446–459.

Swanson, S. J., Sabsevitz, D. S., Hammeke, T. A., & Binder, J. R. (2007). Functional magnetic resonance imaging of language in epilepsy. *Neuropsychology Review*, *17*, 491–504. doi:10.1007/s11065-007-9050-x

Téllez-Zenteno, J. F., Dhar, R., & Wiebe, S. (2005). Long-term seizure outcomes following epilepsy surgery: A systematic review and meta-analysis. *Brain: A Journal of Neurology*, *128*, 1188–1198. doi:10.1093/brain/awh449

Thivard, L., Lehéricy, S., Krainik, A., Adam, C., Dormont, D., Chiras, J., . . . Dupont, S. (2005). Diffusion tensor imaging in medial temporal lobe epilepsy with hippocampal sclerosis. *NeuroImage*, *28*, 682–690. doi:10.1016/j.neuroimage.2005.06.045

University of Oxford. (2008). Free Software Library [Computer software]. Retrieved from http://www.fmrib.ox.ac.uk/fsl

van Atteveldt, N., Roebroeck, A., & Goebel, R. (2009). Interaction of speech and script in human auditory cortex: Insights from neuro-imaging and effective connectivity. *Hearing Research*, *258*, 152–164.

Wada, J., & Rasmussen, T. (2007). Intracarotid injection of sodium amytal for the lateralization of cerebral speech dominance. *Journal of Neurosurgery*, *106*, 1117–1133. (Original work published 1960) doi:10.3171/jns.2007.106.6.1117

Wiebe, S., Blume, W. T., Girvin, J. P., & Eliasziw, M. (2001). A randomized, controlled trial of surgery for temporal-lobe epilepsy. *The New England Journal of Medicine*, *345*, 311–318. doi:10.1056/NEJM200108023450501

Woolrich, M. W., Jbabdi, S., Patenaude, B., Chappell, M., Makni, S., Behrens, T., . . . Smith, S. M. (2009). Bayesian analysis of neuroimaging data in FSL. *NeuroImage*, *45*, S173–S186.

INDEX

Absence seizures, 291
Absolute frame, 212
Abundis, A., 41
ACC. *See* Anterior cingulate cortex
Acioly, N. M., 238
Adamson, L. B., 146
Adderall XR, 136
ADHD. *See* Attention-deficit/
    hyperactivity disorder
ADHD Network, 127–129, 131, 138
Adolescents
    attention training via meditation
        for, 26
    conflict resolution by, 24
    executive control in, 19, 89
Adults
    ADHD prevalence in, 106
    CHRNA4 gene in, 73
    conceptual processing by children vs.,
        276–278
    conflict resolution by children vs.,
        24–25
    conjunction search by, 15
    connectivity between ACC and
        posterior brain areas, 76
    language-vision mapping in, 273–276
    task-switching skills in easy and dif-
        ficult conditions of, 89–93,
        95–98
    task-switching studies for children vs.,
        86–87
Affect, joint attention and, 200–202
Affective control
    and attention, 34
    defined, 12–13
    development of, 24–25
Affective traits, in PLeASES model, 187
Affiliation, gaze grooming and, 159
African Americans, executive attention
    in, 25
Aggression, 43, 44
Aging
    and attention networks, 75–76
    and conjunction search, 15
    and modes of selection, 11, 13–14

and task switching, 22, 94–95, 97–98
and visual search/attention task
    performance, 15–17
Ahadi, S. A., 72
Akshara, 255–266
Alerting network, 35, 63
Allard, M., 306
Allison, T., 198
Allport, A., 86
Alphabetic scripts, non-alphabetic
    scripts vs., 255
Altmann, G. T. M., 274, 275
Altricial (term), 159
Alza Corporation, 136
Amphetamine, in treatment of ADHD,
    105–106, 132, 136
Amso, D., 21
Amsterdam, B., 162
Amygdala, activation of, 64
Analytics (cognitive style), 235
Andersen, R. A., 199
Anderson, L. C., 21
Animals, prosocial behaviors of, 158
Anterior cingulate cortex (ACC), 35, 38
    attention control in conflicts by,
        35–36
    in cognitive and emotional control, 61
    and empathy, 64
    error correction/monitoring in, 65
    and orienting network, 69
    in reward and punishment
        networks, 72
ANTs. *See* Attention network tests
Aoyama, T., 136
Arbib, M. A., 188
Archana S, 147
Arithmetic skills, executive attention
    and, 37
ASDs. *See* Autism spectrum disorders
Asthana, H. S., 218
Attention. *See also specific types, e.g.:*
    Executive attention
    as an organ system, 61
    control in, 12–13
    as regulation of affect, 34

Attentional resources, allocation of, 38
Attention bias, 12
Attention circuit, 128, 129
Attention control, 12–13, 25–26
Attention-deficit/hyperactivity disorder
        (ADHD), 105–117, 127–140
    and abnormal neural circuitry, 129
    and ADHD symptoms without
            attention deficits, 71
    and anatomy/function of dopaminer-
            gic projections, 109–112
    biological basis of, 128–132
    clinical and cognitive characteristics
            of, 106–108
    as cognitive motivational deficit,
            26–27
    and DAT1 gene, 42
    diagnosis of, 107, 108
    and dopamine physiology in,
            112–116
    and error reaction times, 18
    and interparental aggression, 43
    intervention programs for, 45
    methylphenidate treatment of, 41
    stimulant medication for, 131–139
    in stimulant-naive adults, 130, 132
    subtypes of, 107, 108
Attention networks, 61–77
    attention state training for, 74–75
    effects of aging on, 75–76
    and effortful control, 63–65
    and emotional/cognitive self-
            regulation, 62–63
    error correction in, 65
    exercising, 73–76
    genetic factors in development of,
            70–73
    longitudinal study of cognitive and
            emotional control in, 65–68
    parallel control systems for, 68–69
Attention network tests (ANTs), 12,
        14, 39, 63, 67–68
    in affective control studies, 25
    for executive attention, 70
    in studies of executive attention, 18
Attention sharing. See also Joint
        attention
    defined, 175
    in infants, 175–180
Attention state training, 74–75

Attention training, 70–76
    defined, 74
    with meditation, 26
    for preschool children, 45–48
Atypical language dominance, 297–298
Atypical language lateralization,
        293, 298
Autism spectrum disorders (ASDs)
    and attention sharing, 175
    mirror mark test for, 162
    prerequisite learning skills of
            children with, 147–151
Automatic facilitation effect, 22–23
Automatisms, 291

Bakeman, R., 146
Bali, Indonesia, 212, 240–245
Barnett, W. S., 48
Barry, R. A., 49
Bartlett, M. S., 181
Bavalier, D., 15
BDT (Block Designs Test), 218
Becker, M. G., 20
Behavior problems
    and attention/EC, 44–45
    and emotional reactivity, 45
    externalizing, 38
Behavior regulation
    brain mechanisms allowing, 61.
            See also Attention networks
    and conflict resolution, 24
    in infancy, 33
Belsky, J., 72
Bengali language, 255, 256, 259
Benowitz, N. L., 134
Benzedrine, 105
Berger, A., 66
Bernheim, K., 199
Bernzweig, J., 39
Berry, J. W., 233, 235–236
Berteaux, P., 236–237
Bilingualism
    and culture, 226–227
    and executive attention, 48
    in geocentric language and cognition
            studies, 226–227, 242
Binder, J. R., 298
Biological basis, of ADHD, 130
Block Designs Test (BDT), 218
Blushing, 162–163

Body-related spatial representations, 212, 213
BOLD technique, 295–296
Bornstein, M. H., 272
Bradley, C., 105–106
Brain
    anatomical differences between hemispheres, 298
    functional organization of language in, 293–295
    laterality index, 299
    SES and function of, 44
Brain-imaging studies, of cognitive control, 18–19
Brain networks, 61
Breznen, B., 199
Briand, L., 40
Broca, Paul Pierre, 293
Broca's area, 293, 304
Broca–Wernicke–Lichtheim–Geschwind model, 293
Brocki, K., 41
Bronfenbrenner, U., 233
Brooks, R., 146
Bunge, S. A., 18

Campos, M., 199
Cantwell, D., 132
Caregivers. See Infant–caregiver interaction
Carlson, E., 179
Carryover effects, in task switching, 22–24
Catechol-O-methyltransferase (COMT) gene, 40
    and attention networks, 72–73
    and dopamine breakdown, 113
    and executive attention performance, 40–41
    and visual sequencing, 49
Caudate nucleus, 128, 129, 131
Cepeda, N. J., 23
Characters, in scripts, 255
Checa, P., 37
Chiba, A., 201
Children. See also specific headings, e.g.: Young children
    ADHD prevalence in, 106
    attention sharing by, 175

characteristics of human childhood, 159–160
claim of possession by, 164–165
cognitive and emotional control in, 65–68
cognitive self-regulation in, 62–63
color name use/color vision in, 271–273
conceptual processing by adults vs., 276–278
conflict resolution by adults vs., 24–25
and DA diffusion, 40–41
emergence of ethical stance in, 165–167
error correction development in, 65
mirror self-experience for, 161–164
task-switching skills in easy vs. difficult conditions, 93–98
task-switching studies of adults vs., 86–87
Chinese languages
    graphotactic conventions, 259
    radicals in, 263
    symbolism in, 265
Christ, S. E., 19
CHRNA4 gene, 73
Ciong, J., 306
Clerkin, S. M., 41
Cocaine, effects on the brain of methylphenidate vs., 133–134
Cognitive control
    brain-imaging studies of, 18–19
    defined, 12
    task switching in, 12
Cognitive self-regulation
    anterior cingulate areas for, 61
    and attention networks, 62–63, 65–68
    longitudinal study of, 65–68
Cognitive skill acquisition, in children with ADHD, 108
Cognitive styles, 234–240
Cole, M., 234
Color-mediated language-vision mapping, 278–283
Color names, 271–273
Color vision, 271–273
Cómbita, L. M., 26, 41, 49
Communication disorders, 146–147

Complex partial seizures, 291
Compliance, of young children with
    ASDs, 149, 151
COMT gene. *See* Catechol-O-
    methyltransferase gene
Conceptual processing, in adults vs.
    children, 276–278
Concerta, 136, 137
Concrete operations, 238–240
Conflict resolution
    by adults vs. children, 24–25
    cognitive, 62–63
Conflict tasks
    DAT1 gene and scores on, 41–42
    in executive attention studies, 35
Congruent stimuli, 91
Conjunction search, age-related
    changes in, 15
Conscience, EC and, 38, 64
Consistency effect, 258–259, 265, 266
Consonant representation, 259, 260
Control, 12–13, 17–27
    affective, 12–13, 24–25, 34
    of attention, 12–13, 25–26
    of attention networks, 68–69
    cognitive, 12, 18–19
    in developmental cognitive disorders,
        26–27
    effortful. *See* Effortful control
    executive. *See* Executive control
    genetic and experiential effects in,
        25–26
    inhibitory, 19–20, 64–65
Cooper, R. M., 273
Cornoldi, C., 37
Cost of incongruency (task-switching),
    91–96
Covert orienting, 14
Crone, E. A., 22
Cross-cultural studies
    of cognitive styles, 236–240
    of human development, 232–234
Cross-modal mappings, in reading
    development, 263–265
Cue-target interval (CTI), 21–22
Cultural enterprise perspective on
    writing systems, 257
Culture, 211–228, 231–246
    and bilingualism, 226–227
    and cognitive development, 234

    and cognitive styles, 234–240
    geocentric language and cognition
        study, 214–227, 240–245
    in human development studies,
        232–234
    and linguistic relativism, 213–214
    and mirror mark test, 161–162
    and sharing, 165
    transmission of, 233
Cycowicz, Y. M., 18
Czech language, 255, 261

DA. *See* Dopamine
Darwin, Charles, 162–163, 272
Dasen, P. R., 212, 214, 225, 232, 236,
    238, 242
DAT. *See* Dopamine transporter
DAT1 gene, 40–42
    and ADHD, 114–116
    and home environment, 50
    and temperament in children, 26
Davidoff, J., 272, 280
Davidson, M. C., 21, 87, 88
DBH (dopamine-beta-hydroxylase)
    gene, 114
Dead reckoning, 211
Deák, G. O., 174, 179, 181, 193,
    195–196, 200, 201
De Barbaro, K., 201
Decision making
    in children with ADHD, 110
    reward-related, 108
Deckner, D. F., 146
Deep orthographies, 258
Delay aversion, in children with
    ADHD, 108
De León, L., 213
De Liberto, S., 37
DeLoache, J. S., 277
Deaner, R. O., 199
Derryberry, D., 68
Desmond, J. E., 297
Developmental cognitive disorders,
    26–27
Developmental language disorders,
    146–147
Developmental niche, 233
Developmental theories
    of attention, 15–17

of gaze following and related skills, 180

generation of, 180–181

Diacritic form (consonant and vowel representation), 259

Diagnostic and Statistical Manual of Mental Disorders (DSM), ADHD in, 106–107

Diamond, A., 21, 40, 48

Dibbets, P., 22, 87

Difficult paradigms (for task-switching skills)

    for adults, 89–93, 95–98

    for children, 93–98

    defined, 88

    easy vs., 87–98

Diffusion tensor imaging (DTI), 304–305

Dolan, R. J., 198

Dopamine (DA)

    as biologic basis of ADHD, 128–132

    diffusion of, prefrontal cortex, 40–41

    in executive attention network, 39–40

    metabolism of, 72

    and nicotinic cholinergic receptor *CHRNA4*, 73

    physiology of, 112–116

Dopamine-beta-hydroxylase *(DBH)* gene, 114

Dopamine receptor D_4 *(DRD4)* gene, 40, 49, 50, 70

    7-repeat allele, 70–71

    and ADHD, 113–115

    and temperament, 72

Dopamine receptor D_5 *(DRD5)* gene, 113, 114

Dopaminergic projections, 109–112

    mesocortical pathways, 110–112

    mesolimbic pathways, 109–110

    nigrostriatal pathways, 109

Dopamine transporter (DAT), 129

    in ADHD vs. non-ADHD groups, 130–131

    and DA/attention deficit, 130–132

    and dopamine breakdown, 113

    in subjects with ADHD, 113–114

Dörnyei, Z., 236

Dougherty, D. D., 129, 130

Down syndrome, 14

DRD4 gene. *See* Dopamine receptor D_4 gene

DRD5 (dopamine receptor D_5) gene, 114

DSM *(Diagnostic and Statistical Manual of Mental Disorders)*, ADHD in, 106–107

DTI (diffusion tensor imaging), 304–305

Dual modeling problem, 181

Dual-stream model for auditory language processing, 294–295

Dudukovoc, N. M., 18

Dye, M. W. G, 15

EAN. *See* Executive attention network

Easy paradigms (for task-switching skills)

    for adults, 89–93, 95–98

    for children, 93–98

    defined, 88

    difficult vs., 87–98

Eber, J., 22

EC. *See* Effortful control

Echo planar imaging (EPI), 296–297

Ecocultural model of human development, 233

"Ecological map of the child," 233

Ecological systems theory, 233

Educational environment

    as cultural transmission, 233

    and executive attention development, 45–48

Effortful control (EC), 36–39

    and attention networks, 63–65

    control structures related to, 69

    and parenting, 72

    and socioemotional development, 36–38

    and temperament formation in children, 36–37

    terminology, 36

Effortful processing, 12

Egocentric language development, 213–214

Eisenberg, N., 39

Elicitation (of language), 216–220

Ellis, L. K., 38

Eloquent cortex areas, 291

Embarrassment, 163, 164

Emotional reactivity, behavior problems and, 45

Emotional self-regulation

    and affective control, 12–13

    anterior cinglulate areas for, 61

Emotional self-regulation, *continued*
    and attention networks, 62–63,
        65–68
    longitudinal study of, 65–68
Emotions, expression of secondary, 164
Empathy, and effortful control, 39, 64
Empirical mode, 237
Encoding, 221
Endogenous modes of selection, age-
        related changes in, 11, 13–14
Endogenous orienting (Down
        syndrome), 14
Endophenotype, 39
English language, 255
    body-centered spatial notions in, 213
    graphotactic conventions, 259
    Kannada vs., 258, 265
Enns, J. T., 15
Environmental factors
    in executive attention, 42–48
    social environment, 193–195
EPI (echo planar imaging), 296–297
Epilepsy, 289–306
    causes of, 290
    and functional organization of
        language, 293–295
    generalized seizures, 291
    language fMRI for patients with,
        295–306
    language paradigms for epileptic
        patients, 299–304
    partial seizures, 290–291
    presurgical evaluation process, 292,
        297–299
    surgical interventions for, 290–292
ERN (error-related negativity), 38–39
ERPs (event-related potentials), 37
Error processing
    in attention networks, 65
    and response inhibition, 20
Error rates, and task-switch costs,
        92–93
Error reaction times (ADHD), 18
Error-related negativity (ERN), 38–39
Eso, K., 45
Ethical stance, self-consciousness and,
        165–167
European languages, egocentric encod-
        ing in, 213
Event-related potentials (ERPs), 37

Evolution
    and self-consciousness, 159–160
    and writing systems, 257
Executive attention, 33–50
    attention network task in studies
        of, 18
    and COMT gene, 72
    control structures related to, 69
    defined, 12
    for emotion/though regulation, 68
    environmental factors in, 42–48
    and executive attention network,
        34–36
    as executive control process, 17–18
    genetic factors for, 39–42
    individual differences in, 36–39
    interaction of genes and experience
        in, 49–50
    observing development of, 66
    in younger children, 17–19
Executive attention network (EAN),
        34–36
    ANT test of, 63
    and brain state changes, 75
    COMT gene and performance in, 40
    early development of, 67–68
    and educational environment, 45
    effect of attention training on, 48
    and empathy, 64
    and error correction, 65
    individual differences in, 36–37
    in infants, 62
    and parenting, 26
    and socioeconomic status, 44
Executive control, 17–24
    adolescent development of, 89
    response inhibition in, 19–20
    task switching in, 20–24
    task-switching paradigms in studies
        of, 87
Executive function
    with ADHD, 107–108, 111–112
    defined, 107
    and task-switching paradigms, 91
Exercising, of attention networks, 73–76
Existential conundrum, human, 160
Exogenous modes of selection, age-
        related changes in, 11, 13–14
Experiential factors
    in control, 25–26
    in executive attention, 49–50

Exploitation, 201
Exploration, 201
The Expression of the Emotions in Man and Animals (C. Darwin), 162–163
Externalizing behavior problems, 38
Eye contact, of young children with ASDs, 149, 150
Eye direction
    adults' hemodynamic responses to, 198
    discrimination of, 185
    and intraparietal sulcus activation, 198
    representation of, 197–199
Eye gaze. *See also* Gaze following
    and cognitive processing, 276–278
    self-consciousness and others', 159
    and spoken language processing, 273–275
    of young children with ASDs, 149, 151
Eye tracking, color knowledge and, 272–273

Fabes, R. A., 39
Faces
    and gaze patterns, 200
    infants' interest in hands vs., 190
    infants' preferences for, 200
    relative values of toys vs., 187
Fair, D. A., 76
Fairness, 165–166
Fan, J., 41
Fear, and effortful control, 64
Field dependence or independence (FDI), 235–236
Flanker tasks
    and *DAT1* gene, 41
    in executive attention studies, 35
    in executive control studies, 18
Flexibility, mental, 85–86
fMRI. *See* Functional magnetic resonance imaging (fMRI)
Focal epilepsy syndromes, 291, 297–298
Focused attention, developmental trajectory of, 15–16
FoR. *See* Frame of reference
Fossella, J., 40, 41
Fowler, J. S., 130

Fox, P. T., 297, 306
Frame of reference (FoR), 211
    geocentric, 211, 214, 231
    mixed, 213
    in spatial cognition, 212
French language, 259
Friedman, D., 18
Frith, C. D., 198
Frith, U., 198
Frontal lobe, development of, 20
Fuligni, A., 238
Functional magnetic resonance imaging (fMRI), 289, 295
    with BOLD contrast, 295–296
    echo planar imaging, 296–297
    language. *See* Language fMRI
    of motor and cognitive tasks, 290
    time series data from, 297
Functional organization of language, 293–295

Gabrieli, J. D. E., 18
Gambling tasks, 108
Ganea, P. A., 277
Gao, J. H., 306
Gay, J., 234
Gaze following. *See also* PLeASES model of joint attention
    and attention shifts, 184
    and head poses, 185
    in joint attention, 161, 175–180
    neuroconstructivist account of, 197–199
    as predictor of language development, 152
Gehlbach, L., 40
Gelman, S. A., 277
Gender differences, in ADHD expression, 107
Genetic factors
    in ADHD, 114–115
    in control, 25–26
    in development of attention networks, 70–73
    in executive attention, 39–42, 49–50
Geneva, Switzerland, 240–245
Geocentric frame of reference, 211
    as cognitive style, 231
    in language and cognition, 214

Geocentric language and cognition
     studies, 214–227
  in Bali and Geneva, 240–245
  design and sample selection for,
     214–216
  effect of bilingualism in, 226–227
  in Kathmandu, 223–226
  knowledge of NSEW and LRFB, 220
  language and encoding in, 221
  language elicitation in, 216–220
  nonverbal encoding in, 221
  procedure, 219
  in Varanasi, 222–223, 225–226
Geocentric linguistic coding, 213–214
Geocentric spatial representations, 212
German language, 261
Geschwind, Norman, 293–294, 298
Geschwind's territory, 294
Glick, J. A., 234
Glynn, P., 295
Go/no-go tasks, 19
  for attention network, 63
  in children with ADHD, 108
Goss, A. E., 271–272
Goswami, U., 253
Grain size, 266
Grand mal seizures, 291
Granularity, 254, 266
Graphotactics
  conventions of, 259–261
  defined, 259
Greenfield, P. M., 212, 238
Grossberg, S., 199
Guise, K. G., 41
Gupta, R., 19, 20, 24, 97

Habituation (in PLeASES model),
     185–187
Handedness, 218
Hands, infants' interest in faces vs., 190
Head direction
  adults' hemodynamic responses
     to, 198
  representation of, 197–199
Head poses, discriminating, 184–185
Heidrich, A., 45
Hemispheric lateralization tests,
     218–219
Hickok, G., 294, 295
Hindi language, 255, 256, 258–259

Home environment
  and DAT1 gene, 50
  and executive attention develop-
     ment, 42–45
Homeostasis, 131–132
Homeostatic reactions, in synaptic DA
     levels, 132
Homovanillic acid, 114
Horton, C., 18
Hsieh, S., 86
HTR1B gene, 114
5-HTT gene, 114
5HTTPR gene, 49
Huettig, F., 274, 275, 278–280, 282
Human development, integrated
     theoretical framework for cross-
     cultural study of, 232–234
Human existential conundrum, 160
Humans, prosocial predispositions of,
     157–158
Hynd, G. W., 20
Hyperactivity, ADHD and, 106

IBMT (Integrated Body–Mind Training),
     74–75
Iga, T., 136
ILAE (International League Against
     Epilepsy), 290
Imperative stimuli, and task rules in
     task-switching studies, 87
Implicit learning, in children with
     ADHD, 108
Impulsivity (in ADHD), 106
Inattention (in ADHD), 106
Incongruency, cost of, 91–96
Independent locomotion, 160
Indian languages, 256
Individual differences
  in effortful control, 64–65
  in executive attention, 36–39
Infant–caregiver interaction
  and attention sharing, 179
  dynamic properties of, 174
  nonrandom social behavior patterns
     in, 188
  and prerequisite learning skills, 146
  and social behaviors, 173
Infants
  CHRNA4 gene in, 73
  cognitive and emotional control in,
     65–68

cognitive self-regulation in, 62–63
color discrimination in, 271
and error trials, 65
independent locomotion in, 160
orienting network in, 62
parallel control systems in, 68–69
positive affect and COMT gene,
72–73
social knowledge and behavior in,
173. *See also* Joint attention
stimuli preferences of, 190, 199–200
Inherent vowel, 256
Inhibitory control
development of, 19–20
individual differences in developing,
64–65
Integrated Body–Mind Training
(IBMT), 74–75
Intelligence, sensorimotor, 238–240
Interdependent developmental path, 238
International Classification of Diseases
(ICD-10), 107
International League Against Epilepsy
(ILAE), 290
Interparental aggression, ADHD and, 43
Intertrial interval (ITI), 21–22
Intervention programs, for ADHD, 45
Intimacy, and gaze grooming, 159
Intrinsic frame, 212
Intrinsic language, 242
Isaac, W., 20
Italian language, 255
ITI (intertrial interval), 21–22

Jannin, P., 306
Japanese Kanji, 255
Jasso, H., 195–196
Jebara, T., 181
Johnson, E. K., 278–282
Joint attention, 173–203. *See also*
PLeASES model of joint attention
and affect, 200–202
in development of social behaviors/
knowledge, 173–174
and gaze/point following, 175–180
and language development, 152
neuroconstructivist approach to,
197–199
and self-consciousness, 160–161
stimuli preferences and development
of, 199–200

of young children with ASDs, 149,
150
Jokei, H., 305
Jolles, J., 22, 87

Kampe, K. K. W., 198
Kannada language, 254, 256–267
cross-modal associations in, 263–265
English vs., 258, 265
psycholinguistic grain size framework
for, 265–266
script-independent aspects of learning
to read, 267
script-specific aspects of, 256–257
sounds in, 261–263
symbols in, 257–261
Kar, B. R., 19, 24
Kathmandu, Nepal, 223–226
Keller, H., 238
Kerns, K. A., 45
Kesavadas, C., 298
Keys, B. A., 19
Klein, J. T., 199
Klingberg, T., 48
Knowledge
of colors, 272–273
of NSEW/LRFB, 220
social, 173–174
Kochanska, G., 49, 64
Kohs block test, 218
Kolling, T., 200
Kray, J., 22

Lai, S., 306
Language. *See also* Geocentric language
and cognition studies
elicitation of, 216–220
encoding of, 221
functional organization of, 293–295
presurgical lateralization of, 295–297
reading development across languages,
253–255
Language coding schemes, 216
Language comprehension tasks, 300, 304
Language development
egocentric and geocentric systems,
213–214
gaze following as predictor of, 152
and joint attention, 152
Language disorders, prerequisite learning
skills of children with, 146–147

Language elicitation tasks, 216
Language fMRI, 295–304
    challenges with, 305–306
    and diffusion tensor imaging, 304–305
    language paradigms for epileptic
        patients, 299–304
    of left TLE patients, 290
    in presurgical evaluation of epileptic
        patients, 297–299
    presurgical language lateralization
        on, 295–297
    technical considerations of, 304
Language lateralization
    atypical, 293, 298
    in epileptic patients, 295–297, 304
    hemispheric lateralization tests,
        218–219
    laterality index, 299
    in right- vs. left-handed patients, 302
Language paradigms, for epileptic
        patients, 299–304
Language-vision mapping, 271–283
    in adults, 273–276
    color-mediated, by young children,
        278–283
    and color name use/color vision in
        children, 271–273
    and conceptual processing by adults
        vs. children, 276–278
Laterality index (LI), 299
Learning. See also Prerequisite learning
        skills; Temporal difference rein-
        forcement learning (TD-RL)
    in children with ADHD, 108
    reinforcement, 185, 187, 192, 199
Learning mechanisms (PLeASES
        model), 185–187, 190–193
Learning styles, 236
Lee, T. M., 295
Lerner, M., 132
Le Rumeur, E., 306
Levinson, S. C., 228, 246
Levitsky, W., 294, 298
Lewis, J., 195–196
LI (laterality index), 299
Lindenberger, U., 22
Lindgren, M., 276
Linguistic relativism, 213–214
Listening, passive, 300
Logistic growth model, 16

Longitudinal studies
    of cognitive and emotional control
        in attention networks, 65–68
    of joint attention precursors, 182

Macario, J. F., 276
Magnetic resonance imaging (MRI), 63
Mandal, M. K., 218, 219
Mandernach, T., 19
Mani, N., 282–283
Mathematical procedures, 240
Mature cognition, 11
Maynard, A., 238
McCandliss, B. D., 25–26
McCarthy, G., 198
McDonald, S. A., 274
McLaughlin, K. A., 45
Meditation, attention training with, 26,
        74–75
Meltzoff, A. N., 146
Mental flexibility, and task-switching
        skills, 85–86
Merlin, N., 152
MESA Project, 174, 180, 196, 201–202
Mesocortical pathways, in children with
        ADHD, 110–112
Mesolimbic pathways, in children with
        ADHD, 109–110
Metacognitive abilities, and rostrolateral
        region of prefrontal cortex, 163
Methylphenidate
    in ADHD treatment, 41, 132–138
    effects on brain of cocaine vs.,
        133–134
    in PK/PD studies, 133–134
Methylphenidate hydrochloride
        (MPH), 115
Mezzacappa, E., 25
Miller, I., 306
Mind, theory of, 38, 64–65
Mindfulness meditation, 74–75
Mirror mark test, 161–162
Mirror neuron system, 199
Mirror self-experience, 161–164
Mishra, R. C., 214, 225, 227, 235–236,
        242
Mishra, S., 24
Mitchell, D., 272, 280
Modreski, R. A., 271–272
Moen, I., 276

Monoamine oxidase, 113
Monsell, S., 86
Moral sense, ontogenetic root of, 161
Motor timing, in children with ADHD,
    108
Movellan, Javier, 174
MPH (methylphenidate hydrochloride),
    115
MRI (magnetic resonance imaging), 63
Multilingual education, 48
Multimodal Treatment Study of ADHD
    (MTA), 138
Multiple object visual tracking task,
    age-related performance of, 15
Munro, S., 48

Nag, S., 263
Nagai, Y., 188
Nagel, I. E., 76
Nagel, W. A., 272
Naigles, L. G., 277
Naturalistic microbehavioral ethno-
    graphies, and joint attention
    precursors, 182
Nayak, A. S., 295
Negative affect
    and cingulate activity, 64
    and effortful control, 64
    and mirror self-experience, 163–164
    and orienting, 68
Negative mode (emotional reactivity), 45
Nessler, D., 18
Neurocognitive function, SES as predic-
    tor of, 44
Neurocognitive model, attention in,
    34–35
Neuroconstructivist approach (to joint
    attention), 197–199. See also
    PLeASES model of joint attention
Newcorn, J., 130
Nicotinic cholinergic receptor
    CHRNA4, 73
Nigrostriatal pathways, in children with
    ADHD, 109
Nijmegen tasks, 216
Nisbett, R. E., 236, 237
Non-alphabetic scripts, alphabetic
    scripts vs., 255
Nonverbal spatial encoding tasks,
    216–218, 221

Non-WEIRD (Western, educated,
    industrialized, rich, and demo-
    cratic) countries, 13
Norepinephrine, ADHD and, 105
Norman, D. A., 34
Nucleus accumbens, 128, 131
Nyman, M., 39

Object recognition theories, 277–278
Ogawa, S., 295
Okujava, M., 305
Older children
    connectivity between ACC and
        posterior brain areas, 76
    developmental trajectories of
        attention in, 15–17
Opaque orthographies, 258
Operational training techniques, 239
Orienting network, 35
    and ACC, 69
    ANT test of, 63
    early development of, 67–68
    and error correction, 65
    for negative and positive affect
        regulation, 68
Orthography(-ies)
    defined, 293
    and phonology in reading develop-
        ment, 256
    shallow/transparent vs. deep/opaque,
        258
    and symbol-set size, 255–256
Osmotic Release Oral System (OROS),
    136–137
Ozonoff, S., 152

Pandey, G., 218
Parallel control systems (attention
    networks), 68–69
Pardo, J. V., 76
Parent–child interactions
    and attention sharing, 179
    dynamic properties of, 174
    prerequisite learning skills in, 147–149
    speech and gesture modifications in,
        188
Parent–child relationships, and self-
    regulation, 43–45
Parenting
    and ADHD symptoms without
        attention deficits, 71

Parenting, *continued*
and effortful control, 72
and executive attention network, 26
and genetic factors, 71, 72
and orientation to novelty, 69
Partial seizures, 291
Pasolunghi, M. C., 37
Passive listening, 300
Pavese, A., 45
Paz-Alonso, P. M., 41
PD (pharmocodynamic) studies, 133–139
Pelphrey, K. A., 198
Pennington, B. F., 87
Perceptual routines (PLeASES model),
184–185
Perfetti, C. A., 267
Perspectives task, 216
Pervasive developmental disorders
(PDDs), 146. *See also* Autism
spectrum disorders (ASDs)
PES (posterror slowing), 20
Petersen, S. E., 297
Petit mal seizures, 291
PFC (prefrontal cortex), dopamine
diffusion in, 40–41
Pharmacokinetic (PK) studies, 133–137,
139
Pharmocodynamic (PD) studies, 133–139
Phenotype, 39
Philibert, R. A., 49
Phoneme(s), 255
fluency and awareness of, 267
processing of syllables vs., 261–262
reading ability and awareness of, 265
Phonetic markers, stacked, 256–258
Phonology
defined, 293
and language orthography, in reading development, 256
Piaget, Jean, 212, 239, 242n3
Pinuelas, A., 39
PK (pharmacokinetic) studies, 133–137,
139
Platt, M. L., 199
PLeASES model of joint attention, 174,
180–197
affective traits in, 187
experimental results explained by,
195–197
and generation of developmental
theories, 180–181

learning mechanisms in, 185–187
learning signal in, 190–193
main postulate of, 183
methods of testing, 181–182
perceptual routines in, 184–185
predictions from, 188–189
social ecology structures, 188
social environment in, 193–195
and stimuli preferences of infants,
190, 199–200
testing of, 190–197
theory, 182–190
Pluess, M., 72
Plunkett, 276
Poeppel, D., 294, 295
Point following, in joint attention,
175–180
Poiseau, E., 306
Porchet, H.C., 134
Positive affect
and cingulate activity, 64
and COMT gene, 72–73
Posner, M. I., 25–26, 34, 38, 40, 45,
70–72
Possession, and self-consciousness,
164–167
Posterror slowing (PES), 20
Pozuelos, J. P., 41
Prefrontal cortex (PFC), dopamine
diffusion in, 40–41
Premature birth, 159, 160
Prerequisite learning skills, 145–152
of children with autism spectrum
disorders, 147–151
of children with language/
communication disorders, 146–147
future research on, 152–153
and gaze following as predictor of
language development, 152
Preschool children
attention-training exercises for, 45–48
ethical stance of, 166
Presurgical evaluation process for
epilepsy, 292, 297–299
Primary form (consonant and vowel
representation), 259, 260
Proactive aggression, 44
Prosocial disposition of humans, 157–158
Psycholinguistic grain size theory, 254,
265–266

Psychological differentiation, 235
Punishment network, anterior cingulate
    in, 72

Quantitative measures of environment,
    and joint attention precursors, 182
Quinlan, P. T., 274

Race, and executive attention, 25
Radicals (Chinese writing system), 263
Radio-labeled ligands, 129–130
    in ADHD imaging, 113–114
    and DA transport, 129
    defined, 129
Raichle, M. E., 297
Rao, C., 259
Rapid automatized naming (RAN), 265
Rapid naming task, 268
Rasmussen, T., 298
RCI (response-cue interval), 21–22
Reaction time, and switch costs, 24
Reactive aggression, 44
Reading development, 253–268
    across languages, 253–255
    cross-modal mappings in, 263–265
    and diversity of scripts, 255–256
    psycholinguistic grain size framework,
        265–266
    script-independent aspects of,
        267–268
    script-specific aspects of, 256–257
    sounds in, 261–263
    symbols in, 257–261
Reasoning, types of, 237
Reciprocity, and concept of self, 166–167
Recognition, struggle for, 159
Regulatory skills, and serotonin trans-
    porter gene, 49
Reinforcement learning, 185, 187, 192,
    199. *See also* Temporal difference
    reinforcement learning (TD-RL)
Relative frame, 212, 213
Relativism, linguistic, 213–214
Relaxation training, 74–75
Reputation, and self-consciousness,
    158–159
Response-cue interval (RCI), 21–22
Response repetition, and switch costs,
    22–24
Response time, and task-switch costs, 91

Reuptake, 129, 132
Reversed repetition effect, 22–23
Reward cues, gaze and pointing actions
    as, 177, 179
Reward function of attention sharing, 179
Reward/motivation circuit
    with ADHD, 129
    defined, 128
Reward network
    anterior cingulate in, 72
    and gaze information processing, 198
Reward processing, in children with
    ADHD, 110
Reward-related decision-making tasks,
    108
Riding, R., 235
Robledo, M., 176, 200
Rogers, R. D., 86
Rogers, S. J., 152
Rohlfing, K. J., 188
Romski, M. A., 146
Rothbart, M. K., 25–26, 38, 40, 68, 70–72
Rueda, M. R., 25–26, 37, 41, 63, 74

Saccomanno, L., 25–26
Sawada, Y., 136
Saylor, M. M., 277
Schliemann, A. D., 238
School performance, executive attention
    and, 37
Scribner, S., 237–238
Scripts
    diversity of, 255–256
    script-independent aspects of reading
        development, 267–268
    script-specific aspects of reading
        development, 256–257
Search, visual, 14–17
Secondarily generalized partial seizures,
    291
Secondary emotions, expression of, 164
Secondary form (consonant and vowel
    representation), 259, 260
Seizures, 291
Selective attention
    development of, 13–17
    in mature cognition, 11
    and mechanisms of developmental
        cognitive disorders, 26–27
    spatial, 108

Self-concept, 161, 166
Self-consciousness, 157–167
    defined, 158
    development of, 161–164
    and ethical stance, 165–167
    evolutionary context for, 159–160
    and gaze of others, 159
    and joint attention, 160–161
    and possession, 164–167
    and prosocial dispositions of humans,
        157–158
    and reputation, 158–159
Self-experience, mirror, 161–164
Self-regulation
    emotional and cognitive, 62–63,
        65–68
    and error-related negativity, 38–39
    and parent–child relationships,
        43–45
Semantic language-processing tasks, 300
Semantics (term), 293
Sensation seeking, 71
Sensorimotor intelligence, 238–240
Serotonin transporters
    5-HTT, 114
    5HTTPR, 49
SES. See Socioeconomic status
Shallice, T., 34
Shallow orthographies, 258
Sharing, 165–166
Sharp, D. W., 234
Sheese, B. E., 70–72
Sheiner, L. B., 134
Shepherd, S. V., 199
Shutts, K., 277
Simonsen, H. G., 276
Simple partial seizures, 291
Singerman, J. D., 198
Singh, S. K., 218
Sinha, D., 233, 235–236
Sitting tolerance, of young children
        with ASDs, 149, 151
Smith, L. B., 188
Smulders, S. F. A., 22
SNAP-25 gene, 114
Snyder, A. Z., 297
Snyder, C. R. R., 34
Social affiliation, 159
Social behaviors, joint attention in
        development of, 173–174

Social ecology structures (PLeASES
        model), 188, 192, 193
Social environment (PLeASES model),
        193–195
Socialization
    and claims of possession, 165
    executive attention in, 38–39
    and executive network develop-
        ment, 65
    routes to, 64
Social knowledge, joint attention in
        development of, 173–174
Social self-assertiveness, claim of posses-
        sion as, 165
Socioeconomic status (SES)
    and attention development, 42–45
    and bilingualism, 242
    and executive attention networks, 44
    interaction with genes in develop-
        ment of executive attention,
        49–50
    as predictor of neurocognitive
        function, 44
Socioemotional development, and
        effortful control, 36–38
Sohlberg, M. M., 45
Sounds
    mapping of symbols and, 267–286
    in reading development, 261–263
Spatial cognition, developmental
        studies of, 211–212
Spatial conception, egocentric, 213
Spatial mapping
    and intraparietal sulcus activation,
        198
    in PLeASES model, 184
Spatial representations
    body-related, 212
    egocentric, 213–214
    geocentric, 212–214
Spatial selective attention, in children
        with ADHD, 108
Spelke, E. S., 277
Spencer, T. J., 137
Stacked phonetic markers, 256–258
Still, G., 106
Stimulant medication, for treatment of
        ADHD, 106, 132–139
Stimulant-naive adults, 130–132, 138
Stimuli, joint attention and infants'
        preferences for, 190, 199–200

Story-Pictorial Embedded Figures Test
(SPEFT), 218
Striatum, 128
Stroop tasks, 35, 37
Styles, E. A., 86
Styles, S. J., 276
Surge-approaching mode (emotional
reactivity), 45
Surgical intervention (epilepsy),
290–292
Sustained attention, of young children
with ASDs, 149, 150
Swanson, J. M., 132, 134, 136
Switch costs. *See* Task-switch costs
Syllables, 255
awareness of, as predictor or reading
ability, 265
processing of phonemes vs., 261–262
relationship of akshara and, 259–261
Symbols
in Chinese writing system, 265
mapping of sounds and, 267–286
in reading development, 257–261
Symbol-set size, and language orthography, 255–256
Synaptic DA levels, homeostatic
reactions and, 132
Syntactic language-processing tasks, 300
Syntax (term), 293
Syversen, G., 276

Tamil language, 255, 256
Tan, L. H., 267
Tapé, G., 237
Task rules, 87
Task specificity, 243–245
Task-switch costs
and age, 94–95, 97–98
defined, 86
for easy vs. difficult paradigms,
87–93, 95–98
and error rates, 92–93
and response repetition, 22–24
and response time, 91
Task-switching skills, 85–98
of adults in easy vs. difficult conditions, 89–93, 95–98
of children in easy vs. difficult conditions, 93–98
child vs. adult studies of, 86–87

and cognitive control, 12
in easy vs. difficult paradigms, 87–89
and mental flexibility, 85–86
Taylor, C., 167
TD-RL. *See* Temporal difference reinforcement learning
Temperament
and *DAT 1* gene, 26
and *DRD4* gene, 72
individual differences in, 36–37
reactive and self-regulatory aspects
of, 68
Temperature, in reinforcement learning
models, 200–201
Temporal difference reinforcement
learning (TD-RL)
increase in "gain" to external stimuli
in, 201
in PLeASES model, 185–186, 195
Temporal lobe epilepsy (TLE), 290, 305
Teuscher, C., 179, 188
Theory of mind, 38, 64–65
Thomas, J., 48
Thomason. M. E., 18
Thomson, J., 45
Time duration, in children with ADHD,
108
Time estimation, in children with
ADHD, 108
TLE (temporal lobe epilepsy), 290, 305
Tolerance
sitting, 149, 151
of stimulant medication, 132–139
Tonic–clonic seizures, 291
Topological space, 242n3
Torkildsen, J. V. K., 276
Toys
infants' preferences for, 200
relative values of faces and, 187
Training
attention, 26, 45–48, 70–76
and executive attention, 48
Integrated Body–Mind, 74–75
operational, 239
relaxation, 74–75
Transparent orthographies, 258
Trick, L., 15
Triesch, J., 174, 179, 188, 195–196, 199
Troadec, B., 237, 245
Typological perspective, on writing
systems, 257

Universal phonological hypothesis, 267
Urdu language, 258–259
Useful field of view (UFOV), 15–17

Vaidya, C. J., 18
Vajpayee, A., 225
Varanasi, India, 222–223, 225–226
Verbal fluency tasks, 300
Verb generation task, 300, 304
Vision
    color, 271–273
    mapping language to. *See* Language-
        vision mapping
Visual search
    age-related performance in, 15–17
    in studies of attention, 14–15
Visual sequencing, COMT gene and, 49
Vladusich, T., 199
Voelker, P., 72
Voelker, P. M., 70–71
Volkow, N. D., 130, 133, 134, 139
Vowels
    inherent, 256
    representation of, 259, 260

Wada, J., 298
Wang, G.-J., 130, 138
Wassmann, J., 212
Welsh, M. C., 87
Wender, P., 106
Wernicke, Carl, 293
Wernicke's area, 293, 294, 304
Wernicke's Geschwind model, 293–294
White, D. A., 19
Wholists (cognitive style), 235

Witkin, H. A., 235, 236
Woermann, F. G., 305
Wolfe, H. K., 271
Word generation task, 300
Writing systems, 257, 258, 263, 265
Wynn, K., 66

Yamamoto, K., 136
Ye, R., 72
Young, G. S., 152
Young adults, conjunction search by, 15
Young children
    CHRNA4 gene in, 73
    cognitive and emotional control in,
        65–68
    color knowledge in, 272–273
    color-mediated language-vision
        mapping in, 278–283
    conflict resolution by, 24
    and development of executive
        control, 18–19
    ethical stance of, 166
    executive attention in, 17–19
    eye gaze and cognitive processing in,
        276–278
    genetic factors in attention network
        development, 70–72
    parallel control systems in, 68–69
    prerequisite learning skills in. *See*
        Prerequisite learning skills
Yu, C., 188

Zavala, C., 201
Ziegler, J. C., 253
Zukow-Goldring, P., 188

ABOUT THE EDITOR

Bhoomika Rastogi Kar, PhD, is associate professor at the Centre of Behavioral and Cognitive Sciences (CBCS), University of Allahabad. She received her doctorate at the National Institute of Mental Health and Neurosciences (NIMHANS), Bangalore, with Shobini L. Rao as her supervisor in 2003. She has specialized in developmental cognitive neuroscience and neuropsychology. She has a master's degree in psychology and master's degree in medical and social psychology. She has developed a neuropsychological battery for children (as a part of her doctoral thesis) and has studied the growth patterns of neuropsychological functions of Indian children. Her research interests are cognitive development including normative development of attention and control processes and developmental disorders such as dyslexia and attention-deficit/hyperactivity disorder. Her current projects focus on cognitive and affective control, conflict monitoring, bilingualism, and cognitive control using behavioral and electrophysiological methods such as EEG/ERP. She has published several papers, book chapters, and coedited *Advances in Cognitive Science, Volume 2.* She has presented her work at International and National Conferences in India and abroad. She has been collaborating with eminent scholars like Michael I. Posner, University of Oregon; Thomas Lachmann, University of Kaiserslautern, Germany; Shobini L. Rao, NIMHANS, India;

C. Kesavadas, Sree Chitra Tirunal Institute for Medical Sciences and Technology, India; Senthil Kumaran, All India Institute of Medical Sciences, India; and Narayanan Srinivasan, CBCS, University of Allahabad, India. She is consultant editor for the *International Journal of Mind, Brain and Cognition* and is a reviewer for many journals, such as *Archives of Clinical Neuropsychology* and *Psychological Studies*.